FUNDAMENTALS OF TRACK AND FIELD

SECOND EDITION

GERRY CARR

University of Victoria

HUMAN KINETICS

Library of Congress Cataloging-in-Publication Data

Carr, Gerald A., 1936-
     Fundamentals of track and field / Gerry Carr. -- 2nd ed.
         p.   cm.
     ISBN 0-7360-0008-9
     1. Track-athletics.   I. Title.
     GV1060.5.C368   1999
     796.42--dc21

98-52218
CIP

ISBN-10: 0-7360-0008-9
ISBN-13: 978-0-7360-0008-6

Acquisitions Editor: Jeff Riley; **Developmental Editor:** Marni Basic; **Assistant Editors:** Henry V. Woolsey, Chris Enstrom; **Copyeditor:** Heather Stith; **Proofreader:** Lisa Satterthwaite; **Graphic Designer:** Robert Reuther; **Graphic Artist:** Angela K. Snyder; **Photo Editor:** Clark Brooks; **Cover Designer:** Jack Davis; **Photographer (cover):** Tom Roberts; **Photographer (interior):** Tom Roberts, except where otherwise noted. Photos on pages 27, 155, and 260 © Claus Andersen. Photo on page 87 courtesy of Denise Ellis. Photo on page 97 © Joe Rogate. Photo on page 131 © 1998 Photosport/SNS; **Illustrators:** Paul To, Sandra Dailey, Karen Ostrom, and Beth Tarasuk; **Printer:** Premier Print Group

Human Kinetics books are available at special discounts for bulk purchase. Special editions or book excerpts can also be created to specification. For details, contact the Special Sales Manager at Human Kinetics.

Printed in the United States of America   24 23 22 21 20 19 18 17 16

Human Kinetics
Web site: www.HumanKinetics.com

United States: Human Kinetics
P.O. Box 5076, Champaign, IL 61825-5076
800-747-4457
e-mail: humank@hkusa.com

Canada: Human Kinetics
475 Devonshire Road Unit 100,
Windsor, ON N8Y 2L5
800-465-7301 (in Canada only)
e-mail: info@hkcanada.com

Europe: Human Kinetics
107 Bradford Road, Stanningley,
Leeds LS28 6AT, United Kingdom
+44 (0) 113 255 5665
e-mail: hk@hkeurope.com

Australia: Human Kinetics
57A Price Avenue, Lower Mitcham,
South Australia 5062
08 8372 0999
e-mail: info@hkaustralia.com

New Zealand: Human Kinetics
P.O. Box 80
Torrens Park, South Australia 5062
0800 222 062
e-mail: info@hknewzealand.com

CONTENTS

PART II
JUMPING EVENTS

PART III
THROWING EVENTS

PREFACE

This is the second edition of *Fundamentals of Track and Field*. You will find that it follows the same format that was used so successfully in the first edition. This edition offers you improved illustrations, a much more reader-friendly text, and a more attractive layout.

The goal of the second edition has not changed from the first edition, however. Like the first edition, this text is specifically designed to help all the physical educators, teachers, and grass-roots coaches who are faced with the difficult task of teaching track and field under severe time restrictions to large groups of young athletes. The second edition of *Fundamentals of Track and Field* is not directed toward coaches of elite athletes. Instead, this text is meant to help instructors working with beginners and novices, instructors who ask questions such as:

> "What track and field event should I teach first?"
>
> "How do I make the teaching environment as safe as possible?"
>
> "What sequence of lead-ups and drills should I use?"
>
> "How do I make this event an enjoyable experience?"

The second edition of *Fundamentals of Track and Field* answers these questions and expands upon the information that so many readers found valuable in the first edition. Here's a summary of what you'll find in the second edition of *Fundamentals of Track and Field*:

- Suggestions that you can use for planning your track and field program as well as each of your individual instructional sessions
- Methods that you can put into place for improving the level of safety during your instructional sessions, particularly when you're teaching the jumping and throwing events
- A large number of lead-up activities for each event
- A series of drills laid out in sequence and which progress from lead-up activities to the event's basic technique
- Descriptions of major errors that your young athletes are likely to commit and advice on how you can eliminate these errors
- Ideas for graded competitions that you can use at different stages in the learning process
- Suggestions on how you can assess your young athletes' performances
- Recommendations for standards that you can use as a guide when you want to award grades

Fundamentals of Track and Field concentrates heavily on teaching progressions and drills and solving problems of organization, safety, and assessment. This book offers you advice not only on popular track and field events but it also gives you excellent suggestions for events frequently omitted from many track and field manuals. You'll find progressions for teaching the basics of 400-m hurdles, triple jump, pole vault, steeplechase, race walking, and even the hammer throw! These events are becoming increasingly popular at all age levels and with both genders. No longer are events such as the pole vault, triple jump, and hammer throw for men only. The trend in track and field is to make all events available to females.

Fundamentals of Track and Field will show you that you can teach the technique of all the throwing events (even the hammer throw) using substitutes for the competitive equipment. In your instructional sessions, you may decide that teaching the basics of discus using a small rubber ring and teaching javelin by using a ball is as far as you can go. This decision is much better than not introducing the event at all. You will give your young athletes a grounding in the event, and later, when conditions warrant it, you can instruct your young athletes how to throw the competitive implements.

Fundamentals of Track and Field offers you a wealth of information to help you solve the organizational and teaching problems that you might face. Some lead-ups and drills will be perfect for your situation. Others will not. Look at what's offered, and choose what's best for your athletes. While enjoying the challenge and diversity that is offered in the lead-ups and drills, your young athletes will improve in performance and at the same time experience great satisfaction.

One final word about the recommended standards of performance. These standards are nothing more than suggestions that you can use as a guide. They are meant for your instructional classes and certainly not for elite club-level athletes. You should modify these standards according to your particular situation.

ACKNOWLEDGMENTS

I am very much indebted to Roger Burrows for his assistance with the chapter on race walking. My thanks also go to Andy McInnis of Athletics Canada, Brian McCalder of British Columbia Athletics, and James Croft of the Human Performance Laboratory, University of Calgary, for their assistance with the suggested standards of performance.

INTRODUCTION

Teaching the Basics of Track and Field

You must carefully organize the block of time that you allocate to track and field. The overall intent (or goal) of your program must be determined, and you must decide which events you will teach. If your time is limited, you may decide to lead your class for the entire instructional period and teach the basics of only one or two events. In a more favorable setting, you can start out with the whole class as a single group and then move to a station approach after teaching a selection of events. With this approach, you split your class into groups, and different events are practiced at each station. You can move from station to station giving instructions, or you can stay at one station and provide specific assistance.

DETERMINING WHAT TO TEACH

The number of events that you teach will depend upon the following factors:

- The time you have available
- The age, ability, and maturity level of your athletes
- Your knowledge and experience
- Your ability to establish a level of control and discipline such that group activities can operate safely and successfully
- Your class size relative to the available equipment and space
- The availability of assistants and the possibility of team teaching

You will always be faced with the question: "Which event should I introduce first, second, or third in my program?" When answering this question, ask yourself these questions first:

- Will the equipment that I have allow large numbers of athletes to be actively involved?
- Does the event that I want to teach provide a foundation for another event and so provide a teaching sequence that I can follow?
- Does the event require unusually high safety measures—and do these safety measures necessitate that I closely supervise the group practicing this particular event?

Track and field events that are fundamental, low-risk, require the minimum of equipment, and allow a large mixed group to be actively involved (such as sprints, distance running, and relays) should be introduced early in your track and field program. Begin with these events and work your way toward those events that are best taught at stations. The following sections will provide you with some of the major characteristics of track and field events. Knowing these characteristics will help you plan and organize your track and field program.

RUNNING AND WALKING EVENTS

Some running events (such as hurdles) require considerable organization and equipment (particularly if you are setting out flights of hurdles in each lane). Other events (such as sprinting, relays, distance running, and racewalking) do not need so much organization or equipment. Begin with events that require little or no equipment and move later to those that require a higher level of preparation.

Sprinting and Sprint Starts

Sprinting is fundamental to track and field and requires little more than a good running surface. Maximum activity can easily be achieved without the use of equipment. This characteristic means that you can use sprinting as an introduction to your track and field program, but remember that repetitive sprinting by itself can quickly destroy a young athlete's enthusiasm. Don't forget that you can teach the technique of sprinting as part of other activities. Sprinting occurs in chase and tag games, relays, hurdles, long jump, and triple jump.

Relays

Relay racing is one of the most enjoyable activities in track and field. It demands little equipment and adds the excitement of team competition to sprinting. There is a huge variety of relays that you can use, and the thrill of relay racing means that young athletes seldom get bored. Use relays as a means of adding spice to a warm-up and to your workout's culminating activities.

Hurdles

You can introduce hurdles early in your track and field program by using substitutes for competitive equipment. Bamboo canes laid across traffic cones give added organizational flexibility in that novices in your class can hurdle in both directions. Foam-rubber practice hurdles are excellent for reducing the fear of hitting the hurdle, and scissor-style practice hurdles are designed to be lowered to accommodate your smallest class member. Sprint starts and shuttle relays (which require your athletes to sprint back and forth) combine well with hurdling, particularly if your hurdles are designed to be approached from either direction.

The rhythm and pacing taught in hurdling is an important lead-up skill for long jump and triple jump. For this reason, it is worthwhile to teach hurdling prior to these two events. Hurdling also serves as preparation for steeplechase. The 400-m hurdles is an exhausting event and is best introduced to mature athletes who have a background in sprint hurdling (100/110-m hurdles) and sprint endurance training.

Distance Running, Steeplechase, and Race Walking

Distance running is an all-year activity, and like sprinting and relays, it requires only a good surface to run on. Variations in pace, distance, and terrain can make this activity very enjoyable. Because of the cardiovascular benefits of distance running (or repetitive running in games), it should be introduced early to young athletes and made a regular part of their physical education program.

You can teach many of the elements of steeplechase in cross-country running by having your athletes leap ditches, water jumps, and other obstacles. On the track, you can simulate the steeplechase water jump by having your athletes jump up onto a barrier and then down into the sand of the long-jump pit. Couple this simulated water jump with a sequence of practice hurdles, and you'll find it easy to introduce steeplechase to your young athletes.

You can introduce race walking as leisurely walking over specified distances. When you make walking vigorous, it becomes "power walking" and it's an excellent nonconcussive exercise. With changes in technique, power walking can become race walking. You can use walking as an active pause when your athletes run distances, or you can teach competitive walking as an event in its own right. Introduce vigorous walking early in your program to all your athletes and be prepared to offer walking as an alternative to those who are unable to perform some of your more demanding track and field events.

THROWING EVENTS

One of the best ways for you to teach the throwing events and still maintain the highest level of safety is to use easy-to-handle substitutes in place of the competitive implements. Besides dramatically increasing the level of safety, substitutes simplify the learning process and make difficult throwing techniques easier to learn. If you feel that using discuses, javelins, shot, and hammers is too risky in your teaching situation, then consider using the safe substitutes that this text recommends.

You can teach the fundamentals by substituting rubber rings and hula hoops for discuses and balls for shot and javelins. Even the fundamentals of hammer throwing can be taught using basketballs and medicine balls held in nets. (See chapter 14.) You can teach correct technique and even hold competitions with these substitutes. Using substitutes is much better than failing to give your athletes the experience and enjoyment of the throwing events.

When you introduce the throwing events, begin by using lightweight, safe substitutes for competitive implements. If you have enough of this kind of equipment, introduce the throwing event of your choice as a whole-class activity. If you don't have enough equipment to get everyone involved at once, introduce your throwing event as a station activity and supervise that station.

If you are lucky enough to have sufficient competitive implements for the whole class, then use this equipment after you've taught your throwing event using substitute equipment. Remember that using balls, hoops, and other substitutes not only makes the teaching environment safer, it also makes the learning process easier for your young athletes.

Javelin

Of all throwing events, the javelin event most closely resembles the action of throwing a ball. If you start using balls instead of javelins, you can easily teach javelin technique as a whole-class activity. Because the basic throwing action is less complex than other throwing events, javelin throwing (using balls) should be one of the first throwing events you introduce.

Shot Put

The modern shot put event features the glide and rotational technique. The glide technique is more popular and is considered the easier technique to perform. For this reason, introduce the glide technique first. The rotational technique is based on the movement pattern used in the discus throw. Teach this technique only after the glide technique has been mastered, after you've taught the rotational action in the discus throw, and as an experimental technique for mature athletes practicing under your supervision.

The fundamentals of shot put using a glide technique are very easy to learn, and young athletes can quickly achieve a moderate level of success. You can teach the fundamentals of this event as a whole-class activity using small medicine balls, softballs, or even baseballs. If these substitutes are not available and you have only a small selection of competitive shot, wait until you split your class into groups. Then teach shot put as a station activity.

Discus

The discus throw is a rotational event, and the footwork and handhold make it more complex than shot put or javelin. Teach this event after introducing your nonrotational throwing events (javelin and shot put). Rubber rings (quoits) and small hula hoops are excellent substitutes for the discus because they eliminate the problems of holding the discus when the footwork is being taught. Using this very safe equipment, you can teach discus fundamentals to your whole class. Discus throwing using the competitive implement then follows as a station event.

Hammer

The hammer is seldom taught in schools, and at the club level, it generally has fewer devotees than other throwing events. This is unfortunate because many athletes consider the hammer to be one of the most satisfying and pleasurable of all throwing events. However it can be dangerous, and a high level of safety is of paramount importance. A large area of waste land and a throwing cage will be necessary when your athletes practice with the competitive implement. This waste land can be used for discus and shot put, but damage to the turf makes it unfit for other activities.

Don't forget that you can safely teach the technique of hammer throwing by using substitutes for the competitive implement, such as a medicine ball in a net. In this way, you can teach the swings, turns, and release and hold competitions without worrying about turf damage. Usually, the hammer is last of all throwing events to be taught (if it is taught at all). Many instructors avoid this event without realizing that a lot of safe enjoyment can be had if the basic technique is taught using a substitute for the competitive implement.

JUMPING EVENTS

The high jump, long jump, and triple jump are closely related in that their introductory and lead-up activities are very similar. However, these events differ in their organizational demands, and you'll find it is far easier to keep a large group active in the long jump and triple jump than in the high jump. The pole vault is unique as a jumping event in that a pole is used and the athlete travels higher in the air than in other jumping events. Pole vault demands gymnastic ability and a certain degree of fearlessness. Because of its specific physical demands, the pole vault is normally taught as a station activity to a select group.

High Jump

Lead-up activities for high jump without using a crossbar or using $5/16''$ (8 mm) rubber tubing as a crossbar can occur as whole-class activities. This works best if you have more than one set of high-jump standards. A single high-jump station used by a large class generally means minimal activity for each individual, and you should avoid this situation. If you are limited in equipment, you may be forced to introduce high jump as a station activity after the class has been split into groups. You'll work with the high jumpers while other groups practice events that you have previously taught.

Once you have some idea of each individual's high-jumping ability, you can group athletes of similar abilities together. When each group rotates to the high-jump station, the amount of time lost in altering heights is reduced.

Using rubber tubing in place of a regular crossbar not only eliminates the time taken in replacing the crossbar after a failed attempt, but it also removes the discomfort of falling on top of the crossbar. Be sure that the rubber tubing stretches easily and add extra weight to the bases of the high-jump standards or attach them to the ground to prevent them from being pulled down by an athlete who jumps into the rubber tubing.

Always use approved, regulation-size landing pads for the high jump because the flop technique causes athletes to travel a long way in flight and to land on their shoulders and roll back onto their necks. Regulation-size high-jump landing pads are wide, tall, and well-cushioned. The perpendicular height of these pads from the ground prevents your athletes from over-rotating during flight and landing on the back of their necks. Don't use gymnastic crash pads in place of the approved landing pads! They provide neither the area nor the depth to safely accommodate the flop technique. Even tying a group of gymnastic crash pads together is dangerous. An athlete can fall into the join where the pads are tied together.

Long Jump

The construction of oversize jumping pits is one of the simplest and cheapest improvements that you can make to your track and field program. Run-ups can approach from both ends, and a huge square pit will also allow several athletes to jump simultaneously from the side rather than waiting in line at the end of a run-up.

Make the long jump one of the first jumping events you introduce in your program. You can teach this event in combination with the triple jump, or it can follow the triple jump in your teaching sequence. Consider teaching these two jumping events immediately after sprinting, sprint starts, and relays.

Triple Jump

The triple jump is no longer an event for males only, and it is becoming very popular in women's track and field. Many instructors prefer to teach the triple jump before the long jump for the following reasons:

- The rate of improvement in the triple jump is more dramatic than in the long jump, and this improvement boosts enthusiasm.
- Most youngsters consider the triple jump a lot more fun than the long jump.
- The third jump in the triple jump is an elementary long jump.
- Methods of teaching the run-up are similar for both events.

Remember that the repetitive bounding required in the triple jump is stressful for young athletes, and bruised heels and fatigue can occur very quickly. These effects can be counteracted to some degree by using matting where the athletes land after the hop and the step. Even with this cushioning, you will find that fatigue comes quickly in this event, so be ready to provide a visibly tired group with alternative activities that are less demanding.

Pole Vault

The pole vault is seldom taught to the whole class at once. It is usually taught as a station activity with an instructor supervising and assisting. To teach this event adequately, you should have several short, light, flexible training poles. In addition, it is useful to have an elevated ramp from which your athletes can step forward and ride a pole down into sand or onto a pole-vault landing pad. Large, regulation-size landing pads are essential for this event, irrespective of your athletes' levels of performance.

You can waste an immense amount of time in the pole vault adjusting the height of the crossbar and replacing the crossbar after it has been knocked off. Use the $\frac{5}{16}''$ (8 mm) rubber tubing as a crossbar in the same way that it is recommended for use in the high jump. The use of this rubber crossbar will not only save you time, but it will also increase the number of attempts that your athletes make in any one training session.

For even moderate success, young athletes should be able to hang on a pole and have sufficient abdominal strength to elevate their legs at least to the horizontal position. In any instructional group, you will find those who cannot perform these actions. Consider giving these athletes the option of practicing other events when their group rotates to the pole-vault station.

COMBINED EVENTS

After you have taught several events to your athletes, you can give them the opportunity to compete against each other in multiple events. Using a point score for performances, you can have your athletes compete in track and field biathlons (2 events), triathlons (3 events), quadathlons (4 events), and pentathlons (5 events). These combined event competitions can serve as preparation for the more demanding women's heptathlon (7 events) and men's decathlon (10 events).

Biathlons made up of a run and a jump or a run and a throw, and triathlons, consisting of various combinations of runs, jumps, and throws, reward all-around ability and also teach young athletes how scores are kept in combined events. You can periodically offer multievent competitions, and you can also in-clude a multievent competition in a major track meet at the end of your program.

MOVING FROM WHOLE-CLASS TO GROUP ACTIVITIES

You will need to organize groups when you want your class to practice more than one event at the same time. Start your instructional period by teaching your class as a single unit, and then after a series of lessons, divide your class into two large groups. Work with one group while the other practices activities that you've previously taught. Increase the number of groups as you introduce more activities.

There are many ways to organize groups, and all have advantages and disadvantages. Whichever method you decide to use, be sure to set up groups so that you have maximum activity, a high level of safety, and trouble-free rotation from one station to the next. Here are some suggestions to help you achieve these objectives:

- Begin by arranging your athletes in groups according to height and weight.
- After you have introduced high jumping, consider a reorganization of groups based on your athletes' high-jumping ability.
- Provide a large number of substitutes for competitive equipment, particularly in the throwing events. The low cost of these items, in addition to their safety, means that you can introduce events such as the discus, shot put, and javelin as whole-class activities.
- Provide a wide range of weights and sizes of competitive equipment (such as discuses, javelins, shot, pole-vault poles, and practice hurdles). This variation will help you accommodate the differences in body size and strength that are likely to exist in your class.
- To satisfy differing levels of ability, place takeoffs at varying distances from jumping pits. If possible, build two extra-large practice pits, one for the long jump and the other for the triple jump. Using these large pits, you can position take-offs (using short run-ups) at the sides of the pits

as well as at either end. Use take-off areas (or zones) rather than competitive-size take-off boards for both the long jump and the triple jump. A take-off area increases enjoyment because foul jumps are eliminated. It also speeds up the rate of jumping from one athlete to the next.

• Always measure throws with methods that are safe, fast, and easy to administer. Mark arcs on the grass to indicate distances, and then during training, estimate the distances thrown in relation to these arcs. During class, avoid the laborious and time-consuming task of using a tape to measure throws.

• Make the pole vault an optional event for those whose strength-weight ratio prevents them from hanging or swinging on a pole.

PLANNING INDIVIDUAL INSTRUCTIONAL PERIODS

Planning individual instructional periods requires you to make a series of decisions similar to those that you make when you plan your track and field program. Each instructional period must have a series of objectives that you determine prior to instruction. Make each objective lead systematically to the next, not only within each instructional period, but from one instructional period to the next. Divide each instructional period into three sections, such as Introductory, Main, and Closing. Following are some suggestions for what to put in each section.

INTRODUCTORY SECTION

The objective of your introductory section will be the physical and mental preparation of your athletes for what follows in the main section of your instructional period. Your introductory section should contain warm-ups performed by your whole class. These warm-ups will last about ¼ of your total instructional period. During the warm-ups, take the opportunity to explain the tasks that you have planned for the main section of your instructional period.

In your warm-ups, include stretching and flexibility exercises that relate to the events you intend to teach in the main section of your in-

structional period. In addition, don't forget to get everyone involved in some jogging and striding. This type of exercise prepares your athletes for what is to follow. During your introductory section, you can lead your class as a group. If they are more mature, you can allow them to warm up according to the event that they'll be working on in the main section of your instructional period.

MAIN SECTION

The main section of your instructional period should last for about ½ of the total time available. The choice of objectives will depend on what progress you've made in previous classes. These objectives can be any of the following:

• **A lead-up activity for an event that will be new to your class.** For example, provide each athlete in the class with a ball, and you begin teaching the fundamentals of the javelin throw.

• **Improving the technique of an event that you have previously taught.** For example, work to eliminate errors in the relay changeover.

• **Assessment of individual performances in an event that you have already taught.** For example, give a subjective evaluation of your athlete's performance in a particular event. Concentrate on the athlete's technique without assessing the distance thrown, height jumped, or time run. In the discus throw, check the athlete's ability to perform the technique of a standing throw. Assess the athlete's movements without being too concerned about the distance of the throw.

The organizational format you use to achieve these objectives will vary depending on the progress your class has made in past instructional periods. You might work toward the objectives listed previously by instructing the whole class or by instructing smaller groups at a station. Assessing individual performances is best achieved when you are working with a small group.

CLOSING SECTION

The closing section will occupy approximately ¼ of your instructional period. Objectives for this section vary according to what occurred in the main section of your lesson. The closing section can include an activity that brings your class together as a single group, during which you comment on the tasks that were completed and on those that will occur in subsequent instructional periods. The closing section can include an activity that is lighthearted, competitive, and/or has aerobic value (such as a relay or a short distance run). Follow this activity with a warm-down and wrap-up comments.

TEACHING TRACK AND FIELD EVENTS

Most instructors divide the technique of an event that they wish to teach into its basic components. These components are commonly called *phases*. Phases are groups of connected movements that in total make up the techniques of an event. Phases are distinct from one another, but they influence each other like links in a chain. Once you have divided the technique of an event into phases, you select an important and fundamental phase. Using drills, you teach this phase first. You then concentrate on the next important phase.

DIVIDING TRACK AND FIELD EVENTS INTO PHASES

The following examples show you how you can divide the high jump, shot put, pole vault, and hurdles into phases. The most complex of these examples is the hurdles. In this event, the sprint start, sprinting, and hurdle clearances can be considered "events" (or skills) in their own right. Each has its own technique and its important movement phases. Notice also that preparatory movements and mental set are also considered as a phase. An athlete must go through these actions and mental processes to prepare for performing subsequent phases in the event.

High Jump
1. Preparatory movements and mental set
2. Run-up
3. Takeoff
4. Bar clearance
5. Landing

Shot Put
1. Preparatory movements and mental set
2. Glide
3. Putting action
4. Follow-through and reverse

Pole Vault
1. Preparatory movements and mental set
2. Run-up
3. Pole plant and takeoff
4. Hang and upward drive on the pole
5. Bar clearance
6. Landing

Hurdles
1. Preparatory movements and mental set
2. Sprint start
3. Approach to the first hurdle
4. Hurdle clearances
5. Sprint between the hurdles
6. Sprint to the finish

Although all phases link together to give you the technique of an event, you'll always find that it's necessary to teach one phase before another. Start by teaching the phase that you consider to be the most important and fundamental to the event. Modify the required movements in this phase so that novices in your class can perform them easily.

For example, to put the shot using a glide, a beginner must be taught to put the shot from a standing position. The actions that make up a standing throw are taught using balls or lightweight shots, and the speed of movement is reduced so that it is easy to learn. In a discus throw, an athlete learns to perform the phases that make up a standing throw before attempting to throw using a spin across the ring. In hurdling, a novice can work on clearing the leading leg over the hurdle, and do this by walking and stepping over a low hurdle. In the pole vault, beginners can start by standing on an elevated ramp and learn to hang and swing on the pole into sand or a landing pad.

KEY ELEMENTS IN A PHASE

Each phase in a track and field event is made up of a number of key elements. To understand what an element is and to see an element in relation to a phase, think of the technique of an event as a building. Phases are the walls that make up the building. Key elements are the individual bricks. Key elements are essential body positions and movements that occur in a phase. All the phases that make up the technique of a track and field event will have key elements. For example, here are a few (but certainly not all) of the key elements required in a high-jump run-up.

Key Elements in the High-Jump Run-Up

1. A precise number of paces and pace length during the run-up

2. A progressive acceleration throughout the run-up

3. An inward lean into the curve of the run-up

4. A longer penultimate (second to last) stride and lowering of the athlete's center of gravity

5. A shorter last stride and accurate placement of the take-off foot

6. A backward lean and placement the arms to the rear of the athlete's body during the placement of the jumping foot

TEACHING PHASES AND KEY ELEMENTS

Drills used to teach phases and elements are best taught in a particular sequence. A recommended sequence is as follows:

1. Select a fundamental phase in the event (such as a standing throw in shot put, discus, or javelin). Pick out its key elements, and teach each element separately. Thereafter join them together in sequence. Wherever possible, reduce the speed of movement and use modified, easy-to-handle substitute equipment to make your job easier. Correct major errors before moving to the next phase.

2. Teach the next most important phase and its key elements. Work on correcting major errors and joining this phase to the one you previously taught. Progress in this manner until your athletes attempt the basic technique of the whole event.

3. When your athletes attempt the basic technique of the whole event, have them re-peat the correct actions frequently so that the actions become familiar. Progressively increase the speed of movement. Go back and repeat any phases and elements that give your athletes difficulty.

CORRECTING ERRORS IN PERFORMANCE

Errors vary in type and intensity. Beginners tend to commit fundamental errors that involve mistiming and incorrect movements of major body parts. These errors will be easy for you to pick out. Experienced performers tend either to commit minor errors that minimally affect performance or major errors that have become ingrained because of the number of times that they have been repeated. (Errors of the latter type are particularly difficult to eliminate.)

To correct errors, you must have an adequate understanding of the mechanics of the event. In other words, you must know why certain elements exist in a phase and why they have to be performed in a certain manner. The following recommendations relate to the performance of any track and field event. They also relate to the way in which you would analyze the performance of an important phase of an event.

1. Start by watching your athlete perform the complete event.

2. Observe the performance from several directions.

3. Concentrate on the important phases that make up the complete event, and then look at the key elements in each phase.

4. After you have observed the performance several times and made some mental or written notes, home in on what you consider to be the most fundamental error that your athlete is committing.

5. Decide on drills that you will use to correct the error that you have selected. These drills may mean reworking certain actions at reduced speed. The method of correction should be relatively easy for the athlete to perform and, if possible, novel and interesting.

6. Use instructions that are easy for your athlete to understand; don't befuddle

your athlete with needless technical jargon.

7. Insert the corrected element back into its "parent" phase. Have your athlete repeat the complete action at reduced speed and effort.

8. Progressively increase speed and effort.

COMMON TRACK AND FIELD ERRORS

There are many errors that a track and field athlete can commit and it's impossible to discuss them all. The following list is a selection of five common major errors that can occur in any sport as well as in track and field. If you aim to correct these errors and nothing else, you will dramatically improve your athlete's technique! If you correct these five major errors, other minor errors frequently disappear too.

1. **Your athlete isn't positioned correctly when applying force.** There are many examples of this kind of error. Your athlete can be in a poor position at takeoff in the jumps and is unable to apply maximum force to get up into the air. In the throws, the athlete can have a weak, narrow throwing stance and fall (or get thrown) one way when the implement goes the other! Poor foot positioning as your athlete comes out of a sprint start can cause the athlete to stumble from side to side in the lane.

2. **Your athlete isn't using all the muscles that should make a contribution to the performance of the event.** This error is common among novices. In throwing events, athletes fail to make full use of the big muscles of the legs, back, and chest. Instead they try to throw the implement with the arm alone. In the long jump, triple jump, and high jump, athletes fail to swing their arms upward to help lift them up into the air. Adequate arm movement may also be absent in sprinting and hurdling.

3. **Your athlete isn't applying force with the muscles in the correct sequence.** This error is caused by incorrect timing and coordination. In throwing events, athletes commonly use their chest muscles and the muscles of their throwing arm before the big muscles of the legs have made their contribution. In

sprinting, the athlete's arm and leg actions are not synchronized and fail to complement each other. The same problem can occur in the jumping events at takeoff and also during movements performed in the air.

4. **Your athlete doesn't apply force over the optimal distance and/or timeframe.** This error is characterized by your athletes cutting short the application of their muscular force. Their stride length in sprinting and hurdling is too short or, conversely, is exaggerated and too long. In throwing events, the athlete's stance is too small and the athlete's feet are so close together that there is no chance of accelerating the javelin, discus, or shot over the optimal distance. In jumping events, the athlete uses a take-off position that doesn't allow adequate time to drive upward. In pole vault, the athlete is incorrectly positioned below the upper handhold at takeoff and swings up toward the bar either too late or too early.

5. **Your athlete doesn't apply muscular force in the correct direction.** This error seems to be common sense, yet it is very important because it's muscular force that moves an athlete's body (or a throwing implement) in a particular direction. In running events, the leg thrust has to be both horizontal and vertical. The optimal combination of the two helps to drive the athlete at top speed down the track and towards the tape. A sprinter cannot swing the arms across the body; they must be in line with the motion of the legs. In the high-jump takeoff, the athlete has to swing the leading leg upward and turn it back toward the take-off area. This action helps to rotate the athlete in preparation for the bar clearance.

SAFETY IN TRACK AND FIELD

For each event, this text will provide you with suggestions for improving the level of safety. Most of the major problems that you will face are considered in this book, but unfortunately it's impossible to cover all the circumstances that may arise during an instructional session. You must use your own judgment to ensure that your teaching environment is safe and that the skills that you teach are adequate for the age, maturity, and experience of your athletes.

The following comments are intended as a general introduction to the issue of safety in track and field. Specific comments relating to each event will be found in their respective chapters.

RESPONSIBILITY FOR SAFETY

Safety in track and field begins with the planning and layout of the facilities, followed by the manner in which events are conducted or taught. Ground staff, officials, teachers, coaches, and the athletes themselves all play a part in maintaining a high level of safety. Nowadays your legal obligation is to provide a reasonable, prudent, and professional standard of care during your instructional sessions. The word *professional* in this context gives you the responsibility for checking that equipment and facilities are in good order and using the best available methods and practices for teaching and supervising your class.

When you instruct your class, plan to do the following:

- Use teaching techniques, teaching progressions, lead-ups, and drills that take into consideration the ages, genders, maturity, and fitness levels of your athletes.

- Ensure that your equipment, apparatus, and throwing implements are in good order and that they are appropriate in weight and size for the ages and physical maturity of your athletes.

- Teach good safety habits as an integral part of each of your instructional periods, and make your athletes aware of specific dangers that may occur in an activity.

- Use repetition as the key to learning. This guideline applies not only to the teaching and performance of track and field events but also to their associated safety regulations. The fundamental rules controlling the conduct of an event and good safety habits should be reinforced during each of your instructional sessions.

These guidelines are interrelated. In particular, be sure that you select the best teaching progressions relative to the ages, genders, maturity, and fitness levels of your athletes.

What is adequate for a fit adult will be inadequate for an immature youngster. You must know how to modify the movements involved in a track and field event so that they accommodate an individual's physiological and psychological maturity.

The same consideration must be exercised when warning of potentially dangerous conditions. Adequate warning for adults may be inadequate for children. Track and field events themselves are not dangerous, but the way they are conducted can be dangerous. Be sure you know the specific characteristics of each event and the drills that you intend to use. A verbal explanation outlining these characteristics is not enough. You must instruct, demonstrate, and supervise in such a way that dangerous conditions are eliminated and good safety habits are developed by each member of your class.

DISCIPLINE AND CONTROL

Try to establish a high level of control, starting with your first instructional period. Control does not mean removing fun and pleasure from track and field, nor does it mean that you must turn every instructional period into the equivalent of boot camp. Good organization coupled with your leadership not only improves your teaching environment but also enhances safety. Organization and leadership are particularly important if you want your athletes to practice independently at stations.

You may have immature and unreliable athletes in your class who simply cannot be expected to practice without supervision. You cannot expect to progress to group activities if this is the case and you don't have additional assistance. Instead, you must remain in charge until your athletes have developed the required levels of reliability and self-discipline. Any decision to allow young athletes to practice on their own must be based on your careful assessment of their maturity, self-discipline, levels of responsibility, and knowledge of the event and its safety requirements.

When you set up stations, stay at the station where competitive implements are being used for the first time, and position yourself so that other events are also in view. The possibility of moving freely from one station to another will depend on what events you intend your class to practice. The freedom of your movement from one station to the next will also depend on whether safe substitutes for competitive implements are used and whether you are able to vocally and visually control all stations.

One of the difficulties you face in trying to eliminate every possible danger is that you become excessively authoritarian. However difficult it may seem, try to strike a balance between providing a safe environment with one in which your athletes are challenged and want to learn.

A FINAL NOTE

Track and field is a changing sport. Events that were previously only for males are now for men and women. For example, the women's hammer and pole vault will be in the Olympic Games, and sometime soon, you can expect to see a women's steeplechase and a decathlon (rather than the present seven-event women's heptathlon). Make sure the athletes in your classes get the chance to compete in all the events that you teach regardless of their gender.

Part
I

TRACK
EVENTS

1

SPRINTS

Sprinting as a race category includes all distances up to 400 m, with the 400 m classified as a long sprint. The 800 and 1500 m are usually classified as middle-distance races. Distances beyond 1500 m are considered long-distance races.

Most coaches also look on hurdling (from the 100-m hurdles for women to the 400-m hurdles for men and women) as a form of sprinting combined with hurdle clearances. In the seven-event women's heptathlon females compete in the 100-m hurdles and the 200-m sprint. The men's ten-event decathlon includes two sprints (100 and 400 m) and one hurdle race (110-m hurdles).

All track and field events, regardless of whether they are runs, jumps, or throws, require your athlete to make muscular contractions. The energy for a muscle contraction is supplied in two ways: anaerobically and aerobically. The word *anaerobic* means that an athlete's muscles contract by using stored energy supplies existing in the athlete's body. *Aerobic* means that the athlete's muscle contractions use oxygen that is supplied by the cardiovascular system. All athletes have a certain anaerobic and aerobic capacity, which can be increased by training.

Running races ranging from short sprints to distance events makes different demands on the athlete's anaerobic and aerobic capacity. Sprints are anaerobic activities. In anaerobic events, the oxygen demand of the muscles is so high that it surpasses the ability of the athlete's cardiovascular system to supply an adequate amount of oxygen to the muscles. Instead the athlete's muscles make their rapid contractions utilizing chemical processes that set free oxygen stored within the muscle itself. This process means that the oxygen your athlete inhales at the start of a 100-m race doesn't reach the athlete's muscles until the race is finished. After the race is over, the athlete is gasping for air. The athlete's heavy breathing repays the oxygen borrowed from the muscles and simultaneously removes *lactic acid*, which is a waste product produced by muscle contraction.

The requirements for aerobic and anaerobic endurance depend upon an athlete's chosen event. As race distances increase from sprints to the marathon, the athlete has to rely more and more on the aerobic capacity of the heart and lungs to supply the necessary oxygen. During the sprint to the finish in a long-distance race, the situation changes. Now the athlete reverts to using anaerobic energy supplies stored in the body. This change means that an athlete competing in long distance races will need both aerobic and anaerobic endurance. In the short sprints, athletes focus more on developing their anaerobic endurance, but as part of their training they also spend time developing their aerobic endurance.

A season's training for a sprinter is predominantly made up of drills to develop power, good technique, fast reactions, and anaerobic endurance. As the competitive season draws near, the athlete emphasizes quality high-speed sprinting. In this kind of training, the athlete attempts to sprint at top speed while staying as relaxed as possible. Most sprint technique training is completed in the preseason but it is never forgotten during the competitive period. For a beginner faced with a short season and little time to prepare, training should concentrate on basic sprinting technique and the ability to relax while sprinting at top speed.

SAFETY SUGGESTIONS

Because of their simplicity, sprinting events require fewer safety regulations than throwing or jumping events. However, you should consider the following points.

Sprinting is a highly explosive activity that requires powerful, vigorous muscle contractions. In order to reduce the likelihood of muscle tears and pulls make sure that your athletes warm up prior to each training session and, of course, prior to competitions. Begin each training session with light, easy running and flexibility exercises. Increase the intensity with fast striding, short sprints, and practice starts.

Be particularly careful with some of the special activities designed for developing sprint technique, such as high-knee running and high-knee skipping. These activities can produce hamstring pulls and other muscle injuries—so your athletes should be really warm and "loose" before attempting them. This advice applies to more mature athletes as well as to your novices. When you work with beginners, take them step by step through a good warm-up and teach them the value of each activity that you use. Have your athletes memorize the activities and ask one of them to lead the warm-up on the next occasion. Offer advice and correct body positions as your group progresses through the warm-up.

Remember that a complete and thorough warm-up becomes even more important when the weather is cold.

Make sure your athletes have sufficient room to turn and to slow down during sprinting activities. Adequate space is usually not a problem on an open grass area, but it is important when sprinting indoors. Be sure there is sufficient room for deceleration in activities where your athletes sprint to a line and back.

Weight training is an important training activity for modern sprinters, but be aware that it can make an athlete tight and shorten the athlete's muscles. You can counteract this effect by combining weight training with stretching and flexibility exercises. Overuse of weights can be detrimental to sprinting, so keep weight training as a secondary form of training.

When you teach young children to sprint, have them stay in designated lanes and not move off the track or to the center of the track until it is safe to do so; following this rule prevents collisions. Young children should also be taught the use and care of spikes. In hot weather, athletes frequently take their spikes off and run on the infield barefoot. Spikes and spike pins left lying around can cause serious injuries.

Be sure that you strictly control starting pistols and their ammunition. Lock them in a safe place when they are not in use, and never leave a loaded starting pistol unattended. Starting pistol ammunition is designed specifically for track competitions, and it should not be used for any other purposes. You should report the loss of starting pistols to the appropriate authorities.

An excellent substitute for a starting pistol is a pair of starting clappers (see figure 1.1). This simple device is made of two boards

Figure 1.1 Starting clappers.

hinged at the base, with ½ of a black-and-white disk attached to each board. The crack of the boards when they are brought together gives an acoustic signal that starts your athletes. When brought together, the black-and-white halves of the disk also give a visual signal for starting stopwatches.

TECHNIQUE

When sprinting at top speed, the athlete runs on the balls of the feet with the upper body either upright or inclined forward slightly. The arms are flexed 90 degrees at the elbow and swing in the direction of the run. Hands and facial muscles are relaxed. Each leg must drive powerfully to full extension, and the thigh of the leading leg is lifted to the horizontal position. The hips remain at the same height throughout (see figure 1.2).

Officials stop their watches when the athlete's torso crosses the plane of the finishing line. Immediately prior to the finish, your athlete should lean forward and drive the chest (torso) through the tape (figure 1.3). Athletes should always imagine that the finish is 5 meters beyond where it really is to prevent premature deceleration.

TEACHING STEPS
STEP 1. Lead-Ups
STEP 2. Sprinting Technique
STEP 3. Sprint Starts

Figure 1.3 The lean at the finish.

STEP 1: LEAD-UPS

Lead-up activities for sprinting emphasize quick reactions, coordination, and acceleration. Chase, tag games, and relays are excellent for teaching your athletes to react to visual, auditory, and tactile signals; these activities also emphasize the competitive aspect of sprinting.

Shadow Run

Pairs run freely. Athlete A tries to shake off Athlete B, who shadows Athlete A. Athlete B tries to remain within tagging distance of Athlete A throughout (see figure 1.4). On the signal, the athletes change roles. Be sure to use sufficient space in this lead-up activity to avoid collisions.

COACHING TIPS
- Try to shake off your shadow. Accelerate suddenly, and change direction.
- Keep your eye on those around you to avoid collisions.

Figure 1.2 Sprinting technique.

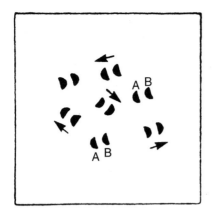

Figure 1.4 Shadow run.

Reaction and Acceleration Drill

Teams (of 3 or 4 athletes) line up behind a starting line. On the signal, the first member of each team sprints to a line or a traffic cone, set 20–25 m away. The athlete then turns and sprints back to tag the next in the team (see figure 1.5). Be sure to allow sufficient space between teams for the turn-around.

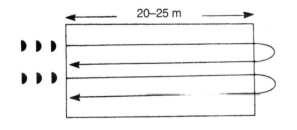

Figure 1.5 Reaction and acceleration drill.

Athletes use different starting positions (for example, sitting, lying, kneeling, or the set position for sprint starts).

Shuttle Relay

Split teams into 2 groups (A and B), with 3 or 4 athletes in each group. On the signal, the first member of Group A sprints to cross a line 20 m away. This athlete then tags the first member of Group B, who sprints back and tags the second athlete of Group A, and so on (see figure 1.6).

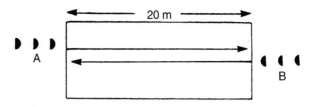

Figure 1.6 Shuttle relay.

VARIATION

Team members exchange a baton or use a hand tag. Athletes can also use different starting positions similar to those listed for the reaction and acceleration drill.

Chase and Tag

Pair off members of Team A with opponents in Team B. All members of Team A run slowly to a line 15 m ahead. The athletes in Team A touch the line with their feet and then accelerate back to the starting line. Members of Team B, in a ready position 4–5 m behind the line, attempt to tag their opponents in Team A after the line has been touched and before members of Team A can get back to the safety of their starting line (see figure 1.7).

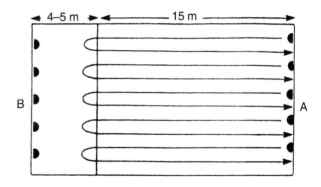

Figure 1.7 Chase and tag.

COACHING TIPS

Team A
- Run slowly to the line; there's no need to sprint.
- When you get near the line, straighten your body for the turn around—you don't want to be leaning forward.
- Pivot quickly and accelerate as fast as you can back to safety.

Team B

- Keep your eye on the line.
- The instant your partner from Team A touches the line accelerate as fast as possible.
- Try to tag your partners before they get back to the starting line.

VARIATION

Place cones on the 15-m line. Members of Team A run to touch (or circle) the cone and sprint back to the safety of their starting line. Vary the starting positions of Team B (for example, kneeling, lying, sitting, or the set position for sprint starts).

Pendular Relay

Divide your athletes into 2 groups with 3 or 4 in each group. The groups face each other 20–25 m apart. Athlete 1 sprints the 20- to 25-m distance, circles around the back of the team, and tags Athlete 2 from the rear (see figure 1.8). Athlete 2 sprints to tag Athlete 3 who has shifted into Athlete 1's position.

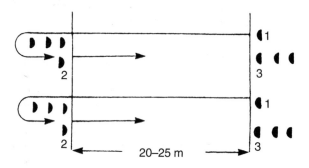

Figure 1.8 Pendular relay.

COACHING TIPS

Crouch down and look back over your shoulder for the tag. Be ready to accelerate.

VARIATION

Have your athletes use a baton, and you determine the type of exchange.

Circle Relay

On the signal, the first athletes in each team (from 4 to 8 teams) sprint around the outside of the circle and tag the second athletes of their teams who have moved out to the cir-

cumference of the circle (see figure 1.9). Athlete 2 repeats the action and tags Athlete 3. Be sure to make the circumference of the circle large enough so that your athletes are able to get sufficient traction when running on the curve!

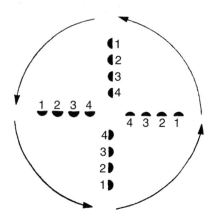

Figure 1.9 Circle relay.

VARIATION

Vary starting positions (for example, sitting, lying, kneeling, or the set position for sprint starts). Have athletes use a baton, and you determine the type of exchange.

STEP 2: SPRINTING TECHNIQUE

The following drills all play a large part in the improvement of sprinting technique. They are set in the following groups:

(a) Drills to improve coordination and sprinting technique
(b) Drills to improve leg power and acceleration
(c) Drills to improve sprint endurance

Select examples from each group when planning an instructional period.

The first set of drills is to improve coordination and sprinting technique. An acceptable method for doing this is to practice the correct elements slowly in a formalized manner. Once your athletes learn the correct actions and grasp the necessary rhythm, their speed of movement increases. Novices in your class will find these drills quite strenuous. Recommended distances are from 10–15 m with 2 or 3 repetitions. Your athletes can use an easy walk as a recovery.

High-Knee Marching

Each athlete marches forward slowly, forcefully driving the thigh of the leading leg up to a horizontal position (see figure 1.10). The arms are flexed 90 degrees at the elbow. The supporting leg extends fully up onto the toes as the athlete lifts the opposing knee.

Figure 1.10 High-knee marching.

COACHING TIPS

- Lift each thigh to a horizontal position.
- Work your arms forward and backward, not across your body.
- Push up vigorously onto your toes with each step.

High-Knee Marching With Extension of the Lower Leg

This drill differs from the previous drill in that the lower leg is extended after the thigh has been raised to a horizontal position (see figure 1.11). The drill is performed in the following sequence:

1. The athlete extends up onto the toes of the left leg, raises the right thigh to a horizontal position, and then extends the right leg. After performing this action, the athlete lowers the right leg and places the right foot on the ground. The left leg does not repeat the action of the right. Instead, the athlete steps forward normally with the left leg. All empha-

sis in this drill is on the right leg only. Repeat 3 or 4 times over distances of 10 to 15 m.

2. Now the emphasis is on the athlete's left leg. The athlete extends up onto the toes of the right leg, raises the left thigh to a horizontal position, and then extends the lower left leg. After performing this action, the athlete lowers the left leg and places the left foot down on the ground. The right leg does not repeat the action of the left. Instead, the athlete steps forward normally with the right leg. All emphasis in this drill is on the left leg only. Repeat 3 or 4 times.

Figure 1.11 High-knee marching with lower-leg extension.

COACHING TIPS

- Keep your vision directly forward, and relax your shoulders.
- Keep your arms held at 90 degrees at the elbows.
- Lift the thigh of your "active" leg as close to horizontal as you can. When your thigh is in the air, kick your lower leg forward. Then relax the leg and lower it.
- Step forward normally with your supporting leg and repeat the action 3 or 4 times.

High-Knee Skipping With Lower Leg Extension

This drill is quite strenuous; 3 or 4 repetitions over 10–15 m, each repetition followed by a rest, are sufficient to begin with for novices. The skipping action is similar to that done with a rope. Instead of walking, as with the previous drill, your athlete mimics skipping a rope. The athlete raises the thigh to a horizontal position and kicks the lower leg forward and out to an extended position (see figure 1.12). The athlete looks straight ahead, holds the arms at 90 degrees at the elbows, and swings the arms forward and backward vigorously.

- Concentrate on your legs; to begin with, forget about your arm action.
- Get the action started by skipping in place. Then move forward very slowly and try to keep the skipping action going.
- Think of a rhythm of "up, extend; up, extend."
- Add the arm action once you have your legs working.

High-Knee Running With Lower Leg Extension

This drill simulates the prancing action of a horse (see figure 1.13). The athlete's forward movement is slow. Your athletes can begin with simple high-knee running and then include the lower leg extension once the rhythm of the high-knee lift is established. Repeat 3 or 4 times over distances of 10–15 m.

- Set up the rhythm while running in place, and then try to move forward at a slow jog.
- Slowly increase the speed of your leg movement.
- Look forward, and keep your arms moving forward and backward throughout. Don't stop your arm action.

Seat Kicks

In this drill each of your athletes moves slowly forward, kicking up the heels to the rear and attempting to hit the buttocks (see figure 1.14). This drill helps to establish the pattern of the athlete's leg movement to the rear of the body. It is also great for stretching and loosening the quadriceps muscles. Be sure to have your ath-

Figure 1.12 High-knee skipping with lower-leg extension.

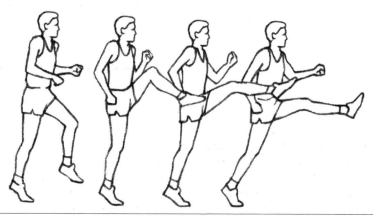

Figure 1.13 High-knee running with lower-leg extension.

Figure 1.14 Seat kicks.

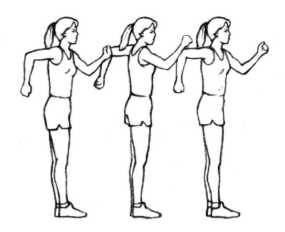

Figure 1.15 Sprint arm action.

letes well warmed up! Repeat 3 or 4 times over distances of 10–15 m.

COACHING TIPS

- Start by running in place and kicking your heels up easily to your rear.
- To begin with, don't try to contact your seat.
- Start moving slowly forward, kicking up your heels higher as you go.
- Concentrate on getting your heels up to your rear.
- Don't worry if you can't hit your seat with your heels to begin with. With practice you'll succeed.

Sprint Arm Action

In this drill, your athletes concentrate on maintaining the angle of the arms at the elbow (90 degrees) together with a forward and backward swing that is parallel to the direction they would run (see figure 1.15). This drill is initially practiced standing still, and then walking, jogging, and

sprinting. For walking, jogging, or sprinting, use 3 or 4 repetitions over 10–15 m.

COACHING TIPS

- Make sure you have the correct angle at the elbows.
- Extend your fingers, and on the upswing point them in the direction that you'd be running.
- Pull your elbows back and upward.
- Don't forget to relax your hands and the muscles of your face.
- Look directly ahead and lean forward slightly.
- When you are jogging and sprinting, let your legs work on their own; concentrate on your arms.

High-Knee Running Followed by Acceleration Sprints

Each athlete moves forward slowly 5 m, emphasizing the high-knee lift without a lower leg extension (see figure 1.16). On your signal,

Figure 1.16 High-knee running and acceleration sprints.

the athletes sprint forward for approximately 10–15 m, accelerating as vigorously as possible. Repeat 3 or 4 times.

COACHING TIPS

- Keep your torso upright when you're performing your high-knee lift. On my signal, sprint forward as fast as you can go. React the instant you hear the signal. Try to "explode" forward!
- Work your arms forward and backward as vigorously as you can, not across your body.
- Look straight ahead; don't lean backward.

Counting Strides Over a Selected Distance

Have your athletes pair off. One athlete sprints 20 m at high speed from a standing start while a partner counts the number of strides the athlete takes to run the distance. Who can run the distance in the least number of strides? Each athlete should concentrate on repetitive and powerful leg thrusts and high-knee lift.

COACHING TIPS

- Concentrate on drive (supporting leg), lift (thigh of the leading leg), and reach (lower segment of the leading leg).
- Look forward; relax the muscles of your face and hands.
- Swing your arms as vigorously as possible.

Testing Leg Speed

Athletes run in place while counting how many leg beats (foot contacts with the ground) they can make in 10 seconds. On the second and third attempts you can try 15 seconds, then 20 seconds. Start the athletes running in place, and then indicate the start and finish of the timed section. (Partners can help count the number of foot contacts.) You can have your athletes count each right and left foot contact, the right only, or the left only.

COACHING TIPS

- Listen to my countdown. I will count "5 4 3 2 1," and then I'll call out the seconds as they pass. Concentrate on counting the number of times you make contact with the ground.

- Lift each foot just clear of the ground each time.
- Concentrate throughout on sheer speed of leg action.
- Use short, fast arm movements.

Sprints at $^1/_2$–$^3/_4$ Speed

The emphasis in this drill is on sprinting at the required speed and maintaining good sprinting form without strain and without tightening up. Each athlete can use a sprint start or a flying start; the distance run depends on the athlete's maturity and fitness. Beginners run 15–20 m. More mature athletes run 25–30 m. Repeat the drill 3 or 4 times with walking rests.

COACHING TIPS

- Think of good leg drive, knee lift, and arm action.
- Let the muscles of your face and hands relax.
- Don't drop your head backward or swing your arms across your body.
- Keep your arms and knees swinging directly back and forward.
- Force your elbows back and up with each arm swing.

Flat-Out Sprinting

Using a flying start, each athlete runs a selected distance marked by two lines. Start the watch when the athlete crosses the first line, and an assistant signals by quickly lowering an arm when the athlete crosses the second line. For beginners, an acceptable distance is 15–20 m. Mature athletes can sprint 30–40 m. The number of repetitions and rest periods will depend on the athlete's fitness and maturity (for example, 2 or 3 repetitions for beginners).

COACHING TIPS

- Work on maintaining good sprinting form throughout; don't tighten up in an attempt to sprint faster.
- Look forward; relax your face and hands, and run on the balls of your feet.

The next 6 drills will help improve leg power and acceleration. These drills are very demanding: use them sparingly with beginners and increase intensity and repetitions slowly. Athletes should practice these drills on a cushioned surface, such as mats or a level grass area. The recommended number of repetitions for beginners is 2 or 3, with walking rests between each effort. (For more examples of this type of training, see chapters 8 and 9.)

Distance Hopping

Each athlete hops 2 or 3 paces with the left leg, and then repeats the same action with the right leg. With each hop, the athletes swing their arms forward and upward and thrust with the legs as powerfully as possible. The thigh of the free leg is lifted to a horizontal position on each hop (see figure 1.17). Repeat this drill 3 or 4 times with short rests in between.

- Swing your arms forward and upward as vigorously as possible to help you gain distance.
- Drive powerfully with your jumping leg.
- Make each hop the same size.
- Don't hop for height; aim for distance.
- Try the hopping sequence from standing and then from a 2 or 3 pace run-up.

Bounding (Striding) for Distance

This drill is a favorite of triple jumpers and is similar to the drill where athletes count their strides over a selected distance. Each bounding stride is long and reaching. Two or 3 bounding strides are performed in sequence (see figure 1.18). Do 3 or 4 repetitions with short rests.

Figure 1.17   Distance hopping.

Figure 1.18   Bounding for distance.

- Lean forward slightly and jump long and low, not upward; try to maintain your forward speed.
- Make each bounding stride about the same size.
- Drive forward and upward with your arms on each stride.
- Try the bounding strides from a standing start and then from a 2 or 3 pace run-up.
- When you use a run-up, don't make your first bounding stride huge and the remaining ones small.

Rabbit Hops

Rabbit hops are two-legged jumps, with 2 or 3 performed in sequence (see figure 1.19). This drill is extremely demanding and is not recommended for athletes who have knee problems. Athletes compete to see who can cover the greatest distance after 3 consecutive jumps. Repeat this drill 3 or 4 times with easy loose walking rests in between.

- Drive forward as powerfully as possible with each jump.

- Be sure to synchronize the actions of your arms by swinging them up and forward as you drive with your legs.

Combinations of Hopping and Bounding Over Low Obstacles

Bamboo canes set across traffic cones are set up to form a series of low obstacles that your athletes have to jump. The obstacles are set in a sequence that requires each athlete to strive for distance on each of 3 or 4 successive jumps (see figure 1.20). Use mats to cushion the athletes' landing. You make up the sequence of required hops and bounds and set the heights of the obstacles and the distances between mats. Have the athletes do 3 or 4 repetitions with short rests in between.

- Don't high-jump the obstacles. Try to jump from one mat to the next without pausing and resting on each landing.
- Use the thrust of your legs and the lift of your arms to get yourself up into the air and from one mat to the next.
- Imagine you are a ball that has been thrown forward and is bouncing along the

Figure 1.19 Rabbit hops.

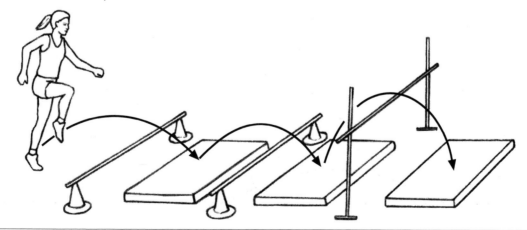

Figure 1.20 Hopping and bounding for distance over obstacles.

ground. Try to simulate in your jumps the series of long, low bounces that the ball would make.

High-Knee Running Backward, Then Forward

Athletes begin by running in place, emphasizing high-knee lift. On your first signal, they shift to slow backward running (with high-knee lift). On your second signal, they revert to slow forward running with high-knee lift (see figure 1.21). Recommended distance for beginners is 5 m backward and then 5 m forward. Have the athletes do 3 or 4 repetitions with short rests in between.

COACHING TIPS

- Keep your knees working high and as fast as possible.
- Listen to the rhythm of your footfalls; try to keep this rhythm fast and regular.
- Lean your upper body slightly backward when you move backward.
- Tilt your body forward to shift to forward running.

Sprinting With Partner Resistance

Using a strap or belt, one athlete pulls another along like a horse pulling a cart. The athlete acting as the horse wears a wide strap or belt around the abdomen. The partner acting as the cart holds the ends of the strap and provides a mobile but gentle resistance (see figure 1.22). Resistance should be sufficient to make the "horse" work as vigorously as pos-

Figure 1.22 Sprinting with partner resistance.

sible, as though sprinting flat-out. Both horse and cart move forward 10 m at a speed equivalent to a fast jog. You need a surface that will provide good traction. Athletes change positions after 2 or 3 repetitions.

COACHING TIPS

Horse

- Lean forward and work your legs and arms as hard and fast as you can. See if you can get yourself going faster and faster and overcome the resistance of the "cart."

Cart

- Don't stop the horse from moving forward. Give just enough resistance so that the horse can lean forward and work the legs and arms as vigorously as possible.

Figure 1.21 Backward and forward high-knee running.

- Lean backward enough so that the resistance is the right amount.

The following drills are intended to improve leg power and acceleration for a mature athlete who has progressed beyond elementary sprinting drills. This athlete must have developed additional leg power during the off-season through weight training and other complementary activities.

Running, Bounding, and Jumping Up Stairs

In this drill, athletes run, bound, hop, and jump up stairs (see figure 1.23); as the athletes' leg power increases, steeper stairs with greater depth are used. Drills of this nature are familiar to football players who run and bound up stadium steps as part of their training. Introduce these drills on steps that are low (shallow) and wide enough to allow plenty of room for each landing and takeoff. Begin by having your athletes run up the stadium steps. Then use combinations of different types of jumps. Experienced athletes may also bound down shallow stairs using a controlled double-leg or single-leg takeoff and a single-leg or double-leg landing. Note: Drills of this type demand excellent control and can be stressful on the legs.

COACHING TIPS

- Keep your eyes on the steps throughout.
- Drive as powerfully as you can, and lift your thighs with each jump.

- Remember to swing your arms forward and upward.
- Rest and breathe deeply once you have reached the top of the steps.
- Walk down if you are really tired at the top.

Depth or Rebound Jumping

Depth jumping (often called rebound jumping or *plyometrics*) develops explosiveness and elastic rebound in the leg muscles. In these drills, the athlete's muscles perform a lengthening contraction when the athlete cushions the landing after jumping down from height. Then immediately the muscles perform a shortening contraction as the athlete rebounds up again. A common method for an athlete to perform this drill is to step or jump down from the top of a vaulting box onto the floor and then immediately rebound up onto another box (see figure 1.24).

Many athletes in sprints, jumps, and throws use these drills as part of their training. Keep in mind that rebound jumping drills are very strenuous. They are recommended for physically mature athletes who have already developed power in the legs with considerable bounding, jumping, and weight training (squats). These drills are not intended for novices. For several more examples of this type of training together with coaching tips, see chapter 9.

Sprint endurance can be developed by many kinds of drills. The following are some examples.

Figure 1.23 Running, bounding, and jumping up stairs.

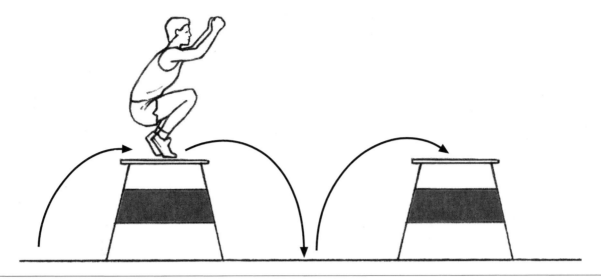

Figure 1.24 Rebound jumping.

Rolling Sprints

Athletes in teams of four (or more) jog or run slowly around the track. At your signal, Athlete D sprints to the front of his or her team. On your next signal, Athlete C sprints to the front, then Athlete B, and finally Athlete A (see figure 1.25). To increase the intensity of the drill, reduce the time between your signals and/or increase the size of teams. One full lap of a 400-m track is adequate for beginners.

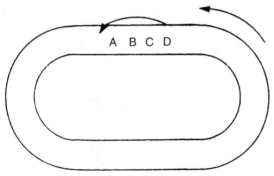

Figure 1.25 Rolling sprints.

Running Inclines

Athletes run up moderate inclines of 250 to 400 m at ½, ¾, and full speed (see figure 1.26). You can increase intensity by changing the following factors:

(a) Increasing the number of repetitions

(b) Reducing the rest period between repetitions

Continuous Relay

Form a team of 9 members. Each team member runs 50 m on a 400-m track. Athlete 1 runs 50 m and then passes a baton or tags Athlete 2 (see figure 1.27). Athlete 1 then waits at 2's position for the next round of exchanges. Athlete 9 moves into Athlete 1's position to receive the tag (or baton) from Athlete 8.

Fartlek

This drill uses a cross-country course of 2 or 3 miles. Athletes alternate short bursts of sprinting with jogging. (See chapter 4 for a more detailed explanation of Fartlek.)

Interval Sprints

Interval sprints are excellent for developing your athletes' anaerobic endurance. In these drills, your athletes sprint the curve and jog or walk the straightaway on a 400-m track (see figure 1.28), or they sprint 50 m and jog or walk 200–300 m. Intensity can be increased by increasing the number of repetitions (from 3 or 4 to begin with) and by reducing the length of time taken to rest.

The length and type of rest depends on the fitness and performance ability of each athlete. The athlete's pulse rate provides a good measure of fitness. When the athlete's pulse falls below 120 beats per minute at the end of the rest, the next repetition can begin. If the pulse stays above 120, the intensity of

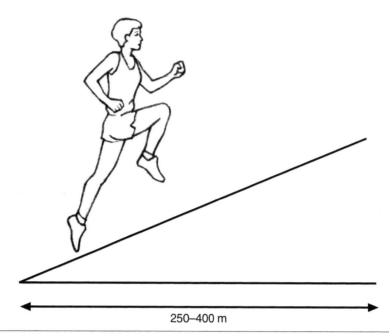

250–400 m

Figure 1.26 Running an incline.

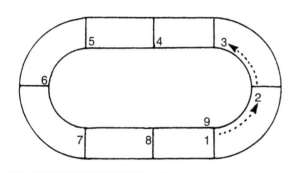

Figure 1.27 Continuous relays.

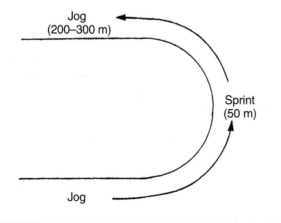

Jog
(200–300 m)

Sprint
(50 m)

Jog

Figure 1.28 Interval sprints.

training is too high and should be reduced. (For a more detailed discussion of interval training, see chapter 4.)

There are many drills which you can use to introduce intense sprint training to your more mature athletes. Some examples follow.

Repetition Sprint Starts With Maximum Effort Over 40 to 60 Meters

For this drill, each athlete goes through a complete sequence of commands for a sprint start. At the sound of the gun, the athlete sprints flat-out for 40–60 m. After a short rest, the athlete sprints the distance again. The selected distance and the number of repetitions will depend on individual fitness and ability. For example, an athlete might do 4 or 5 repetitions with a 2–3 minute pause between each. Repetition sprints improve the athlete's sprint endurance, coordination, and power.

Repetition Sprints From a Flying Start

In this drill, the athlete accelerates slowly over 20 m and then sprints with maximum effort for 20–30 m (see figure 1.29). The distance and the number of repetitions depends on individual fitness and ability. For example, an ath-

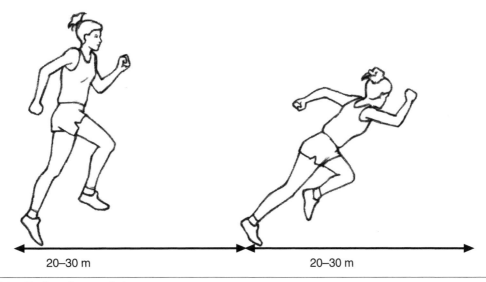

Figure 1.29 Sprints from a flying start.

lete might do 2 or 3 repetitions with rest pauses of 2–3 minutes between each repetition. This drill improves the athlete's sprint endurance and develops the athlete's ability for relaxed high-speed running.

Ins and Outs

"Ins and Outs" is a common name given to periods of high-speed sprinting followed by equal distances of loose, relaxed, fast running. For example, an athlete runs 100–150 m in the following manner: 20 m of relaxed, fast running (an "out"), 20 m at high speed (an "in"), and then another "out" of 20 m of relaxed, fast running (see figure 1.30). The objective is to improve the athlete's sprint endurance, sprint technique, and coordination.

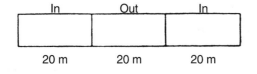

Figure 1.30 Ins and Outs.

Repetitive Relays

Athlete A accelerates over 40 m and passes a baton or tags Athlete B. Athlete A takes the position of B, who accelerates to Athlete C. Athlete C jogs, and then accelerates to tag Athlete D, who is waiting at the start to repeat the process (see figure 1.31). The objective of this drill is to improve sprint endurance.

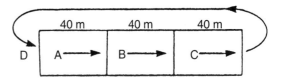

Figure 1.31 Repetitive relays.

100-Meter Repeats

Athletes run these repeats of 100-m distances at 80 to 90 percent of their 100-m best performances. The number of repetitions varies depending on fitness, and the rest period should be long enough to allow for full recovery. (This type of training is often used by 400-m runners and improves the athlete's sprint endurance.)

STEP 3: SPRINT STARTS

After you issue the "on your marks" command, each athlete is positioned in the blocks with the body weight resting equally on the rear knee and the hands. Arms are shoulder-width apart, and the hands are just to the rear of the line. The fingers and thumb form a V. Shoulders are rotated forward, 7–8 cm (3″–4″) ahead of the hands.

The athlete's stronger leg normally drives from the front block, because contact with this block is longer. The forward foot on the blocks is commonly 1¾–2 of the athlete's foot lengths from the starting line. The rear foot on the blocks is usually 1½ of the athlete's foot lengths behind the front foot (see figure 1.32). Breathing is steady and regular.

Figure 1.32 Two views of the "on your marks" position.

In the set position, the athlete is like a coiled spring. The athlete's seat is raised up and moved forward so that the angle of the leading leg is approximately 80 to 90 degrees at the knee. The rear leg is 110 to 130 degrees at the knee. The athlete's body weight is equally supported by arms and legs, and both feet are well in contact with the blocks. The athlete's back and head form a straight line. Vision is forward and toward the ground. The athlete holds the shoulders in a position that is slightly ahead of the vertical plane of the hands (see figure 1.33). On the set command, the athlete inhales and holds the breath.

At the sound of the gun, the athlete's forward leg extends vigorously and the knee of the rear leg is driven forward (see figure 1.34). The arms work vigorously to counterbalance the powerful action of the legs. The athlete inclines the body forward for the first 5–6 m of the race. Beyond this distance, the athlete as-

Figure 1.33 Set position.

sumes a more upright sprinting position for the rest of the race. By 40 m, the athlete is fully upright.

Most athletes use one of three basic block positions. These positions vary in the distance between the front and rear block and in the distance that the blocks are set from the line. Selection of these distances is determined by the body position required following the set command. The block positions used by each athlete depend upon the athlete's body length, leg length, leg power, and coordination. Leg length is the most important single characteristic for determining block positions. Figure 1.35 illustrates the three basic block positions.

Position A shows the greatest distance in foot lengths between the forward foot and the rear foot. This type of starting position is often called an *elongated* start and is frequently used by athletes with long legs. Position C shows the shortest distance between the front and rear blocks. This starting position is often called a *bunched* or *bullet* start and is used by athletes with shorter legs. The most commonly used stance is Position B, which is simply called a *medium* start.

Starting Practice

Each athlete walks forward, stops, and places both feet together on a line. On your signal each athlete leans forward slowly. Once their

Figure 1.34 Drive from the blocks.

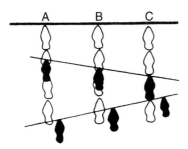

Figure 1.35 Three basic starting block positions: (A) elongated; (B) medium; (C) bunched.

body weight is tilted sufficiently to require a step forward, the athletes sprint forward 15–20 m (see figure 1.36).

COACHING TIPS

- Let's see who can tilt forward the furthest and begin sprinting without stumbling.
- Keep your knees swinging directly forward when you accelerate; avoid turning the knees and feet outward.

- Drive with your legs as powerfully as possible as you accelerate.
- Lift your thighs to a horizontal position.
- Lift your elbows as high as possible to the rear with each arm swing.

Touch the Ground Drill

Athletes jog slowly in line abreast. On your signal, each individual touches the ground with both hands, momentarily simulating a set position, and immediately sprints 10–15 m (see figure 1.37). The athletes then resume jogging, and on your next signal, they repeat the set position and sprint. Repeat this drill 3 or 4 times.

COACHING TIPS

- Don't worry about your body position when you touch the ground.
- Be sure the fingers and thumb of both hands touch the ground simultaneously on each signal.

Figure 1.36 Leaning followed by sprinting.

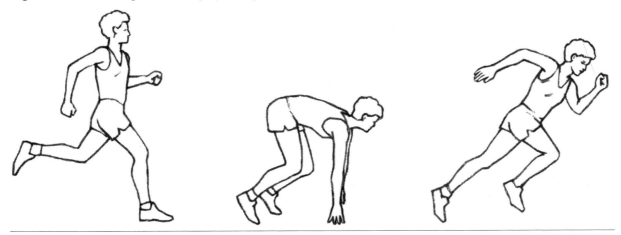

Figure 1.37 Touch the ground drill.

- Accelerate as fast as you can immediately after you've touched the ground.

Developing Explosive Drive From the Set Position

Athletes jog slowly in line abreast. On your signal, each athlete makes a small jump upward and rotates 180 degrees in the air. The athletes drop from their 180-degree spin into a momentary set position from which they immediately sprint for 10–15 m (see figure 1.38). On your next signal, athletes repeat the sequence. Dropping from a small jump into a set position and driving out of the set position helps athletes develop a feel for the explosive response needed in a sprint start.

COACHING TIPS

- Don't jump high in the air as you turn around; otherwise, you will collapse into the set position.
- Only the feet and hands touch the ground in the set position; don't sink all the way down onto your knees.
- Incline your body forward and work your arms and legs as vigorously as possible as you accelerate from your momentary set position.

VARIATION

Athletes are in line abreast. They move slowly backward with high-knee lift until you give a signal. They immediately drop into the momentary set position and sprint forward to cross a line that is 10 m ahead. They form in line abreast again and repeat the sequence.

Running Lines and Practicing the Set Position

Draw chalk lines on the ground 5 m apart. From a standing start position, your athletes run to the farthest line (25 m), jump and turn, drop momentarily into a set position, run back to the start, jump and turn, drop into a set position, run to the next nearest line (20 m), and repeat (see figure 1.39).

COACHING TIPS

- This drill is not a race; run at medium speed, and use a low jump for the turnaround.
- Drive with your legs as vigorously as possible out of the set position.

"On Your Marks, Get Set, Go"

Using a standing start, athletes lean forward and relax down into the "on your marks" position. On your command, each raises into the set position. You move from one athlete to the next and correct individual positions. On your signal, athletes sprint for 10–15 m.

COACHING TIPS

- Make sure your arms are shoulder-width apart.
- Your thumb and fingers should form a V just to the rear of the starting line.
- Move your shoulders slightly ahead of your hands with the "on your marks" command. Then simply raise your seat up

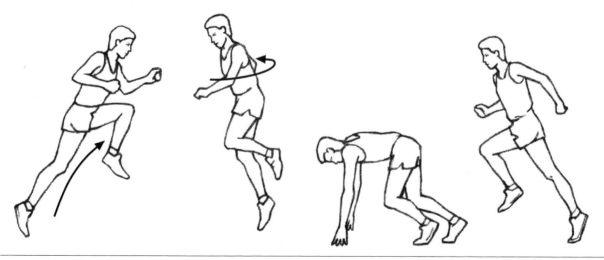

Figure 1.38 Jumping, rotating, landing in a set position, and then accelerating.

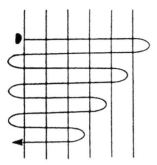

Figure 1.39 Running lines.

and forward when you hear the "get set" command.

- Concentrate on achieving the correct angle at your knees with the set position (80 to 90 degrees at your front knee and 110 to 130 degrees at your rear knee).

- On "go," work your arms and legs as vigorously as possible to drive yourself forward out of the set position.

- Don't lift your head upward or jump straight up with the "go" command.

- Try to thrust vigorously down the track so that after 4 or 5 strides you are in a sprinting position.

Partners as Starting Blocks

Using a partner as starting blocks, each athlete can work through a complete sprint start sequence, experimenting with various foot distances between the front and rear blocks (see figure 1.40). Assist each individual in finding the correct block positions. Athletes with longer legs will find the correct starting position by setting their blocks further apart and further from the starting line.

COACHING TIPS

- If you are acting as blocks for your partner, be ready to resist the leg drive that will occur when the "go" command is given.

- When you act as blocks, lean backward, straighten your arms, and be sure to turn your fingers to the rear. This position makes you more stable and helps you to resist the backward drive of the athlete practicing the start.

Sprint Start and Acceleration Practice

At your signal, athletes practice sprint starts and accelerating from starting blocks. Partners act as judges at the finish line 20–30 m away. A second line is set 3–5 m beyond the finish line. Initially, you should require your athletes to run through the tape and continue sprinting to the second line. Once your athletes understand that they must sprint through the finish, they can try pushing their chests forward at the tape (see figure 1.3, on page 4). Avoid having novices attempt an excessive lean at the finish, because this lean will cause them to stumble. Practice this drill on 25–30 m of straightaway, and then practice on a curved segment of track.

COACHING TIPS

Starting on the curve

- Line up your starting blocks on the curve so that you sprint toward the inside edge of the lane.

- Lean inward as you sprint around the curve and swing your right arm more powerfully than the left.

- Keep your feet parallel to the curve; don't turn your feet or knees outward.

- Look forward and swing your arms forward and backward, not across your body.

- Sprint through the tape as though the finish is at the second line.

- When practicing a lean, drive your chest ahead of your arms and lean toward the tape when you are approximately one full stride away. Don't jump at the tape or lean too early, or you will stumble.

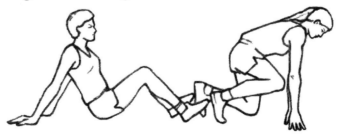

Figure 1.40 Using a partner as starting blocks.

COMMON ERRORS AND CORRECTIONS

SPRINT TECHNIQUE

Error	Reasons	Corrections
The athlete runs in a sitting position. The legs never fully extend.	The driving leg is not extending, and the upper body is inclined backward.	The athlete should practice leg-strengthening activities, sequence hopping with right and left leg, running on inclines, and bounding strides mixed with sprinting.
The athlete's arms do not swing back and forth parallel to the direction of run.	The athlete's shoulders and torso twist and rotate during the sprint, and the line of vision is not toward the finish. The athlete's head swings around, and the arms swing across the chest.	The athlete must work to correct the arm action while running in place or sprinting at ½ and ¾ speed. The athlete's line of vision should be on a target that is set directly ahead.
The athlete runs with the head tilted back or with the upper body inclined backward.	The athlete is tense and straining to run as fast as possible. The athlete's vision is not directly ahead. The athlete may have weak abdominal muscles.	The athlete should practice running in place, and then change to running backward followed by running forward. Emphasize the correct angle of the athlete's head and torso and have the athlete sprint while consciously relaxing the muscles of the face and hands. Have the athlete practice starts emphasizing the correct position of the head and torso. The athlete should also perform strengthening and flexibility exercises for the back and abdomen.
The athlete has poor forward and upward thrust of the thigh of the leading leg.	The athlete may have weak quadriceps, poor flexibility in the hip area, or poor coordination between arms and legs.	The athlete should practice high-knee running, skipping and bounding exercises, and repetitive hopping and jumping. Weight-training exercises that develop leg strength and flexibility exercises for increasing range of motion will also be of assistance.

→

Error	Reasons	Corrections
The athlete doesn't run in a straight line down the track but weaves around within the lane.	The athlete may be running with the head back or with the eyes closed or may be straining too much and tightening up during the run.	The athlete should emphasize running along a line, with the vision directly ahead, consciously trying to relax rather than strain. Repetition sprints with increasing speed on each sprint and emphasizing the correct head and torso position are helpful.
The athlete appears extremely tense. Fists are clenched, shoulders are tight, and muscles of the face are tense.	Tension is caused by inexperience and lack of training emphasizing relaxation while running at speed. The athlete feels that tension equals maximum effort and speed.	Have the athlete practice running with the muscles of the face and neck relaxed and the fingers loose (as though carrying an egg in the fingers of each hand).

SPRINT START

Error	Reasons	Corrections
In the set position, the athlete's shoulders stay behind the hands, and the athlete's center of gravity remains to the rear and over the legs.	The line of the athlete's center of gravity has not been shifted sufficiently forward toward the hands. The athlete's shoulders are not moved far enough forward. The blocks may be too far back from the starting line.	Correct the positioning of the blocks. Have the athlete practice elevating the seat and shifting the shoulders forward so that they are slightly ahead (in front) of the hands.
In the set position, the angle of the athlete's leading leg is too small (less than 90 degrees).	The starting blocks are set too close to the line. The athlete's seat is not raised high enough in the set position.	Correct the starting position. Using a partner who observes and provides corrections, have tho athlete work at lifting into the correct starting position.
In the set position, the angle of the athlete's leading leg is too large (more than 90 degrees).	The blocks may be too far from the line. The athlete has no knowledge of the correct body position in the set position. The athlete's legs are almost fully extended, and the athlete's seat is lifted too high in the set position.	Correct as for the previous error.
In the set position, the athlete's back remains parallel to the ground.	The athlete's head is raised, and the athlete's vision is on the finish line. The blocks may be too far apart. The athlete is not sure of how to lift the body up and forward into the set position.	Correct the athlete's line of vision, instructing the athlete how to rise into the set position and to look at a point approximately 1–1½ meters ahead of the hand position. Set blocks closer together.

→

Error	Reasons	Corrections
The athlete stands up or jumps up out of the blocks when the gun goes off. The athlete's initial strides from the blocks are short and weak.	Immediately after the gun is fired, the athlete elevates the upper body and raises the head and the line of vision. The athlete has poor drive from the blocks and during the strides that follow. The athlete may also have poor leg power.	Correct the angle of the athlete's body out of the blocks during the first 2 to 3 strides. Have the athlete practice working the arms and legs vigorously immediately after the gun is fired. Improve the athlete's leg power with jumping, bounding, hopping, and weight training.
The athlete stumbles or staggers from the blocks.	The athlete has poor arm action and drive from the legs. The athlete's legs are thrust out to the sides instead of in the direction of the run. The athlete may have poor leg power.	When the gun fires, the athlete must drive vigorously from the blocks; arms must work as vigorously as legs. The athlete should also work on leg-strengthening activities.

ASSESSMENT

1. **Assess the following theoretical elements as taught during instructional sessions:**
   a. Fundamental rules governing sprinting and sprint starts.
   b. Good safety habits for use in sprinting and sprint starts.
   c. Basic elements of sprinting and sprint start technique.
   d. Basic elements of sprinting and sprint start training.
2. **Assess the performance of technique during the following stages of skill development:**
   a. Sprinting over varying distances (for example, 50–200 m) using a flying start.
   b. Sprint start and acceleration from the blocks.
   c. Sprint start, acceleration from the blocks, maintenance of sprinting form over selected distances, and sprinting through the tape.

   CRITICAL FEATURES OF TECHNIQUE TO OBSERVE DURING ASSESSMENT

   Sprint Start

   ✓ Positioning of the blocks.
   ✓ Body alignment and positioning of the hands, shoulders, and seat following the "on your marks" command.
   ✓ Body alignment and positioning of the seat relative to the shoulders in the set position.
   ✓ Line of vision and angle assumed at the knees following the "get set" command.
   ✓ Leg drive, arm action, inclination of the body, and acceleration over the first 10 m following the "go" command (sound of the gun).

Sprinting Technique

- ✓ Extension of the driving leg and knee lift to the horizontal position on the athlete's leading leg.
- ✓ Running on the balls of the feet.
- ✓ Relaxation of the hands, shoulders, and facial muscles.
- ✓ The shoulders held steady.
- ✓ The line of vision held directly ahead.
- ✓ Position and movement of the arms (held at 90 degrees at the elbows and swung directly forward and backward).
- ✓ Moderate inward lean of the body for sprinting on the curve of the track.

Form at the Finish

- ✓ Position of chest (thrust forward at the tape).
- ✓ Continuation of sprint well beyond the finish.

3. **Hold graded competitions to help develop motivation and technique.**

a. Athletes use a sprint start and compete over varying distances (40– 100 m) on the straightaway.

b. Athletes repeat the start and race distances on the curve.

c. Athletes compete in handicap races held over distances ranging from 60–100 m. You set handicaps according to your knowledge of the athletes' abilities. For example, the distance between athletes at the finish can be used for a distance handicap at the start of the next race. An athlete who wins by 5 m in one race is set 5 m back at the start of the next. Or handicap athletes so that superiority of $\frac{1}{10}$ of a second in sprinting 100 m is translated into a handicap of 1 m at the start.

d. Partners measure how far the athletes can run in a certain number of seconds. You control the watch and the whistle.

SUGGESTED STANDARDS OF PERFORMANCE—SPRINTS

MALE		DISTANCE		
Age		100 m	200 m	400 m
12-13	Satisfactory	16.0	33.0	78.0
	Good	15.0	31.0	73.0
	Excellent	14.0	29.0	69.0
14-15	Satisfactory	15.0	31.0	72.0
	Good	14.0	28.5	68.0
	Excellent	13.0	27.0	64.0
16-17	Satisfactory	14.5	30.0	68.0
	Good	13.5	28.0	64.0
	Excellent	12.5	26.0	60.0
18-19	Satisfactory	14.0	28.5	65.0
	Good	13.0	26.5	61.0
	Excellent	12.0	24.5	57.0

FEMALE		DISTANCE		
Age		100 m	200 m	400 m
12-13	Satisfactory	18.0	39.0	85.0
	Good	16.8	36.0	80.0
	Excellent	15.8	33.0	76.0
14-15	Satisfactory	16.5	36.0	79.0
	Good	15.5	33.0	74.0
	Excellent	14.5	31.0	70.0
16-17	Satisfactory	16.0	34.0	77.0
	Good	15.0	31.0	72.0
	Excellent	14.0	29.0	68.0
18-19	Satisfactory	15.5	33.0	72.0
	Good	14.5	30.0	67.0
	Excellent	13.5	28.5	63.0

All standards measured in seconds.

2

RELAYS

The two types of sprint relay for males and females in the Olympic Games are the 4 × 100-m relay and the 4 × 400-m relay. The objective in the 4 × 100-m relay is for athletes to pass the baton while sprinting at top speed. A nonvisual (or blind) pass is used. This means that the baton receiver does not look back or turn and reach back for the baton. The 4 × 100-m relay has three changeover zones; each one is 20 m in length. Prior to each changeover zone is a 10-m acceleration zone. The rules of the event permit the baton receiver to accelerate within the 10-m acceleration zone provided that the baton is subsequently exchanged within the 20-m changeover zone.

In the 4 × 400-m relay, only the first lap and the first bend of the second lap are run in lanes. The incoming athlete is moving at a slower speed than the athlete in the 4 × 100-m relay, so there are no changeover zones. Also, a visual exchange is used rather than a blind pass, which means the baton receiver looks back and reaches back for the baton. The baton receiver concentrates on taking the baton out of the baton carrier's hand rather than being given the baton.

In the 4 × 100-m relay, elite athletes usually place a check mark a precise distance from the start of the acceleration zone. The baton receiver begins accelerating when the baton carrier hits this check mark. A call from the baton carrier indicates when the baton receiver must reach back for the baton. Usually the exchange occurs approximately 5 m prior to the end of the changeover zone.

With practice, the baton receiver knows exactly where the exchange will occur and will reach back for the baton at this point. It is up to the baton carrier to see that the baton is passed safely. An excellent 4 × 100-m relay team exchanges the baton at top speed. Good arm stretch during the exchanges ensures that athletes run the shortest possible distance during their legs of the relay. It is not unusual for athletes using superb changeovers to beat a team made up of much better sprinters.

All the various methods for passing the baton have advantages and disadvantages. This chapter explains four methods. Two are elementary and recommended for novices. In both these elementary exchanges, the athlete receiving the baton shifts it from the receiving hand to the other hand. So if an athlete receives the baton in the right hand, then the athlete immediately shifts it to the left hand.

For more experienced athletes, this chapter offers two alternate exchanges: the alternate upsweep exchange and the alternate downsweep exchange. With these methods, the baton stays in the receiving hand. With each baton pass, the baton alternates from the right hand of one athlete to the left hand of the next and so on. Of these two advanced exchanges, the alternate downsweep is recommended.

SAFETY SUGGESTIONS

Relays involve large numbers of athletes, and it is important that officials control changeover zones well. After passing the baton, athletes must stay in their lanes rather than immediately moving to the infield of the track. Slower teams can be coming up on the inner lanes. Officials must also control the movements of athletes to and from baton exchange areas; this control will minimize the risk of excited and/or fatigued athletes wandering into throwing sectors, or disturbing athletes in other events. The safety precautions concerning sprints and sprint starts discussed on pages 3–4 also apply to relays.

TECHNIQUE

There are two fundamental exchange techniques used for passing the baton. They are used in both the elementary and advanced exchanges and differ only in the way in which the baton is passed by the incoming runner.

These fundamental exchange techniques are the upsweep technique and the downsweep technique.

THE UPSWEEP TECHNIQUE

In the upsweep technique, the baton carrier passes the baton with an upward, pushing motion. The baton is thrust as far as possible into the hand of the baton receiver. The baton receiver grips the baton between the V formed by the fingers and the thumb of the receiving hand (figure 2.1a). Figure 2.1b shows a close-up of the baton being passed up into the V formed by the hand of the baton receiver.

The upsweep technique can be applied to three methods of baton exchange: the outside exchange, the inside exchange, and the alternate upsweep exchange. The outside and inside exchanges are elementary methods and are recommended for novices. The technique used in the alternate upsweep exchange is advanced and is recommended for more mature and experienced athletes.

THE DOWNSWEEP TECHNIQUE

In the downsweep technique, the baton carrier passes the baton with a downward, forward-pushing motion onto a platform provided by the hand of the baton receiver, who reaches back to grip the upper $\frac{1}{3}$ of the baton (figure 2.2a). In this action, the forward push of the baton is emphasized by the incoming runner. Figure 2.2b shows a close-up of the baton being passed to the platform formed by the hand of the baton receiver.

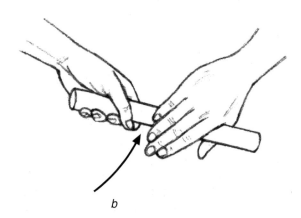

a b

Figure 2.1 Two views of the upsweep baton exchange.

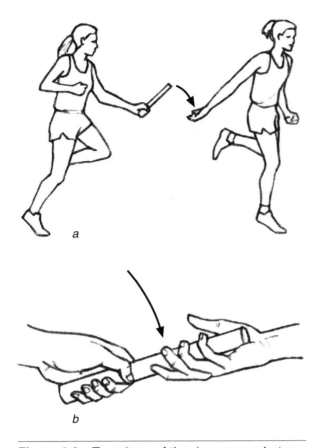

a

b

Figure 2.2 Two views of the downsweep baton exchange.

The downsweep technique is most commonly used in the alternate downsweep exchange. Like the alternate upsweep exchange, the alternate downsweep exchange is an advanced method of passing the baton. Elite relay teams vary in their choice of these two techniques. The majority of elite teams use the alternate downsweep exchange.

ELEMENTARY OUTSIDE AND INSIDE BATON EXCHANGES

Both the elementary outside and inside exchanges require the baton receiver to shift the baton from the receiving hand to the opposing hand. These exchanges are so named because the athlete carrying the baton runs to the outside or to the inside ½ of the lane to pass the baton. (In the outside exchange the baton carrier runs to the outside ½ of the lane. Using the inside exchange, the baton carrier runs to the inside ½ of the lane.) In both exchanges, the baton carrier passes the baton

with an upsweep motion into the V formed by the fingers and thumb of the baton receiver. The baton receiver then shifts the baton immediately from the receiving hand to the opposing hand in preparation for the next changeover. This aspect of the outside and inside exchanges classifies both as elementary exchanges and less efficient than the alternate exchanges where no hand shift of the baton occurs. Figure 2.3 shows the baton receiver receiving the baton and shifting the baton from one hand to the other.

Characteristics of the Elementary Outside Exchange

With this exchange, the baton carrier carries the baton in the left hand, passing it with an upsweep motion. The baton receiver receives the baton in the V formed by the thumb and fingers of the right hand. During the exchange, the baton carrier runs to the outside of the lane, while the baton receiver waits on the inside of the lane looking back over the right shoulder. The left foot is forward, and a standing or modified crouch start is used. (See figure 2.17 on page 39)

The baton receiver receives the baton in the right hand and immediately shifts it to the left hand. This athlete then runs from the inside of the lane toward the outer half of the lane in preparation for passing the baton in the next exchange. The first, second, and third athletes in the team repeat the exchange in this fashion. The fourth athlete in the team has no need to cut across the lane and runs the shortest possible distance to the finishing line. Figure 2.4 shows an overhead view of each athlete running toward the outer half of the lane in order to pass the baton into the right hand of the next athlete on the team.

Advantages of the Elementary Outside Exchange

The upsweep action of this exchange complements an athlete's sprint arm action. In addition, the baton receiver receives the baton in the right hand, which is most commonly the favored hand. Because the method of baton exchange is the same for the whole team, it means you can easily substitute or shift athletes from one position to another. Finally, the outside exchange is easy for youngsters to learn.

Figure 2.3 Receiving (a) and shifting (b) the baton for inside and outside exchanges.

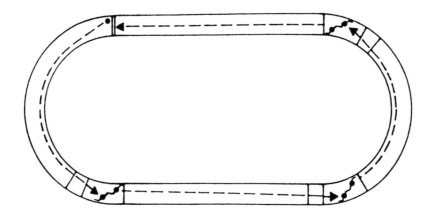

Figure 2.4 Outside exchange.

Disadvantages of the Elementary Outside Exchange

This type of exchange temporarily hinders the sprinting actions of the second and third athletes, who must shift the baton from one hand to the other. (The athlete running last on the team has no need to shift the baton.) In addition, the first and third athletes on the team (the curve runners) run further using the outside exchange than they would using the inside exchange.

Characteristics of the Elementary Inside Exchange

The baton carrier carries the baton in the right hand, passing the baton with an upsweep motion. The baton receiver receives the baton in the V formed by the thumb and fingers of the left hand. For this exchange, the baton carrier runs to the inside of the lane while the baton receiver waits on the outside of the lane, looking back over the left shoulder. The right

foot is forward, and a standing or modified crouch start is used.

The baton receiver receives the baton in the left hand and immediately shifts it to the right, running from the outside of the lane toward the inside half of the lane for the next exchange. The first, second, and third athletes in the team repeat the exchange in this fashion. The fourth athlete in the team has no need to cut across the lane and runs the shortest distance to the finishing line. Figure 2.5 shows an overhead view of each athlete running toward the inner half of the lane in order to pass the baton into the left hand of the next athlete on the team.

Advantages of the Elementary Inside Exchange

The upsweep exchange complements sprint arm action, and because the method of exchange is the same for the whole team, substituting or shifting athletes from one position to another is easier. The first and third athletes (the curve runners) run shorter distances using the inside exchange as compared with the outside exchange. Looking back for the baton carrier is more comfortable when the baton receiver is standing on the outside of the lane. Finally, the inside exchange is easy for youngsters to learn.

Disadvantages of the Elementary Inside Exchange

The second and third athletes must shift the baton from one hand to the other, which hinders the sprinting action. (The athlete running last on the team has no need to shift the baton from one hand to the other.) Athletes receive the baton in the left hand, which is commonly a less-favored hand.

ADVANCED EXCHANGES: THE ALTERNATE UPSWEEP EXCHANGE AND THE ALTERNATE DOWNSWEEP EXCHANGE

Elite relay athletes use two advanced baton exchanges: the alternate upsweep exchange and the alternate downsweep exchange.

Advanced Alternate Upsweep Exchange

In the alternate upsweep exchange, the baton carrier swings the baton upward into the V formed by the palm and thumb of the baton receiver's hand (see figure 2.1). This action is exactly the same as used in the elementary outside and inside exchanges. However, in the advanced exchange, the baton receiver does

not shift the baton from one hand to the other, but keeps it in the receiving hand. The baton carrier must give as much of the baton to the receiver as possible. To do this, both athletes try to make the giving and receiving hands touch during the exchange.

Advantages of the Advanced Alternate Upsweep Exchange

The sprinting action of the second and third athletes on the team is not hindered because there is no shift of the baton from one hand to the other. These two athletes also run the shortest possible distance to pass the baton because they run in a straight line, not diagonally across the lane (which was required in the elementary exchanges). In addition, the upward sweep of the baton complements the arm action used in sprinting.

Disadvantages of the Advanced Alternate Upsweep Exchange

Because each athlete in the team has a specific task to perform, rearranging or substituting athletes within a team is more difficult. With this exchange, each athlete receiving the baton has progressively less of the baton to grasp. This problem frequently forces athletes to readjust their grip on the baton, often by hitting the base of the baton on their thigh. This adjustment greatly increases the risk of dropping the baton (particularly during the last exchange).

Advanced Alternate Downsweep Exchange

Using the advanced alternate downsweep exchange, the baton carrier grips the base of the

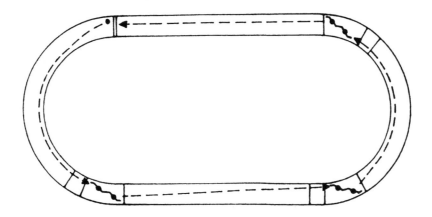

Figure 2.5   Inside exchange.

baton and passes it with a pushing downsweep motion into the raised palm of the baton receiver, who grips the upper extremity of the baton (see figure 2.2). Once the baton receiver gets the baton, the receiving hand is rotated down, under, and then forward. This rotation means that the upper extremity of the baton becomes the base, and the baton is ready for the next exchange.

Advantages of the Advanced Alternate Downsweep Exchange

This exchange allows for the greatest possible distance between the two athletes during the exchange. The baton carrier grips the lower ⅓ of the baton, and the baton receiver grips the upper ⅓; consequently the distance between the two athletes is two outstretched arms plus ⅓ of the baton. As with the alternate upsweep exchange, the second and third athletes on the team have shorter distances to run, and there is no shift of the baton from one hand to the other.

Disadvantages of the Advanced Alternate Downsweep Exchange

The pushing downsweep action of this exchange is contrary to sprint arm action, and efforts to achieve arm stretch and baton distance between the two athletes can cause a loss of rhythm and sprinting speed. Because each athlete in the team has a specific task to perform, rearranging or substituting athletes within a team is more difficult.

Common Characteristics of the Advanced Alternate Upsweep and Downsweep Exchanges

Both of these advanced exchanges have several common characteristics. These charac-

teristics are outlined in the following sections.

Positioning of Team Members The positioning of team members in the lane is the same for both techniques; both exchanges require the first athlete to pass the baton on the inside half of the lane, the second to pass the baton on the outside half of the lane, and the third to pass the baton on the inside half of the lane. Figure 2.6 shows the routes followed by each athlete on the team.

First Exchange The first athlete runs along the inside half of the lane, carrying the baton in the right hand. The second athlete on the team waits on the outside half of the lane, looking back over the left shoulder. As the first athlete approaches, the second athlete accelerates along the outside half of the lane and receives the baton in the left hand where the baton remains. The second athlete continues to run along the outside half of the lane.

Second Exchange The third athlete waits on the inside half of the lane, looking back over the right shoulder. As second athlete approaches (with the baton in the left hand), the third athlete accelerates along the inside half of the lane and receives the baton in the right hand. With the baton remaining in the right hand, the third athlete continues to run along the inside half of the lane.

Third Exchange The fourth athlete waits on the outside half of the lane, looking back over the left shoulder. As the third athlete approaches (with baton in right hand), the fourth athlete accelerates along the outside half of the

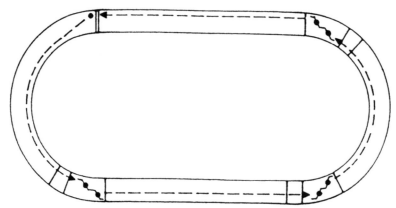

Figure 2.6 Positioning of relay team members in alternate exchanges.

lane and receives the baton in the left hand. With the baton remaining in the left hand, the fourth athlete runs directly toward the finish.

DUTIES OF 4 × 100-METER RELAY TEAM ATHLETES

Each athlete of a 4 × 100-m relay team performs specific duties, which apply regardless of whether the team uses an elementary or an advanced exchange.

First Athlete

The first member of the team must be a reliable starter (no false starts), run well on the curve, and be skilled at handing off the baton. This athlete runs approximately 105 m from the start to the point where the baton is exchanged.

Second Athlete

The second member of the team must be skilled at receiving and handing off the baton and able to sprint well over long distances. This athlete can be tall, because there are no curves to run. The second member of the team runs approximately 125 m from the acceleration zone to the point where the baton is exchanged.

Third Athlete

The third member of the team must be good at receiving and handing off the baton, an excellent curve runner, and able to sprint over long distances. This athlete runs approximately 125 m from the acceleration zone to the point where the baton is exchanged.

Fourth Athlete

The fourth member of the team must be skilled at receiving the baton and able to maintain good form while sprinting under pressure; this athlete must have plenty of fighting spirit. The fourth member of the team runs approximately 120 m from the acceleration zone to the finishing line.

TEACHING STEPS

STEP 1. Lead-Ups
STEP 2. Drills for Elementary and Advanced Baton Exchanges

STEP 1: LEAD-UPS

The following lead-up activities progress toward the outside and inside exchanges. These lead-up activities emphasize games of chase and tag, sprint starts (see chapter 1), and modified baton exchanges.

Chase

Mark out an area 20 m by 20 m. Athletes of Team 2 run freely within the area; Team 1 athletes stand on the perimeter (see figure 2.7). On your signal, one athlete from Team 1 attempts to tag any athlete from Team 2. If tagged, that athlete must leave the area. The first athlete of Team 1 sprints back and tags any athlete on the team, who tries to tag another athlete from Team 2. How much time did Team 1 take to tag all the athletes of Team 2? Teams change roles when all athletes of Team 2 have been tagged.

VARIATION

Set a time limit: How many of the opposing team are tagged within the time limit? Or allow pairs of the chasing team to enter the area to tag their opponents. If you have a larger area, have one complete team chase the other: Who is last to be tagged? How much time did it take?

Red Versus White

Pairs sit facing each other 1–2 m (3'–6') apart; one athlete from each pair is "red," the other is

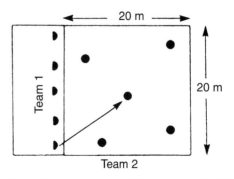

Figure 2.7 Chase.

"white." When you call "red," the red athletes must react as fast as possible by leaping up, turning, and sprinting to the safety of a line 10 m to their rear without being tagged by the whites, who leap up at the same time (see figure 2.8). If the call is "white," the reverse occurs.

COACHING TIPS

- Use this drill as a chance to practice your sprint start. When you turn to sprint away, roll sideways from sitting into a set position and work your arms and legs as powerfully as possible, as though from a sprint start.

VARIATION

Athletes lie or kneel in their starting positions. This variation may require some adjustment in the 1–2 m spacing so that the chase remains competitive.

Touch and Go

Athletes in Team A assume standing start positions. Athletes of Team B run to touch with their feet a line 4–5 m from Team A. Athletes in Team B turn and attempt to sprint to safety behind a line 15–20 m to the rear (see figure 2.9). Members of Team A cannot start pursu-

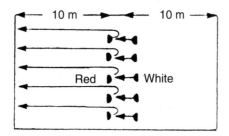

Figure 2.8 Red versus white.

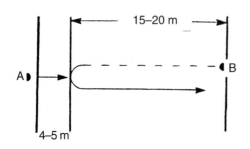

Figure 2.9 Touch and go.

ing until those in Team B have touched the 4–5 m line. Athletes in Team A attempt to tag those in Team B before they reach the safety of the starting line 15–20 m away.

COACHING TIPS

Team B

- Run slowly to the line; be prepared to turn and accelerate in the opposing direction.
- After you have pivoted around, drive with your legs and work your arms vigorously as you accelerate.

VARIATION

Team A begins in a set position. On the signal, athletes in Team B run to pick up tennis balls or relay batons placed on the 4–5 m line. The athletes in Team B then turn and sprint to the safety of the starting line.

Tag

Teams of 3 or 4 athletes line up to the rear of a starting line (A). The first athlete of each team races to a line 20–25 m away (B) and then back to the starting line to tag the next athlete in the team, who repeats the sequence (see figure 2.10). Each athlete goes to the rear of the team. Which team finishes first?

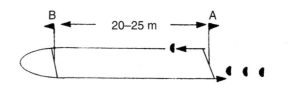

Figure 2.10 Tag.

VARIATION

Athletes can use different starting positions (such as lying, kneeling, sitting, or the set position for sprint starts). You can also place cones 20–25 m away from each team and have team members run around the cones instead of to a line. For another variation, a baton can be handed (visually from the front) from one team member to the next.

Shuttle Relay With Baton Exchange

Choose teams and then split each team into two groups (A and B). Groups A and B face each other 20–25 m apart. The first athlete from Group A sprints to pass a baton to the first athlete of Group B, who sprints back to pass the baton to the second athlete of Group A (see figure 2.11). The race is over when all athletes on a team have changed sides.

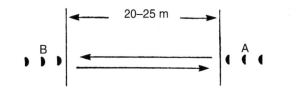

Figure 2.11 Shuttle relay with baton exchange.

Pendular Relay

Set up posts 20–25 m apart. Athletes from each team sprint around Post B and tag the next athlete on their team to the rear of Post A (see figure 2.12).

Pendular Baton Relay

Using the same organization as in the pendular relay, athletes perform the same drill but now carry a baton. The first athlete sprints around Post B, back around the rear of the team, and hands the baton to the next athlete who stepped out from the team in order to be ready to receive the baton. Both athletes visually control the exchange of the baton (see figure 2.13). The first athlete can use a sprint start.

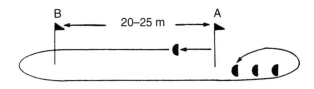

Figure 2.12 Pendular relay.

COACHING TIPS

Baton receiver

- Begin running when the baton carrier is 3–4 strides away. In this exchange, look back and extend your arm backward to receive the baton. This type of exchange is similar to what you'd use in the 4 × 400-m relay.

Circular Relay

Athletes stand in a line inside a circle. The first athlete, standing at the circle's edge, sprints around the outside of the circle, and the next athlete on the team moves to the circumference and assumes a sprint set position. A tag on the shoulder from the incoming runner sets this athlete going. Be sure to make the circumference of the circle large enough to give sufficient traction; too tight a curve will cause athletes to slip (see figure 2.14).

Circular Relay Using Check Marks and Batons

Use the same setup as for the circular relay and place a check mark on the circumference of a circle 3–4 large strides back from the starting point for each team. When the first athlete

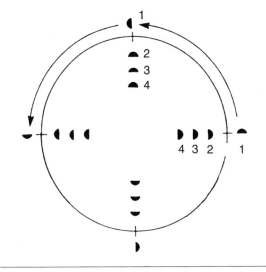

Figure 2.13 Visual baton exchange.

Figure 2.14 Circular relay.

has started sprinting around the circle, the second member of the team moves to the starting point and watches for the first athlete to reach the check mark. When the first athlete hits the check mark, the second athlete turns and starts accelerating. Both athletes attempt to pass the baton while sprinting fast. Don't emphasize a particular exchange at this stage in the teaching sequence. Any type of exchange is acceptable.

COACHING TIPS

- Look back for the baton carrier. When the baton carrier hits the check mark, turn and start running at that instant.
- Try to pass the baton without stopping.

STEP 2: DRILLS FOR ELEMENTARY AND ADVANCED EXCHANGES

You can use the following drills for teaching all exchanges, whether elementary or advanced. The main elements of each drill are the same, although the specifics of the baton pass will depend on the type of exchange you decide to teach. The following drills use an elementary outside exchange as an example.

Static Baton Exchange Practice

Teams of 3 or 4 athletes stand 1½ m apart, one behind the other. This distance is sufficient to require good arm stretch during the baton exchange. The athlete at the back of each team holds a baton. Athletes pass the baton with the left hand to the right hand of the ath-

lete in front (see figure 2.15). The baton carrier calls "stick" or a similar verbal command. On this call, the baton receiver places the right hand back to receive the baton, holding the right arm angled at approximately 45 degrees. The baton is swung up into the V formed by the thumb and fingers. The baton receiver immediately shifts the baton from the right hand to the left.

When the athlete at the front of the team gets the baton, all team members rotate 180 degrees and repeat the drill. To avoid confusion, it is a good idea to use different calls for each team. In addition, be sure to separate the teams sufficiently one from the other so that there is no confusion among the baton receivers who will be answering the call from the baton carriers.

COACHING TIPS

Baton carrier

- Hold the base of the baton and rotate your hand downward so the baton forms a straight line from the forearm.
- Swing the baton upward into the V of the receiving hand, making sure you don't hit your teammate's fingertips.
- Try to give the receiving athlete the top ⅓ of the baton.

Baton receiver

- Hold your hand steady with your arm back at about 45 degrees; don't wave your hand around, and be sure that your thumb and fingers are spread apart.
- Grip the top ⅓ of the baton with your hand. Immediately bring the baton across

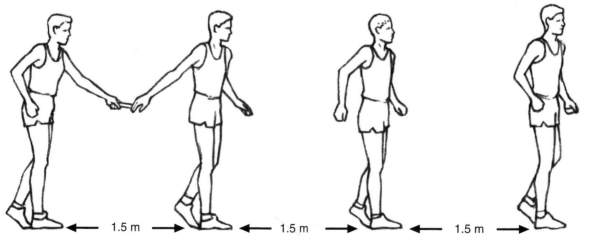

Figure 2.15   Static baton exchange.

the front of your body and grip its base with the opposite hand. In this way, you'll be ready to pass the baton in the next exchange.

Static Baton Exchange Using Sprint Arm Action

Groups of 2, 3, or 4 athletes stand 1–1½ m apart, one behind the other. Each athlete assumes a slight forward body lean and mimics the arm action used when sprinting. At the call, the receiver's hand is placed back, and the baton carrier in each group passes the baton to the receiver. The receiver immediately shifts the baton from the right to the left hand, repeats the sprint arm action (but not the leg action) 2 or 3 times, and then calls for the next exchange.

COACHING TIPS

- Flex your arms at the elbows and swing them back and forth slowly.
- Lean your upper body forward as though sprinting.
- Listen for the call and immediately put your hand back to receive the baton.
- When you get the baton, immediately shift it to your other hand, and then mimic the sprint arm action for at least 2 or 3 arm cycles before making the call for the next exchange.

Baton Exchange Practice: Jogging Slowly

During this practice, you can use the same organization as in the previous drill. Athletes in each group must maintain a distance of two arms' stretch plus ⅓ of the baton between the baton carrier and baton receiver. If there are 3 or 4 in a group, then they must all position themselves the same distance apart as they jog forward slowly. On the call, the baton exchanges are begun with the baton being passed forward from the athlete at the back of the group to the athlete in front. If athletes are in pairs, the rear athlete can pass the baton and then run ahead to receive the next pass.

VARIATIONS

You can use the following variations when you have groups of 3 or 4. Make sure that your athletes run slowly at first:

(a) The baton is dropped to the side after the last exchange. The athletes pass by, and the rear athlete picks up the baton to repeat the sequence of passes. (This method only works well if all athletes are moving forward slowly. Otherwise, the 2 or 3 athletes in front will outdistance the athlete who must pick up the baton from the ground.)

(b) After passing the baton forward, the athlete at the rear of the team sprints to the front of the team. This sequence can be repeated continuously.

(c) The athlete at the front of the team (who will be last to receive the baton) steps to the side and allows the 3 athletes to the rear to pass by. They then repeat the sequence of passes from the rear to the front.

COACHING TIPS

- Be sure to run slowly, and concentrate on the baton passes.
- Always position yourself the correct distance from the other athletes on your team.
- Fully extend your arm when passing or receiving a baton.
- Don't put your arm back to receive the baton until you hear the call.

Baton Exchange Practice

Have your athletes practice this drill at ½–¾ speed, and then have them attempt it at full speed. When your athletes are running fast, they must maintain the required distance between team members. Have the athlete at the front of each team set the pace. Those to the rear then establish the correct distances between each athlete for passing the baton.

COACHING TIPS

Baton carrier

- Wait until all team members are running at the same pace and have established the correct distance before calling "stick" or "hand."
- Look for the hand of the receiving athlete when you call "stick."
- Stretch out your arm to pass the baton. Don't run onto the heels of the athlete in front of you.

Baton receiver

- When you hear the call, put your arm back and hold it steady to receive the baton.

- Spread your fingers and thumb wide to provide a good target.

- Don't wave your arm around. Put it back and keep it steady.

- As soon as you receive the baton, shift it from the right hand to the left in order to be ready to call for the next exchange.

Practicing the Advanced Alternate Upsweep Exchange

Make up teams, each consisting of 3 or 5 athletes. The athletes begin jogging slowly in single file. After the front athlete has established the pace, those to the rear set the passing distance of 2 arms' distance. The baton carrier holds the baton in the right hand, gripping it at the base. After calling "stick," the baton carrier makes the pass with an upsweep motion into the left hand of the receiving athlete.

Athletes continue to pass the baton using alternating passes (right to left, left to right, and so on) until the baton gets to the front of the team. Odd numbers of 3 or 5 per team means that the baton will always finish in the right hand of the athlete in front. Once the baton is passed to the front, the teams can turn around and repeat the practice. The athlete at the front now becomes the athlete at the back, with the baton starting again in the right hand.

COACHING TIPS

Baton carrier

- Be sure your baton hand contacts the receiver's hand during the exchange; give as much of the baton as possible.

- Remember that with each pass, the receiving athlete gets less and less of the baton to hold; grip as close to the base of the baton as you can.

Baton receiver

- Once you receive the baton, don't shift it from one hand to the other. Grip as close to the base of the baton as possible.

- Avoid trying to readjust your hold on the baton (e.g., by pressing the base of the

baton against your thigh). If you grip the baton properly, you won't have to do this!

Alternate Downsweep Exchange Practice

Make up teams containing 3 or 5 athletes in each team. The athletes begin jogging slowly in single file. After the athlete at the front has established the pace, those to the rear set the passing distance of 2 arms' stretch plus $\frac{1}{3}$ of the baton. The baton carrier holds the baton by its base in the right hand. With the call of "stick," this athlete pushes the baton downward onto the platform formed by the left hand of the receiving athlete. Gripping the upper $\frac{1}{3}$ of the baton, the receiving athlete rotates the baton hand down, forward, and upward and prepares to pass the baton with a downsweep push onto the right hand of the next athlete in line.

Athletes alternate passing the baton in this fashion to the front of the team. Odd numbers of 3 or 5 per team means that the baton will always finish in the right hand of the athlete in front. Once the baton is passed to the front, the teams can turn around and repeat the practice. The athlete at the front now becomes the athlete at the back, with the baton starting again in the right hand.

COACHING TIPS

Baton carrier

- Immediately after calling "stick," push the baton down onto the hand of the receiving athlete and give only the upper $\frac{1}{3}$ of the baton.

- Don't smash the baton down onto the receiver's hand! Remember that the upper $\frac{1}{3}$ of the baton will become the base of the baton when the receiving athlete rotates the hand forward for the next pass.

Baton receiver

- Be sure to extend your receiving arm back horizontally to provide a flat platform as a target for the athlete who's going to pass you the baton.

- Keep your arm steady, and once you've gripped the end of the baton, simply rotate it down, forward, and upward so that you are ready to make the next pass.

Introduction to the Acceleration Zone, Changeover Zone, and Use of Check Marks

(a) This drill is practiced without the use of a baton. Pair off athletes who have approximately the same sprinting ability. One will act as the baton receiver and will stand ready on a line with a check mark initially placed 4–6 m (i.e., 5–6 long strides) to the rear. The incoming athlete, acting as the baton carrier, sprints from a line 20–25 m back from the check mark (see figure 2.16). When the incoming athlete hits the check mark, the outgoing athlete turns and sprints as fast as possible toward a line 25 m ahead. The incom-ing athlete attempts to catch up with the outgoing athlete about 5 m prior to the 25-m line. Ask each pair of athletes to adjust their check marks so that the tag occurs when both are sprinting flat-out and when they are 5 m short of the 25-m line.

(b) Now have your athletes use a baton and practice the exchange method that you select. The athletes will have to adjust the position of the check mark to allow for variations in sprinting speed and the fact that they become fatigued with each repetition of this drill. Be sure to tell your athletes to make allowance for the two arms' stretch and the baton distance that is required between the baton carrier and the receiver. The receiver should wait for the baton carrier to hit the check mark and then turn and accelerate.

Crouched Starting Position of the Athlete Receiving the Baton

You can use the previous drill to teach the baton receiver the use of a crouched position and how to look back over the shoulder for the incoming baton carrier. Figures 2.17a and 2.17b show two variations for the crouched position. Figure 2.17b uses a single hand for support and simulates the set position for sprint starts. Other skills to teach at this time include making sure that the baton receiver

Figure 2.17 Two variations of the crouched starting position used in relay changeovers.

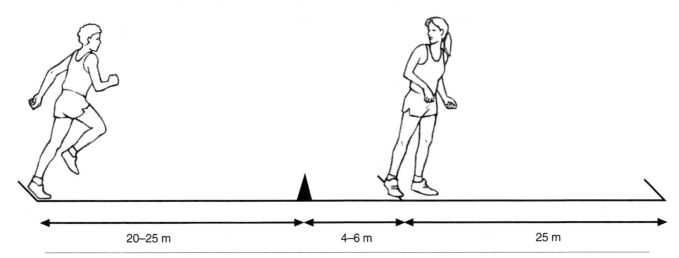

| 20–25 m | 4–6 m | 25 m |

Figure 2.16 Introduction to use of checkmarks.

knows where to stand in the lane, which shoulder to look back over, and how to reach back with the receiving hand only on the call of the baton carrier.

COACHING TIPS

Baton receiver

- Accelerate as vigorously as possible as soon as you see the baton carrier hit the check mark; stay in your ½ of the lane until you receive the baton.

- It's the job of the baton carrier to catch you and give you the baton, so don't slow down.

- Listen for the call of "stick;" only then do you put your arm back for the baton. Don't put your arm back until you hear the call. If you run continuously with your arm back, you'll lose speed.

- The complete baton exchange should take no more than 2-3 strides.

Baton carrier

- If you are required by the exchange to run on the inside half of the lane, be sure that you do so.

- Don't run directly behind the baton receiver; otherwise you might step on each other.

- Call "stick" and reach out with your arm and the baton only when you are within distance to make the pass, not before.

- Don't run with the baton arm continuously outstretched. It'll ruin your sprinting speed!

Baton Exchange on the Track Using Acceleration and Changeover Zones

This drill is similar to the prior drills, with the exception that the athletes now use the 10-m acceleration zone and the 20-m changeover zone on the track (see figure 2.18). Athletes work in pairs and practice the exchange that you have selected. In this drill, it is useful to have a third athlete observe and help to establish the positioning of check marks. Athletes should also practice the baton exchange running from the straightaway into the curve, from the curve into the straightaway, in the tighter inner lanes, and in the less-tight outer lanes.

Repetitive Acceleration and Changeover Zone Practice

This drill requires a two full-size changeover and acceleration zones and 25 m between each (see figure 2.19). When the baton carrier (Athlete 1) passes the check mark, the receiver, (Athlete 2), who is ready at the start of the 10-m acceleration zone, sprints to receive the baton in the 20 m changeover zone. Athlete 2 then sprints to pass the baton to Athlete 3, who is waiting in the acceleration zone. Check marks are initially placed 4–6 m back from the acceleration zone and are adjusted if necessary by an observer after changeover has occurred. After passing the baton, Athlete 1 turns and immediately runs back to take the starting position of Athlete 2, and Athlete 2, after passing the baton, runs to take the position of Athlete 3.

Additional athletes can also be included in this practice so that each baton carrier has a longer rest period between sprints. You may

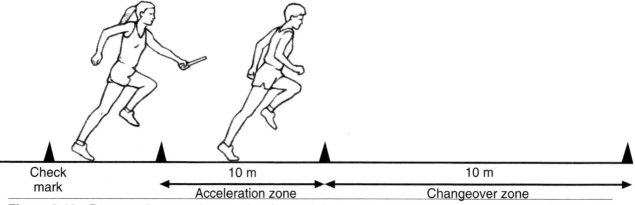

Check mark   10 m   10 m

Acceleration zone   Changeover zone

Figure 2.18 Baton exchange using acceleration and changeover zones.

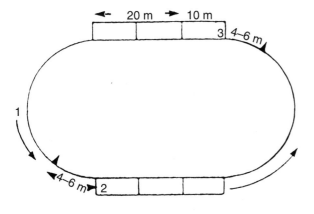

Figure 2.19 Repetitive acceleration and changeover zone practice.

also find that young athletes need not use the full 10 m of the acceleration zone. The line indicating the start of the acceleration zone can be used as the check mark for the baton carrier. The baton receiver then stands within the 20 m of the changeover zone. This setup gives a young sprinter a line to use as a check mark and ensures that the baton exchange occurs in the changeover zone and not in the acceleration zone (which is illegal!).

Continuous Relay Practice Using 8 Athletes

In this drill you use check marks, but you don't use specific changeover zones. Eight athletes form a practice group, and each runs 50 m of a 400-m track (see figure 2.20). After passing off the baton, the athletes jog back to their original starting positions to receive the baton the second time around.

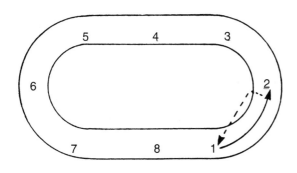

Figure 2.20 Eight-runner continuous relay practice.

Continuous Relay Practice Using 9 Athletes

In this drill, each athlete sprints 50 m. There are no marked acceleration or changeover zones. Athletes 1 and 9 are stationed at the start. Athlete 1 carries the baton and passes it to Athlete 2. Athlete 1 takes the position of Athlete 2 to receive the baton the second time around. Athlete 9 steps onto the track to fill the position vacated by Athlete 1 (see figure 2.21).

If you decide that your athletes use an alternate exchange, then the first athlete will carry the baton in the right hand. On the next circuit, this athlete must receive and pass the baton with the left hand. This setup means that all athletes must remember that if they receive in the left on one occasion, they will receive in the right on the next. This type of alternation also requires that athletes receiving in the left hand stand in the outer half of the lane, looking back over their left shoulder. The reverse occurs the next time they receive the baton. They will receive in the right hand, stand on the inside of the lane, and look back over the right shoulder.

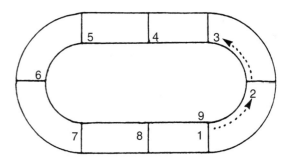

Figure 2.21 Nine-runner continuous relay practice.

COACHING TIPS

Baton carrier

- If you're carrying the baton in your right hand, remember you must run along the inside half of the lane.
- If you're carrying the baton in your left hand, remember you must run along the outside half of the lane.

Baton receiver

- If you're not sure where you should stand to receive the baton, look back to see in what hand the baton carrier has the baton.
- If the baton carrier is carrying the baton in the right hand, you'll stand on the outside ½ of your lane, looking back over your left shoulder, and receive the baton in your left hand.
- If the baton carrier is carrying the baton in the left hand, you'll stand on the inside half of your lane, looking back over your right shoulder, and receive the baton in your right hand.

Continuous Relay Practice Using 12 Athletes

Each athlete sprints the full 100 m plus additional distances for acceleration and changeover. Athlete 1 sprints around the curve, passes the baton to Athlete 2, and then goes to the end of the team stationed at the first changeover. Athlete 2 sprints the straightaway, passes the baton to Athlete 3, and then goes to the end of the team stationed at the second changeover, and so on (see figure 2.22). Immediately after the first athlete from each changeover group has received and sprinted away with the baton, the next athlete steps onto the track. An alternate exchange will demand an ability to receive and pass the baton with either hand. Athletes will also have to know in which half of the lane they should stand to receive the baton.

COACHING TIPS

See coaching tips for the preceding drill.

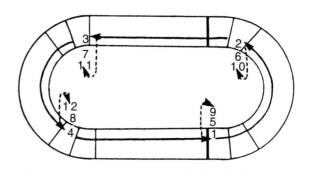

Figure 2.22 Twelve-runner continuous relay practice.

COMMON ERRORS AND CORRECTIONS

ELEMENTARY AND ADVANCED ALTERNATE EXCHANGES

Error	Reasons	Corrections
The baton receiver is not ready for the exchange and starts too late or too early.	The baton receiver is unsure of his/her duties and poorly estimates the speed of the baton carrier.	The baton receiver needs more practice on the exchange; reassess check marks and specific duties of each athlete.
The baton receiver looks back during the exchange.	The athlete is afraid of not receiving the baton or of dropping it during the exchange. The athlete poorly estimates the speed of the baton carrier and is unsure of the accuracy of the check marks.	Corrections are the same as for the previous error. Provide the athletes with more practice in pairs, and work on developing the confidence of the baton receiver.

→

Error	Reasons	Corrections
The baton receiver runs with the hand back and arm extended for several strides prior to receiving the baton.	The baton receiver is unsure when he/she is going to receive the baton and is afraid of not receiving the baton.	Corrections are the same as for the previous two errors. The athletes need more practice on the exchange. The baton carrier must know when to call, and the baton receiver should know at what point in the changeover zone the baton carrier will call.
The two athletes drop the baton during the exchange.	The baton carrier may not be holding the lower $1/3$ of the baton. In the upsweep exchange, the baton receiver may not be spreading the thumb and fingers of the receiving hand to form a V. In the downsweep, the baton receiver may not have provided a horizontal platform on which the baton carrier can place the upper $1/3$ of the baton. The baton receiver may be allowing the hand to wave around so that it presents an unsteady target.	Provide athletes with more practice on the required exchange. Concentrate on the correct arm and hand actions by both athletes. Practice the exchange standing, then walking, and then finally running. Emphasize the correct distance between the two athletes.
In the elementary exchanges, the baton receiver forgets to shift the baton from the receiving hand to the other hand or performs this action immediately prior to passing the baton to the next athlete.	The baton receiver is unsure of duties or is nervous and distracted.	Corrections are the same as for previous drills. Have athletes practice the reception and the immediate shift of the baton from one hand to the other. The last athlete in the team will not need to shift the baton from one hand to the other after receiving it.
The baton carrier stretches out the baton arm too early and disrupts his/her sprinting rhythm.	The baton carrier is anxious and is unsure of where the exchange is going to occur.	Have the athletes practice the required baton exchange. Establish where the exchange will occur, and have both athletes practice maintaining good sprinting action until within baton-passing distance.

→

Error	Reasons	Corrections
The baton carrier slows down prior to the exchange.	The baton carrier is anxious or afraid of the exchange and is unsure of where the baton exchange should occur. The athlete may have poor sprint endurance.	Establish where the exchange will occur, and have the athletes practice the baton exchange at full speed. Have the athletes practice sprint endurance training (see chapter 1).
The baton carrier runs onto the heels of the baton receiver.	The athletes are forgetting which part of the lane they should run in during the exchange. The baton receiver starts sprinting too late.	Have the athletes practice the baton exchange at full speed. If the athletes use the elementary outside exchange, then the baton carrier must run to the outside $1/_2$ of the lane. For the elementary inside exchange, the baton carrier runs to the inside $1/_2$ of the lane.
The baton carrier leaves the lane immediately after passing the baton to the baton receiver.	The athlete lacks knowledge of rules controlling relay races.	Make sure all athletes know the rules governing the event.
The last athlete of the team, upon receiving the baton, shifts it from one hand to the other.	The athlete doesn't understand the duties required of the last athlete on the team. The athlete is excited or anxious.	More practice will help all the athletes on the team develop control and reduce anxiety. The last athlete must learn to receive the baton and sprint as fast as possible toward the finish. In all exchanges (elementary and advanced), the last athlete in the team has no need to shift the baton from one hand to the other.
The baton exchange occurs outside of the changeover zone.	The baton receiver may have started before the baton carrier hit the check mark. The check mark is positioned wrongly for the sprinting ability of the two athletes.	Practice the exchange again, making sure that the check mark is positioned correctly for the two athletes involved. Make sure that the baton receiver starts only when the baton carrier hits the check mark and not before.

→

ADVANCED ALTERNATE UPSWEEP EXCHANGE

Error	Reasons	Corrections
The baton receiver is forced to hit the baton on the thigh in order to shift the grip to the base of the baton.	The baton carrier is not gripping the base of the baton but is holding the middle, so this athlete incorrectly gives the baton receiver the top $\frac{1}{3}$ of the baton. The athletes are too far apart when they complete the exchange, and the baton receiver receives an insufficient portion of the baton.	The baton carrier must grip the baton at the base and give as much of the baton as possible to the baton receiver. The athletes' hands must touch during the exchange. After the exchange, the baton receiver should be gripping as close to the base of the baton as possible. Practice the exchange again, making sure that the baton receiver starts running only when the baton carrier has hit the check mark.
The baton carrier has great difficulty in getting the baton into the hand of the baton receiver.	The baton receiver may not be holding the receiving arm at the correct angle (approximately 45 degrees) or may be allowing the arm and hand to wave around so that it presents an unsteady target.	Have the athletes practice the exchange repeatedly. The baton receiver should accelerate vigorously with the correct upper body lean and take into account this upper body lean when holding the arm back. The receiving arm should be held steady and at the correct angle.

ADVANCED ALTERNATE DOWNSWEEP EXCHANGE

Error	Reasons	Corrections
The baton carrier has great difficulty in passing the baton to the baton receiver.	The baton receiver is not holding the receiving arm high enough so that the baton can be placed downward onto the palm of the hand. The baton receiver may be accelerating without enough forward lean in the upper body. The baton receiver may be allowing the receiving arm to wave around and present an unsteady target.	Have the athletes practice the exchange again. The baton receiver must accelerate vigorously while maintaining the correct upper body lean. When the arm is placed back, the athlete should hold the arm close to horizontal. The arm and receiving hand should be held steady.

→

ADVANCED ALTERNATE DOWNSWEEP EXCHANGE

Error	Reasons	Corrections
The baton receiver is forced to hit the baton on the thigh in order to shift the grasp to the base of the baton.	The baton carrier has not given the baton receiver the upper $\frac{1}{3}$ of the baton. The athletes are too close together during the exchange.	The baton carrier should hold the baton by its bottom $\frac{1}{3}$ and give the upper $\frac{1}{3}$ to the baton receiver. Athletes should be 2 arms' length (plus $\frac{1}{3}$ of the baton's length) apart during the exchange. The athletes should repeatedly practice maintaining this distance at walking pace, and then at a sprinting pace.

ASSESSMENT

1. **Assess the following theoretical elements as taught during instructional sessions:**
   a. Fundamental rules governing the 4 × 100-m relay.
   b. Good safety habits for use in the 4 × 100-m relay.
   c. Basic elements of the technique of the 4 × 100-m relay.
   d. Basic elements of training for the 4 × 100-m relay.

2. **Assess the performance of technique during the following stages of skill development:**
   a. Pairs of athletes demonstrate a selected elementary exchange. Use check marks, but don't use acceleration or changeover zones.
   b. Pairs of athletes demonstrate a selected advanced alternate exchange. Use check marks, but don't use acceleration or changeover zones.
   c. Pairs of athletes demonstrate a selected exchange. Use check marks and acceleration and changeover zones.

   CRITICAL FEATURES OF TECHNIQUE TO
   OBSERVE DURING ASSESSMENT

   Alternate Downsweep Exchange

   ✓ Positioning of the check mark by the baton receiver.
   ✓ Proper carrying of the baton by the baton carrier and sprinting in the inner or outer $\frac{1}{2}$ of the lane as required.
   ✓ The call by the baton carrier and a pushing downsweep action with the baton.
   ✓ Body position and alignment of the baton receiver on the inner or outer $\frac{1}{2}$ of the lane (as required) while waiting for the baton carrier.
   ✓ Line of vision and acceleration of the baton receiver once the baton carrier passes the check mark.

✓ Position of the receiving arm and hand by the baton receiver following the call of the baton carrier.

3. **Hold graded competitions to help develop motivation and technique.**

   a. Teams of 2 athletes race 100 m using a selected exchange. Use check marks, but don't use specific acceleration or changeover zones.

   b. Teams of 6 athletes race 6 × 50 m, 300 m in total. Use check marks, but don't use specific acceleration or changeover zones.

   c. Teams of 8 athletes race 8 × 50 m: 400 m in all. Use check marks, but don't use specific acceleration or changeover zones.

   d. Teams of 4 athletes race 4 × 100 m under full competitive conditions.

SUGGESTED STANDARDS OF PERFORMANCE—RELAYS		
MALE		**DISTANCE**
Age		**4 × 100 m**
12-13	*Satisfactory*	65.0
	Good	61.0
	Excellent	57.0
14-15	*Satisfactory*	61.0
	Good	57.0
	Excellent	53.0
16-17	*Satisfactory*	59.0
	Good	55.0
	Excellent	51.0
18-19	*Satisfactory*	57.0
	Good	53.0
	Excellent	49.0
FEMALE		**DISTANCE**
Age		**4 × 100 m**
12-13	*Satisfactory*	72.0
	Good	68.0
	Excellent	64.0
14-15	*Satisfactory*	67.0
	Good	63.0
	Excellent	59.0
16-17	*Satisfactory*	65.0
	Good	61.0
	Excellent	57.0
18-19	*Satisfactory*	63.0
	Good	59.0
	Excellent	55.0

All standards measured in seconds.

3

HURDLES

Modern hurdle races include the 100- and 400-m hurdles for women and the 110- and 400-m hurdles for males. Hurdling is also required in the men's 3,000-m steeplechase. In the heptathlon, females compete in the 100-m hurdles, and in the men's decathlon, males compete in the 110-m hurdles.

Today's hurdlers tend to be tall, with excellent hurdling technique and tremendous sprinting ability. These qualities are particularly evident in the men's 110-m hurdles, where the hurdles are 1.067 m (3′6″), and in the women's 100-m hurdles, where the hurdles are .838 m (2′9″). In the 400-m hurdles, the lower hurdles (.914 m [3′] for males and .762 m [2′6″] for females) allow for a less-exaggerated hurdling technique. In all hurdling events, excellent sprinting ability is absolutely essential.

The technique of hurdling has changed little over the past 30 years. In the 100/110-m hurdles, elite athletes aim for three strides between each hurdle. They attempt to spend as much time as possible on the ground sprinting and, conversely, as little time as possible in the air over each hurdle. This strategy re-

quires superior hurdling technique, which can only be developed through a concentrated program of sprinting, hurdling, and related flexibility exercises.

Hurdle heights and race distances are adjusted for age and gender. Young athletes run shorter distances using fewer hurdles, which are set at lower heights than those used by adults. Hurdle heights, distances between hurdles, and race distances are also less for females than for males. As young athletes become more mature, they work progressively toward adult specifications.

Hurdling teaches rhythm, pacing, tempo, and an appreciation of stride count and stride length. The benefits of hurdle training carry over into the jumping events, where these factors are particularly important.

SAFETY SUGGESTIONS

Be sure that you select hurdles that suit the age and ability of your athletes. Nothing destroys a young athlete's enthusiasm or ingrains poor technique faster than knowing that any contact with a hurdle will cause pain. For this reason, avoid using competitive hurdles until novices in your classes have developed an adequate hurdling technique over practice hurdles. Practice hurdles can be made from many materials, ranging from light bamboo canes balanced on traffic cones to polystyrene foam and rubber hurdles specifically designed and manufactured for the beginner.

During your instructional sessions, be sure to adjust the number and height of hurdles as well as the distance between the hurdles. Adjustments of this type accommodate age, body size, and ability. For beginners, too many hurdles set at competitive heights turn the event into a series of mini-high jumps. Using a large number of hurdles will also increase the likelihood of stumbling and tripping as fatigued youngsters struggle to clear all the barriers. Teach novices that competitive hurdles are cleared in one direction only, although this rule does not apply to bamboo canes balanced on traffic cones or to hurdles specifically designed to be hurdled in either direction.

Start teaching hurdles by using low obstacles that are 15–30 cm (6″–12″) in height. Then move to low practice hurdles (at approximately knee height) using short distances between each hurdle and progress slowly to competitive standards. After your athletes are familiar with hurdles set in a straight line, they can then attempt sprint endurance hurdling over longer distances (200, 300, and 400 m, for example). These distances will demand the following abilities:

(a) Crossing hurdles set on the curve of the track

(b) Hurdling with either leg

(c) Altering the tempo of running and stride length between hurdles as fatigue increases

Don't forget that hurdle height and distances in between the hurdles must also be varied according to your athletes' seasonal levels of fitness. In the off-season, reduce the heights and distances between hurdles, particularly if you're coaching the 400-m hurdles. A simple guide is for you to check the stride pattern of the athlete and position the hurdles accord-

ingly. Set the hurdles low enough so that an easy clearance is possible and adjust distances and heights as performance and fitness improves.

The ability to hurdle cannot be improved solely by clearing hurdles. The closer that hurdles approach competitive height, the greater the demand placed on superior technique. An athlete improves technique by performing related stretching exercises, most of which are aimed at increasing flexibility in the hip area.

100/110-METER HURDLES

There is tremendous variation in the specifications of hurdle races leading up to the senior-level 100/110 m hurdles. The Hurdle Specifications (table 3.1) shows how the specifications progressively increase the hurdle height and the distance run.

As young athletes mature, the heights of the hurdles and the distances the athletes race are increased. Regardless of height and distance, the basic hurdling technique remains the same. Athletes run three strides between the hurdles and the most important qualities are sprinting speed and good hurdling technique.

TECHNIQUE

The athlete accelerates toward the hurdle. At takeoff, the upper body is angled forward, and the leading leg vigorously extended. The arm on the side of the body opposite the leading leg reaches forward and counter balances the action of this leg. Once the athlete crosses the hurdle, the athlete then drives the leading leg down toward the ground, forcing the body forward toward the next hurdle. The trailing leg, which is flexed at the knee, is brought forward and upward and reaches out toward the next hurdle. The sprinting action between hurdles is powerful and aggressive. The athlete's shoulders and hips stay parallel to the hurdles throughout, and there is minimal rise and fall of the athlete's body when crossing each hurdle (see figure 3.1).

TABLE 3.1   HURDLE SPECIFICATIONS

Age Range	Distance run	Number of hurdles	Hurdle height (m)	Distance to first hurdle (m)	Distance between hurdles (m)	Distance to the finish (m)
Females 12-13	80 m	8	.762	12	7.5	15.5
Males 12-13	80 m	8	.762	12	8.0	12
Females 14-15	80 m	8	.762	12	8.0	12
Females 16-17	80 m	8	.838	12	8.0	12
Males 14-15 and 16-17	100 m	10	.762	13	8.5	10.5
Females 18-19	100 m	10	.762	13	8.5	10.5
Females 18-19	100 m	10	.838	13	8.5	10.5
Males 16-17	110 m	10	.914	13.72	9.14	14.02
Males 18-19	110 m	10	.990	13.72	9.14	14.02
Junior international competition	110 m	10	1.067	13.72	9.14	14.02
Males 14-15 and 16-17 Females 14-15 and 16-17	300 m	7	.762	50	35	40
Males 16-17	400 m	10	.838	45	35	40
Males 18-19	400 m	10	.914	45	35	40
Females 16-17	400 m	10	.762	45	35	40
Females 18-19	400 m	10	.762	45	35	40

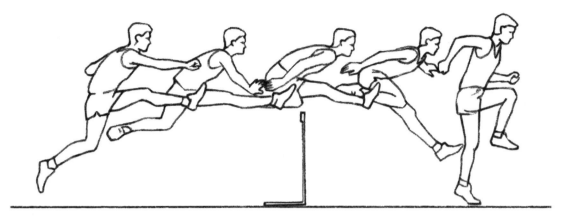

Figure 3.1 Hurdle technique.

TEACHING STEPS

STEP 1. Lead-Ups

STEP 2. Introduction to Hurdling Technique

STEP 3. Sprint Start and Approach to the First Hurdle

STEP 1: LEAD-UPS

Lead-up activities for hurdles are intended to satisfy several objectives:

- To get young atletes accustomed to running and clearing a series of low obstacles
- To develop a stride pattern so that a precise number of paces is used between each obstacle
- To cross each obstacle leading with the same leg

During these introductory lead-up activities, the actual technique of hurdling is deemphasized. The primary purpose is to develop rhythmic running and jumping over each low obstacle.

Jumping Low Obstacles

Select obstacles that your athletes have to clear that are at knee height (bamboo canes set on traffic cones). Set up several lanes of obstacles. Arrange the obstacles so that your athletes can clear them easily and have plenty of space to ready themselves for the next clearance (see figure 3.2). To begin with, emphasize nothing more than running and clearing the obstacles.

Clearing Low Obstacles in Shuttle Relays

Include low obstacles (mats) in shuttle relays. The athletes are required to clear each mat (set crosswise) and tag their teammate for the return run (see figure 3.3). Don't worry about the clearance technique or the number of paces taken between the obstacles in these relays. Make sure that your athletes don't slip on the landing side of the mats.

Developing a Stride Pattern

Mark pairs of lines on the ground in the manner shown in figure 3.4. Variations in distance will allow for differences in your athletes' stride lengths. Place your athletes in lanes according to their leg length, height, and sprint speed. Each athlete runs and jumps the spaces marked by each pair of lines. If an athlete has to reduce stride length in one lane, then shift this athlete to a lane where the spaces between lines are larger. Teach your athletes to use a 5-pace rhythm between each clearance. Later have them attempt a 3-pace rhythm between each clearance. When trying the 3-pace rhythm your athletes may have to shift back to a lane where the distances between each clearance are closer together. Don't worry if the clearances are a series of small high jumps.

Selecting the Leading Leg

All athletes tend to lead with one leg rather than the other when crossing a hurdle or when jumping the lines laid out in figure 3.4. A simple method for helping young athletes find their leading leg is laid out in the following coaching tips.

Figure 3.2 Jumping low obstacles.

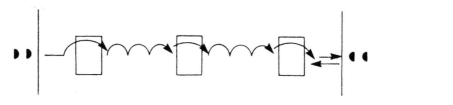

Figure 3.3 Shuttle relay over low obstacles.

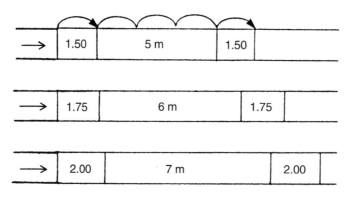

Figure 3.4 Developing a stride pattern.

- Stand with your feet together. Then lean forward until you overbalance and step forward. The leg that you place forward will be your leading leg; try leading with this leg as you clear the space between the lines.

- If you feel cramped in one lane, move to the next lane where the lines are further apart.

- Count a rhythm of "over-1-2-3-over-1-2-3-over" to help you as you run the 3 paces between each clearance.

Developing a Stride Pattern and Clearing Low Obstacles

Use the lines that you laid out in the last drill. Set low obstacles between each pair of lines, placing each obstacle ⅔ of the distance from the first of each pair of lines (see figure 3.5). Obstacles can be low hurdles, bamboo canes balanced on traffic cones, or ropes held lightly by other athletes. To begin with, set the height of the obstacles at 15–30 cm (6"-12"). Each athlete takes off from the first line to clear the

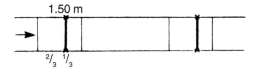

Figure 3.5 Developing a stride pattern and clearing low obstacles.

obstacle. The athlete runs 3 paces to the next clearance.

Be sure that you emphasize the following: (a) that each athlete try to run moderately fast, (b) that each athlete keep each clearance low rather than making it a high jump, and (c) that each athlete try to maintain a 3-pace rhythm between each clearance. Don't worry about clearance techniques. This drill is meant to teach a feel for the takeoff, pacing, and rhythm between obstacles.

COACHING TIPS

- The hurdles (obstacles) are very low so that you can avoid making each clearance look like a high jump.

- If you find that you have to stretch in your three paces to get to the hurdles, then move to another lane where the hurdles are closer together.

- As you gain confidence and run faster, you will find that you have to move again to a lane where the obstacles are further apart.

STEP 2: INTRODUCTION TO HURDLING TECHNIQUE

Many of the drills used to introduce hurdling technique are similar to those used to develop good sprinting technique. This close relationship exists because a successful hurdler must be an excellent sprinter, and the emphasis on high-knee lift, lower-leg extension, and vigorous arm action is essential for both sprinting and hurdling. Some of the following drills are tiring for beginners. A recommended distance for each drill is 8–10 m.

High-Knee Marching

Each athlete marches forward slowly, lifting the thigh of the leading leg forcefully up to a horizontal position. The arms are flexed at 90 degrees at the elbows and swing forward and backward. The supporting leg extends fully up onto the toes as the opposing knee is lifted.

The athlete works the arms as vigorously as possible, pulling the elbows back and up. Begin this drill by emphasizing the thigh lift with one leg only; thereafter, have the athlete elevate each thigh in sequence. (See figure 1.10 on page 7 in chapter 1.)

COACHING TIPS

- Concentrate on lifting each thigh to the horizontal position. Be vigorous as you lift each thigh upward.

- Push up onto your toes with your supporting leg. If you are lifting your left leg upward, then push up onto the toes of your right foot.

- Work your arms vigorously forward and backward, not across your body.

High-Knee Marching With Extension of the Lower Leg

Each athlete practices high-knee marching with an extension of the leading leg in the following sequence. The athlete's right leg takes a normal step forward. The left thigh is then raised to a horizontal position. When the left thigh is in the horizontal position, the lower leg is extended so that the whole leg is horizontal. The athlete's left leg is then lowered, and the sequence is repeated. (See figure 1.11 on page 7 in chapter 1.)

VARIATIONS

1. The athlete's right leg takes a normal step forward. The left thigh is raised to horizontal and the lower leg extended. The athlete's left leg is then lowered. The athlete steps forward normally with the right leg and normally with the left leg. Now the right thigh is raised to the horizontal position, and the lower leg is extended. The rhythm for this drill is right leg step, left leg raise, right leg step, left leg step, right leg raise, and so on.

2. Once the action of raising the thigh and extending the lower leg is understood, the athlete then shifts to performing the action with each successive step. The athlete takes each step precisely and slowly, kicking out the lower leg after lifting the thigh to the horizontal position.

COACHING TIPS

- Keep your vision directly ahead. Relax your shoulders.

- Keep your arms flexed 90 degrees at the elbows. Swing them back and forth vigorously.
- Lift your thigh as close to horizontal as possible. When the thigh is horizontal, kick the lower leg forward as close to horizontal as possible and step down to repeat.

High-Knee Running

Each athlete practices high-knee lift while moving forward at a slow jog. The athlete's thighs are raised to the horizontal position or above (see figure 3.6). The knees remain flexed throughout with no extension of the lower leg. Athletes work their arms vigorously. This drill will be quite strenuous for novices. Recommended distance is 10–15 m with 2 or 3 repetitions.

Figure 3.6   High-knee running.

COACHING TIPS
- Look forward and try not to lean backward.
- Concentrate on raising your thighs as close to horizontal as possible. Don't extend the lower leg in this drill. This comes later!
- Keep your arms swinging strongly back and forth to balance your leg action.

High-Knee Running With Lower-Leg Extension

This drill simulates the prancing motion of a horse. Have your athletes begin with high-knee running and then include the lower-leg extension once the rhythm of the high-knee lift is established. This drill will be particularly exhausting for novices. Recommended distance is 10–15 m with 2 or 3 repetitions. (See figure 1.13 on page 8, chapter 1.)

COACHING TIPS
- Set up your rhythm while running in place and then move forward slowly.
- Concentrate on raising your thigh to a horizontal position and then kicking out your lower leg.
- Use a rhythm pattern of "up, out; up, out."

Simulated Hurdling Action

The basic hurdling action is demonstrated first by you in a mechanical fashion and as slowly as possible. Initially you need not use any hurdles. (See figure 3.7.) Then you can use low hurdles. Your athletes can follow behind you and copy your actions. Emphasize just the leg actions at first. Tell your athletes not to worry about their arm actions.

The sequence of movements is as follows: The left (leading) leg is elevated, and the lower leg is kicked out as close to horizontal as possible. The left leg is then lowered and the foot placed on the ground. The right (trailing) leg is turned outward, flexed at the knee, and rotated upward and forward at the hip. It is then swung around and forward and placed down on the ground.

Figure 3.7   Simulated hurdling action.

- Lift the knee of the leading leg to a horizontal position and kick out the lower leg. Then lower the leg to the ground.
- Turn the trailing leg out to the side, flex it at the knee, and bring it forward up and under your arm. Rotate the leg to the front, and step forward.

Leading-Leg Action: No Extension of Lower Leg

In this drill, your athletes walk along the side of a low hurdle, and only the leading leg crosses the hurdle. If the leading leg is the right, the athlete walks along the left side of the hurdles, and the right leg crosses the hurdle. The opposite sequence occurs if the leading leg is the left. The athlete lifts the thigh of the leading leg so that the foot clears the hurdle (see figure 3.8). The hurdle must be low enough that no lower leg extension is necessary. The low hurdle will make this drill easier. The athlete steps over the hurdle and places the foot of the leading leg on the ground and moves on to the next hurdle. This drill concentrates specifically on the elevation of the thigh of the leading leg. No trailing-leg clearance of the hurdle occurs. Athletes repeat the sequence over 3 low hurdles.

- Be sure to flex your leading leg at the knee as you lift your leg upward.
- Lift the leading leg directly forward and upward; don't swing it sideways and up.

Step over the hurdle, and place your foot down on the ground.

- If the leading leg is your right leg and it has cleared the hurdle, then step forward normally with the left leg and move to the next hurdle to repeat the same action.
- Concentrate only on the action of the thigh of the leading leg. Don't concern yourself at this point about the action of your arms or the trailing leg.

Leading Leg: High-Knee Lift With Lower Leg Extension

Athletes first walk, then later jog slowly with a high-knee lift action along the side of the low hurdles. Each athlete lifts the thigh of the leading leg above the horizontal position and extends the lower leg over the hurdle (see figure 3.9). If the leading leg is the right leg, the left leg will simply step forward. The athlete does not simulate the trailing leg action. Use 2 or 3 hurdles. After your athletes have walked through the drill, they should repeat it at a slow jog, emphasizing good technique throughout.

- Position yourself so that you have enough room for your leading leg to be extended without hitting the hurdle.
- Lift the thigh of your leading leg above the horizontal position and kick your heel forward to extend the lower leg.
- Lean forward so that you can place the leading leg on the ground.

Figure 3.8 Leading-leg action with no lower leg extensions.

a   *b*

Figure 3.9 Two views of lower-leg extension over the end of the hurdle.

Partner Practice for Trailing-Leg Action

Pair off the athletes. One of the athletes in the pair stands on the leading leg at the side of a low hurdle. The trailing leg will be the only leg crossing the hurdle. If the athlete's leading leg is the left leg, then the athlete stands on the left side of the hurdle. A partner holds the athlete's outstretched arms and also makes sure that the athlete is leaning forward. The athlete practicing the drill brings the trailing leg slowly up and over the hurdle and then down to the ground (see figure 3.10). The same action is repeated several times slowly and then at increasing speed.

COACHING TIPS

- Make sure you position yourself next to the hurdle so that your trailing leg can easily clear the hurdle.

- Concentrate on bringing the trailing leg up, around, and forward, with the knee of the leg coming up toward your chest.

- Turn the foot of the trailing leg out so that it moves horizontally over the top of the hurdle. Don't allow the toes to droop down; otherwise, they will clip the hurdle.

- Perform the action slowly and mechanically at first, and then slowly increase your speed.

Trailing-Leg Action Only

The athlete walks along the side of low hurdles. The athlete steps next to the end of the hurdle with the leading leg. Only the trailing leg clears the hurdle (see figure 3.11).

VARIATION

The thigh of the athlete's leading leg is raised to clear an imaginary hurdle. (No lower-leg

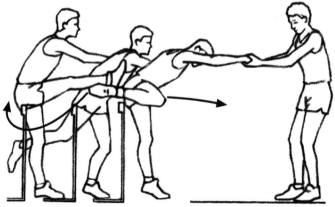

Figure 3.10 Partner practice for trailing-leg action.

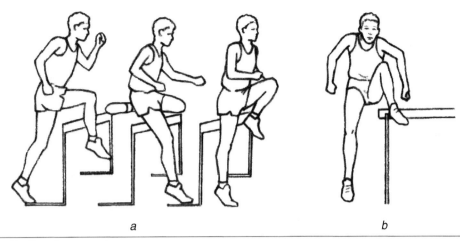

Figure 3.11 Trailing-leg practice.

extension occurs). When the athlete places the leading leg back down on the ground, the trailing leg is then brought over the hurdle. After this movement pattern is established, athletes can repeat the drill at a slow jog.

COACHING TIPS

- Imagine you are clearing a low hurdle with the leading leg. If your leading leg is the right, then reach forward with the left arm.
- Lift the thigh of the trailing leg upward and outward to clear the hurdle.
- Raise the toes of the trailing leg to a horizontal position so that they do not hit the hurdle.
- Bring the knee of the trailing leg up and forward, simultaneously swinging the arm on the same side to the rear.

Walking Hurdle Clearance With No Leading-Leg Extension

In this drill, the athlete approaches the hurdle directly from the front at walking speed. The hurdle is set low enough so that leading-leg clearance is possible without full leading-leg elevation and extension. The leading leg crosses the hurdle and is placed down on the ground. The athlete then brings the trailing leg over the hurdle and walks to the next hurdle to repeat the same action (see figure 3.12). Make sure that each athlete gets close enough to the hurdle so that the leading leg can easily clear the hurdle and be placed on the ground. The under thigh of the leading leg should not contact the hurdle. You can increase the intensity of this activity by having each athlete move from one hurdle to the next using a prancing, high-knee lift action. This activity is strenuous for beginners; 2 or 3 hurdles in sequence is recommended. Repeat 2 or 3 times.

COACHING TIPS

- Try to lean your upper body forward as you raise your leading leg. Maintain this lean when the leading leg contacts the

Figure 3.12 Walking hurdle clearance with no leading-leg extension.

ground because it will make clearing the trailing leg easier.

- Work your arms vigorously during the hurdle clearance to counter balance your leg action.

Walking Hurdle Clearance With Leading-Leg Extension

This drill differs from the preceding one in that the thigh of the leading leg is now raised to a horizontal position and the lower leg is extended. Each athlete walks between the hurdles. The leading leg is raised and extended for the hurdle clearance. The leading leg crosses the hurdle and steps down on the ground (see figure 3.13). The trailing leg is brought quickly over the hurdle. You can increase the intensity of this drill by requiring a high-knee lift at jogging speed between the hurdles.

COACHING TIPS

- After raising the thigh of the leading leg, kick out the heel to assist in extending the lower leg.
- Aim for snappy actions during the hurdle clearance.
- Concentrate on the actions needed to clear the hurdle.

Hurdle Clearance From a Running Approach

Use only one low hurdle to begin with in this drill. Your athletes approach the hurdle at a slow jog. Over low hurdles, they will not need

to lean their upper bodies excessively, but some forward upper body lean should be apparent. As your athletes gain confidence, progressively increase the speed of approach.

COACHING TIPS

- As you jog toward the hurdle, raise your knees high and swing your arms vigorously.
- The faster you approach, the further back you will have to take off. Incline your upper body slightly toward the hurdle at takeoff.
- Make your hurdle clearance as snappy as possible, and after you've completed the clearance, jog for another 5–10 m. Don't slow down immediately after clearing the hurdle.

Clearance of 2 Hurdles With 3 Paces in Between

Set up 3 or 4 lanes with 2 practice hurdles in each lane. Use sponge rubber practice hurdles if you have them available. Otherwise, use low-height competitive hurdles. Alternate a lane that has hurdles with one that has no hurdles. In the first lane with hurdles, hurdles will be set 6 m apart. In the second lane with hurdles, hurdles will be set 7 m apart. The third lane with hurdles will have them set up 8 m apart, and the fourth lane with hurdles will have them set 10 m apart.

In the empty lanes, athletes test their approach and pacing and also mimic two hurdle clearances. Partners mark the take-off positions for each of the 2 simulated hurdle clearances.

Figure 3.13 Walking hurdle clearance with leading-leg extension.

Judging from the take-off marks, and with your assistance, your athletes then choose the lane in which they feel they would be able to perform 3 paces between each hurdle and also manage a successful hurdle clearance. Challenge the athletes to see if they can progress to the lane where the hurdles are furthest apart.

- In the empty lane, sprint fast, putting in 2 simulated hurdle clearances with 3 paces in between. Your partner will check your take-off spot for the first and second hurdle. Then move to the lane where the hurdles are the right distance from your take-off spots.

- If you clear the first hurdle successfully but find yourself too close to the second hurdle, move to a lane where hurdles are further apart.

- Drive low and hard at the first hurdle and sprint hard to the next hurdle.

- Avoid high-jumping the second hurdle.

- As you get more confident, you'll find yourself running faster and clearing the hurdles at greater speed. When this happens, expect to move to a lane where the hurdles are further apart.

STEP 3: SPRINT START AND APPROACH TO THE FIRST HURDLE

If your athlete uses 8 strides to reach the first hurdle, then the athlete should position the trailing leg forward and the leading leg back in the starting blocks. Some long-legged athletes use 7 strides to the first hurdle, in which case the leading leg is put forward in the blocks. Using 9 strides is also acceptable for beginners. Figure 3.14 shows two stride patterns to the first hurdle, one using 8 strides and the other using 9. The athlete's body is inclined forward coming out of the blocks and becomes almost upright after the fifth and sixth stride in the approach to the first hurdle. The athlete should accelerate to the first hurdle and continue to accelerate after crossing this hurdle.

Clearance of One Low Hurdle From a Standing Start

Set up single low practice hurdles in lanes that alternate with lanes containing no hurdles. Vary the distance 11–13 m from the starting line. In the first lane, the hurdle will be 11 m from the starting line. Then there will be a vacant lane. In the next lane, the hurdle will be 12 m from the starting line. You'll then have a vacant lane, and in the next lane, the hurdle will be 13 m from the starting line. You'll need to have one more vacant lane.

Have your athletes begin by running in a vacant lane along the side of the hurdles. The athlete uses a standing start with the left foot forward if the athlete hurdles with the right leg as the leading leg. Have a partner mark the eighth stride. This mark will be the take-off spot for the clearance of the first hurdle. The distance of the take-off spot from the hurdle should be approximately ⅔ the total

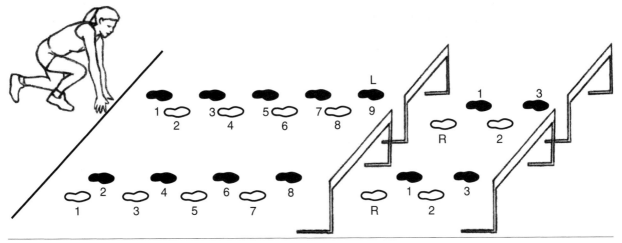

Figure 3.14 Sprint start and approach to first hurdle.

distance taken to clear the hurdle. Have your athletes try the following options if they find during these preliminary practices that the hurdle is too far away for a comfortable clearance:

(a) Have the athlete shift to a lane where the hurdle is closer to the starting line. Then when the athlete's confidence improves and speed increases have the athlete shift back to a lane where the hurdle is further away from the starting line.

(b) Instruct your athlete to put the opposing foot forward at the start and use 9 strides to the first hurdle. The athlete can revert back to 8 strides as confidence improves and speed increases.

COACHING TIPS

- Aim for powerful acceleration from the standing start.
- Be sure to run aggressively toward the hurdle.
- Try to use good hurdling technique as you clear the hurdle.
- If you find that you are too close to the hurdle at takeoff, trying hurdling in the lane where the hurdle is 1 m further from the starting line.

Clearance of 2 Hurdles From a Sprint Start

When you add an additional hurdle, you can adjust the distance of the second hurdle from the first and set the second hurdle lower than the first hurdle. As speed and confidence increase, the athlete works toward 8 strides to the first hurdle and 3 strides to the second.

Competition Over 2 Hurdles

When your athletes compete against each other, it helps them to develop an aggressive approach to clearing the hurdles. For this practice, vary the distance of the hurdles from the start in each lane. Set some hurdles at 11 m from the start, some at 12, and others at 13. The second hurdle in each lane can also vary in distance from the first. The total distance to the finish (25 m) is the same for each lane. Your athletes will need to know which distance is best for them prior to competing over 2 hurdles.

COACHING TIPS

- Get the leading leg down to the ground as fast as possible as soon as it clears the hurdle.
- Be aggressive with your arm action. Bring your trailing leg over the hurdle as fast as possible.
- Run as aggressively as possible between the hurdles and all the way to the finish.
- Aim for continuous acceleration.
- Don't high-jump the hurdles. Try to stay in the air for as little time as possible.

Increasing the Number of Hurdles

As your athletes' ability improves, progressively increase the number of hurdles from 2 to 5. Be ready to reduce the height of the hurdles and to adjust the distance between each hurdle. Urge your athletes to work toward competitive distances and heights relative to their age. Further improvement in hurdling technique will occur through repeated hurdle clearances, sprinting practice, and improved flexibility.

COMMON ERRORS AND CORRECTIONS

100/110-METER HURDLES

Error	Reasons	Corrections
The athlete's approach to the first hurdle is irregular, and the stride pattern from the start to the first hurdle varies with each attempt.	The athlete is anxious, unsure of the approach and pacing to the hurdle, and probably is afraid of the hurdle clearance. The athlete straightens up too soon from the blocks, and vision is not focused on the first hurdle. The athlete has insufficient body lean and drive at the hurdle and poor leg power.	Use low, lightweight (e.g., foam rubber) practice hurdles. Instruct your athlete to run alongside the hurdle, practicing starts and pacing to the first hurdle. Have your athlete maintain an upper body lean from the blocks until the fifth and sixth stride and attack the hurdle with as much aggressive acceleration as possible. Exercises to develop the athlete's leg power will improve the athlete's drive from the blocks.
The athlete jumps over the hurdle.	The athlete straightens up prior to clearing the hurdle. The approach is too slow to the hurdle, and the athlete is either overstriding or or cutting the strides short prior to the takeoff. The action of the leading leg and opposing arm are weak and ineffectual. The pacing to the hurdle is incorrect.	The athlete should maintain the forward lean of the upper body during the sprint to the first hurdle and during the hurdle clearance. The opposing arm (to the leading leg) should be thrust forward during the hurdle clearance. The athlete must also sprint aggressively at the hurdle so that take-off position is the right distance from the hurdle.
The leading leg is excessively flexed throughout the hurdle clearance.	The takeoff is too close to the hurdle, and the athlete has no forward extension of the lower leg after the thigh is elevated. The athlete may have poor flexibility.	Adjust the athlete's approach and stride pattern to the hurdle. Have the athlete practice the hurdle technique with and without hurdles, emphasizing the extension (kick-out) of lower leg after lifting the thigh close to a horizontal position. Stretching and flexibility exercises will be essential.

→

Error	Reasons	Corrections
The leading leg is not lifted directly at the hurdle.	The takeoff is too close to the hurdle, and the athlete is swinging the leading leg in a looping fashion rather than directly toward the hurdle. The athlete may have poor flexibility.	Readjust the athlete's stride pattern and approach to the hurdle. Have the athlete practice the hurdle technique over a series of low hurdles. During clearance, the athlete should concentrate on driving the leading leg directly toward the hurdle. The athlete should work on flexibility exercises for the hip and thigh area.
The trailing leg and foot are not raised sufficiently. The knee or foot of the trailing leg hits hurdle.	The athlete is failing to bring the trailing leg forward parallel to the hurdle and allows the foot of trailing leg to hang down. The athlete may have poor hip flexibility.	Have the athlete work on flexibility and stretching exercises for the hip and thigh area. Use partner exercises, emphasizing the correct trailing-leg action.
The trailing leg is brought through far too early. Both feet hit the ground at the same time after the hurdle clearance.	The downward thrust of the leading leg after clearing the hurdle is far too slow. The athlete is not bringing the trailing leg through high enough after crossing the hurdle or is not driving the trailing leg "down the track" toward the next hurdle after making the clearance. The athlete jumps the hurdle.	Emphasize a downward, backward thrust of the leading leg after it crosses the hurdle. Instruct your athlete to drive low and hard at the hurdle with the leading leg and opposing arm. Check the athlete's take-off position and stride pattern prior to the hurdle. The athlete should work on trailing-leg clearance drills using a partner and a low hurdle.
The athlete straightens up immediately after clearing the hurdle.	The athlete jumps the hurdle and slows down after clearing the hurdle. The upper body is elevated after hurdle clearance.	The athlete must have the correct stride length prior to the hurdle takeoff. There must be a strong forward drive of upper body, leading leg, and opposing arm. The athlete must keep the upper body angled forward even after crossing the hurdle.
The athlete lands too far away from the hurdle.	The takeoff is too close to the hurdle, and the athlete is jumping the hurdle. The downward and backward action of the leading leg is slow after the hurdle clearance.	Readjust the athlete's stride length so that the take-off position is further from the hurdle. The athlete must increase the speed of the downward and backward stabbing action of the leading leg.

Error	Reasons	Corrections
The athlete loses speed between hurdles.	The athlete is jumping the hurdle and using poor arm and leg action between hurdles. There is no drive toward the next hurdle, and the athlete's body is too upright. The athlete may be afraid of hitting the second hurdle.	Have the athlete practice driving at the first and second hurdles and get back into sprinting as fast as possible after each clearance. The athlete can improve arm action and leg drive with repetitive bounding and hopping.

ASSESSMENT

1. **Assess the following theoretical elements as taught during instructional sessions:**
   a. Fundamental rules governing the 100/110-m hurdles.
   b. Good safety habits for use in the 100/110-m hurdles.
   c. Basic elements of 100/110-m hurdles technique.
   d. Basic elements of training for the 100/110-m hurdles.

2. **Assess the performance of technique during the following stages of skill development:**
   a. Clearance of 1 hurdle from a standing start.
   b. Clearance of 1 hurdle from a flying start.
   c. Clearance of 1 hurdle from a sprint start using starting blocks.
   d. Clearance of 2 hurdles using 3 strides between the hurdles. The athlete approaches the first hurdle from a sprint start using blocks, and the second hurdle is adjusted in distance to accommodate the athlete.
   e. Clearance of 2 hurdles using 3 strides between the hurdles, with hurdles set at competitive distances. The athlete approaches the first hurdle from a sprint start using blocks.
   f. Clearance of 3, 4, and 5 hurdles using 3 strides between the hurdles. The athlete approaches the first hurdle from a sprint start using blocks.

   CRITICAL FEATURES OF TECHNIQUE TO OBSERVE DURING ASSESSMENT

   - ✓ Aggressive sprinting from the blocks to the first hurdle and between hurdles.
   - ✓ Upper body lean toward the hurdle.
   - ✓ Extension of the leading leg and opposing arm toward the hurdle.
   - ✓ Forceful downward drive of the leading leg after crossing the hurdle.
   - ✓ Movement of the trailing leg (forward, upward, and reaching out toward the next hurdle).
   - ✓ Minimal rise and fall of the hips and minimal break in sprinting form when the athlete crosses the hurdles.
   - ✓ Shoulders and hips remaining parallel to the hurdles throughout.

3. **Hold graded competitions to help develop motivation and technique.**
   a. Competitors sprint 25 m, crossing 1 hurdle. Adjust hurdle height and distance to the hurdle for each individual.
   b. Competitors sprint 50 m, crossing 3 hurdles. Adjust hurdle height and distances between hurdles for each individual.
   c. Competitors compete over 5, 7, and 10 hurdles, with hurdle height and distances set according to age level.

400-METER HURDLES

The 400-m hurdles is an extension of the sprint hurdle races and is usually considered an event for more mature athletes. Occasionally, 200-m and 300-m hurdle races are held, but these distances are now more commonly used as training for the 400-m hurdles. This event is built upon a foundation of long sprints (400- to 600-m sprints) and sprint hurdling (100- and 110-m hurdles). Coaches normally introduce young athletes to the 400-m hurdles after building a background in sprint endurance training, sprinting, and hurdling over 100/110 m hurdles. As a result, the 400-m hurdles tends to be a specialist event for the more senior of school-age competitors.

The 400-m hurdles demands excellent hurdling ability combined with a high level of sprint endurance. Besides being an excellent runner over 400 m, a 400-m hurdles specialist must be able to lead with either leg over the hurdles, to run the 400-m hurdles in any lane, to hurdle efficiently irrespective of the tightness of the bend, and efficiently change the number of strides between the hurdles as fatigue increases.

The hurdling technique in the 400-m hurdles is similar to that of the 110-m and 100-m hurdles, but it is less exaggerated because the hurdles are lower in height. The positioning of the hurdles around the track is the same for males and females (45 m to the first hurdle and 35 m between each of the 10 hurdles).

TECHNIQUE

Because the hurdles are lower, the clearance action in the 400-m hurdles is less exaggerated than in the 100/110-m hurdles. The upper body is more upright, and there is less forward lean during the hurdle clearance. The leg action for 400-m hurdles is similar to that of the 100/110-m hurdles; the athlete lifts the thigh of the leading leg to a horizontal position and extends the lower leg forward for the clearance. The opposing arm is brought forward to balance this action. The trailing leg is flexed at the knee and rotated forward horizontally to clear the hurdle. The knee of the trailing leg is rotated upward and inward as the leg is brought into line for the next stride (see figure 3.15). The athlete aims for a smooth, fast clearance, changing tempo and stride pattern between hurdles and leading with left or right leg as the need arises.

TEACHING STEPS

STEP 1. Lead-Ups

STEP 2. Development of Sprint Endurance

STEP 3. Hurdling With a Right-Leg and Left-Leg Lead

STEP 4. Establishing a Stride Pattern for the Approach to the First Hurdle (and to Subsequent Hurdles)

Figure 3.15 400-m hurdles technique.

STEP 1: LEAD-UPS

Review lead-ups and drills for the 100/110-meter hurdles in this chapter and review lead-ups and drills for sprinting and sprint starts on pages 4 to 6 in chapter 1.

STEP 2: DEVELOPMENT OF SPRINT ENDURANCE

Review drills for the development of sprint endurance on pages 14 to 17 in chapter 1 and on pages 82 to 83 in chapter 4.

STEP 3: HURDLING WITH A RIGHT- AND LEFT-LEG LEAD

Two of the most important characteristics of 400-m hurdles races are as follows:

- The 400-m hurdles is run counterclockwise around the track with some hurdles positioned on the curve. This means a left-leg lead over hurdles set on the curve is better than a right-leg lead.
- Athletes face the onset of fatigue in the second half of a 400-m hurdles race. Consequently, a left-leg lead over the hurdles in the first half of the race may be changed to a right-leg lead over some hurdles in the second half of the race.

These characteristics require the athlete to practice crossing the hurdles with a right- and left-leg lead and to learn to cross hurdles set on the curve of the track. The drills in this section build toward these objectives.

Review drills for 100/110-m hurdling in this chapter.

Hurdling Clearance at Walking Speed

Set 3 or 4 hurdles 15–23 cm (6″–9″) below competitive height, arranging them so that only the athlete's leading leg crosses the hurdle. Athletes walk and step over each hurdle, leading with the right leg over the first and the left leg over the second, or vice versa (see figure 3.16). On each occasion, the athlete brings the trailing leg around the side of the hurdle.

COACHING TIPS

- Be slow and precise in your actions.
- Try to get comfortable leading with your nonfavored leg.
- Mimic the action of your trailing leg, but concentrate on the actions of your leading leg.

Hurdle Clearance at Jogging Speed

Set up hurdles as in the preceding drill. The athlete slowly jogs toward each hurdle, emphasizing high-knee lift. The leading leg crosses the hurdle, and the trailing leg is brought around the side of the hurdle. The right leg leads over one hurdle and the left leg over the next.

COACHING TIPS

- Emphasize your high-knee lift.
- Lift the thigh of the leading leg and extend your lower leg to cross the hurdle.
- Work on lifting your nonfavored leg directly toward the hurdle. Kick your heel forward to extend the lower leg.

Hurdle Clearance With an Even Number of Strides Between the Hurdles

Set up hurdles so that your athletes take 4–6 easy running strides between hurdles. Only the

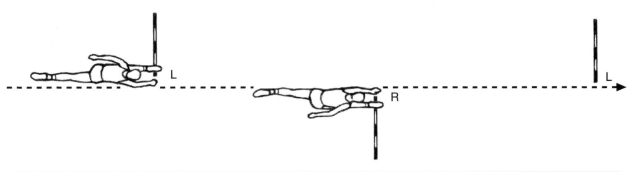

Figure 3.16 Hurdle clearance at walking speed.

athlete's leading leg crosses the hurdle; the trailing leg is brought around the side of the hurdle. The even number of strides between the hurdles will require an alternate leg lead.

COACHING TIPS

- Be sure to lead with an alternate leg each time.
- Don't alter the stride pattern so that you lead with your favored leg.

Hurdle Clearance With 2 Strides Between Hurdles

Reduce the distance between low hurdles so that the athletes can take 2 easy strides between the hurdles. This drill will demand good coordination and an alternate leg lead over each hurdle. Only the leading leg crosses the hurdle; the trailing leg is brought around the side of the hurdle.

COACHING TIPS

- Concentrate on your nonfavored leg.
- Use a rhythm of "drive, 1, 2; drive, 1, 2; drive, 1, 2" as you cross the hurdles.
- Reach forward with your opposing arm to balance the leading-leg action.

Lead-Leg Clearance Only: 2 Strides Between Hurdles

Adjust the distance between 2 hurdles so that your athletes can run 2 strides in between at greater speed. Only the leading leg crosses the hurdle.

Trailing Leg Clearance Only: 2 Strides Between Hurdles

Have your athletes repeat the previous 4 drills with only the trailing leg crossing the hurdle. The leading leg steps along the side of the hurdle.

COACHING TIPS

- Walk up to the hurdles and lift the trailing leg slowly and mechanically over each hurdle.
- Concentrate on developing the correct action, particularly when using the nonfavored trailing leg.
- When running faster, use strong arm actions and lean your upper body forward

as you bring your trailing leg over the hurdle. This lean makes it easier to clear your trailing leg over the hurdle.

- Simulate the action of the leading leg even though it is not crossing a hurdle.

Hurdle Clearance: Alternate-Leg Lead

Place the hurdles in a line and have your athletes cross them directly from the front (with both the leading and trailing legs crossing the hurdle). Arrange the hurdles to give your athlete 4 or 6 strides in between the hurdles. This number of strides will require an alternate-leg lead. To begin with, reduce the hurdle height. The athlete can then practice over hurdles that are set up to allow 2 strides in between each hurdle.

Alternate-Leg Lead Over Hurdles Set on the Curve of the Track

In the 400-m hurdles, 5 of the 10 hurdles are set on the curves of the track. To prepare for this situation, arrange hurdles as in the previous drill, but place them on the curve of the track. Athletes practice taking 8 strides between each hurdle. Then the athletes practice taking 6 strides and subsequently 4 strides between each hurdle. Shift the hurdles to an inside lane to have your athletes experience hurdling around a tight curve.

COACHING TIPS

- This drill will show you that it is more comfortable to have a left-leg lead over hurdles set on the curve, particularly when running on the tighter inside lane.
- The inward lean to the left as you run around the track will help you clear the right (trailing) leg.
- A right-leg lead will feel awkward, but it may have to be used, particularly on the last curve, when you are tired. Be sure to run directly at the hurdle so the leading leg crosses the hurdle well toward the outer edge of the hurdle. If you do this, your trailing leg (and foot) will completely cross the hurdle. If your leg and foot don't cross the hurdle, you will be disqualified! (See figure 3.17 for an illustration of an illegal clearance.)
- As a beginner, you will find it easier to run directly at hurdles set on the curve of

Figure 3.17 Illegal 400-m hurdle clearance.

the track for at least 2 strides prior to the hurdle and run straight at least 2 strides after the hurdle. This strategy will help you avoid disqualification. When you are more experienced, you will be able to cross the hurdles at more of an angle.

Alternate-Leg Lead With 10–14 Strides Between Each Hurdle

Progressively increase distances between hurdles so that your athletes take 10, 12, and 14 strides between each hurdle. The even number of strides demands an alternate leg lead over each successive hurdle. The athlete can begin using hurdles set alternately in adjacent lanes and arranged for leading-leg clearance only. As the athlete's confidence increases, place the hurdles in the same lane so that both the leading leg and trailing leg cross the hurdle.

Hurdle Clearance Using Uneven Strides Between Hurdles

Set distances between hurdles so that the athlete now takes an uneven number of strides (9, 11, or 13) between each hurdle. This number of strides will require the same leg lead over each hurdle.

STEP 4: ESTABLISHING A STRIDE PATTERN FOR THE FIRST HURDLE AND BETWEEN SUBSEQUENT HURDLES

The number of strides taken over the competitive distance of 45 m to the first hurdle varies considerably for each athlete. How many strides the athlete takes will depend on which leg is forward in the blocks and the stride length taken to the first hurdle. In addition, the stride pattern and tempo of approach to the first hurdle helps establish the subsequent number of strides taken between the next 5 or 6 hurdles.

The athlete's level of sprint endurance is particularly important in the 400-m hurdles. Sprint endurance, coupled with the athlete's natural stride length, determines the number of strides taken between hurdles, especially in the latter ½ of the race. At this stage of the race, fatigue will require an increase in the number of strides taken between hurdles. For example, at the fifth hurdle, a 15-stride pattern may be changed to a 17-stride pattern. To change from 15 to 17 strides, the athlete's stride length must be shortened to include 2 additional strides. Athletes sometimes change their stride patterns 3 times within a race.

The stride patterns that elite athletes take to the first hurdle vary from 21–24 strides. Elite athletes then use stride patterns ranging from 13–17 strides between the next 5 or 6 hurdles and thereafter use up to 19 strides between the remaining hurdles.

Approach to the First Hurdle

The method for teaching the approach to the first hurdle in 400-m hurdles is the same as for 100/110-m hurdles. The number of strides the athlete uses will depend on individual characteristics. An even number of strides in the approach to the first hurdle requires the starting blocks to be set up so that the trailing leg is forward. Initially, the athlete should run by the side of the first hurdle. A partner can help by noting pacing and take-off position for the first hurdle and deciding the number of strides to use. If a 22-stride approach is too difficult, the athlete should switch to 23 or 24 strides. Adjust the starting blocks accordingly.

Approach and Clearance of 2 Hurdles With Competitive Distance (35 m) Between the Hurdles

To practice this drill, start by placing the second hurdle in the adjacent lane. The athlete clears the first hurdle (in 22 paces, for example) and runs past the second hurdle, noting the pacing and deciding on the number of strides to use (15, for example) prior to takeoff for the second hurdle. The second hurdle is then placed in the lane, and the athlete repeats the start and attempts both hurdle clearances. A partner can assist in assessing the stride pattern and determining the number of strides to take between hurdles.

Stride and Tempo Variation Using 2 Hurdles

The athlete uses varying stride patterns (for example, 17, 18, and 19) while running between the hurdles. This variation familiarizes the athlete with the change to a shorter stride length, faster tempo, and increased number of strides between the hurdles.

Approach and Clearance of 3, 4, and 5 Hurdles Set at Competitive Distance

Set 5 hurdles at competitive distances and add a 15-m distance after the last hurdle. The distance of 45 m to the first hurdle, 35 m in between the hurdles, and 15 m at the finish totals 200 m. Repetition of this distance, with specific controls set on the speed of the run, the number of repetitions, and the rest period becomes an excellent form of interval training. (For more information on interval training, see pages 80 to 82 in chapter 4).

VARIATION

Elite athletes will frequently set 3 or 4 hurdles on the straightaway facing one direction, and in the adjacent lane, set 3 or 4 hurdles facing the opposing direction. In repetitions of this distance, athletes will use a flying start. They then run "down" one lane, turn, and run immediately "up" the other lane. Placing the hurdles in adjacent lanes reduces the amount of labor required to place hurdles around the track.

Combinations of Hurdles and Distances

Variations in distance and the number of hurdles help the athlete develop stamina and a feel for pacing and rhythm between the hurdles. The athlete practices changes in stride patterns over distances in which hurdles are included in the latter part of the run. Choose the number of repetitions for each run and the rest periods taken in between according to the athlete's level of fitness. The type of interval training used by a 400-m hurdler is similar to that of the 400-m sprinter.

Here are some examples:
- 50 m followed by 200 m (with 5 hurdles).
- 200 m (with 5 hurdles) followed by 100 m flat.
- 100 m followed by 200 m (with 5 hurdles).
- 150 m followed by 200 m (with 5 hurdles).
- 200 m (with 5 hurdles) followed by 150 m flat.

VARIATIONS

- 200 m (with 5 hurdles) followed by 200 m flat.
- 300 m (with 7 hurdles) followed by 100 m flat.
- 200 m flat followed by 200 m (with 5 hurdles).
- 100 m flat followed by 300 m (with 7 hurdles).

This type of training helps to improve the athlete's level of sprint endurance. In competitions, the athlete must try to maintain the required stride pattern between the hurdles and clear the last two hurdles successfully. The competitor with the greatest endurance and best hurdling technique is least affected by fatigue and will be required to make fewer adjustments in tempo, stride length, and hurdling technique.

Checking the Athlete's Pace Judgment Over 400-Meter Hurdles

You can compare times taken at various parts of the race by timing the contact of the leading leg with the ground after it passes over specific hurdles. These times will give you a measure of the quality of the athlete's sprint endurance and hurdling technique. In general, the second half of the 400-m hurdle race should be run no more than 2 seconds slower than the first half.

COMMON ERRORS AND CORRECTIONS

400-METER HURDLES

Note: Errors in basic hurdling technique are found in the error and correction table for the 100/110-m hurdles on page 61.

Error	Reasons	Corrections
The athlete is disqualified because the trailing leg does not cross the hurdle.	The athlete leads with the right leg over the hurdle and runs too close to the inside edge of the lane or leads with the left leg and runs too close to the outside edge of the lane. The athlete fails to hurdle over the center of the	The athlete should aim to cross the hurdle in the center. Two strides prior to takeoff, beginners should line themselves up with the center of the hurdle (rather than approaching the hurdle at an angle).
The athlete hits the hurdles, struggles to reach the hurdles, and slows down prior to hurdles. The athlete has difficulties with rhythm and pacing between the hurdles.	The athlete is not reaching the first hurdle with the correct pacing and cadence and destroys rhythm and pacing. In the latter part of the race, the athlete uses an inaccurate change to an increased number of strides between hurdles. The athlete has inadequate sprint endurance and may be anxious.	The athlete should improve sprint endurance. Work on the approach to the first hurdle and the pacing between hurdles. Have the athlete practice a change-up in tempo and a reduction in stride length to accommodate fatigue in the latter part of the race.

ASSESSMENT

1. **Assess the following theoretical elements as taught during instructional sessions:**
   a. Fundamental rules governing the 400-m hurdles.
   b. Good safety habits for use in the 400-m hurdles.
   c. Basic elements of 400-m hurdling technique.
   d. Basic elements of training for 400-m hurdles.

2. **Assess the performance of technique during the following stages of skill development:**
   a. Approach and clearance of 2 hurdles. Require an even number of strides between the hurdles so that both right-leg and left-leg leads are required.
   b. Approach and clearance of 2 hurdles set at competitive heights and distances. Set the hurdles on the straightaway and then on the curve of the track.

   c. Approach and clearance of 5 hurdles over 200 m set at competitive heights and distances.

   d. Approach and clearance of 5 hurdles set over the final 200 m of a 400-m track. The first 200 m do not contain hurdles.

   e. Running of 400-m hurdles under full competitive conditions.

CRITICAL FEATURES OF TECHNIQUE TO OBSERVE DURING ASSESSMENT

✓ Stride control and approach to the first hurdle and between subsequent hurdles.

✓ Use of a less-exaggerated clearance of the hurdle in 400-m races.

✓ Hurdle clearance on the curve using left- and right-leg leads.

✓ Tempo and stride adjustment over hurdles set in the last 200 m.

3. Hold graded competitions to help develop motivation and technique.

   a. Athletes compete using 3 hurdles set over 150 m. Two hurdles are set on the straightaway and one on the curve. Hurdle height is adjusted to the age and gender of the individual.

   b. Athletes compete using 3 hurdles set over 150 m. All hurdles are on the curve, and hurdle height is adjusted to the age and gender of the individual.

   c. Athletes compete using 5 hurdles set over 200 m. Three hurdles are set on the curve. Hurdle height is adjusted to the age and gender of the individual.

   d. Athletes compete over 300 m, with 5 hurdles set in the first 200 m.

   e. Athletes compete over 400 m, with 5 hurdles set in the first 200 m.

   f. Athletes compete over 400 m, with 5 hurdles set in the final 200 m.

   g. Athletes compete over 400-m hurdles under full competitive conditions.

SUGGESTED STANDARDS OF PERFORMANCE—HURDLES

MALE		DISTANCE				
Age		**80 m**	**100 m**	**110 m**	**300 m**	**400 m**
12-13	*Satisfactory*	17.5				
	Good	16.0				
	Excellent	14.0				
14-15	*Satisfactory*		21.0		58.0	
	Good		19.5		54.0	
	Excellent		18.5		51.0	
16-17	*Satisfactory*		20.0		56.0	
	Good		19.0		51.0	
	Excellent		18.0		48.0	
18-19	*Satisfactory*			20.5		79.0
	Good			19.0		74.0
	Excellent			18.0		68.0

FEMALE		DISTANCE			
Age		**80 m**	**100 m**	**300 m**	**400 m**
12-13	*Satisfactory*	20.5			
	Good	19.0			
	Excellent	18.0			
14-15	*Satisfactory*	18.5		63.0	
	Good	17.0		59.0	
	Excellent	16.0		56.0	
16-17	*Satisfactory*	17.5		61.0	
	Good	16.0		57.0	
	Excellent	15.0		54.0	
18-19	*Satisfactory*		20.0		86.0
	Good		18.5		80.0
	Excellent		17.5		74.0

All standards measured in seconds.

4

DISTANCE RUNNING

For young athletes, any distance from 800 m on up is considered as a long run. At the elite level, 800 m is looked on as a long sprint, 1,500 m as a middle-distance race, and competitions beyond 1,500 m are long-distance races. In the women's heptathlon, the longest distance race is the 800 m. In the men's decathlon, it is the 1,500 m.

Training for all races from sprints to long-distance races requires improvement of the athlete's anaerobic and aerobic endurance. An athlete's aerobic endurance is controlled by the ability of the athlete's heart, lungs, and circulatory system to supply oxygen to the athlete's muscles for a long, sustained effort. Training for aerobic endurance is characterized by long runs at moderate speed.

Anaerobic endurance is the capacity of the athlete's muscular system to operate using fuel stored in the muscles themselves. Training for anaerobic endurance is characterized by all-out effort over distances that are frequently shorter than the race distance. (Pages 2–3 in chapter 1 discuss in detail the differences between aerobic and anaerobic endurance).

Sprinting places extreme demands on an athlete's anaerobic capacity. As the competitive distance increases, there is progressively less demand for anaerobic endurance and greater demand for aerobic endurance. Figure 4.1 shows the approximate demands placed on an athlete's anaerobic and aerobic energy systems in relation to race distance. This diagram indicates that distance runners cannot be satisfied with just aerobic training. An athlete must be able to maintain a fast pace over a long period of time, and then be able to sprint when necessary. For this reason, training for distance racing is designed to improve both the athlete's aerobic and anaerobic endurance.

Novices training for long-distance races must begin in the off-season and work progressively toward the competitive season. Emphasizing volume (long, slow runs) before intensity (repetitive, high-speed runs), a novice trains for the competitive season in the following manner:

1. The athlete begins with work on aerobic endurance.
2. After developing a base of aerobic endurance, the athlete shifts to activities that

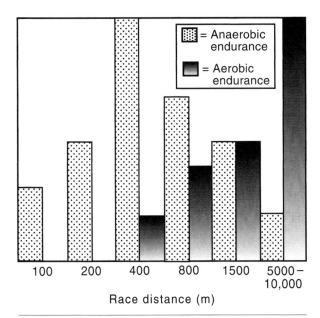

Figure 4.1 Energy demands of distance running.

are designed to develop a mix of aerobic and anaerobic endurance.

3. Training is completed with activities that emphasize anaerobic endurance specific to the athlete's competitive event.

Figure 4.2 shows a simplified season's program.

When you plan a season's training for novices, you should work through the 5 teaching steps listed in this chapter. Fall, winter, and spring are taken as the pre-competition or off-season periods, and summer is considered as the competitive period. You will have to adjust your training sessions if the athlete's competitive period occurs in the spring instead of the summer. Athletes concentrating on cross-country races in the fall and winter and distance competitions in the summer will find themselves faced with two competitive seasons. Plan for them to have a break between the two seasons.

SAFETY SUGGESTIONS

The popularity of distance running, from jogging to serious marathon running, has increased dramatically in recent years. Unlike many other track and field events, distance running can be practiced virtually anywhere and requires minimum equipment. In spite of its simplicity, you must consider certain safety precautions.

Always take into consideration the safety of your athletes when you plan cross-country routes and jogging trails. Try to plot the course so it doesn't cross traffic lanes. Inform your local police and provide competition marshals if you plan to hold a race that is likely to interrupt local traffic patterns. Check your cross-country course for hidden and visible dangers such potholes, tree roots, and sharp rocks. Plan to avoid trail bottlenecks that could cause your athletes to run into each other.

When running on roads, your athletes should run toward the traffic, well to the side of the road, and wear reflective, easy-to-see colors. Athletes should be particularly careful at intersections and if possible run with partners. Running alone can be dangerous, especially on isolated or empty trails.

For both training and competition, always take into account the age of your athletes, the length of the run, the number of athletes involved, and the type of weather that you expect during the run. Excessive heat demands fluid replacement, and extreme cold requires warm clothing such as a hat, gloves, tights, or a track suit. Your athletes should wear comfortable clothing that will not chafe the skin. Good-quality running shoes are essential.

The start and finish of cross-country races must always be well-marshaled. The start should be wide and long enough so that the athletes can separate themselves with the minimum of jostling. The finish must also be wide enough to allow exhausted athletes to sprint directly to the finish without bumping or spiking each other. Course marshals must be able to position each athlete according to finish with the minimum of fuss. Treatment for injuries must also be available.

A good warm-up is an essential part of distance training and should include loosening, stretching, and light flexibility exercises. These exercises can be followed by easy running in which your athletes emphasize stretching out and striding. You can use some accelerative activities (pick-ups) to get the athlete's legs moving quickly. The sequence of exercises and the duration of a warm-up will vary according to your preferences and those of your athletes. The purpose of a warm-up is to make the

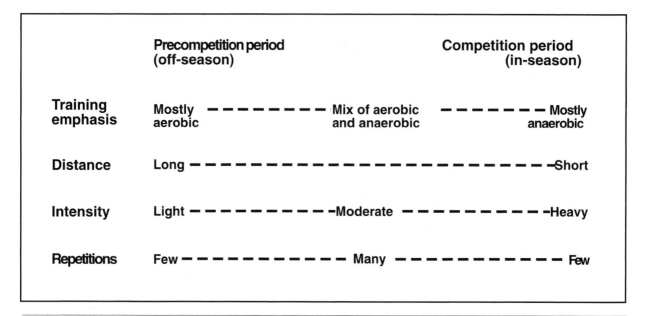

	Precompetition period (off-season)		Competition period (in-season)
Training emphasis	Mostly aerobic	‒ ‒ ‒ ‒ ‒ ‒ ‒ Mix of aerobic and anaerobic	‒ ‒ ‒ ‒ ‒ ‒ Mostly anaerobic
Distance	Long ‒ Short		
Intensity	Light ‒ ‒ ‒ ‒ ‒ ‒ ‒ ‒ Moderate ‒ ‒ ‒ ‒ ‒ ‒ ‒ ‒ ‒ Heavy		
Repetitions	Few ‒ ‒ ‒ ‒ ‒ ‒ ‒ ‒ ‒ ‒ Many ‒ ‒ ‒ ‒ ‒ ‒ ‒ ‒ ‒ ‒ ‒ Few		

Figure 4.2   A season's training program for distance running.

athlete's body warm and get the cardiovascular system working well; for many, the warm-up is as much psychological as it is physiological.

You must develop your distance-running program for young athletes slowly and carefully. Distance running should not be the only way in which you get young athletes to run long distances. Plenty of running occurs in other sports as well, such as soccer, basketball, and field hockey. Many of these sports will help develop the young athlete's aerobic endurance. If your young athletes complain frequently of soreness or try to avoid running, your approach may be wrong. Emphasize fun, variety, and progressive development.

You will need to know how much and what type of running will produce a training effect and what is excessive and can lead to injuries. With beginners, use game situations that allow momentary pauses. If you are going on a distance run, begin by using a run-walk. In this way, you'll have an opportunity to visually assess your young athletes. Flushed faces, gasping, and other obvious signs of discomfort are signals to cut back on the demand.

When you are planning a distance running program for young athletes, be sure that you emphasize activities that have a training effect that is more aerobic than anaerobic.

Anaerobic training is particularly demanding for a young developing body, and activities that develop anaerobic endurance should occupy a minimal part of your program until your young athletes are in their late teens. At that age, you can intensify anaerobic training. Remember also that athletes must have rest and recovery days after demanding training sessions. This recovery time is beneficial for the athlete both physiologically and psychologically.

TECHNIQUE

The distance runner's technique is characterized by an upright body position. Some forward lean can occur during phases of acceleration. The stride length in shorter distance races is moderate to long. In long-distance races, the stride length is somewhat shorter. The athlete's knee lift and leg drive depend upon the distance the athlete is running and also the phase of the race. When the athlete is sprinting to the finish, the knee lift will be high; during nonsprinting phases, knee lift is less exaggerated. The athlete's arm action always balances the motion of the legs (see figure 4.3). It should be vigorous and powerful when the athlete is sprinting and moderate to minimal during nonsprinting phases of the race.

Figure 4.3 Distance running technique.

STEP 1: LEAD-UPS

The following lead-up activities are designed to get your young athletes running repetitively. The fun of the activities diverts the athletes' attention from the amount of running being done.

Relays, Chase, and Tag

Although these activities do not require continuous running (which is what best produces a base of aerobic endurance), they help condition your athletes' muscles and cardiovascular system. See also chapter 1, pages 5–6, and chapter 2 for examples of various types of relays and games of chase and tag.

Games

Sports, such as basketball and soccer, that emphasize repetitive running interspersed with short rests help prepare young athletes for more specific aerobic training that will follow later. Repetitive running and passing a ball over selected distances (e.g., while running the width or length of a soccer field) are good aerobic lead-up activities.

STEP 2: AEROBIC ENDURANCE TRAINING (OFF-SEASON PRECOMPETITIVE PERIOD)

Long-distance running is considered as an excellent method for developing aerobic endurance. The following examples suggest ways in which you can introduce this form of training to your athletes. You need not introduce these activities in sequence, because they all develop aerobic endurance. By varying the activity, you will maintain interest.

Long Runs

Long runs are usually performed in a steady state. This means that the athlete runs at a speed which allows the athlete's oxygen demands to be met by the oxygen inhaled. Have your athletes run on trails, fields, roads, and tracks at a slow to moderate speed. Emphasize variety, and instruct your athletes to progressively increase intensity by running the same distance at a faster speed or by running a longer distance at the original speed. The recommended distance for beginners is 2–3 km (1.24–1.86 mi.).

Timed Runs

In this activity, your athletes run continuously for a specific time period rather than for a particular distance. You can have them increase intensity by attempting to run for a longer time period. A recommended time period for beginners is 8–15 minutes.

Long Runs in Performance Groups

Divide your athletes into groups. Choose a leader for each group. The leaders carry stopwatches and take their groups on 14-minute runs (7 minutes out and 7 minutes back). Faster groups will run further during the 14-minute time period. Increase the time that your athletes run as they become fitter.

Quality Distance Runs

Quality runs are distances run faster than the steady state speed used for long runs. Use these runs after your athletes have developed some aerobic endurance from long, steady runs and from Fartlek (a later section in this chapter has an explanation of Fartlek). Distances that were previously run at an easy pace are run faster. Emphasize the maintenance of speed. Quality runs are considered the first step toward paced or tempo training in which your athletes learn to maintain a particular pace over a selected distance. In a quality distance run, your athletes will run 1–2 minutes faster over a measured route that was previously run easily in 15–20 minutes.

Handicap Distance Races

Your athletes can also perform a quality run in the form of a handicap distance race. Athletes start running over a known route singly, in pairs, or in groups, with time advantages so that the fastest athletes start last. A typical handicap race can occur in the following man-

ner: The slowest pair of athletes are given 30 seconds or a minute advantage over the next pair. This time advantage is repeated down to the fastest athletes, who start last and with the greatest timed handicap. Set the handicaps so that each group of athletes has a reasonable chance of catching those in front of them and the athletes arrive at the finish close together. This type of run is ideal for cross-country courses and can provide fun and motivation for both slow and fast athletes. (Note: The most obvious disadvantage of this type of race is that an athlete's inability to run fast is emphasized by being positioned as an early starter in the race.)

Fartlek

The objective of Fartlek (a Swedish word meaning "speed play") is to provide variation in terrain and running intensity (see figure 4.4). Fartlek also provides considerable choice in the activities performed, which can range from pauses during which calisthenics are performed to flat-out sprinting. The course should go through wooded areas, across fields, up inclines, and should allow for periods of slow, easy jogging and walking. For mature athletes, the choice of when to run fast or slow is left to the individual. For young athletes, you should control the pace and the activity. Remember that Fartlek should not degenerate into a meaningless social excursion. A course lasting 15–20 minutes including walks and calisthenics is recommended for beginners.

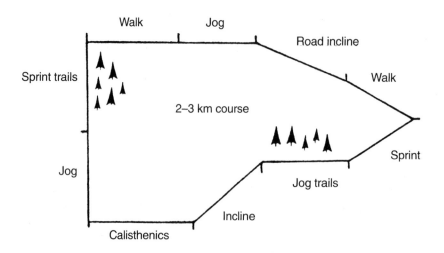

Figure 4.4 Fartlek training.

STEP 3: POWER AND RESISTANCE TRAINING (OFF-SEASON PRECOMPETITIVE PERIOD)

Power and resistance training occurs at the same time of the year as aerobic endurance training, during the off-season precompetitive period. The objective of power and resistance training is to develop muscular power that will assist distance running. This type of training is not intended to develop needless muscular bulk. Power and resistance training can include light weight training as well as running in sand, snow, up hills, and in water.

Deep-Water Running

Deep-water running is a popular form of resistance training for distance athletes. Using flotation devices where necessary and keeping their bodies upright, athletes run circuits in the deep end of a swimming pool, working against the resistance of the water. Normally there is no contact with the bottom of the pool, although this kind of activity is also beneficial in waist-deep water in the shallow end of the pool. You can adapt your land workouts for use in the swimming pool. In this way, the drills simulate the long runs of aerobic training or the run-recovery-run characteristics of interval training.

Pool training is also excellent for maintaining the fitness levels of injured athletes while they recover. Exercising in water allows an injured athlete to continue training and to use joint areas such as the foot, ankle, knee, and hip, which could become more seriously injured if training were to continue on land. Deep-water running provides diversion for your athletes and a pleasant change of activity.

Weight Training

Distance runners can also practice various forms of weight training. Weight training for runners usually takes the form of circuits of exercises using light weights (30–50 percent of maximum), high repetitions (15–30), and short recovery periods (30–60 seconds).

STEP 4: MIXING AEROBIC AND ANAEROBIC TRAINING (MID-SEASON PRECOMPETITIVE PERIOD)

Once you have helped your athlete develop an aerobic base through long runs, Fartlek, and quality runs, you should then intensify training. You can do this by increasing the pace of each run, being sure that you carefully regulate the length of the run and the type of recovery taken between runs. You will need to specify how long each individual run should be and take note of the distance accumulated in each workout.

What training effect you desire for your athletes is contingent upon the way you design their workouts. For example, you can gradually change the athletes' workouts so that anaerobic training predominates over aerobic. You can make this change by having your athletes work on intensified Fartlek. Thereafter, you introduce the athletes to paced running (tempo running), which in itself is a preparation for interval training.

Intensified Fartlek

In intensified Fartlek, the terrain is still varied and interesting, and the distance is the same as before, but greater effort is required throughout. Replace walking recovery periods with jogging, make sprinting sections longer and more vigorous, and intensify and quicken the pace throughout. This activity differs considerably from the more leisurely approach taken to Fartlek when it is initially introduced.

Pace or Tempo Training

Pace training is frequently called *tempo* training. The two terms refer to the controls placed on the speed that an athlete must run to cover a particular distance in a set time. Athletes are initially introduced to this type of training through quality distance runs and intensified Fartlek. A feeling for running at a particular speed becomes very important when your athletes begin work on interval training.

Introducing Pace or Tempo Training to Novices

Have your athletes gather around you. Start a stopwatch, and while you look at your stopwatch, ask the athletes in your group to estimate (by raising their hand) when 30 seconds have elapsed. Compare their estimates with the correct time. Then repeat this practice with other times (such as 20 seconds, 45 seconds).

COACHING TIPS

- Close your eyes and imagine the second hand moving on a clock. Say "now" and raise your hand when you think the stopwatch has reached 30 seconds.
- Make this activity competitive; see who can get closest to the actual time.

Estimating the Duration of a Run

Put athletes in teams and have each team run in single file. Instruct the leaders of each team to take their team over a random course and then bring them back to the starting place in exactly 45 seconds (see figure 4.5). The leaders have to estimate the 45-second time frame. Change leaders and times with each run.

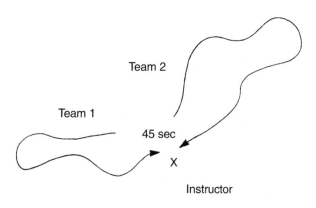

Figure 4.5 Estimating the duration of a run.

COACHING TIPS

- Stay together in your teams.
- Leaders can chose the route for their team.
- Only the leaders are responsible for estimating the 45-second time frame.
- Each team must arrive back together.

Estimating Pace and Tempo on the Straightaway

Instruct groups of your athletes to run 50 m in 15 seconds on the straightaway (see figure 4.6). Call times as the athletes pass the 50-m

mark. Don't allow your athletes to suddenly increase their speed to arrive at the finish on time. They must try to set the correct pace from the start. Athletes walk or jog back to the start. Use the same distance and time requirement 2 or 3 times so your athletes establish a feel for the required pace. Then use differing times for subsequent occasions so that your athletes can practice faster and slower paces of running.

COACHING TIPS

- Try to get a feel for how quickly you must run to cover the distance in the required time.
- Don't bound or strain to increase your stride when you run.
- After accelerating from the start, try to keep your stride length the same throughout the run.

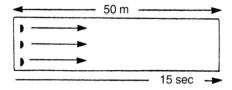

Figure 4.6 Estimating pace and tempo on a straightaway.

Estimating Pace and Tempo on a Triangular Course

Divide your class into three teams. Each team begins at a different corner of a triangular course laid out on the grass with 50 m to each side (see figure 4.7). Tell each team of athletes how long they must spend running to get to the next corner and indicate that they must arrive exactly when your whistle blows. You blow your whistle at selected times (for example, 15 seconds for beginners). Those who arrive early must run in place. Those who are slow must catch up and then adjust their running speed to be more accurate over the next 50 m. A short rest period (10 seconds light jogging on the spot) may be necessary at each corner to allow less fit athletes to recover.

COACHING TIPS

- Running this course is no different than running 50 m in 15 seconds on the straightaway.

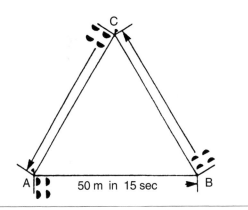

Figure 4.7 Estimating pace and tempo on a triangular course.

- Try to arrive at the corner flag exactly when the whistle blows.
- Try to avoid having to run in place by arriving early at the corner.

VARIATION

Athletes run a full circuit of the course in 45 seconds. A double blast of your whistle indicates that your athletes must run a circuit in 40 seconds. After one slow and one fast circuit, they can take a walking recovery period (you select the time and distance of the recovery period). You can increase the intensity of this type of training in the following ways:

(a) Move to a square course

(b) Have your athletes jog rather than walk during the recovery period

(c) Have your athletes run faster circuits

Estimating Pace and Tempo on a 400-Meter Track

Put flags or traffic cones at 50-m intervals around a 400-m track (see figure 4.8). Your

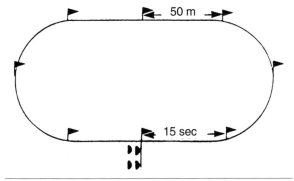

Figure 4.8 Estimating pace and tempo on a track.

athletes must maintain a set pace (for example, 15 seconds for 50 m) so that they arrive at each flag exactly when your whistle blows.

Pace and Tempo Training in Teams

Two teams of athletes start together at the same spot but run in opposing directions around the track (see figure 4.9). Each team must maintain the correct tempo (for example, 200 m in 40 seconds) in order to arrive exactly together on the opposing side of the track. They pass each other and continue to run, meeting again on the side of the track where they started. Flags placed every 50 m around the track, coupled with 10-second whistle blasts, can help your athletes pace themselves. Require a faster pace for more mature athletes.

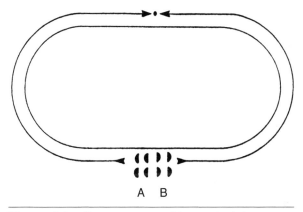

Figure 4.9 Group pace and tempo training.

Pace Training Using Varying Distances

Athletes run different distances in the same time period (for example, 50, 60, and 70 m, each in 20 seconds). The different distances will force a change in pace for each distance.

COACHING TIPS

- Reduce stride length and tempo for the short distances.
- Increase stride length and tempo for the longer distances.
- Try to relax as you run.
- Swing your arms forward and backward, not across your body.
- Keep your vision forward and your head up. Don't roll your head or let it drop back.

Interval Training

Interval training requires an athlete to perform a series of runs and to take a short recovery period after each run. This kind of training is usually performed on the track and as such is highly formal, repetitious, and disciplined. Take this fact into consideration when working with school-age athletes.

Most forms of interval training use an incomplete or partial recovery period after each run. An incomplete recovery period means that the athlete's heart rate is not allowed to fully return to a resting level. This means that a specific work load is continuously placed upon the athlete's cardiovascular system. The athlete's cardiovascular system responds by becoming more powerful and efficient.

Interval training has many variations. Each variation depends on the balance of aerobic and anaerobic endurance that you and your athletes wish to achieve. All forms of interval training systematically vary the following:

- The distance run
- The number of times the distance is run
- The speed of each run
- The length of the recovery period between each run
- The type of activity that occurs during the recovery period (walking, jogging)

The variables listed above are all interrelated. Each is adjusted according to the athlete's level of fitness and the specific intent of the training. Here are some examples:

- **Distance.** Training distances vary considerably (from 50–1,500 m) and depend on the length of race the athlete is training for. The distance the athlete runs is related to the speed of each run, the number of repetitions performed, and the duration and type of the recovery periods.
- **Number of repetitions.** The number of repetitions that the athletes uses depends on the distance of the run, the speed of the run, and the duration and type of each recovery period.
- **Speed.** The speed of the run is usually modified so that the athlete's heart rate returns to 120 at the *end* of each recovery period. The speed of the run will de-

pend on the distance of the run, the number of repetitions, and the duration and type of the recovery period.

- **Duration of recovery.** The recovery period may last from less than 1 minute to 5 minutes or more. As with the type of recovery, the duration of the recovery period depends upon the speed of the run, the distance of the run, and the number of repetitions performed. The type and duration of recovery period used will depend upon the time taken for the athlete's heart to return to 120 beats.
- **Type of recovery.** The type of recovery used by the athlete may be a walk, a slow or fast jog, or a slow run. The type of recovery (and its duration) depends on the speed of the run, its distance, and the number of repetitions performed.

Interval Training Designed to Develop Aerobic Endurance

This type of training develops the athlete's stamina and basic endurance. It forms a foundation for other types of interval training that follow. It is characterized by short distances (50–200 m), short recovery periods (1 minute or less), and a large number of repetitions (10–15). Because of the short recovery periods, the athlete is forced to run the next repetition with an incomplete recovery. In this way, the athlete's cardiovascular system continuously works under stress. As a result it becomes more powerful and develops the capacity to recover quickly.

Athletes who compete in the long sprints (400 m) need less aerobic endurance than anaerobic endurance. However, they still need to train to improve their aerobic endurance, and for this reason, the 400 m is included in table 4.1.

Introduction to Interval Training on a Square Course

Introduce your athletes to interval training at the same time as they work on paced or tempo training. The repetitive runs that you had your athletes perform around a triangular course, although used to develop a feel for paced or tempo running, are also a simplified form of interval training. The triangular course that you used previously can be expanded to a square course, as shown in figure 4.10.

Competitive Distance	Training Distance	Speed of Run	Number of Repetitions	Duration of Recovery	Type of Recovery
400 m	50-200 m	Fast-Moderate	10-15	10-60 s	Walk, jog, or run
800 m	100-200 m	Moderate	10-15	10-60 s	Walk, jog, or run
1,500 m	100-200 m	Moderate	10-15	10-60 s	Walk, jog, or run
3,000 m	100-200 m	Moderate	10-15	10-60 s	Walk, jog, or run

TABLE 4.1 EXAMPLE OF AEROBIC INTERVAL TRAINING

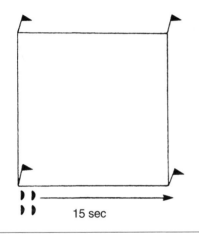

Figure 4.10 Interval training on a square course.

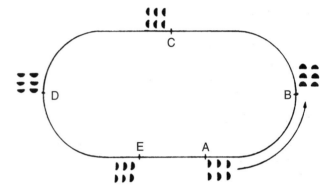

Figure 4.11 Introduction to interval training on the track.

Have teams of athletes start at the corner flags and run to reach the next corner flag at the same time as your whistle blast (after 15 seconds, for example). Require a specific type of recovery period (jogging in place) at each flag. Set the speed of the run, the number of repetitions, and the length of the recovery period according to the levels of fitness of your athletes. Athletes run each 50-m side of the square in 15 seconds, followed by a 15-second recovery (easy jogging in place). After 4 circuits, assign a circuit of walk recovery.

Introduction to Interval Training on the Track

Have 5 teams of your athletes walk around the 400-m track. Position the teams so that they are 80 m apart. Team A runs at medium tempo to catch up with Team B; at that point, Team A walks again (see figure 4.11). Team B then runs to catch up with Team C. Team B walks, and Team C runs to catch up with Team D. Team C walks, and Team D runs to catch up with Team E. Team E runs to catch up with Team A. Have your athletes repeat this sequence around the track. Determine the tempo of running and the number of repetitions according to the fitness levels of your athletes. The recovery period will be the walk.

Interval Training Designed to Develop a Mix of Aerobic and Anaerobic Endurance

Interval training that includes fast to moderately fast runs builds stamina at a pace close to competitive conditions. The athlete's basic endurance improves, and at the same time the athlete's muscles become used to working anaerobically. Because the runs are generally fast, the recovery periods must be longer. Distances will vary considerably. The number of

		TABLE 4.2 EXAMPLE OF AEROBIC/ANAEROBIC INTERVAL TRAINING			
Competitive Distance	Training Distance	Speed of Run	Number of Repetitions	Duration of Recovery	Type of Recovery
400 m	100-300 m	Fast	3-10	1-5 min	Walk, jog, or run
800 m	200-400 m	Fast-moderate	3-10	1-5 min	Walk, jog, or run
1,500 m	200-800 m	Fast-moderate	3-10	1-5 min	Walk, jog, or run
3,000 m	200-1,000m	Moderate	3-10	1-5 min	Walk, jog, or run

runs that you demand will depend upon the intent of the training (aerobic or anaerobic) and the athletes' levels of fitness. Table 4.2 shows an example of this type of training. It is best to start with a light workload and then progressively increase the intensity.

Interval Sprints

Athletes run short distances (50–100 m) at high speed, and then recover by walking 50–100 m. The number of repetitions depends upon fitness. Increase the intensity of the training by changing the walk to a jog.

There are many ways you can design interval training to develop a mix of aerobic and anaerobic endurance. Some examples follow:

Equal Distances and Recovery Periods

Athletes sprint for 25 seconds and recover for 25 seconds by jogging slowly. This sequence is performed for 3 or 4 repetitions.

Interval Relay

Form a team of 3 athletes. Athlete A sprints at top speed to pass the baton to athlete B, and then jogs to recover. Athlete B runs to pass the baton to athlete C and recovers after the pass (see figure 4.12). Each athlete sprints 5 × 200 m to cover a distance of 1,000 m. (3,000 m in total for the team.)

Pyramid (Ladder) Sprints

In this drill, you progressively increase the sprint distance or the duration of the sprint. After your athletes reach the top of the "pyramid" or have climbed the "ladder," you pro-

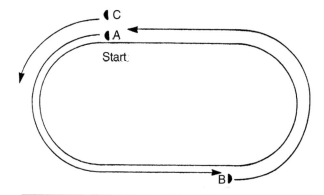

Figure 4.12 Interval relay.

gressively decrease the distance run or its duration. For example, athletes run a pyramidic program of 50, 100, 150, 200, 150, 100, and finally, 50 m. Or they sprint for 10, 15, 20, 15, and 10 seconds. You select the type and duration of the recovery period depending on your athletes' levels of fitness.

STEP 5: ANAEROBIC ENDURANCE TRAINING (IN-SEASON COMPETITIVE PERIOD)

This kind of training is frequently called "quality" or "speed" training. It requires your athletes to run at maximum or close to maximum speed. Like other types of interval training, it uses a run-recovery-run sequence. However, it is not considered true interval training because it doesn't work on the principle of partial recovery after each run. Instead, the high speed of each run requires a complete recovery.

The drills used for this type of training are similar to those designed to develop a mix of aerobic and anaerobic endurance. The difference is that this type of training always requires maximum or close to maximum speed with each repetition. It's intended to develop the athlete's speed and stamina sufficiently for the athlete to maintain relaxed and controlled sprinting technique while running flat-out. Because of the high speed required, few repetitions are used. Quality training adds a final polish to the athlete's preparation and establishes a feel for the pace used during the race. This training is performed just before the competitive season and during the competitive season. Table 4.3 provides a sample schedule for this type of training.

TABLE 4.3 EXAMPLE OF QUALITY TRAINING

Competitive Distance	Training Distance	Speed of Run	Number of Repetitions	Duration of Recovery	Type of Recovery
400 m	100-200 m	Fast	2-4	Sufficient to allow full recovery	Walk, jog, or run
800 m	200-600 m	Fast	2-4	Sufficient to allow full recovery	Walk, jog, or run
1,000 m	200-800 m	Fast	2-4	Sufficient to allow full recovery	Walk, jog, or run
2,000 m	300-1,000 m	Fast	2-4	Sufficient to allow full recovery	Walk, jog, or run
3,000 m	300-1,000 m	Fast	2-4	Sufficient to allow full recovery	Walk, jog, or run

COMMON ERRORS AND CORRECTIONS

DISTANCE-RUNNING TECHNIQUE

Error	Reasons	Corrections
The athlete uses an uneconomical style of running. Leg drive and arm swing are incorrect.	The athlete's leg drive may be forcing the athlete's body upward rather than forward. The arm swing is across the chest rather than back and forward in line with the direction of run.	The athlete should practice bounding and hopping, stressing correct leg drive. Emphasize running without rise and fall of the hips. Have the athlete concentrate on the correct forward and backward arm swing and the correct angle of flexion at the elbow.

→

Error	Reasons	Corrections
The athlete leans backward while running. The head is back or is allowed to "roll around."	The athlete has an incorrect chest (torso) and head position, and the vision is not directly ahead. The athlete may have weak abdominal and trunk muscles (or tense back muscles).	Have the athlete run with the head forward and the vision ahead. Have the athlete do strength and flexibility exercises for the back and abdomen.
The athlete swings the shoulders (and head) from side to side while running.	This error can also be caused by the arms swinging across the chest. The athlete has poor concentration on running technique, and the athlete's vision is not directly ahead. The athlete can be straining to keep up with other competitors.	Use activities that concentrate on running technique. Have the athlete practice arm swinging, parallel and in the direction of the run, while standing, and then while running. Improve the athlete's aerobic and anaerobic fitness.
The athlete uses poor drive or extension of the leg while running. The athlete has an appearance of sitting while running or demonstrates bent-legged running.	The athlete uses no extension or leg thrust during the run and has poor leg power and hip flexibility.	Assign exercises for increasing the athlete's leg power and hip flexibility. Hopping, bounding, jumping, and hurdler's flexibility exercises are all good for leg power.
The athlete appears tense while running.	Tension results from poor running technique, exhaustion, poor preparation for the distance run, and inadequate flexibility.	The athlete must concentrate on relaxing the facial muscles and the hands (no fists). The athlete should work to improve his/her aerobic/anaerobic endurance, and improve flexibility through related stretching exercises.

ASSESSMENT

1. **Assess the following theoretical elements as taught during instructional sessions:**
   a. Fundamental rules governing distance running.
   b. Good safety habits for distance running.
   c. Basic elements of distance-running technique.
   d. Basic elements of training for distance running.

2. **Assess the performance of technique during the following stages of skill development:**
   a. Long runs of varying types.
   b. Pace and tempo runs.
   c. Interval training.
   d. Quality/speed training.

CRITICAL FEATURES OF TECHNIQUE TO
OBSERVE DURING ASSESSMENT

✓ Overall appearance of relaxed, easy running style.

✓ An upright body position with minimal body lean.

✓ Moderate knee lift and arm swing.

✓ Arms and legs work directly forward and backward.

✓ A rolling support from the heel to the ball of the athlete's foot.

✓ Minimal lift and fall of the hips with each stride.

✓ Variation in the tempo of running and stride control according to demand.

3. **Hold graded competitions to help develop motivation and technique.**

   a. Athletes compete in a 12-minute run. How much distance is covered?

   b. Athletes compete over distances selected according to age and ability.

   c. Athletes compete singly in a handicap distance race. Start each athlete on the basis of prior performances, giving the weakest athlete the greatest time advantage.

   d. Athletes compete in pairs in a handicap race; members of each pair pace each other. Start each pair on the basis of prior performance, giving the weakest pair the greatest time advantage.

   e. Athletes predict the times they can achieve in pacing themselves over a specified distance, and scores are awarded for proximity to the predicted time. You set a maximum time for the course on the basis of previous performances.

   f. Teams compete against each other, simulating a cycle pursuit race. In this type of race, two teams of athletes start on opposing sides of the track; the group that gains distance on its opposition at the end of a specified time is the winner.

   g. Individuals compete against each other on an orienteering run. Using maps and a compass and markers positioned around the course, the athletes compete over a specified distance. Base the distance and difficulty level on the ability levels of the competitors.

   h. Athletes compete in distance competitions over 800; 1,500; 3,000; 5,000; and 10,000 m. Distances are chosen according to age, ability, gender, and maturity.

SUGGESTED STANDARDS OF PERFORMANCE—DISTANCE RUNNING

MALE		DISTANCE		
Age		**800 m**	**1,500 m**	**3,000 m**
12-13	Satisfactory	3:15	6:40	
	Good	3:05	6:10	
	Excellent	2:55	5:50	
14-15	Satisfactory	3:00	6:00	13:00
	Good	2:50	5:40	12:10
	Excellent	2:40	5:20	11:30
16-17	Satisfactory	2:50	5:40	12:10
	Good	2:40	5:20	11:30
	Excellent	2:30	5:00	10:50
18-19	Satisfactory	2:40	5:30	11:40
	Good	2:30	5:10	11:00
	Excellent	2:20	4:50	10:20

FEMALE		DISTANCE		
Age		**800 m**	**1,500 m**	**3,000 m**
12-13	Satisfactory	3:40	7:40	
	Good	3:25	7:10	
	Excellent	3:15	6:50	
14-15	Satisfactory	3:20	7:10	16:00
	Good	3:10	6:40	15:00
	Excellent	3:00	6:20	14:00
16-17	Satisfactory	3:10	6:50	15:30
	Good	3:00	6:20	14:00
	Excellent	2:50	6:00	13:10
18-19	Satisfactory	3:10	6:40	15:00
	Good	2:55	6:10	13:30
	Excellent	2:45	5:45	12:20

Standards measured in minutes and seconds.

5

STEEPLECHASE

The steeplechase, as a track and field event, is derived from cross-country running and obstacle course races. It combines distance running, hurdling, and water jumps. At present, steeplechase is a track event for males only.

The hurdles and the water-jump barrier used in the steeplechase are heavy, solid barriers that are made to support the weight of several athletes at the same time. They are not designed to be knocked over in the manner that occasionally occurs in the 100/110-m and 400-m hurdles. The rules of the steeplechase allow the athlete to jump on and off the water-jump barrier and (if the athlete wishes) to use the same technique in clearing the steeplechase hurdles. Most athletes use hurdling technique to clear the steeplechase hurdles, and as they get tired they may jump onto the hurdle and off again. Athletes normally jump on and then off the barrier set in front of the water jump. However, some elite Kenyan athletes hurdle this barrier and clear almost all of the water pit at the same time! This is far too dangerous to be attempted by young athletes. Steeplechase competitors are permitted to vault over the barriers, although this method is seldom used because it is so inefficient.

The water jump used in steeplechase has a barrier (which the athletes step up and onto) and a 3.66-m (12′) water pit, which the athlete must jump across or run through. The common practice is to jump up onto the 91.4-cm (3′) barrier with one leg and use the same leg to thrust across the water. Occasionally, an elite athlete will jump from the barrier and totally clear the water, but most athletes land with one foot in the water and step out with the other.

For athletes over 19 years of age, the competitive steeplechase distance is 3,000 m with the water jump most frequently on the inside of the track. Each lap is slightly less than 400 m (approximately 390 m). A 3,000-m steeplechase race contains 28 hurdles and 7 water jumps. A 2,000-m race has 18 hurdles and 5 water jumps, and the 1,500-m race 12 hurdles and 3 water jumps. The latter two races are usually run by athletes below the age of 19.

An athlete who chooses steeplechase as his event needs to be an excellent distance and cross-country runner and a good hurdler, with sufficient power and endurance to perform efficiently over the water jump and the hurdles. One of the biggest difficulties a steeplechaser faces is in estimating the approach and take-off position for the hurdles and the water jump. Increasing fatigue coupled with jostling from other runners makes this issue more and more critical as the race progresses.

SAFETY SUGGESTIONS

Steeplechase is a demanding distance race. In terms of fatigue, a 1,500-m steeplechase race is generally considered equal to a 3,000-m race on the flat. Young athletes are usually introduced to steeplechase by way of cross-country running. Their initial experiences with steeplechase should be over short distances that require only a few hurdle and water-jump clearances.

It is particularly important that your young athletes learn to jump on and off the steeplechase hurdles before attempting to hurdle them. In addition, your athletes should develop a good aerobic base through long runs and interval training. The stamina that is developed through this kind of training means that fatigue will take longer to affect the quality of their hurdle and water-jump clearances. A young athlete training for steeplechase must develop the ability to recognize the onset of fatigue and be able to decide when to switch from using a hurdling technique over the steeplechase hurdles to the easier method of jumping on and off.

To maintain a high level of safety, check all steeplechase hurdles and the water-jump barrier to make sure that they are stable and capable of withstanding the impact and weight of several athletes jumping on and off at the same time. Replace the tops of the hurdles and the water-jump barrier when they become splintered, and make sure the floor of the water-jump pit is smooth and covered with approved matting. This matting is necessary because it cushions the athletes when they jump down from the barrier into the water. Empty the water from the water-jump pit and restrict access when the pit is not in use.

Competitors in the steeplechase should wear well-fitting spikes that drain well and are comfortable to run in when wet. A good safety practice is to have athletes walk into the water jump with their spikes on, totally immerse their feet (and shoes), and then retighten the soaked laces. Track shoes can stretch when they become wet, and this precaution prevents them from becoming loose and uncomfortable during a race.

It's best to use a simulated water jump during instructional sessions when your athletes are not wearing spikes. You can have athletes jump onto a steeplechase hurdle and then from the hurdle into the sand of the long-jump pit (see figure 5.5). Even though the surface of the hurdle is likely to remain dry, be aware that wet grass or sand on top of the hurdle can cause an athlete not wearing spikes to slip. Keep hurdle surfaces brushed clean of sand and dirt, particularly when athletes in your classes are wearing rubber-soled shoes.

The preparation for clearing the hurdles and the water jump is an essential part of steeplechase training. Elite athletes become accustomed to bumping and jostling and to maneuvering and adjusting their approach for each of the hurdles and the water-jump barrier. Even though bumping occurs, athletes are expected to respect the rules and avoid cutting in and disrupting the approach of other competitors. The first hurdle in a steeplechase race is purposely made longer from one end to the other so that at the start of the race, athletes who are bunched close together can clear the hurdle without incident.

Teach your athletes to approach all hurdles (and the water-jump barrier) straight on so that the contact of the foot with the hurdle and the barrier's upper surface is at a right angle. In a race, this line of approach becomes particularly important when the hurdles and the water jump barrier become wet on top. When the water jump is positioned on a curve of the track, your athletes should run wide so that the approach to the water-jump barrier is more direct.

Athletes in a steeplechase race should try to avoid running behind their opponents when they approach a hurdle or the water jump barrier. They should shift to the side to get a clear view. In this way, if a competitor trips and falls, others are not taken down as well. Teach your athletes to avoid pausing after landing in the water at the water jump. More athletes will be following and jumping down from the water-jump barrier.

For indoor training, gymnastic vaulting boxes can substitute for a hurdle or the water-jump barrier, providing that you make sure that assistants keep the box stable. Outdoors, a steeplechase hurdle set in front of the long-jump pit provides a good substitute for the competitive water jump, particularly as landing in the sand simulates the drag of the water. Be sure you rake the sand.

When you work with young athletes, concentrate on careful progressive development. Increase the competitive distance and the number and height of the barriers as fitness and maturity develop. For beginners, 1 or 2 interlocking vaulting-box sections, 30 to 60 cm (1'–2') tall, set in front of the long-jump pit, substitute adequately for a water jump.

TECHNIQUE

The steeplechase water-jump clearance is made up of a precise approach to the water-jump barrier, a single-leg takeoff and landing on the barrier, and a strong thrust from the barrier to land in the shallow portion of the water jump. Takeoff, landing on the barrier, and takeoff from the the barrier to land in the water should be fluid and continuous.

WATER JUMP CLEARANCE

At about 10 to 15 m prior to the water jump, the athlete accelerates in order to jump up onto the barrier. The takeoff usually occurs 1½–2 m (5'–6'6") prior to the barrier. The athlete's upper body leans forward, and the free leg is flexed so that the instep can be placed on the barrier.

Once on the barrier, the athlete's supporting leg flexes to approximately 90 degrees. The upper body leans forward so that the athlete passes low over the barrier, rather than rising upward. When the athlete's body has passed over the supporting leg, the athlete's spikes grip the forward edge of the barrier in preparation for the push out over the water. The athlete thrusts forward with the leading leg, aiming to land 30–40 cm (12"–16") prior to the far end of the water jump. The athlete extends the arms on the landing to maintain balance (figure 5.1).

TEACHING STEPS
STEP 1. Lead-Ups
STEP 2. Development of Aerobic and Anaerobic Endurance
STEP 3. Steeplechase Hurdle and Water-Jump Clearance

Figure 5.1 Technique for clearing the steeplechase water jump.

STEP 1: LEAD-UPS

All lead-up drills for distance running and hurdling are excellent preparation for the steeplechase. Lead-ups that develop stamina (see chapter 4), hurdling ability (see chapter 3), and explosive leg power (see chapters 1 and 9) are particularly helpful. Weight-training exercises for the legs and rebound jumping (see chapters 8 and 9) are excellent for improving leg strength.

The steeplechase hurdle has the same dimensions as the barrier in front of the water jump. This similarity means you can use a steeplechase hurdle as a substitute for the water-jump barrier and a long-jump pit as a substitute water jump. Once accustomed to landing in sand, your athletes can then progress to clearing a water jump. Throughout these practices, your athletes should also train to develop a reasonable hurdling technique over low sprint hurdles (see chapter 3). When the athlete can easily clear 91.4-cm (3') sprint hurdles, the same technique can be applied to steeplechase hurdles.

STEP 2: DEVELOPMENT OF AEROBIC AND ANAEROBIC ENDURANCE

A steeplechase competitor requires both aerobic and anaerobic endurance. See chapters 1 and 4 for drills to develop the athlete's aerobic and anaerobic endurance.

STEP 3: STEEPLECHASE HURDLE AND WATER-JUMP CLEARANCE

Jumping on and off a Vaulting Box

In this drill, you can use a vaulting box that is progressively built up in sections to competitive steeplechase height (91.4 cm or 3'). Have your athletes start at low heights and use a mat to cushion their landing. The athletes jump up onto the box and push off onto the mat. If they take off from the floor on the right foot, they will step up on to the box using the left foot and use the left leg to push away from the box.

It's important that your athletes learn to judge their take-off position relative to their approach speed and also learn to take off using either leg. The athlete should swing the arms and free leg forward and upward to help get up onto the box. Once on the box, the athlete rotates forward over a flexed supporting leg, keeping the body low and the torso inclined forward. The athlete then uses a strong drive forward with the leading leg to jump from the box (see figure 5.2). The arms are used to help maintain balance during the landing.

Be sure to have spotters gripping the ends of the vaulting box to ensure that it will not tilt when an athlete jumps up onto it and pushes away from it. Your athletes should learn to run directly at the box so that their approach run is at right angles to the long axis of the box. Any other approach angle may cause the athlete to slip and fall when jumping onto a wet competitive steeplechase barrier.

COACHING TIPS

- Use your favored leg to jump up onto the hurdle from the ground. (Chapter 8 contains activities to select the favored leg.)
- Run wide from the curve and line yourself up so that you are running directly toward the center of the vaulting box.
- Swing the thigh of your leading leg upward and drive strongly from your jumping leg.
- Use your arm swing to assist you in getting up onto the box.
- Stay low over the box; don't straighten up.
- Jump long and low down to the ground.
- Use your arms to help maintain balance in the landing.
- Keep moving forward. Don't pause after you've landed. In a race, other competitors can be right behind you.

Using a Vaulting Box and Two Low Sprint Hurdles in a Circuit

To be comfortable in this drill, your athlete must be able to hurdle over low hurdles. Variations in the size of this circuit and the positioning of the vaulting box and hurdles develops the athlete's ability to assess the distance of the takeoff for the jump on to the box, and clearance of the two hurdles. At least 15 m should be available for acceleration toward the vaulting box. Use check marks set 6–8 strides prior to the vaulting box to help novices judge their approach and takeoff. Start by setting the box low and then progressively increase its height up to 91.4 cm (3'). Initially set your hurdles below this height. Don't forget to have two ath-

Figure 5.2 Jumping on and off a vaulting box.

letes stabilize the vaulting box so that it doesn't tip over when your athletes jump on and off it.

Figure 5.3 shows a circuit that you can set up outdoors or indoors. You can put the vaulting box on the track or place it in front of the long-jump pit so that the vaulting box and the long-jump pit simulate the steeplechase water jump.

COACHING TIPS

- Try to lengthen your stride rather than shorten it when modifying your paces for the takeoff to the vaulting box.
- Accelerate toward the vaulting box; don't slow down.

Using a Steeplechase Hurdle to Simulate the Barrier in Front of the Steeplechase Water Jump

A steeplechase hurdle is a good substitute for the barrier in front of the steeplechase water jump, because both are the same height and width (see figure 5.4). Chalk a square on the ground to indicate the 3.66 m (12′) of the water jump. Teach your athletes the following:

(a) To adjust their approach so that their take-off is accurate for jumping onto the hurdle

(b) To correctly place their foot on top of the hurdle

(c) To clear a distance that in competition will land them in the shallow water at the far border of the water jump

COACHING TIPS

- Be sure to accelerate toward the hurdle.
- Contact the hurdle with your instep; allow your foot to roll on the top of the hurdle so that the instep of the foot grips the far side of the hurdle.
- Lean forward and flex the supporting leg on the hurdle so that your body rotates low over the hurdle. (Don't try standing up on the hurdle.)
- Drive low and forward toward the landing.
- Use the swing of the leading leg to assist in driving your body outward for the landing.
- Use your arms for balance in the landing.

Combining a Steeplechase Hurdle and the Long-Jump Pit to Simulate a Steeplechase Water-Jump Clearance

Place a steeplechase hurdle at the edge of the long-jump pit. Athletes jump up onto the hurdle and jump down into the sand of the long-jump pit. The drag of the sand simulates the effect of the water in the water jump. Mark a square in the sand of the long jump pit to simulate the perimeter of the 3.66 m (12′) of the water jump. Intensify this drill by including additional hurdles and increasing the distance run (figure 5.5).

COACHING TIPS

- Concentrate on driving low and forward into the landing.

Figure 5.3 Steeplechase training circuit.

Figure 5.4 Jumping on and off a steeplechase hurdle.

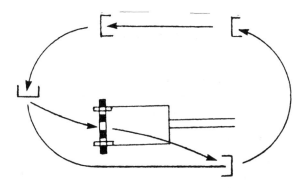

Figure 5.5 Simulated steeplechase and water-jump clearance.

- Do not relax in the landing; keep moving forward.
- Aim to land in the sand close to the line indicating the far perimeter of the steeplechase water pit. This is where the shallow water will be.

Jumping Onto the Water-Jump Barrier and Clearing the Water Jump

Your athletes now graduate to the competitive steeplechase water jump. Each athlete jumps up onto the barrier and aims to clear all but the final few centimeters of water. One foot lands in the water, and the other steps forward out of the water to continue running. Teach the athlete that the single-legged landing in the water is an "active" landing from which the athlete must move quickly forward. There's no pause or rest after the landing!

COACHING TIPS

- The single-legged landing in the water is a landing from which you push forward.
- Don't relax when you land.
- Your next stride should be clear of the water.

Using Hurdling Technique to Clear Steeplechase Hurdles

Competitive steeplechase hurdles cannot be set at a height lower than 91.4 cm (3'). They are massive and can hurt an athlete who hits them awkwardly. Have your novices jump on and off steeplechase hurdles until they develop an adequate hurdle clearance technique over sprint hurdles. It is an advantage to be able to hurdle with either leg leading. For greater con-

fidence in clearing the 91.4-cm steeplechase hurdles, the athlete must be comfortable in hurdling sprint hurdles set at 98 cm (3'3"). See chapter 3 for drills and coaching tips to develop hurdling technique (figure 5.6) and the ability to hurdle with an alternate leg lead.

Clearing a Steeplechase Water Jump and Steeplechase Hurdles in Distance Training

Position the steeplechase water jump and steeplechase hurdles in various sections of middle-distance training runs. By varying the positions of the barriers, you will force athletes to adjust their approach and stride pattern. If several of your athletes train together, they will make each other modify their stride patterns for the takeoff to the hurdles under competitive conditions.

You can design a course so that your athletes clear the steeplechase water jump and hurdles several times in the first part of a middle-distance training run and then complete the remaining part of the run without any barriers to clear. You can also set up the course so that the steeplechase water jump and hurdles are in the middle part of a middle-distance training run. The athletes complete the first and last third of the run without barriers to clear. The most challenging variation for the athletes is for you to set up the course so the athletes must clear the steeplechase water jump and hurdles in the last part of a middle-distance training run.

Figure 5.6 Steeplechase hurdle clearance.

STEEPLECHASE WATER-JUMP CLEARANCE

Error	Reasons	Corrections
The athlete's pacing and rhythm of approach to the water jump are poorly judged. The athlete takes stutter steps prior to takeoff.	The athlete has had insufficient practice on the approach. The athlete is anxious and has poor endurance. The athlete is blocked by other competitors and is not able to assess the pacing to the water jump until it is too late.	The athlete needs repetitive practice of approach and clearance of the water jump. Use check marks to help the athlete develop a feel for distance in final strides prior to takeoff. Teach the athlete to move into a clear position so that assessing pacing prior to takeoff is easier. Have the athlete work on improving aerobic endurance.
The athlete loses momentum after jumping onto the barrier and hesitates prior to clearing the water jump. The athlete jumps down into the deeper water.	The athlete takes off too far away from the barrier or jumps too high and lands on the barrier with an erect upper body and/or straight legs.	Instruct the athlete to use check marks for the 6-8 paces prior to the takeoff. A marker for the takeoff will also be useful. The athlete must keep the upper body low and forward when landing on the barrier. The athlete must flex at the hips and knees to keep the center of gravity low and to provide the drive forward and out over the water jump.
The athlete lands in the middle of the water.	The approach to the water jump is too slow. The athlete has poor drive from the barrier with the supporting leg and poor transfer of momentum from the arms and leading leg. The jump from the barrier may be upward rather than forward.	Help the athlete improve his aerobic endurance, and work to speed up the athlete's approach to the water jump. Use repetitive bounding and jumping to improve the athlete's jumping technique to strengthen the athlete's legs. nstruct the athlete to flex the supporting leg on the barrier, to keep low, and to thrust out across the water and not upward.
The athlete loses speed after landing in the water.	The athlete jumps upward from the barrier and relaxes and hesitates after landing in the water.	The athlete must lean forward and drive forward and outward from the barrier, concentrating on keeping the body moving forward after landing in the water. Vigorous arm swing will assist in keeping the body moving.

| | |

ASSESSMENT

1. **Assess the following theoretical elements as taught during instructional sessions:**

   a. Fundamental rules governing steeplechase competition.

   b. Good safety habits for use in steeplechase training.

   c. Basic elements of steeplechase technique.

   d. Basic elements of steeplechase training.

2. **Assess the performance of technique during the following stages of skill development:**

   a. A simulated water-jump clearance using a steeplechase hurdle and the long-jump pit or a simulated water-jump clearance using a vaulting box and gymnastics mats.

   b. A water-jump clearance using the competitive equipment.

   c. A jump-on/jump-off steeplechase hurdle clearance.

   d. A steeplechase hurdle clearance using hurdling technique.

   e. A series of steeplechase hurdle and water-jump clearances occurring during the first third, second third, and latter third of a distance run. (Tempo and stride adjustment in the run-up for the hurdle and water-jump clearances are challenged by the differing levels of fatigue that occur.)

   CRITICAL FEATURES OF TECHNIQUE TO OBSERVE DURING ASSESSMENT

   Water-Jump Clearance and Jump Clearance of a Steeplechase Hurdle

   ✓ Stride adjustment and acceleration toward the steeplechase water-jump barrier (or a steeplechase hurdle).

   ✓ Vigorous drive with the take-off leg, forward body lean, and flexion in the leading leg at takeoff toward the barrier. The thigh of the leading leg is raised to a horizontal position during the takeoff.

   ✓ Low carriage of the upper body over a flexed (90 degrees) supporting leg on the barrier.

   ✓ Strong forward and downward drive from the barrier. The arm actions assist balance on the landing.

   ✓ A landing on the leading leg that both cushions and drives the athlete forward.

   (For the steeplechase hurdle clearance using hurdling technique, see 100/110-m hurdles and 400-m hurdles assessment in chapter 3.)

3. **Hold graded competitions to develop motivation and technique.**

   a. Individuals compete in cross-country runs that include water jumps, hurdles, and similar obstacles.

   b. Runners compete in steeplechase competitions that are graded according to age and experience. Runners compete over 1,500, 2,000, and 3,000 m.

SUGGESTED STANDARDS OF PERFORMANCE—STEEPLECHASE				
MALE		**DISTANCE**		
Age		**1,500 m**	**2,000 m**	**3,000 m**
16-17	Satisfactory	7:00	8:00	
	Good	6:30	7:30	
	Excellent	6:00	7:00	
18-19	Satisfactory	6:00	7:30	11:30
	Good	5:30	7:00	11:00
	Excellent	5:00	6:30	10:30

Standards measured in minutes and seconds.

6

RACE WALKING

Race walking was included in the early modern Olympic Games, and over the years males have raced over a number of different distances. These distances have ranged from 1,500 m offered in 1906 in Athens to the longest distance of 50 km first offered in 1932 in Los Angeles. For males, the two established distances are 20 km and 50 km. In 1992 in Barcelona, females were finally offered a race walk competition of their own of 10 km. The distances of 10 km for females and 20 and 50 km for males are now the standard distances for most international competitions. These distances were used in Atlanta in 1996.

At the competitive level, race walking is controlled by a set of simple rules that are intended to make sure that the competitor is walking and not running. These rules specify that race walking must entail a progression of steps taken in such a way that to the trained eye of the official no apparent loss of contact with the ground occurs. An additional rule states that the athlete's leg that is swung forward for each step cannot be flexed at the knee from the moment the foot contacts the ground. This leg must stay straight (or "locked") until it has reached a vertical position below the athlete's

body. It is this repetitive straight-legged position, together with the forward and downward rotation of the athlete's hips, that gives race walking its familiar flowing style of movement.

It is important to realize that the athlete's motion is assessed by an official's eye and not by high-speed cameras. Elite race walkers, and fast walking of any kind, has a "flight phase" when both feet are—for a brief instant—off the ground. This instant can certainly be detected by the lens of a camera, but the human eye does not capture this action so quickly. It is only when the flight phase is apparent to the eye of a judge that a race walker is declared to be infringing the rules.

Today there is growing support for walking as a lifetime activity. It is performed as an individual form of exercise and also used as an active rest for those who jog and run. In schools it's a form of exercise in which most children can participate—even those whose physical condition prevents them from involvement in other sports.

Leisurely walking, which most of us do at some time during the day, can easily be intensified so that it becomes what is loosely called "power walking." In power walking, the action is made vigorous by additional movements such as greater arm and leg swing. Athletes can also increase resistance by using hand weights, weight vests, and/or ankle weights. Power walking is certainly a vigorous form of exercise, and it provides an excellent workout!

As far as technique is concerned, power walking is very different from the smooth high-speed actions of a top-class race walker. At the elite level, race walking is fast, efficient, and dynamic. Race walking technique is designed for speed, and you certainly won't see the exaggerated actions characteristic of power walking.

In this chapter you will be offered a series of teaching progressions that lead from easy walking to race walking. Given the fitness benefits of power walking, you can include it in your walking program. But don't use power walking as a lead-up to race walking, and don't teach the exaggerated swinging motions of power walking as part of race walking technique. They're detrimental to a good race walking technique.

You'll notice that this chapter suggests that you draw on drills and teaching progressions offered in chapter 4 (Distance Running). Be prepared to adapt the training principles outlined in that chapter to your instruction in race walking. Apart from technique training, the workouts used by distance runners and race walkers are very similar.

SAFETY SUGGESTIONS

The popularity of walking and jogging has increased dramatically in recent years. Walking, in particular, has been recognized as an activity that not only improves general health but is less concussive than running or jogging. Its more gentle effects on the body—particularly on the lower back, hips, and knee joints—means that it's a great lifetime activity and, as you are probably aware, a favorite with seniors. Like distance running and jogging, recreational walking can be practiced virtually anywhere and requires little more than adequate clothing, a good pair of walking shoes, and a fairly level surface to walk on. If your athletes intend to compete in race walking, they will need shoes that are more flexible and that have less padding than normal walking shoes. Many race walkers train and compete using light shoes designed for distance running. These shoes are commonly called "racing flats."

In spite of the ease with which you can practice walking, there are certain safety precautions to consider. These safety precautions, briefly outlined below, are discussed in greater detail in chapter 4.

Easy walking requires little to no warm-up, although some preliminary stretching and light calisthenics are certainly beneficial. Begin by having your athletes walk slowly, and then progressively increase the intensity so that walking becomes more vigorous and demanding. Once your athletes are used to walking vigorously, you should direct your attention to teaching them the technique of race walking. For variety, you can integrate race walking with periods of brisk normal walking, jogging, and short bursts of sprinting.

Whether your athletes race walk for fitness or intend someday to compete, be sure to take into account their age relative to the distance that you wish them to walk and the vigor of the walking action that you demand. Vigorous walking, whether you concentrate on race walking technique or not, uses a lot of energy and is very demanding. In hot weather, fluid replacement is necessary. Cold weather will require warm clothing, such as a hat, gloves, tights, or a track suit.

TECHNIQUE

The race walking technique used by elite athletes is a perfect combination of speed and efficiency. It may surprise you to know that elite athletes are able to travel at over 15 kph (9.3 mph) while still satisfying the rules of the event. To reach such high speeds, race walkers use a smooth, fast, flowing technique which can be broken down into three closely connected phases. These are (a) the "double support" phase, (b) the "traction" phase, and (c) the "thrust" or "drive" phase.

THE DOUBLE SUPPORT PHASE

The double support phase is a very brief phase, when both the athlete's feet are in contact with the ground. It occurs after the athlete has pushed forward with the rear leg and the front foot has just contacted the ground. The athlete's center of gravity is between the feet and slightly to the rear of the front foot. The front leg will be straight by the time it has contacted the ground (see figure 6.1c).

Figure 6.1 Race-walking technique.

THE TRACTION PHASE

The traction phase begins once the leading leg has been brought forward and the athlete's front foot has made contact with the ground. The leading leg is already straight, so there will be no flexion at the knee. The front foot lands with the athlete's center of gravity almost directly above it, and the foot "claws," or pulls, the ground backward. The traction phase resembles the action of a spinning wheel that thrusts itself forward as its rim contacts the ground. The athlete's center of gravity smoothly passes forward over the leading leg without any rise and fall. The contraction of the athlete's hamstring and gluteal muscles (i.e., the muscles to the rear of the thigh and the buttocks), together with the forward momentum that has built up with each stride, contribute to the traction phase (see figure 6.1d and e)

THE THRUST OR DRIVE PHASE

The thrust or drive phase occurs at the same time that the ground is being pulled backward in the traction phase. When one leg is ahead of the body, the rear leg is simultaneously thrusting the athlete forward. Once the thrust from the rear leg is complete, the leg is flexed at the knee and ready for the leg to be brought forward again. The athlete should avoid swinging or kicking the heel upward when the knee is flexed (see figure 6.1a–c).

INDIVIDUAL TECHNICAL ELEMENTS

Within the three phases just described, there is a series of specific actions that provide the most important elements of race walking technique. These are as follows:

FOOT POSITIONING

The race walker's feet are placed directly in front of each other, so that the athlete moves forward along as straight a line as possible.

HIP ACTION

The rotary forward and downward action of the hips is probably the most recognizable characteristic of race walking technique, yet it varies in degree according to the individual athlete's hip mobility. The hip on the leading leg side of the athlete's body is thrust forward and downward with each stride. This action carries the leading leg forward and helps to keep the path of the athlete's center of gravity horizontal. The cyclical motion of the hips is counterbalanced predominantly by the swing of the athlete's arms and to some degree by some countermotion of the shoulders. Stride length and the maintenance of a fast tempo are promoted by this hip action.

THE ARMS

The race walker's arms are flexed at the elbows. The angle at the elbows varies so that a piston-like movement of the forearm occurs as the athlete moves forward. The intention of the arm swing is to help the athlete move forward as efficiently as possible. The athlete's shoulders are relaxed rather than hunched upward so that the athlete's hands brush past the hips during their forward and backward swing. This low position of the hands is brought about by the relaxed low carriage of the shoulders, not by the athlete allowing the arms to straighten at the elbows.

THE ATHLETE'S OVERALL BODY POSITION

The athlete's body is upright, although there can be some slight forward lean from the feet. Leaning from the hips either forward or backward is detrimental to an efficient technique.

RHYTHM AND CADENCE

The high-speed motion characteristic of an elite race walker comes from a combination of good technique, coupled with excellent strength, speed, flexibility, and endurance. The athlete makes sure that the arms are not swung forward and upward nor backward and upward. The rear foot is kept low during its recovery and not kicked upward. There is a pronounced rotary motion of the hips. The stride length is optimal and is not so large that the forward foot acts as brake or an axis that forces the athlete's body to lift upward. All of these factors contribute to a smooth, fast horizontal flow of the athlete's center of gravity as each step is taken.

TEACHING STEPS

STEP 1. Introduction to Race Walking

STEP 2. Race Walk Technique Training

STEP 3. Long-Distance Walking With Short Segments Emphasizing Race Walk Technique

STEP 4. Technique and Rhythm Training Over Longer Distances

STEP 5. Preparing for Competitive Race Walking

You can progressively intensify normal walking for your athletes so that it becomes a highly vigorous form of exercise. You can also use walking at selected tempos as a form of active rest when your athletes train for distance running. The drills that follow progress from easy to vigorous walking. During each of these drills you can emphasize one or two technical elements of race walking. Later you can progress to drills where you concentrate completely on race walking technique.

STEP 1. INTRODUCTION TO RACE WALKING

Introduce race walking to your class with minimal emphasis on technique and maximum emphasis on activity and enjoyment. Your initial objective is to have your athletes appreciate that vigorous walking is an energetic and demanding activity.

Make-Believe Race Walking

As an introduction to your class, begin with some fun! Ask all your athletes to race walk 50 m. Give them no instruction, allowing them to copy the race walking movements that they have seen at track meets or on television. Some of your athletes will have a good kinesthetic sense of what race walking is all about and distinguish themselves as natural walkers. Use these athletes as group leaders in some of the later drills.

VARIATION

8 × 50 m race walk relay; 8 runners per team, with each athlete race walking 50 m.

COACHING TIPS

No instruction should be given other than the following:

- Running is not allowed.
- Everybody must race walk.

Easy Walking

Easy walking is nonvigorous normal walking. While your athletes are walking, emphasize one technical element essential to race walking, such as walking in a straight line. Vary the speed of walking from slow to moderately fast. Easy walking can be performed on roads and trails as well as on the track. For working on walking in a straight line, it is best to use the lines on a track. Start with a distance of 800 m (875 yd.). Progressively increase the distance up to 2–3 km.

- When on the track, choose a lane line to walk along and walk so that each of your feet land on the line.
- Make sure that each foot points straight ahead when you place it on the line.
- Keep your head up and look ahead. Don't look down at your feet.

Timed Walks

In this drill your athletes walk for a specific time period rather than a specific distance. You can again include some work on race walk technique as part of this drill. Repeat the practice for walking in a straight line and include some coaching tips on your athletes' arm action. Begin with 20 minutes. Over the course of your program, progressively increase the time that your athletes walk to 30–40 minutes.

- On the track, choose a lane line to walk along, and make sure that each of your feet lands on the line.
- Make sure that each foot points straight ahead when you place it on the line.
- Keep your head up and look ahead.
- Flex your arms at the elbows.
- Swing your arms back and forth so that your forearms swing parallel to the line you're walking along.
- Think of your arms as pistons moving horizontally back and forth. Don't swing your arms upward to your front or to your rear.
- Try to make the heel of your hand brush your hips as your arms swing back and forth.

Easy Walking With Segments of High-Tempo Walking

In this drill you intersperse easy walking with more aggressive faster walking. Repeat the coaching tips that you used previously. Your main objective in this drill is to have your ath-

letes experience high-tempo walking. Begin with easy walking. Then on your signal have your athletes reduce their stride length to approximately $^3/_4$ of its original length, and increase the cadence of their walking. Now each step will be performed faster. Have your athletes swing their arms vigorously forward and backward. Start with a distance of 400 m which is made up of 30-m segments of easy walking followed by 20-m segments of high-tempo walking. As your athletes get fatigued, reduce the 20-m segments of high-tempo walking to 15 m, and with increased fatigue, from 15 m to 10 m. When your athletes become more accomplished, you will increase the total distance walked to 800 m, and you'll make fewer reductions in the distance of the high-tempo segments.

- Remember to keep your arms flexed at the elbows and to swing your forearms back and forth parallel to the direction you are walking.
- Swing your arms vigorously back and forth.
- Try not to swing the arms upward at the front or the rear.
- Imagine a straight line ahead of you, and walk directly along this line.
- Cut your stride down a little so that you can make each stride faster.
- Try not to turn your feet out as you walk.

High-Tempo Walking in Pairs

Here are two drills that emphasize high-tempo walking.

a. Have your athletes walk normally side by side in pairs. On your signal the athletes on the right reduce their stride length as before and simultaneously increase their walking tempo. The athletes on the left walk with a normal stride length and try to keep up with their partners. They walk in this fashion for 20 m. On your second signal, both athletes walk normally for 20 m. On your next signal, the athletes on the left reduce their stride length and increase their walking tempo. The athletes on the right walk with a normal stride length and try to keep up with their partners. They walk in this fashion for the next 20 m. Have your athletes perform some easy, relaxed walking, and then repeat the drill. Both athletes may be surprised to see how an increased walking tempo coupled with a shorter stride length produces higher speeds.

b. Pair off your athletes and have one walk at a moderate tempo, applying the technical elements that you have emphasized so far. The second athlete jogs behind the walker and on your signal provides a constant but gentle push from the rear for 15–20 m. The extra thrust from the rear will make the walker experience both the speed and the effort needed to maintain such a high tempo. Have your athletes repeat this drill and then change positions.

COACHING TIPS

- When you walk at high speed, you must still keep your feet pointing forward and walk along the line in front of you.
- Keep your arms flexed at the elbows, and swing your forearms forward and back like pistons.
- Concentrate on the forward and backward movement of your arms. Don't swing them up in the air.
- Keep your vision forward, and don't drop your head down or let it fall backward.

Vigorous Walking in Performance Groups

Divide your class into performance groups based on your assessment of their ability to walk vigorously and at speed. Choose your natural walkers as leaders for each group. Leaders take their groups over a random course that the leader selects for 15 minutes out and 15 minutes back. The leaders are required to mix high-tempo walking with easy walking. Each group can follow cross-country routes or road routes. With subsequent sessions, intensify the demand by increasing the time to 20 minutes out and 20 minutes back.

Handicap Walking Competitions

Set up a handicap race in which all of your athletes walk a distance you select as fast and as vigorously as they can. Have your athletes start in groups of 2 or 3 according to ability. Set up timed handicaps so that the slowest walkers start first and the fastest walkers start last. Try to set the handicaps so that all athletes arrive at the finish close together. A distance of 2–3 km is adequate for this drill.

Fartlek Walking

The Swedish Fartlek method of training for distance runners is explained in on page 76. You can use a similar Fartlek course for walking as you previously used for distance running. This means your athletes walk up inclines, through forested areas, and on long flat sections. Be sure to include sections where your athletes can walk more casually or stop to perform a series of calisthenics according to your demand. You control the length of the sections that are walked vigorously and those that are walked at a more relaxed pace. Plan an interesting course with pleasant changes in terrain. Start with a course 2–3 km in length and later increase the distance to 4–5 km.

STEP 2. RACE WALK TECHNIQUE TRAINING

In the following drills, your athletes work more intensely on race walk technique. In the first 4 drills, have them practice various technical elements repeatedly. Don't expect them to learn each technical element immediately. All require frequent repetition. The drills can be performed on a track or a similar flat surface. Each technique segment lasts 50 m and is followed by 50 m of easy walking for recovery. Repeat the technique segments 5 times for a total of 250 m.

Action of the Arms and Hands and Body Position

Walk 50 m, concentrating on arm and hand action and body position. After hitting the 50-m mark, turn and walk easily back to the start. Repeat the technique segment 5 times for a total of 250 m.

COACHING TIPS

- Bend (flex) your arms at your elbows. Swing your arms back and forth in time with your leg action. Keep your forearms parallel to the ground and in line with the direction you're walking.

- Make sure your arm swing originates from the shoulders and is forward and backward and not across the chest.
- Swing your elbows backward but only so far that your hands reach the midline of your body.
- Make your normal stride quicker by shortening the length of each stride. A quick stride rhythm will help to generate more push as you move forward.
- Look directly forward and keep your torso upright

Stride Length

Walk 50 m, concentrating on stride length. Follow this with 50 m of easy walking for recovery. Repeat the technique segment 5 times for a total of 250 m.

COACHING TIPS

- Make your normal stride quicker by shortening the length of each stride.
- A quick stride rhythm will help to generate more push as you move forward.

Straightening the Leading Leg

Walk 50 m, concentrating on straightening the leading leg. Follow this with 50 m of easy walking for recovery. Repeat the technique segment 5 times for a total of 250 m.

COACHING TIPS

- Straighten your leading leg the instant it contacts the ground. (Later you will learn to straighten this leg immediately prior to its contact with the ground.)
- If you pull backward with your leading leg by tightening the thigh muscles, you'll find that it will help you to straighten the leg.
- Start by working on your favored leg for 10 paces, and then switch to your nonfavored leg.
- Alternate from favored to nonfavored (for instance, from right leg to left leg) for 10 paces each for the full 50 m.

Thrust With the Rear Leg

Walk 50 m, concentrating on thrusting the rear leg. Follow this with 50 m of easy walking for recovery. Repeat the technique segment 5 times for a total of 250 m.

COACHING TIPS

- Concentrate on driving forward when your favored leg is to the rear of your body. Do this for 10 paces, then switch to the nonfavored side for 10 paces.
- Don't push upward—push forward. Alternate from favored to nonfavored for 10 paces each for the full 50 m.
- Don't kick your rear heel up in the air when you flex your rear leg to bring it forward.
- Flex your rear leg just enough to skim it forward above ground level.
- As you bring forward your rear leg, lift the toes upward toward your shin so that there is a 90-degree angle between the upper surface of your foot and your shin.

Action of the Hips

Young athletes will vary greatly in their hip mobility. This variation is seen even in competitive race walkers at the elite level. The action of the hips plays an important role in all race walking. However, a lack of the classic hip roll is not in itself a barrier to progress.

The following drills have as their objectives (a) making sure that the athlete's leading foot contacts the ground near to or vertically below the athlete's center of gravity and (b) lengthening the athlete's stride without resisting the athlete's forward motion. The following four drills will help you to teach these actions.

On-the-Spot Hip Roll Drill

Stand with your feet together with your hands on your hips. Keep your heels on the ground and bend your left leg as much as possible while your right leg remains straight. Now straighten the left leg and bend the right as you did with your left. This motion is the same as in the Rumba, a Latin American dance. Repeat this action 10 times.

COACHING TIPS

- Can you feel the hip on the bent leg side rotating forward and downward? The movement you're feeling is the basic racewalk hip action.

- Some of you will be a little stiff in your hips and ankles, and this will initially restrict your movement. With practice you will loosen up!

Lift and Shift Drill

Sit on the ground or on the gym floor with your legs extended in front. Progress forward by lifting and shifting each hip (i.e., buttock) forward alternately. Rest after you have made 10 "seat shifts" in total, then repeat.

COACHING TIPS

- Hold your arms extended sideways, and don't allow them to touch the ground.
- Concentrate on the following movements: lift, shift, lower, lift, shift, lower!

One-Hip Thrust Drill

Perform this drill while walking 50 m on the track straightaway. Start with both feet together.

Thrust your right hip deliberately forward to take one long step with the right leg. Count this as step 1. Then take 3 normal steps. Now you are ready to step forward again with the right leg, emphasizing the action of the right hip. After 2 or 3 repeats of 50 m concentrating on the right hip, try the same action with your left hip.

Two-Hip Thrust Drill

Perform this drill while walking 50 m on the track straightaway. Concentrate on driving forward with the left and then the right hip with each successive stride.

COACHING TIPS

- Try to think of "hip forward" rather than "leading leg forward."
- When the foot of your leading leg contacts the ground, it should already be moving backward. Try to get your bodyweight above this foot as soon as you can. Don't kick your leading leg out far in front of you.

STEP 3. LONG-DISTANCE WALKING WITH SHORT SEGMENTS EMPHASIZING RACE WALK TECHNIQUE

In Step 3, increase the overall distance that your athletes walk vigorously, and inter-sperse vigorous walking with segments in which they concentrate on race walking technique.

Repetitions of 1-Minute Technique Training

For a warm-up, have your athletes perform some light calisthenics and walk easily for 3 minutes. Then have them begin this drill by walking normally (but briskly) for 1 minute. Normal walking for 1 minute is then alternated with 1-minute segments during which your athletes concentrate on race walking technique. Repeat the coaching tips that you used earlier during your 50-m repeats. When a 1-minute race walking technique segment is completed, have your athletes go back to normal vigorous walking for another minute. Keep up these alternating minutes of technique training and nontechnical walking until they have practiced their race walking technique 5 times. Then put in a longer 3-minute segment of nontechnical vigorous walking, and start the 1-minute alternating segments for a second sequence. Here's a summary of this drill:

a. 3-minute warm-up (walking plus light calisthenics).

b. 1 minute of vigorous walking.

c. 1 minute of race walking technique training.

d. Repeat steps b and c 4 more times in sequence.

e. 3 minutes of vigorous walking.

f. Repeat steps b, c, and d.

g. 3 minutes of easy walking as a cooldown.

COACHING TIP

Your coaching tips for the 1-minute race walk technique segments will be the same as for those used in the 50-m repeats.

STEP 4. TECHNIQUE AND RHYTHM TRAINING OVER LONGER DISTANCES

In Step 4, increase the distance over which your athletes concentrate on race walking technique.

Technique and Rhythm Drill

This drill is performed on the track or a straight, flat stretch of road. Previously you had your athletes work on race walking technique over 50 m. In this drill, you will have your athletes race walk over a distance of 100 m at a speed that allows them to concentrate specifically on technique and rhythm.

If you use the 100-m straightaway on the track, the easy walking segments occur when your athletes return to the start for another 100 m of technique training. Begin by having your athletes race walk 4 times for 100 m during which they concentrate on technique. Progressively increase the amount of technique training until your athletes reach a total distance of 800 m made up of 2 sets of 4 repetitions of 100 m.

COACHING TIPS

- Pick one of the lines dividing the lanes of the straightaway. Walk along this line so that your body is moving along a perfectly straight path. In this way you will not be moving from side to side, and there will be no loss of speed or stride length. Don't turn your feet out.
- Begin by concentrating solely on pulling the ground back toward you with your right front foot every time it lands. Concentrate on this action for 10 paces. Then do the same with the left foot.
- When you are working on pulling the ground back with the right foot, be sure you straighten the right leg. Concentrate on this action for 10 paces. Then do the same with the left leg.
- Now concentrate solely on driving with your right rear leg. Do this for 10 paces, then switch to concentrating on the left leg.
- Roll your left hip forward and down when your right leg supports you. Then repeat the same action with the right hip when your left leg supports you.
- Keep your arms flexed and swing your forearms back and forward like pistons, not up in the air.
- Reduce any arm motion across your chest to a minimum.
- Keep your torso upright.

- Try to follow a smooth, flat path as you travel forward. There should be no up-and-down motion in your body.

STEP 5. PREPARING FOR COMPETITIVE RACE WALKING

If your athletes are interested in competitive race walking, you must have them work on improving their technique and also on their anaerobic and aerobic endurance. There is no reason why your athletes should not continue running or performing other fitness activities as long as the race walking techniques are consistently practiced. Work on race walking technique and on building endurance in the manner suggested in step 2 of this chapter. Remember that beginning race walkers do not compete in long races early in their careers. Competitive race walking is an endurance *and* a technique event. For your younger athletes, races should be no more than 800 m (and even shorter distances for the very young). Recommended distances for various age groups are shown at the end of this chapter. The traditional Olympic distances are for well-trained athletes only!

Here are some general suggestions for when you work with your aspiring race walkers:

a. Refine your athlete's race walking technique over short distances at least twice a week. Concentrated technique training over 100 m is excellent for this purpose. However, there is nothing to be gained by going past the point of technique breakdown. So increase your athletes' distances gradually. Performing 2 repetitions of 50 m well is much better than 1 repetition of 100 m performed with poor technique.

b. Have your athlete race walk long distances so that they build up basic endurance but don't expect them to maintain good race walk technique for the whole distance. This will come with practice. Be sure to include running and other vigorous activities as part of their training so that your athletes build up aerobic and anaerobic endurance. Some walkers build their endurance and technique by mixing race walking and running in the following manner, working toward a goal of 60 minutes of race walking:

Run out for 15 minutes and race walk back.

Race walk out for 20 minutes and run back.

Run for 10 minutes, race walk 5 minutes, and repeated 2, 3, and then 4 times.

Work toward a goal of 60 minutes of racewalking.

c. Apply the principles of interval training at least once a week to your athletes' race walk training. This means that you should vary the *distance* your athletes race walk, the *number of times* (or reps) they race walk this distance, the *tempo* (i.e., the speed) that they race walk the required distance, the *length of the recovery time* between each repetition, the *number of times* each group (or set) of repetitions is repeated, and the *rest period* taken between each set.

When you are using interval training, be sure that your athletes avoid practicing to the point where their technique disintegrates! Shorten the distances of the intervals, reduce the speed of the interval, or give more rest if you see that your athletes' technique is deteriorating. For whatever the reason, don't let your athletes continue training if good technique is no longer apparent.

Here is an example of a session of interval training for race walking:

Three sets of 3 reps of 1½ minutes of race walking with a 1-minute recovery between each repetition. Take 3 to 4 minutes of rest between sets, or sufficient rest to allow the heart rate to return to 120 beats. This is written as 3 × (3 × 1½ min)—1-min recovery between reps, 3–4 min rest between sets.

Over a number of weeks the workload is be intensified in the following manner:

3 × (3 × 2 min)—1½ min rest between reps, 3–4 min rest between sets.

4 × (3 × 1½ min)—1 min rest between reps, 3–4 min rest between sets.

4 × (3 × 2 min)—1½ min rest between reps, 3–4 min rest between sets.

3 × (5 × 1 min)—45 secs rest between reps, 3-4 min rest between sets.

3 × (6 × 1 min)—1 min rest between reps, 3–4 min rest between sets.

3 × (5 × 1 min)—30 secs rest between reps, 3–4 min rest between sets.

An Example of a Yearlong Training Program for Race walking

A yearlong training program for race walking is planned in much the same way as for the distance runner. The following program tells you what you should have your athlete work on during the off-season, the precompetitive season, and finally the competitive season.

OFF-SEASON

Much of your athletes' off-season training should be directed toward the development of a good aerobic base. This means that your athletes build up an aerobic base through a mix of race walking and running over long distances. General conditioning will be improved with circuit training and weight training. In addition, their general mobility will be improved with a good, all-inclusive program of flexibility exercises and specific mobility exercises directed toward race walking.

PRECOMPETITIVE SEASON

In your athletes' precompetitive period, the emphasis shifts to tempo training over short and long distances and interval training in which they walk short distances at fast race walking speed with incomplete rest periods in between each repetition. Your athletes will also use distance running to increase endurance. In circuit training and weight training, have them concentrate on light fast actions. General mobility exercises are continued as before.

COMPETITIVE SEASON

During the competitive season, your athletes will take part in race walking competitions that are carefully scheduled to fit in with their training. In between competitions they should continue to practice some intensive interval training and high-speed race walking over long and short distances. The objective is to maintain the quality and fitness built up during the off-season and the precompetitive season and to be at peak condition for selected competitions.

COMMON ERRORS AND CORRECTIONS

Error	Reasons	Corrections
The athlete is not progressing along a straight line, and distance is being lost with each stride.	Your athlete's feet are being placed down on the ground with the toes turned outward, or the athlete is stepping across the body with each stride.	Have your athlete concentrate on the positioning of each foot along an imaginary line that is straight ahead of the body. The athlete's feet should be placed down on the ground directly ahead.
The athlete's leading foot is contacting the ground flat. There is audible slapping noise as the whole of the foot contacts the ground.	The leading leg may still be flexed at the knee when the foot contacts the ground. The toes of the leading foot are allowed to point downward toward the ground.	Instruct your athlete to straighten the leading leg by contracting an the quadriceps muscles prior to contact with the ground. Tell the athlete to lift the toes of the leading foot upward so that the heel contacts the ground before the rest of the foot. Check the pick-up of the rear foot. The heel should be kept low and not kicked up to the rear of the athlete. Check the action of both legs and the position of the feet. The correct motions must be performed on both sides of the body.
The athlete's leading leg is not fully extended prior to contacting the ground with the leading foot. The athlete may also have a high knee lift similar to that of a runner.	The athlete is allowing flexion to continue too long in the leading leg as it is swung forward. It is also possible that the athlete is kicking the heel of the rear foot upward, causing the rear leg to be prematurely flexed and the flexed leg to be lifted too high.	Have your athlete walk slowly and concentrate on straightening the leading leg immediately prior to the foot contacting the ground. Contraction of the quadriceps muscles and turning the toes of the leading foot upward will assist in making this action occur. The athlete should try to keep the rear foot in contact with the ground longer and pull the toes of the rear foot upward rather than positioning them downward as the foot leaves the ground. The athlete may need to strengthen the quadriceps and lengthen (increase the flexibility of) the hamstring muscles.

→

Error	Reasons	Corrections
The action of the athlete's hips is incorrect. The movement of the athlete's hips tends to be side to side (lateral) rather than forward and downward.	There can be several reasons for this error. The athlete may not have a kinesthetic sense of the correct forward and downward rotation of the hips. The athlete's hip mobility may be limited, and lateral rotation can be caused by incorrect shoulder and arm motion.	Use slow-motion skill exercises so that the athlete can experience the motion of the hip driving forward and downward in a cyclic manner. Have your athlete practice driving the hip forward and downward while the leg on the same side of the body extends to make contact with the ground. Make sure that the athlete's arms swing forward and backward and that there is minimal rotation of the athlete's torso.
The position of the athlete's upper body is incorrect. The athlete is either leaning too far forward or too far backward. The athlete's upper body may be swinging excessively side to side.	A slight forward lean starting from the feet is acceptable. Your athlete may not be keeping the torso perpendicular and the vision straight ahead. The arm swing may be forward and upward or backward and upward. Forward lean can also be caused by poor conditioning and fatigue. Backward lean, which is less common than forward lean, may be caused by posture defects brought about by an imbalance in the strength of the abdominal muscles and the muscles of the lower back.	Check that the carriage of the head and the line of vision is correct. The head should be upright with the line of vision directly ahead. Instruct the athlete to avoid leaning forward from the waist and to resist thrusting the abdomen forward. Improvement in muscular endurance, general flexibility, and abdominal and lower-back strength will be of great assistance in correcting these errors. Have your athlete racewalk with the line of vision directly ahead. The athlete's arm swing should be predominantly back and forth, and there must be no upward motion of the arm at the extremities of the swing. The athlete should also concentrate on keeping the rear foot on the ground long enough for it to provide the optimal amount of drive. Stretching and flexibility exercises coupled with concentrated efforts at walking with a correct body position will help to eliminate poor posture.

→

Error	Reasons	Corrections
The athlete's arms swing forward and upward, backward and upward, or are swung across the midline of the body.	The athlete incorrectly feels that a vigorous upward swing of the arms both forward and backward assists forward motion.	Have your athlete drive the arms forward and backward so that the forearms move parallel to the ground. The hands should brush the hips as they swing back and forth. If the athlete's arms are swung excessively across the midline of the body, tell the athlete to turn the hands outward and have the base of the hands and forearm brush the hips as they move forward and backward.
The athlete's shoulders are hunched upward and/or swing excessively toward the left and the right.	Hunching the shoulders is usually caused by tension and fatigue as the athlete struggles to maintain a high racewalk tempo. The shoulder swing is probably caused by arms being swung across the midline of the body and by excessive rotation of the upper body.	Instruct your athlete to relax the shoulders and to lower the elbows. If the athlete's shoulders are being swung toward the left and right, check for an incorrect arm swing and correct as instructed before. Instruct your athlete to keep the chest facing the direction of the walk and to avoid rotating the chest away from this direction.
The athlete is allowing the head to drop either forward or backward.	Dropping the head forward or backward is generally caused by fatigue.	Improve the general conditioning of the athlete and strengthen the muscles of the athlete's neck and upper body. Instruct the athlete to race walk while looking directly ahead.
The athlete's center of gravity follows an up-and-down wave motion rather than moving forward along a horizontal plane.	There is insufficient forward and downward rotation of the hips as the extended supporting leg passes under the athlete's body. The athlete's arms and shoulders are lifting up and down far too much from the toes. The forward swing of the nonsupporting leg is lifting the athlete too much. The direction of thrust from your athlete's rear leg is not forward enough and too much upward.	Have your athlete concentrate on lowering the hip on the side opposing the supporting leg. The arms should not be swung forward and upward or backward and upward to the degree that they lift the athlete's torso and shoulders.

Error	Reasons	Corrections
Your athlete is visibly losing contact with the ground and is warned by the judges. The athlete's leading foot is not making contact with the ground before the rear foot has left the ground.	The placement of your athlete's leading foot on the ground is slow. The athlete is flexing the rear leg and lifting it from the ground before the front foot makes contact.	Have your athlete reduce speed and work to get the front foot down on the ground faster (before the rear foot has broken contact with the ground). Have your athlete concentrate on pulling, or "clawing," the ground back with the heel of the leading leg.
Your athlete's racewalking motion looks "militaristic" and lacks fluidity.	Your athlete is far too stiff and immobile in the hip region and in the shoulder girdle and could be trying to incorporate power-walking characteristics into the technique of racewalking.	Have your athlete work on flexibility exercises that concentrate on the hip area and shoulder girdle. The athlete should practice running on the spot with the left arm moving across the torso while the right leg steps across in front of the left and vice versa. Trunk twisting exercises and hurdler's mobility exercises should be practiced. Once the extended supporting leg is to the rear of the body, the leg is flexed for its movement forward again. The arms should be flexed at the elbows and not swung in an extended position from the shoulders.

ASSESSMENT

1. **Assess the following theoretical elements as taught during instructional sessions.**
    a. Fundamental rules governing race walking.
    b. Good safety habits for race walking.
    c. Basic elements of race walking technique.
    d. Basic elements of training for race walking.

2. **Assess the performance of technique during the following stages of skill development.**
    a. Normal walking with race walking technique assessment applied to the position of the head, the shoulders, the carriage of the torso, the swing of the arms, and the position of the hands.
    b. Race walking hip action performed on the spot (i.e., Rumba hip action).
    c. Race walking technique performed at slow-to-moderate speeds.

   d. Race walking technique performed at moderate to fast speeds with changes in rhythm and acceleration.

CRITICAL FEATURES OF TECHNIQUE TO
OBSERVE DURING ASSESSMENT

Race Walking Technique

- ✓ Keeping the supporting leg straight during the support phase.
- ✓ Obtaining a full thrust from the rear leg.
- ✓ Providing traction and a backward "clawing" motion with the front leg and foot.
- ✓ Walking along a straight line.
- ✓ Holding the arms close to 90 degrees at the elbow, and using minimal movement across the chest during the arm swing.
- ✓ Avoiding shoulder and arm lift at the forward and rear extremities of the arm swing.
- ✓ Using a forward and downward rolling hip action to assist in achieving optimal stride length, cadence, and to avoid an upward and downward movement of the athlete's center of gravity.

3. Hold graded competitions to help develop motivation and technique.

  a. Ask your athletes to predict the times they can achieve for vigorous normal walking over a specified distance. Scores are awarded for proximity to the predicted time.

  b. Ask your athletes to compete against each other on an orienteering walk. Using maps, a compass, and markers positioned around the course, your athletes compete over a specified distance. Base the distance and difficulty level on the ability levels of the competitors.

  c. Have teams of athletes race walk against each other, simulating the team pursuit race in cycling. In this type of race, two teams of athletes start on opposing sides of the track; the group that gains distance on its opposition at the end of a specified time (or distance) is the winner. You select the time or distance according age and ability.

  d. Have male and female athletes compete in race walking competitions over 100, 200, 400, 600, and 800 m.

  e. Have older and more mature athletes compete in race walking competitions over 1,500, 3,000, 5,000, 7,500, and 10,000 m (0.93, 1.86, 3.1, 4.6, and 6.2 mi., respectively).

SUGGESTED STANDARDS OF PERFORMANCE—RACE WALKING

MALE		DISTANCE				
Age		**800 m**	**1,500 m**	**3,000 m**	**5,000 m**	**10,000 m**
12-13	*Satisfactory*	5:15				
	Good	4:45				
	Excellent	4:15				
14-15	*Satisfactory*		9:15			
	Good		8:45			
	Excellent		8:15			
16-17	*Satisfactory*		8:45	18:30		
	Good		8:15	17:30		
	Excellent		7:45	16:00		
18-19	*Satisfactory*			18:00	29:00	65:00
	Good			16:30	27:00	60:00
	Excellent			15:30	25:00	55:00

FEMALE		DISTANCE			
Age		**800 m**	**1,500 m**	**3,000 m**	**5,000 m**
12-13	*Satisfactory*	5.30			
	Good	5.00			
	Excellent	4.30			
14-15	*Satisfactory*	10.15			
	Good	9.30			
	Excellent	8.45			
16-17	*Satisfactory*		9.30	20.00	
	Good		9.00	19.00	
	Excellent		8.30	17.30	
18-19	*Satisfactory*			19.30	33.00
	Good			18.00	31.00
	Excellent			17.00	29.00

Standards measured in minutes and seconds.

Part
II

JUMPING EVENTS

7

HIGH JUMP

The high jump exists in the Olympic Games as an individual event and also as one of the events in the men's decathlon and women's heptathlon. High jumpers today all use the Fosbury Flop technique. Athletes find the flop technique easy to learn, and youngsters are attracted to its dramatic method of bar clearance.

SAFETY SUGGESTIONS

The backward rotation that occurs during flight in the Fosbury Flop causes athletes to land on their shoulders and frequently on the backs of their necks. Landing pads that are too low to the ground (relative to the height being jumped) allow too much backward rotation in flight. This rotation can cause injury to the neck and shoulders when the athlete drops onto the landing pads. Because of this danger, you must use landing pads that are specifically designed for high jumping. Such pads are noted for their absorbency, their large landing area (5 × 4 m), and the fact that the landing surface is at least 1–1½ m above the ground. The extra height from the ground stops athletes from over-rotating backward while in flight.

Flop jumpers tend to have flight paths that cause them to cross the landing pads diagonally and land in the corners. Approved landing pads are designed so that these corner areas have as much support as the center of the pad. Don't use any landing pad that will allow the athlete to "bottom out." Nor should you try to create a landing area out groups of gymnastic crash pads. Even when the mats are tied together by the mat handles, an athlete can fall into the join where the mats contact each other.

During training, rubber tubing is an excellent teaching aid and is preferable to the normal competitive crossbar. You can make a substitute crossbar by threading 8 mm ($^{5}/_{16}$″) rubber tubing through 5 or 6 brightly colored sponge rubber plugs. If you use this tubing, make sure that the rubber crossbar stretches adequately and that the high-jump standards are attached to the ground at the base or have additional weights placed on them. This stops the standards from being dragged inward if an athlete fails in an attempt. You can obtain this rubber tubing from your local hardware store. (See also chapter 10, page 171 for information on the use of the same rubber tubing as a crossbar for the pole vault.)

Run-ups for the high jump should be firm and give good traction for each successive athlete. Grass and artificial surfaces can become slippery and dangerous when wet; under these conditions, athletes should wear spikes. The design of high-jump spikes is critical for good traction on the takeoff. The shoe on the jumping foot not only has spikes on the sole but also additional spikes on the heel to prevent slipping during the last stride prior to takeoff. Many athletes use short spikes or none at all on the leading (swing-up) leg.

Successful flop jumping at the elite level requires the athlete to have excellent flexibility and to perform a back arch (hyperextension) during the bar clearance. This high level of flexibility is developed slowly and systematically through gymnastic-type flexibility exercises.

TECHNIQUE

The flop high-jump run-up is fast, and the last portion of the run-up is curved in toward the bar. The tightness of this curve varies from one athlete to the next. At takeoff, the athlete drives upward off the jumping foot, simultaneously thrusting the leading leg upward and then back toward the run-up. This rotary action of the leading leg helps to turn the athlete's body into a back layout position for the bar clearance.

During the bar clearance, the athlete's arms, which are swung upward at takeoff, are usually brought into the sides of the athlete's body, and the athlete's vision is directed along the line of the bar toward the far high-jump standard. When the shoulders cross the bar, the athlete's back is arched, and the hips are pushed upward. After the athlete's seat has passed over the bar, the athlete flexes at the hips, and the legs are brought toward the chest. The athlete's head and shoulders lift upward. The athlete then relaxes to land on the back and shoulders on the landing pads (see figure 7.1).

TEACHING STEPS
STEP 1. Lead-Ups
STEP 2. Flop High Jump Using a Short (3-Stride) Run-Up
STEP 3. Flop High Jump Using an Extended (Curved) Run-Up

STEP 1: LEAD-UPS

All jumping, bounding, and sprinting activities are excellent preparation for the high

Figure 7.1 The flop high-jump technique.

jump. Drills used for sprinting (chapter 1), the long jump (chapter 8), and the triple jump (chapter 9) are excellent preparation for the high jump.

High-Knee Marching

With each step the athlete drives the thigh of the leading leg up to a horizontal position or above. The athlete drives up onto the toes of the supporting foot, works the arms vigorously back and forward, and drives the knee of the leading leg upward as powerfully as possible. The recommended distance is 10–15 m with 3 or 4 repetitions. (See figure 1.10 on page 7 in chapter 1.)

High-Knee Running

Each athlete runs slowly, concentrating on raising the thigh of the leading leg to the horizontal position or above. The athlete drives up onto the toes of the supporting foot throughout. The recommended distance is 10–15 m with 3 or 4 repetitions. (See figure 3.6 on page 54 in chapter 3.)

Long Bounding Strides

With each stride, the athlete drives forward and upward to cover as much ground as possible. The thigh of the athlete's leading leg is thrust up to the horizontal position, and the arms are swung vigorously throughout (see figure 7.2). The driving leg extends powerfully and vigorously with each bounding stride. Recommended distance is 10–15 m with 3 or 4 repetitions.

COACHING TIPS

- Swing your arms forward and upward as strongly as you can with each bounding stride.
- Try to achieve a wide stride position at the midpoint of each bounding stride.
- Try to get a feeling of floating at the midpoint of each stride.

Jumping to Head a Suspended Volleyball or Soccer Ball

Suspend balls 30–60 cm (1′-2′) above the heads of your athletes. From a run-up of 3 to 5 strides, each athlete jumps to head the ball, using a single-footed takeoff (see figure 7.3).

COACHING TIPS

- Try to lean slightly backward prior to takeoff.
- Jump directly upward.
- Swing your arms and leading leg upward as vigorously as possible at takeoff.

VARIATION

Have your athletes compete in a jump-and-reach competition. Athletes stand sideways by a wall and reach up with chalked fingers of the hand nearest the wall to make a mark. They rechalk their fingertips, and then take a 3- to 5-stride approach parallel to the wall. They jump off one foot to reach as high as possible above their original chalk mark. Who can achieve the greatest distance between their original chalk mark and the one they make when they jump?

Figure 7.2 Bounding strides.

Figure 7.3 Heading a suspended ball.

A Squat Jump Over the Bar

Substitute rubber tubing for the competitive crossbar and set your high-jump standards in front of the long-jump sand pit. Have your athletes approach directly from the front and squat-jump over the bar to land in a standing position in the sand (see figure 7.4). (A squat jump is a jump where the athlete keeps the torso as close to upright as possible, but flexes the legs and pulls them upward in a squat position for the bar clearance). This drill encourages your athletes to jump directly up-

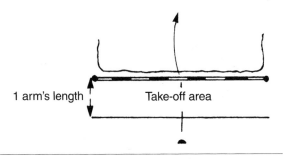

Figure 7.4 Squat jump over the bar.

ward. (Don't forget to put additional weight on the base of your high-jump standards and rake the sand so that it is level and soft to land in).

COACHING TIPS

- Drive up off the ground as powerfully as possible.
- Swing your leading leg and arms upward at takeoff.
- Stretch up and extend your body upward at takeoff.
- Keep your head up; don't lean forward in the jump.
- Take off one arm's length from the bar.

Marking a Take-Off Line for a Squat Jump Over the Bar

Set your rubber crossbar 7 cm (2″–3″) above the top of the landing pads. Mark a take-off line on the ground at approximately one arm's length back from the bar (see figure 7.5). Tell your athletes that they must not jump from further back than the line. This take-off line will make them jump upward rather than long-jump over the bar.

A Squat Jump Using a 3-Stride Approach

Have each of your athletes set their take-off spot one arm's length back from the bar. Starting with the feet together, each athlete measures 3 running strides back from the take-off spot at an angle of 35 to 40 degrees to the bar (see figure 7.6a). This angle of approach is going to be used later when your athletes rotate onto their backs for the flop bar clearance. Use traffic cones to guide your athletes along the pathway of the run-up. An athlete approaching from the bar from the left begins with the feet together and starts the run-up by stepping forward with the right foot. The athlete will use a right, left, right run-up and take off from the right leg (see figure 7.6b).

COACHING TIPS

- In this drill, keep your approach strides the same length.
- Use a powerful bounding jump to squat-jump over the bar.
- Drive the thigh of your leading (left) leg up to a horizontal position or above.

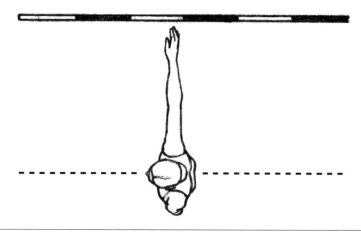

Figure 7.5 Marking the take-off line for a squat jump over the bar.

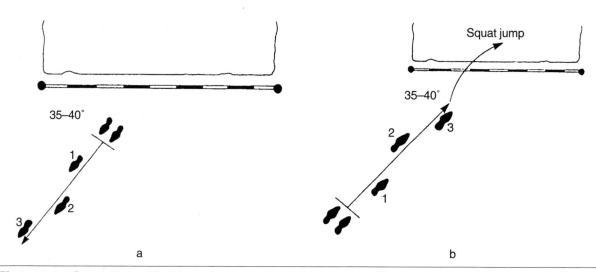

Figure 7.6 Squat jump with a 3-stride approach.

- Hold your head high and keep your upper body erect.
- Swing your arms to help you jump upward.
- Pull your legs up tight underneath you and lift your knees as high as possible.

STEP 2: FLOP HIGH JUMP USING A SHORT (3-STRIDE) RUN-UP

The sequence of drills used for a flop high jump from a short 3-stride run-up begins with specific drills designed to accustom your athletes to the back layout bar clearance. To begin, no run-up is used in these drills. Once your athletes are accustomed to the bar clearance, the short 3-stride run-up is added.

Orientation to Backward Jumping

Facing away from the landing pad, each of your athletes jumps backward to land flat-backed on the landing pads (see figure 7.7). The athlete's heels must be no more than two foot lengths from the base of the landing pad at takeoff. No crossbar of any type is used in this drill.

COACHING TIPS

- Try to lift your hips upward during the jump so that your back lands flat on the landing pad.
- Relax your body as you land.
- Don't just fall back on the pad. Jump upward so that you drop back onto the pad.

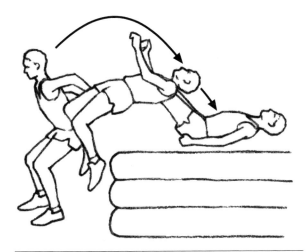

Figure 7.7 Backward jumping.

Backward Jumping With Leg Elevation

The starting position for your athletes is the same as in the previous drill. Athletes now land on their backs with their legs elevated. Be sure that your athletes jump upward, arch their backs a little during flight, and then flex at the hips to lift their legs upward (see figure 7.8). No crossbar of any type is used in this drill.

Figure 7.8 Backward jumping with leg elevation.

COACHING TIPS

- Think of this drill as an upward and backward jump followed by a sit-up in the air.
- Jump upward, drop your shoulders and head back, and then pull your knees toward your chest.
- Point your feet up in the air.

Backward Jumping With Leg Elevation Using an Elastic Crossbar

Use your rubber tubing as a crossbar. Each athlete performs the same action as in the previous drill (see figure 7.9). Initially you should set your crossbar just above the height of the landing pad. Raise the crossbar beyond hip height to chest height for your better athletes.

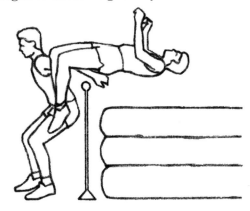

Figure 7.9 Backward jumping over rubber tubing used as a crossbar.

Use of Minitrampoline by Experienced Athletes

Experienced athletes often use a minitrampoline or jump backward off a vaulting box to give themselves additional height and time in the air (see figure 7.10). A minitrampoline provides more height and time for the athlete to practice the visual timing of the bar clearance. Adjust the minitrampoline so that it slopes toward the landing area. This drill is not recommended for beginners.

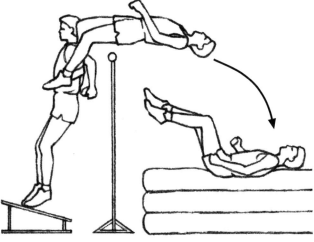

Figure 7.10 Using a minitrampoline to assist in backward jumping.

COACHING TIPS

- Look across your shoulder at the bar to time the bar clearance of your legs. Arch your back above the bar, and when your seat has crossed the bar, pull your knees toward your shoulders to clear your legs.
- Be sure to flex your legs at the knees.

Elementary Flop Using a Straight Three-Stride Run-Up

In this drill, use your rubber tubing as a crossbar. Set the takeoff ¼ of the crossbar's length in from the nearest standard and 1 arm's length away from the bar (see figure 7.11 for these positions). Have your athlete use an angle of 35 to 40 degrees for the run-up. Starting with feet together, the athlete runs back 3 fast strides from the takeoff spot. A partner marks the third stride. The athlete begins the run-up from the left side starting with the right foot (right foot, left foot, right foot, jump). (See figure 7.11a.) Approaching from the right side, the athlete begins the run-up with the left foot. Figure 7.11b shows a run-up from the right side of the bar. You can use traffic cones or markers to guide the foot positions.

COACHING TIPS

- Accelerate toward the bar during your run-up.
- Place your take-off foot down quickly (directly in line with your run-up) and drive the knee of your leading leg vigorously upward.
- Once your knee is as high as possible, rotate your knee and thigh back toward the center of the run-up. This action will rotate you so your back is toward the bar.

- Look across your shoulder at the bar to time the clearance of your legs.
- Arch your back above the bar. When your seat has crossed the bar, pull your knees toward your shoulders to clear your legs over the bar.
- Be sure to flex your legs at the knees.

STEP 3: FLOP HIGH JUMP USING AN EXTENDED (CURVED) RUN-UP

There are many variations in the way an elite athlete approaches the bar. Some athletes use a run-up that has a gentle curve throughout. Others start their run-up with a gentle curve and finish with a tight curve as they accelerate toward the take-off spot. Finally, there are those athletes who use a run-up that is straight for a number of paces, but that finishes with a curved approach to the bar. All these variations reflect personal preferences, and no one approach is technically superior.

In general, a fairly tight curve occurs in the last 5 strides before takeoff. The number of strides taken in the run-up ranges from 9 to 15. The number of strides and the positioning of check marks is also a matter of personal preference. Frequently elite athletes use 2 check marks. The first check mark is often positioned where the first stride falls in the approach to the bar. The second check mark is frequently placed 5 strides prior to the takeoff as shown in figure 7.12. In all cases, the run-up is characterized by continuous acceleration.

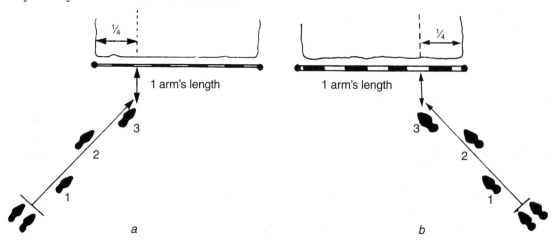

Figure 7.11 Elementary flop with a straight 3-stride run-up from the left (*a*) and from the right (*b*).

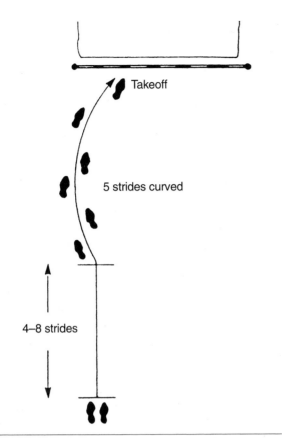

Figure 7.12 Technique for the curved run-up.

Body Position During the Run-Up

The athlete leans forward gently at the start of the run-up and accelerates toward the bar. The acceleration is smooth and continuous throughout the run-up. During the curved part of the run-up, the athlete leans in toward the center of the curve (figure 7.13). The second to last stride is usually longer than the last stride

Figure 7.13 Body position during the run-up.

before takeoff. The characteristic curve in the run-up helps the athlete to get a good takeoff and an optimal layout position over the bar.

Curve Sprinting

This drill will prepare your athletes for the curved flop run-up. Athletes sprint a figure eight, alternately leaning to the right and then to the left (see figure 7.14). Each athlete leans into the curve. The curves are moderate and should not slow the athletes' running speed.

COACHING TIPS

- Be sure to lean into the curve of the run-up so that your bodyweight is on the inside of the curve each time.

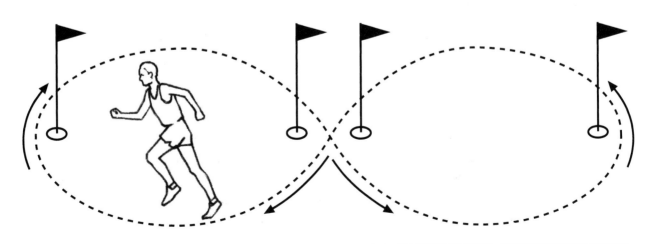

Figure 7.14 Curve sprinting.

• Don't lean so much that you stumble. Lean just enough that you can handle the curve as you run.

Orientation to a Curved Run-Up

This drill has a similar objective as the preceding one. Mark two circles of 7 m (approximately 20'–23') in diameter on the ground. Athletes who approach the bar from the left side and take off from the right foot will run clockwise around one of the two circles (see figure 7.15). Athletes who approach the bar from the right side and take off from the left foot will run counterclockwise around the other circle. The speed of the run should be sufficient to make the athletes lean in toward the center of the circle.

COACHING TIPS

• Run fast and lean into the curve.

• Lean just the right amount so that you don't stumble as you run.

• Place each foot parallel with the line marking the curve of the circle.

Elementary Curved Run-Up

This run-up is adequate for novices and young athletes who are attempting the flop from a curved run-up. Have an athlete approaching from the left measure a run-up in the following manner:

Set the take-off spot one arm's length in toward the run-up from the bar and $\frac{1}{4}$ of the crossbar's length in from the left high-jump standard (see figure 7.11). Take 1 large stride to the left from the left high-jump standard, and take 2 strides from this point back into the run-up as shown in figure 7.16a. Mark this spot. This mark will indicate the position of the second stride in the run-up and the start of the curve toward the bar. Measure a 5-stride run-up back from the take-off spot. Approaching the bar, the athlete's first 2 strides will be straight and the final 3 strides will be curved. The run-up will resemble an inverted letter *J*. Each run-up will differ slightly according to individual stride length. Increasing confidence and faster approaches will necessitate changes in the run-up. Figure 7.16b shows a similar run-up from the right side of the bar. The first

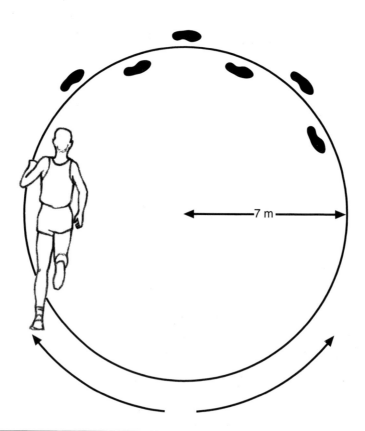

Figure 7.15 Orientation to a curved run-up.

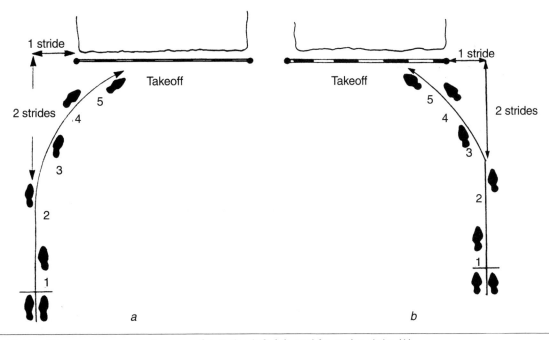

Figure 7.16 Elementary curved run-up from the left (*a*) and from the right (*b*).

pace for a run-up from the right side is taken with the left foot.

Increasing the Length of the Run-Up

As your athletes develop confidence, they will need to enlarge and adjust their run-up to allow for a greater approach speed. The take-off spot will still be $1/4$ of the crossbar's length inward from the nearest high-jump standard. The following sequence will assist in setting up a 9-stride run-up. Adjustments will have to be made relative to individual stride length and speed of approach.

The take-off spot is $1/4$ of a crossbar length in toward the center of the crossbar, measured from the nearest high-jump standard. The take-off spot is shifted back from the bar to just beyond 1 arm's length (75–90 cm or 30"-36"). This distance allows for an increase in the speed of approach. Measure 3–4.5 m (10'-15') directly to the left from the left standard and 6–9 m (20'-30') back into the run-up (5 paces from the bar). This measurement marks the start of the curved part of the run-up. Measure 4 more strides in a straight line back from the fifth stride to give a 9-stride run-up (see figure 7.17a).

An athlete begins a 9-stride run-up from the left side with the right foot (assuming that the athlete starts with the feet together). One or 2 check marks on the run-up will assist in making the run-up accurate. If 2 check marks are used, place the first check mark where the first stride falls in the approach to the bar. Place the second check mark 5 strides prior to takeoff. With improved technique (and leg strength), the athlete can lengthen the run-up beyond 9 strides to 11 and 13 strides. Figure 7.17b shows the run-up for an athlete approaching from the right side of the bar. The first stride of the run-up from this side is taken with the left foot.

COACHING TIPS

- Make sure that your takeoff is in the right spot. If you are jumping into the bar, your take-off spot is too close. If you are dropping onto the bar, your takeoff is too far away.
- Adjust your take-off spot a single foot-length, and repeat until your take-off spot is correct.
- Count your strides aloud as you approach the bar.
- Remember you are running 4 straight strides and 5 curved.
- Try to hit your check marks as you approach the bar.

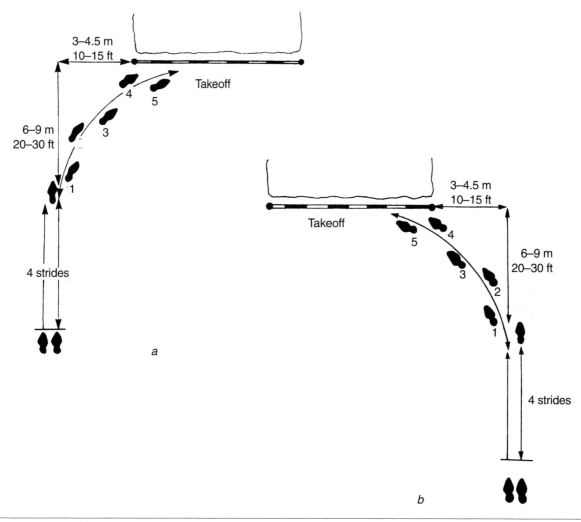

Figure 7.17 Increasing the run-up length from the left (*a*) and from the right (*b*).

Developing the Arm Action and Stride Length During the Last 3 Approach Strides

Figure 7.18 shows the last 2 strides taken by a high-jump athlete approaching from the right side of the bar. Notice the forward-backward movement of the arms and the backward lean of the body prior to takeoff. To practice this action, lead your athletes (first slowly and mechanically) through the required movement pattern of the last 3 strides. Once your athletes learn the movement pattern, they can practice the actions at a faster speed. If mistakes are made, make your athletes go back to performing the actions slowly and mechanically and then progressively increase the speed of motion again.

The sequence of actions for jumps approaching the bar from the right side (and jumping from the left foot) is as follows:

1. The athlete stands with feet together. The athlete's arms are extended downward at the side of the athlete's body.

2. The athlete steps forward one medium-size stride with the left foot, keeping the arms at the side of the body.

3. The athlete then steps one long stride with the right foot. Simultaneously both arms are swung forward ahead of the body.

4. The athlete steps forward one short stride with the left foot, simultaneously tilting the upper body slightly backward. At the same time, the athlete swings the arms backward so that they are now both to the rear of the body.

5. Finally, the athlete jumps directly upward from the left foot, driving the thigh

Figure 7.18   Arm action and body positioning during the last two approach strides.

of the right leg up to a horizontal position and simultaneously swinging the arms forward and upward. (During this learning sequence, the jump upward is a small jump, no more than 1'–2' in the air.)

COACHING TIPS

- Make your second to last stride a long one. Swing your arms forward ahead of your body.
- Place your jumping foot down on the ground for the last stride as quickly as possible.
- Make your last stride shorter than your second to last stride.
- As you step out onto the take-off spot with your jumping foot, swing your arms to the rear of your body.
- When you jump upward, swing both your arms forward and upward at the same time.

Skipping Backward With a Rope While Moving Forward

In learning the last 3 strides of the flop run-up, young athletes sometimes have difficulty rotating the arms backward while simultaneously moving the body forward. Skipping backward with a rope while moving forward is an excellent method to teach the backward rotation of the arms (see figure 7.19).

COACHING TIPS

- Start skipping in place with the rope rotating backward, and then slowly move forward.
- Keep the rope rotating backward.

Long Bounding Strides With Arm Swinging

If skipping rope backward while moving forward is too difficult, your athletes can practice bounding forward with long strides, swinging the arms forward on one stride and backward on the next (see figure 7.20).

Arm Action and Stride Length Adjustment During the Run-Up

This drill does not require a crossbar. Place marks on the run-up or use traffic cones to

Figure 7.19   Backward rope skipping.

Figure 7.20 Bounding with arm swings.

indicate the size of the last 3 strides (see figure 7.21). In the second-to-last stride, the athlete moves the hips forward ahead of the torso, setting up a backward lean. The athlete's arms are swung from a forward position to a backward position as the athlete steps forward for the last stride.

COACHING TIPS

- Step well forward in your second-to-last stride and lean back.
- "Slide" (or push) your hips ahead of your chest, lean back, and swing your arms backward.
- Put your jumping foot down quickly for a short stride, and swing your arms and leading leg forward and upward for the takeoff.

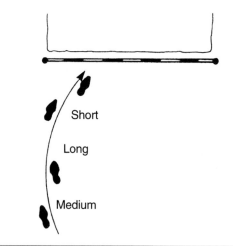

Figure 7.21 Stride length during the last 3 strides of the run-up.

COMMON ERRORS AND CORRECTIONS

Error	Reasons	Corrections
The athlete leans forward toward the bar at takeoff.	The last two strides of the run-up are too small. The athlete's body-weight is forward and toward the bar during the last 2 strides of the approach.	Have your athlete practice the run-up with the last strides marked on the ground. Emphasize placement of the athlete's jumping foot with the heel placed down first and then rolling forward onto the flat of the foot and up off the toes of the jumping foot for the take-off. Emphasize a backward body lean prior to takeoff.
The athlete leans the upper body sideways toward the bar at takeoff.	The athlete's take-off foot is placed parallel to the bar at takeoff.	Mark the run-up with a line and draw the position of the take-off foot on the ground (diagonally toward the crossbar). Have the athlete concentrate on placing the foot parallel to this line at takeoff.
The athlete takes off with the back already turned toward the bar.	The athlete is anticipating the back layout position. The athlete's takeoff foot is pointing back toward the run-up. The curve of the run-up is too tight.	Mark the correct position for the athlete's take-off foot. Use visual cues ("Look along the line of the crossbar") to control body position. The athlete should reduce the tightness of the curve.
The athlete has difficulty getting into a back layout position over the bar.	The athlete has insufficient curve in final part of run-up and does not lean into the curve of the run-up. The athlete has poor rotary action of the leading leg during the thrust up toward the bar. take-off.	Mark the correct position of the take-off foot. Instruct the athlete to increase the tightness of the curve of the run-up. Have the athlete emphasize a thrust of the leading leg up and then back toward the run-up at
The athlete crosses the bar in a sitting position, knocking the bar off with the seat.	The athlete lifts the thighs or shoulders too early during the bar clearance. The athlete's head is lifted to look at the bar before the seat has crossed the bar.	After the takeoff, the athlete must drop the leading leg down and press the hips up-ward. The athlete should drop the head back and use side-ways vision toward the cross-bar to visually time the ele-vation of the legs over the bar.

→

Error	Reasons	Corrections
The athlete crosses the bar with the side of the body nearest the bar rather than with the back.	The athlete uses insufficient rotation around the long axis of the body (from head to feet) and insufficient rotation of the leading leg back toward the run-up.	Instruct the athlete to use a 3-stride run-up emphasizing the upward and inward rotation of the leading leg. The leading leg must be turned away from the bar and back toward the run-up. The athlete should emphasize a strong lean into the curve when using a longer run-up. A tighter curve in the run-up may also be necessary.
The placement of the athlete's take-off foot varies with each jump.	The athlete's stride length in the run-up varies with each approach. The athlete's run-up is poorly established.	Measure the athlete's run-up and use control markers. Work on building uniform acceleration throughout the run-up. If necessary, use control markers (traffic cones) for each of the athlete's strides.
The athlete slows down before takeoff.	The athlete is anxious about the takeoff. The athlete's stride length is incorrect in the final phase of the run-up.	Have the athlete practice the run-up and takeoff without using a crossbar. Use markers for positioning the last 3 strides. Make the athlete concentrate on uniform acceleration throughout the run-up.
The athlete's run-up speed is not translated into height.	The athlete's run-up is too fast (or too slow). The athlete uses no backward body lean at take-off and no inward lean into the curve. The athlete's take-off foot is incorrectly placed. The athlete's leg power may be poor. The length of each of the last 3 strides may be incorrect.	The athlete should start the run-up slowly and accelerate throughout, tighten the curve of the run-up, and/or lean more into curve. The athlete should point the take-off foot diagonally toward the crossbar and lean back at take-off. The athlete can also improve eg power to assist in takeoff. The arms should be back when the take-off foot is planted and then swung up toward the bar at takeoff. Have the athlete work on the correct length of the last 3 strides of the approach.
The athlete has no upward arm swing at takeoff.	The athlete has not established the correct arm action and has not synchronized this arm action with the last 3 strides of the run-up.	Have the athlete go back to the drills that establish the arm actions for the last 3 strides of the run-up. The athlete should jump lower heights concentrating on the action of the arms and the correct stride length during the last 3 strides.

ASSESSMENT

1. **Assess the following theoretical elements as taught during instructional sessions:**

   a. Fundamental rules governing the high jump.

   b. Good safety habits for use in the high jump.

   c. Basic elements of high-jump technique.

   d. Basic elements of training for the high jump.

2. **Assess the performance of technique during the following stages of skill development:**

   a. Backward jumping and flop bar clearance (elastic crossbar is used).

   b. Flop high jump from a 3-stride non-curved run-up.

   c. Flop high jump from a 5-stride curved run-up.

   d. Flop high jump from 9- and 11-stride curved run-ups.

      CRITICAL FEATURES OF TECHNIQUE TO
      OBSERVE DURING ASSESSMENT

      ✓ Measurement of the run-up and positioning of check marks.

      ✓ Acceleration through the run-up and inward lean into the curve of the run-up.

      ✓ Shift of the hips ahead of the upper body in the final strides of the takeoff.

      ✓ Synchronization of the arm actions with the last 3 strides of the run-up.

      ✓ Positioning and alignment of the take-off foot immediately prior to takeoff.

      ✓ Upright trunk and elevated head at takeoff.

      ✓ Upward drive of the arms and the knee of the leading leg during takeoff.

      ✓ Rotation of the thigh of the leading leg back toward the run-up at takeoff.

      ✓ Lowering of the leading leg and the elevation of the hips over the bar.

      ✓ Rotation of the body to a layout position.

      ✓ Vision along the line of the crossbar towards the far high-jump standard.

      ✓ Flexion at the knees and hips to clear the bar.

      ✓ Relaxed landing on the shoulders with the arms spread.

3. **Hold graded competitions to help develop motivation and technique.**

   a. Athletes use a backward jump and flop clearance to clear an elastic crossbar.

   b. Athletes compete in a flop high-jump competition using a straight 3-stride run-up.

   c. Athletes compete in a flop high-jump competition using a curved 5-stride run-up.

   d. Athletes compete in a flop high-jump competition using a run-up with stride length chosen according to individual preference.

SUGGESTED STANDARDS OF PERFORMANCE—HIGH JUMP

MALE

Age		Height
12-13	Satisfactory	1.20 m (4'0")
	Good	1.30 m (4'3")
	Excellent	1.40 m (4'7")
14-15	Satisfactory	1.30 m (4'3")
	Good	1.40 m (4'7")
	Excellent	1.50 m (5'0")
16-17	Satisfactory	1.40 m (4'7")
	Good	1.50 m (5'0")
	Excellent	1.60 m (5'3")
18-19	Satisfactory	1.50 m (5'0")
	Good	1.60 m (5'3")
	Excellent	1.70 m (5'7")

FEMALE

Age		Height
12-13	Satisfactory	1.05 m (3'5")
	Good	1.15 m (3'9")
	Excellent	1.25 m (4'1")
14-15	Satisfactory	1.10 m (3'7")
	Good	1.25 m (4'1")
	Excellent	1.35 m (4'5")
16-17	Satisfactory	1.15 m (3'9")
	Good	1.30 m (4'3")
	Excellent	1.40 m (4'7")
18-19	Satisfactory	1.25 m (4'1")
	Good	1.40 m (4'7")
	Excellent	1.50 m (5'0")

8

LONG JUMP

For many years, the long jump was an event that sprinters enjoyed as a diversion from sprinting. Today, athletes specialize in this event, although it is still common for sprinters to be great long-jumpers and vice versa. The long jump exists as an separate event in the Olympic Games, and it is also included as one of the events in the men's decathlon and the women's heptathlon.

Two major techniques are used in long jumping: the hang technique and the hitch-kick technique. The hitch-kick is the more popular, but both techniques have been used by elite athletes to reach distances in excess of 8.83 m (29'). The hang and the hitch-kick are patterns of movements the athlete uses while in flight. In the hang technique, the athlete appears to temporarily hang in the air during flight. In the hitch-kick, the athlete cycles the legs during flight. Each technique is intended to counteract the unfavorable forward rotation imparted to the athlete at takeoff. If the hang or the hitch kick were not performed, the athlete's feet and legs would contact the sand earlier than necessary, and the resulting distance would be shorter.

Both the hang and hitch-kick require a fast run-up, similar body positions at takeoff, and similar actions for the landing in the sand. Most young athletes will have difficulty performing the hitch-kick, because it requires considerable speed and sufficient time in the air to perform well. However, an elementary long jump (which requires minimal leg and arm movement in the air) and a rudimentary form of the hang technique are well within reach of young athletes. Remember that the most important requirements in this event are speed and spring. An athlete does not have to perform a hitch-kick or a hang to jump good distances.

SAFETY SUGGESTIONS

The sand in a long-jump pit should be fine, well-raked, level, and slightly wet to avoid dust. It should be deep enough (no less than 38 cm or 15") to prevent jarring when the athletes land. It should be frequently searched for debris and covered when not in use. The edges of the pit must be designed so as not to injure the athlete, although they must be well-defined so that sand does not scatter out of the pit. A long-jump pit must be surrounded by a wide grass or open area that is well away from walls, trees, fences, and other obstacles. The pit should be positioned so that long jumpers are not in any danger from throwing events.

Brooms, rakes, and spades must always be stacked well clear of the pit and not left lying around. Your officials should ensure that no jump is made while the pit is being raked. The take-off board should be firmly fixed to the ground and lie flush with the surface of the run-up. The run-up must provide a firm but comfortable approach and be swept clear of dirt and sand. Any depressions near the take-off board should be filled in and made level. Take-off boards narrower in width than 20 cm (8") should not be used, because these are likely to cause foot injuries. Another consideration is that grass and certain types of artificial surfaces can become slippery when wet and dangerous unless your athletes wear spikes.

Elite athletes in the long jump (and the triple jump) prepare in the off-season by sprinting, training to develop anaerobic endurance, and working on a variety of dynamic jumping activities that develop the explosive elastic quality of the athletes' legs. Called *plyometrics*, *depth jumping*, and more commonly *rebound jumping*, these activities require the athlete to simulate the rebound of a bouncing ball. These drills place considerable stress on the joints and muscles of the athletes' legs. They are not recommended for young and physically immature athletes.

TECHNIQUE

The following descriptions of the hang and hitch-kick give the main elements of each technique. Elite athletes will perform these techniques with some individual variations.

THE HANG TECHNIQUE

After a fast run-up, the athlete drives up powerfully at takeoff. The athlete's leading leg, which is initially flexed and driven upward, is then extended and brought backward to join the take-off leg. Both legs, in their extended positions, are thrust to the rear of the body. The arms circle downward, backward, and then upward and forward. With the arms momentarily above the head, the athlete appears to hang in the air. The athlete's legs are flexed and thrust forward, and as they extend for the landing, the athlete's arms circle forward. As soon as contact with the sand is made, the athlete's legs flex at the knees, and the upper body moves forward and over the feet. The athlete's arm actions assist in driving the athlete forward beyond where the feet make contact with the sand (see figure 8.1).

THE HITCH-KICK TECHNIQUE

After a fast run-up, the athlete drives up powerfully at takeoff. The athlete's leading leg, which is initially flexed at the thigh, is extended so that the athlete assumes a momentary stride position in flight. The leading leg is rotated backward in its extended position. Both legs are then flexed and brought forward for the landing. The arms rotate forward and then backward, balancing the action of the legs and also assisting in thrusting the ath-

Figure 8.1 The hang technique.

lete forward in the landing. The characteristic cycling action of the legs is called a hitch-kick. The athlete extends both legs for the landing, as the arms circle forward and then backward. Upon contact with the sand, the knees flex, and the athlete's upper body moves beyond the landing spot in the sand (figure 8.2).

TEACHING STEPS

STEP 1. Lead-Ups

STEP 2. Elementary Long Jump and Run-Up

STEP 3. The Hang Technique

STEP 4. The Hitch-Kick Technique

STEP 1: LEAD-UPS

Athletes in the long jump and the triple jump use similar lead-up activities. Both events require excellent sprinting ability and explosive leg power. In this chapter, you will find some demanding drills that develop leg power. For beginners, 3–4 repetitions with short rests between each repetition are recommended. (See chapter 1 for activities that develop sprinting ability and anaerobic endurance.)

Hopping for Distance and Finding the Favored Jumping Leg

Measure the distance each athlete can achieve in 3 successive hops from a standing start with the right leg only (see figure 8.3). Measure the distance gained from the same action performed with the left leg only. The leg that produces the greater distance is the preferred jumping leg. The athlete will use this leg to push from the ground in the long jump takeoff.

COACHING TIPS

- On each hop, drive the thigh of your leading leg (nonjumping leg) up to horizontal.
- Jump for distance, not height, with each hop.
- The leg with which you jump further will be your favored leg.
- Remember which leg is your favored leg.

Bounding for Distance

In this lead-up activity, the thigh of the athlete's leading leg is lifted to horizontal with each bounding stride. The athlete should strive for long strides, reaching for distance with each one. (See figure 1.18 on page 12 in chapter 1.)

COACHING TIPS

- Swing your arms up and forward with each bounding stride.
- Try to achieve a wide stride position at the midpoint of each of your bounding strides.
- Try to get a feeling of floating at the midpoint of each of your bounding strides.

Figure 8.2 The hitch-kick technique.

Standing Long Jump Using a 2-Legged Takeoff

In this drill, the athlete uses a strong swing of the arms coupled with a double-legged drive to cover as much distance as possible (see figure 8.4). Have your athletes perform this drill from the edge of the long-jump pit. Measure the distances jumped. Who can jump the furthest?

- Thrust with your legs as powerfully as possible and combine this action with a strong swing of your arms.

- Immediately after you take off, pull your legs forward underneath you to cover as much distance as possible.

Standing Long Jump Using a Single-Legged Takeoff

This drill is similar to the drill used when bounding for distance except that both legs are brought together for the landing (see figure 8.5). Athletes jump using their favored and nonfavored legs for the takeoff. Have the athletes perform this drill from the edge of the long-jump pit. Measure the distances jumped. Who can jump the furthest?

- Push with the jumping leg as powerfully as possible.

- Swing the thigh of your leading leg up to horizontal at the same time that you push with your jumping leg. Reach out with both legs for the landing.

- Use your arms in the same fashion as with the two-legged jump. Swing them up and forward in unison with your leading leg.

Distance Jumping Competition

From a line, your athletes see how far they can jump with 3 continuous and successive 2-footed jumps (see figure 8.6). Who can go the furthest?

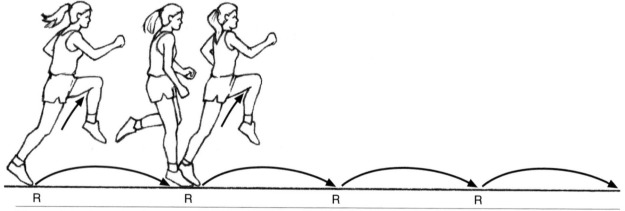

Figure 8.3 Hopping for distance.

Figure 8.4 Standing long jump with a 2-legged takeoff.

Figure 8.5 Standing long jump with a single-legged takeoff.

Figure 8.6 Distance jumping competition.

- Don't put everything into the first of your 3 jumps.
- To get the longest distance, all 3 of your jumps must be fairly equal in length.
- Avoid jumping upward. Jump low and forward.
- Try to avoid collapsing downward at the end of each of your jumps.

VARIATION

Make up teams with 3 or 4 athletes per team. The first athlete in a team completes 3 successive 2-footed jumps (or 3 bounding strides). The next member of the team adds 3 more jumps of the same type at the spot where the previous athlete completed 3 jumps. Which team can accumulate the greatest distance?

Circle Jumping

Divide your class into teams with 5 members per team. Lay a series of hoops (3 or 4) on the grass in front of each team. Each team member hops or bounds according to your command from hoop to hoop (see figure 8.7). Initially place the hoops close to each other, and then set them progressively farther apart to demand long reaching strides and explosive leg action. Be sure that the hoops don't slip if an athlete lands on them. If there is any likelihood of this occurring, use traffic cones instead. The athletes attempt to land next to the cones.

Figure 8.7 Circle jumping.

COACHING TIPS

- Use a forward and upward swing of your arms to help with each of your jumps.
- Drive forward as powerfully as you can from your jumping leg.
- Concentrate on lifting your leading thigh to horizontal with each successive jump.
- Keep your vision forward; don't let your head drop backward.
- Don't relax when you land; try to claw the ground backward immediately upon landing with your supporting foot.
- Experiment by starting the series of jumps from your right foot and then from your left. Which foot gives you the greatest distance?

Hopping and Bounding Over a Series of Low Obstacles

Each athlete hops, bounds, or jumps (as you require) over a series of low obstacles. The athlete's arms are swung upward, and the thigh of the athlete's leading leg is driven up to horizontal with each jump. (See figure 1.20 in chapter 1.)

COACHING TIPS

Your coaching tips will be the same as for the previous drill.

Jumping From a Beat Board and a Low Box

Athletes pace back a 3-stride run-up from a gymnastic beat board. They step from the beat board onto a low box and take off from their favored leg to land on a soft mat or in the sand of the long-jump pit (see figure 8.8).

COACHING TIPS

- Accelerate as you approach the beat board and low box.
- Start your 3-stride run-up from your other leg if you find yourself jumping off the box from your nonfavored leg.
- Drive up strongly from the box.
- Use your arms and the leading leg as before. Swing them upward as strongly as possible.

STEP 2: ELEMENTARY LONG JUMP AND RUN-UP

At takeoff in an elementary long jump, each athlete drives off a fully extended jumping leg and flexes the leading leg with the thigh raised to horizontal. The athlete's upper body is perpendicular, the vision is ahead, and the athlete's arm actions compliment those of the legs. When the athlete is in flight, the leading leg extends and the jumping leg trails behind so that the athlete is momentarily in a stride position. For the landing, the athlete's jumping leg is brought forward so that both legs extend forward together. The athlete's arms and upper body reach forward, and the legs flex at the knees upon contact with the sand (see figure 8.9).

Landing in a Kneeling Position From 3 Bounding Strides

The athlete takes 3 bounding strides in sequence. On the third, the athlete takes off from

Figure 8.8 Jumping from a beat board and a low box.

Figure 8.9 Elementary long-jump technique.

the favored leg, holding the thigh of the leading leg horizontal and landing in the sand pit with the thigh still in the same position (see figure 8.10). Notice that the athlete lands in a 1-legged kneeling position with the leading leg forward and flexed at the knee. For this drill, be sure the sand is well-dug and loose.

COACHING TIPS

- At takeoff, swing (drive) the thigh of your leading leg to horizontal and hold it in this position through to the landing. Don't be tempted to lower it while you're in the air.

Standing Jumps Over a Mound of Sand

Build up a mound of sand lengthwise down the center of the long-jump pit. Fashion the mound of sand to become progressively higher and wider along its length. Instruct your athletes to perform 2-legged standing jumps over the mound (see figure 8.11). Jumping over a mound will force your athletes to pull their legs up under their seat to get over the top of the mound, and then extend them for the landing. If your athletes are successful jumping across one cross-section of the mound, they move to attempt a higher and wider section.

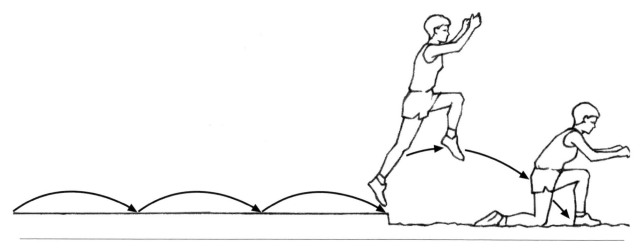

Figure 8.10 Jumping to kneeling in a sand pit from 3 bounding strides.

Figure 8.11 Standing jumps over a mound of sand.

Each athlete begins by using a 2-footed take-off. After competing in this fashion, they then take off from a stride position with the jumping foot placed forward. The rear leg is swung forward and upward to become the leading leg at takeoff.

COACHING TIPS

- Extend your legs strongly at takeoff, and then flex them quickly to get over the top of the mound.

- Pull your legs up under your seat and extend them forward for the landing.
- Bend at your knees and hips on the landing.
- Reach forward with your arms so you don't sit backward when you land.

An Elementary Long Jump From an Elevated Takeoff

The athlete uses a short run-up (3 strides), steps onto a low box (1 section) on the third stride, and takes off from the box to jump into the sand (see figure 8.12). The run-up sequence for an athlete starting with the feet together and taking off the left foot is as follows: left foot, right foot, left foot (step up onto the box), jump. The elevated takeoff allows time in the air for the athlete to achieve a good stride position in the air and then to bring both legs forward for the landing. Make sure the box is stabilized and will not tip.

Beat Board Takeoff

Athletes repeat the preceding drill but from a lower elevation. For example, you can substitute a gymnastic beat board or a low wooden ramp for the top section of the vaulting box.

Takeoff from Ground Level

Remove the gymnastic beat board and have your athletes repeat the same drill as before from ground level.

Measuring a 9-Stride Run-Up

Here's a sequence for working out a run-up for young athletes:

Figure 8.12 Elementary jump from an elevated takeoff.

1. Each athlete stands in stride position, facing back down the run-up with the toes of the nonjumping (nonfavored) foot placed against the leading edge of the take-off board. The leading edge will be the edge of the take-off board nearest the sand.

2. The athlete runs 9 strides back down the run-up, with the first stride taken by the jumping foot.

3. You or an assistant counts each footfall of the athlete's jumping foot in a sequence of 1, 3, 5, 7, and 9 (this counting method is easier and less confusing than counting every stride).

4. Mark the ninth stride. This mark will give an approximate starting point for the athlete's run-up. The athlete places the nonjumping foot on the mark and takes the first stride toward the pit with the jumping foot. An uneven number of strides in the run-up will put the jumping foot on the board for the takeoff.

5. You can use check marks at the first and fifth strides of the run-up for additional accuracy (see figure 8.13).

As each athlete attempts a 9-stride run-up, you should stand by the take-off board and note the relationship between the position of the take-off foot and the take-off board. Help the athletes adjust the start of their run-up so that their take-off foot lands on the board as close to the leading edge of the board as possible. If the athlete takes off beyond the leading edge of the board, check by how far the athlete has "fouled" and move the start of the run-up back the same distance. If the athlete takes off before reaching the board, check how far the athlete is short of the board and move the start of the run-up forward the same distance. Be sure that these errors are not caused by irregular strides during the run-up. If they are, consider using a third checkpoint in the run-up.

VARIATION

For another method of determining an approximate run-up for beginners, pair off your athletes (A and B). Athlete A will be active, and athlete B will measure the run-up for athlete A. After athlete A has been given a run-up measurement, the two athletes change places and the following process is repeated:

1. Lay out a 50 m (approximately 165') tape next to the curb of the track straightaway so that you can look down at the tape and read the measurements.

2. Starting at the zero end of the tape, athlete A sprints as fast as possible down the straightaway.

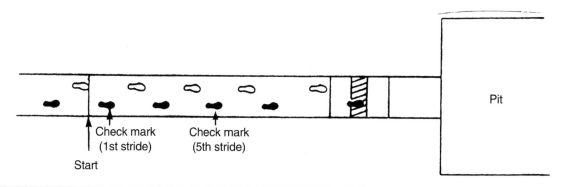

Figure 8.13 A 9-stride run-up with check marks at the first and fifth strides.

3. Athlete B stands back about 20 m (approximately 60') from the midpoint of the tape and selects the approximate spot where athlete A reaches top speed. Athlete B marks this distance with a peg or traffic cone next to the tape.

4. Athlete A goes back to the start and, after a short rest, sprints down the straightaway a second time. Before sprinting, athlete A calls out to athlete B "right" or "left" to indicate the jumping foot. Starting the run-up with the same foot as before, athlete A now sprints down the straightaway, counting aloud every alternate stride while sprinting. (Another option is to have athlete B count aloud every contact of the jumping foot during the run-up.)

5. Athlete B notes the position of A's jumping foot nearest A's top speed marker. This distance is read off from the tape and given to athlete A. Athlete A now knows the number of strides used to reach top speed and also knows how far this distance is from the take-off board.

6. This distance is transferred to the long-jump run-up by placing the zero end of the tape on the leading edge of the take-off board.

Using a Take-Off Area

Young athletes get discouraged if they repeatedly commit a foul by jumping from beyond the take-off board. During training, one way of eliminating this problem is to use a take-off area. A take-off area can be a chalk-marked area or a large board (80 cm–1 m or 2'6"–3'3" wide) set flush in the runway with a regular take-off board marked on it in a central position (see figure 8.14). Young athletes aim to jump from the take-off board, but if they miss it doesn't matter—all jumps taken from within the take-off area are considered valid. Distances are measured from the take-off spot to the landing in the sand. A take-off area makes young athletes more relaxed during the run-up and less concerned about hitting an exact spot for the take-off.

Teaching the Length of Each of the Last 3 Strides

Athletes must learn to lengthen their penultimate (second to last) stride and shorten the final stride prior to takeoff. This action lowers their center of gravity and tilts their body backward, placing it in an optimal position for takeoff. Teach your athletes to use a sequence of medium, long, short as indicators of the length of the last three strides before takeoff. You can have your athletes practice these stride length changes by using a gymnastic beat board and the top section of a gymnastic vaulting box. The athletes step from the beat board to the box top, and then take off from the box top to land in the sand or on soft matting (see figure 8.15).

To practice this drill put a mark on the run-up to indicate the start of the medium stride. The athlete's average sprinting stride length is used for the length of the medium stride. Use a traffic cone to indicate the landing from the medium stride. Make the distance from the traffic cone to the beat board 15–30 cm (6"–12") longer than the athlete's medium stride. The distance from the beat board to the vaulting box top will be approximately 15 cm (6") shorter than the medium stride. Have each athlete practice this drill by using a 3-stride approach beginning with their feet together at

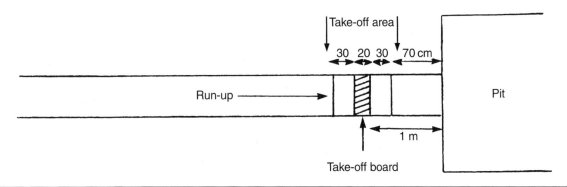

Figure 8.14   Using a take-off area.

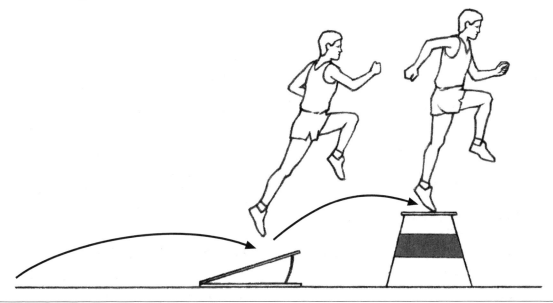

Figure 8.15   Rhythm and placement of the last 2 strides.

the start of the medium stride. A right-footed jumper will make one medium-length stride starting with the right foot. The sequence for a right-footed jumper will be right foot (medium), left foot (long), right foot (short), jump.

COACHING TIPS

- Stretch upward immediately prior to takeoff.
- Look forward, not downward, at takeoff.
- Reach out with your stride onto the beat board, and then shorten your last stride onto the box top for your takeoff.
- Concentrate on making the changes in stride length, not on jumping far.

Practicing Stride Length Variations From a 5-Pace Run-Up

Increase the run-up from 3 paces to 5. Remove the beat board and the vaulting box. Put marks on the run-up that your athletes try to hit during their run-up. Traffic cones positioned by the side of the run-up will help in this drill. The marks on the run-up and the traffic cones will indicate the medium stride, the longer penultimate stride, and the shorter last stride (see figure 8.16). An athlete who takes off from the right foot will start with the feet together and take the first stride in the run-up with the right foot.

COACHING TIPS

- Try to hit the markers as you perform your 5-pace run-up. Remember that your first, second, and third strides will be sprinting strides during which you will be accelerating.
- Try to stretch out in your fourth stride.
- Put your jumping foot down quickly for the short fifth stride.
- I'll call out a rhythm as you approach the takeoff. The "daaa" sound indicates that

Figure 8.16 Shortening the final stride.

your stride should be a long one. The quick "da" will indicate the short fifth (last) stride.

Stride:	1	2	3	4	5	jump
Vocal Cue:	daa	daa	daa	daaaa	da	dap
Stride Length:	med	med	med	long	short	

Practicing Stride Length Control From a 13-Pace Run-Up

Elite athletes use check marks on their run-up to make sure that they are accurate with their takeoff and don't make a foul jump. The choice of where to position these check marks varies from one athlete to another. Figure 8.17 indicates two check marks on a 13-stride run-up. It also shows the stride length changes that occur on the second-to-last and final stride of the run-up.

In Figure 8.17, the athlete is starting the run-up with the left foot forward and the right foot back. The first stride of the run-up is taken with the right foot. Put a check mark at the first stride and another check mark 5 strides prior to the board. Position the take-off board within a take-off area. Have your athletes aim to jump from the take-off board. Elite athletes often use 19 strides or more for their run-ups. Place check marks in the same manner that they have been placed for the 13-stride run-up if you want your athletes to work up to a 15-, 17-, and finally a 19-stride run-up.

STEP 3: THE HANG TECHNIQUE

While in flight during the hang technique the athlete will momentarily extend both legs downward. The athlete's legs and arms are then rotated to the rear and the hips are pushed forward. A powerful contraction of the athlete's abdominal muscles coupled with flexion of the legs and forward rotation of the arms prepares the athlete for landing in the sand. To obtain the characteristic "hanging" position in flight, you'll find it necessary to get young athletes to push their hips forward. This action will help the athlete's legs and arms to move in the opposing direction (see figure 8.1).

Learning to Drive the Hips Forward

Using a 5-pace run-up and jumping from a beat board, each athlete takes off as though performing an elementary long jump. In flight, the athlete pushes the hips (the front of the lower abdomen) forward to contact a bamboo cane held loosely by another athlete or by you. Hold the bamboo cane 1 m in front of the beat board in the manner shown in figure 8.18.

VARIATION

Two athletes stand 1 m away from the takeoff with their arms loosely outstretched to form a double "gate." The athlete taking off pushes the stomach forward to open the "gate."

COACHING TIPS

- At takeoff, thrust the thigh of the leading leg up and forward.
- Drive powerfully with the jumping leg.
- Once in the air, lower the leading leg and push your stomach forward to contact the cane or to open the "gate."
- Athletes who are holding the cane or forming the "gate" with their arms: be sure that

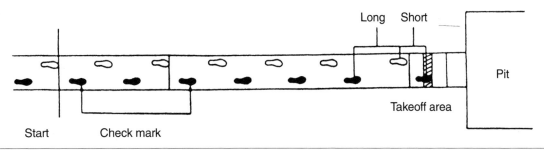

Figure 8.17   A 13-stride run-up with two check marks.

Figure 8.18   Driving the hips forward.

you don't resist the forward movement of the athlete who's jumping!

Learning the Arm Action of the Hang Technique

Pair off your athletes according to size and bodyweight. One jumps upward. The partner assists the jumper by gripping the athlete's waist from the rear and lifting upward (see figure 8.19). A forward, downward, backward and forward circling of the arms is initiated the instant the athlete jumps upward.

COACHING TIPS

Jumper

- Remember that the motion of your arms is forward, down, back, up, and then forward again.

Figure 8.19   Arm action of the hang technique.

- Try to complete the arm action while you are in the air.

Lifter

- Time your lifting action to coincide with the jumper's upward thrust.

Emphasizing the Arm Action in the Hang Technique

An athlete stands in stride position with the leading leg on a box top and the favored or jumping foot to the rear. This stance simulates the position that the athlete assumes after driving upward in the air from the takeoff. The athlete positions both arms ahead of the body and then pushes off with the leg that is on the box top. The arms simultaneously circle backward and then forward. (See figure 8.20.)

COACHING TIPS

- Remember that the leg you've placed on the box will be the one you drive up in the air at takeoff. It's not your jumping leg!
- Put your arms forward. As you take off, swing them back, up, over, and then forward.
- Immediately after takeoff, flex your legs and pull them forward for the landing in the sand.

Practicing the Hang Technique From Height

Place 2 vaulting boxes lengthwise, one behind the other in front of the sand pit. Make them

2–3 sections tall and be sure they're stable. Athletes step along the top of the boxes, taking off from the end (see figure 8.21). The additional height provides time in the air to attempt the hang technique.

COACHING TIPS

- After takeoff, drop your leading leg backward and push your stomach forward.
- Circle your arms backward and then forward.
- As your arms come forward and downward, flex your legs and lift them up toward your arms for the landing.

Practicing the Hang Technique From Reduced Height

Set a beat board 1 stride (1 m) away from 1 or 2 sections of a vaulting box set crosswise. If necessary, use other athletes at the ends of the box sections to hold the box stable. Using a slow 3-stride approach, the athlete steps onto the beat board with the jumping foot, and then steps up onto the box top with the leading leg to push off and attempt the hang technique (see figure 8.22). The extra height will give the athlete time to hang the legs downward and then pull them forward for the landing.

COACHING TIPS

- Be sure to measure the 3 strides so that your favored leg lands on the beat board. The step up onto the vaulting box will

Figure 8.20 Emphasizing arm action in the hang technique.

Figure 8.21 Practicing the hang technique from vaulting boxes.

Figure 8.22 Practicing the hang technique from reduced height.

force your leading leg into a position that you will use at takeoff.

- Approach slowly to begin with, and then gradually speed up your run-up.

- Circle your arms forward and down from beat board to box top, and then backward and then forward as you jump from the box top to the sand.

- Extend your leading leg downward in the air, and then flex both legs to pull them forward to meet your arms for the landing in the sand.

Put a long plank of wood along the top of a mound of sand. Make sure the plank is completely stable. Using the favored leg to take off, the athlete jumps from the end of the plank down the incline of the mound of sand (see figure 8.23). The extra time in the air will make

Figure 8.23   Jumping down a sand incline.

it easier to complete the leg and arm action of the hang technique.

Attempting the Hang Technique From Reduced Height

The athlete attempts the hang technique taking off from the ground or from a beat board (see figure 8.24). The athlete uses a 3–5-stride run-up and now takes off from the favored leg. Your coaching tips will be the same as for the previous drills.

Hang Technique With Extended Run-Up

The athlete performs the hang technique into the sand pit using an extended run-up. When appropriate you can have the athlete build up to a 13-, 15-, 17-, or 19-stride run-up. Your coaching tips will be the same as for the previous drills.

STEP 4: THE HITCH-KICK TECHNIQUE

Swinging the Leading Leg Up and Forward

Using a short run-up, have your athletes jump from the edge of the sand pit into the sand

holding the thigh of the leading leg at horizontal throughout. The athlete lands in the sand in a kneeling position, with one leg forward and one leg back (see figure 8.25). Make sure that the sand is well-dug and soft so that landing in a kneeling position is comfortable.

COACHING TIPS

- Swing (drive) the thigh of the leading leg to horizontal and hold the leg in that position through the landing.
- Land in a kneeling position. Don't bring both of your legs together for the landing.

Swinging the Leading Leg Up in a Flexed Position, and Scissoring This Leg Backward in the Air

From a 3-stride run-up, and using a beat board and a single section of a vaulting box for take-off, athletes jump to land in a kneeling position. Each athlete attempts to drive the thigh of the leading leg upward and while in the air straighten the same leg and swing it backward. Simultaneously the take-off leg is brought forward and flexed for a kneeling landing (see figure 8.26). Each athlete should land in a kneel-

Figure 8.24 The hang technique from reduced height.

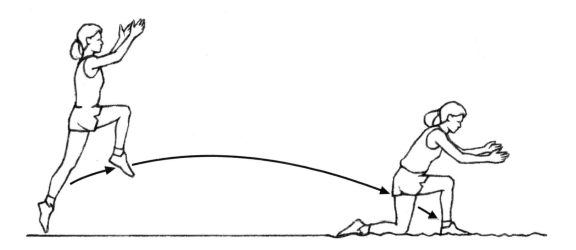

Figure 8.25 Emphasis on the action of the leading leg in the hitch-kick technique.

ing position with the take-off leg ahead. Be sure the sand is well-dug and soft.

- Lift the thigh of the leading leg to horizontal, straighten it, and swing it backward.
- Bring the take-off leg forward so that your legs scissor in the air (change position in the air).
- Land in a kneeling position with your take-off leg in front; don't bring your legs together for the landing.

Practicing the Hitch-Kick Leg Action

Using a 5-stride run-up, the athlete takes off from a beat board or a single section of a box. The leading leg, which is flexed at take-off, is extended and swung backward. To practice the backward motion of the leading leg, the athlete tries to kick a bamboo cane backward that is placed approximately 1.5–2 m (5'–6') ahead of the takeoff and .5–.75 m (1'–2') from the ground (see figure 8.27). The bamboo cane can be set on two supports or lightly held by another athlete. The athlete can begin this practice by landing in a kneeling

Figure 8.26 Scissoring the legs while in flight.

Figure 8.27 Practicing the hitch-kick leg action.

position in the sand with the jumping leg ahead. Then the athlete can try landing with both feet together.

COACHING TIPS

- Lift the leading thigh to horizontal, and then straighten the leg and swing the leg backward.
- Try to claw the bamboo cane backward with the foot of the leading leg.
- Land in a kneeling position with the take-off leg ahead.

- Now try landing with both legs brought forward together.

Attempting the Full Hitch-Kick Action From a Beat Board

The athlete takes off from a beat board and cycles the leading leg to the rear and then brings it forward again in a flexed position for the landing (see figure 8.28). The arms rotate forward, downward, backward, and then forward again to counter balance the actions of the legs. The drill in which the bamboo cane is

Figure 8.28 Practicing the full hitch-kick action from a gymnastic beat board.

clawed backward can still be used if it helps the athlete initiate the backward cycling rotation of the leading leg.

- Begin by concentrating on the leg action during this drill. Don't worry about your arm action.
- Lift the thigh of the leading leg, and then straighten it and swing (or pedal) the leg backward.
- Then flex your leading leg and bring it forward to join the jumping leg for the landing.

Practicing the Full Hitch-Kick Without Additional Take-Off Height

Because take-off assistance is now removed, only your better athletes are likely to succeed with this drill. Have your athletes use an extended run-up and remove the beat board that was used in the previous drill. If an athlete doesn't have sufficient speed and spring, you'll find that the hitch-kick will degenerate into an aimless wriggling of the legs. It will detract from the jump rather than be of any assistance. In the majority of cases, you will find that young athletes are unable to complete a full hitch-kick in the air and that they are better off using the hang technique.

A 2½-stride hitch-kick is completed in the following manner. The athlete extends the leading leg forward at takeoff (this is stride 1). The leading leg is then cycled to the rear and the jumping leg is brought forward (this is stride 2). Finally, the leading leg is brought forward to join the jumping leg for the landing (this is the final ½ stride). Considerable height and time in the air is required to perform these movements efficiently.

COMMON ERRORS AND CORRECTIONS

ELEMENTARY LONG JUMP AND RUN-UP

Error	Reasons	Corrections
During the run-up, the athlete appears tense and fails to run in a straight line.	The athlete's head position and line of vision are incorrect; the athlete closes the eyes or looks down during the run-up. The athlete has poor sprinting technique.	Emphasize uniform acceleration and correct head and arm action. Have the athlete work on improving sprinting technique, concentrating on correct arm and leg action.
The athlete stutter-steps and takes off on the wrong foot. There are repeated irregularities in the run-up.	The athlete's run-up, starting position, and stride length varies with each jump. The athlete becomes tense prior to the takeoff.	Remeasure and check the accuracy of the athlete's run-up and check marks. Have the athlete practice sprinting on the track, emphasizing good technique and controlled acceleration. The athlete should begin the run-up in the same manner each time. Drills that use a take-off area rather than a take-off board will help to get the athlete to relax and produce a good accelerative run-up.
The athlete looks down at the take-off board at the moment of takeoff.	The athlete is unsure of the run-up and is tense prior to takeoff.	Have the athlete perform repetitive run-ups, with an emphasis on using check marks. Use a take-off area rather than a take-off board. Instruct the athletes to keep their vision directly ahead.
The athlete gets height but not distance.	The athlete's run-up is not accurate; the athlete uses the wrong stride length on the take-off stride. The athlete has too much backward body lean prior to and during takeoff.	Have the athlete practice the run-up with the second-to-last stride occurring on a beat board and the takeoff from a single section of a vaulting box. A predetermined distance from beat board to box top will help the athlete get used to the correct stride length. Markers on the run-up for the three strides prior to takeoff will be of assistance.

→

Error	Reasons	Corrections
The flight path of the jump is low and close to the ground; the athlete has no time in the air. The athlete's feet hit the sand too early.	There's no drive from the athlete's take-off leg, and the athlete's upper body is angled too far forward at takeoff. The thigh of the leading leg is poorly elevated at takeoff, and the athlete uses no extension of the legs at the end of flight. The athlete is physically weak in the legs and abdomen.	Have the athlete practice repetitive bounding and jumping, keeping the upper body perpendicular and the thigh of leading leg lifted to horizontal at takeoff. Emphasize reaching out with the feet for distance immediately prior to landing. Have the athlete remeasure and check the run-up and stride lengths for accuracy. Sit-ups and leg strengthening exercises will assist in strengthening the athlete's abdomen and quadriceps.
The athlete lands in the sand in a sitting position (or sits back after landing in the sand).	The athlete leans backward at takeoff and has no flexion at the knees when the feet hit the sand. The athlete's arms are not thrown forward during the landing to help shift the upper body forward.	Have the athlete practice standing long jumps using a 1- or 2-footed takeoff. Emphasize flexion at the athlete's knees during landing to allow the hips to move forward. A vigorous swing will assist in this action.

HANG TECHNIQUE

Error	Reasons	Corrections
The thigh of the athlete's leading leg is not lifted to horizontal at takeoff.	The athlete is too concerned with backward thrust of the leading leg in the hang technique. The takeoff is rushed.	Have the athlete repeat the elementary long jump, emphasizing the elevation of the thigh of the leading leg The athlete should also practice the hang technique from a raised take-off so that there is sufficient time to concentrate on the correct leg action.
The athlete lands upright in the sand pit. There is no forward "reach" of the athlete's legs.	The athlete has too much forward lean at takeoff. There's no height in the athlete's jump so that after the extension of the legs, there's not enough air time to bring them forward. The athlete has poor flexion at the knees and hips, so the legs are not brought forward from a hang position. The athlete has weak abdominals.	Instruct the athlete to practice the hang technique from elevation, emphasizing the upward drive of the thigh of the leading leg. The athlete should practice 2-footed standing long jumps and also work on improving abdominal strength.

→

Error	Reasons	Corrections
The athlete's flight is performed in a bunched or squatting position.	The athlete's jumping leg is not fully extended at takeoff and does not remain to the rear for the hang action to occur. The athlete's leading leg is not first driven forward and upward in a flexed position and then to the rear in an extended position. Both legs are driven to the rear for hang action.	Have the athlete repeat repetitive hopping, bounding, and 2-legged jumps, emphasizing a powerful thrust with the jumping leg. Rework the lead-up drills for the hang technique.

HITCH-KICK TECHNIQUE

Error	Reasons	Corrections
The athlete's leg actions in the hitch-kick lack amplitude. They appear hurried and reduced in range. The hitch-kick technique is incomplete by the time the athlete hits the sand.	The athlete has insufficient time in the air to complete the required movements of the hitch-kick technique. The physical requirements of this technique are too difficult for the athlete.	The athlete should return to the elementary long jump and progress to the hang technique. Then have the athlete work through the hitch-kick lead-up drills again. If these drills are too difficult, then have the athlete stay with the hang technique until the speed of takeoff and height in the air are improved. Leg power exercises will assist in improving spring and speed.
The athlete's leading leg is flexed throughout the hitch-kick.	The athlete does not extend the leading leg after the takeoff and does not drive the leg backward.	Repeat the drills for landing in a kneeling stride position in the sand. Practice pedaling backward a bamboo cane with the leading leg.

ASSESSMENT

1. **Assess the following theoretical elements as taught during instructional sessions:**
   a. Fundamental rules governing long-jump competition.
   b. Good safety habits for use in long jump.
   c. Basic elements of long-jump technique.
   d. Basic elements of training for the long jump.
2. **Assess the performance of technique during the following stages of skill development:**
   a. Jumping from an elevated takeoff and using a short (3–5-stride) run-up.
   b. Jumping from a take-off area and using a short (3–5-stride) run-up.
   c. Jumping from a take-off area and using an extended (9–11-stride) run-up.
   d. Jumping from a take-off board and using an extended (9–11-stride) run-up.

CRITICAL FEATURES OF TECHNIQUE TO OBSERVE
DURING ASSESSMENT

Hang Technique

✓ Use of an extended run-up with 2 check marks.

✓ Stride adjustment prior to takeoff.

✓ Backward inclination of the athlete's body at contact with the board.

✓ Strong upward drive at takeoff.

✓ Elevation of the thigh of the athlete's leading leg to the horizontal position.

✓ Lowering of the thigh of the athlete's leading leg and the backward thrust of both legs in an extended position.

✓ Forward, downward, and backward circling of arms.

✓ Forward motion of the athlete's legs to a flexed position; then extension of the athlete's legs to join the arms for the landing.

✓ Flexion at the knees and hips after landing, allowing the athlete's body to move beyond the point of contact with the sand.

Hitch-Kick Technique

✓ Use of an extended run-up with 2 check marks.

✓ Stride adjustment prior to takeoff.

✓ Backward inclination of the athlete's body at contact with the board.

✓ Powerful upward drive at takeoff.

✓ Elevation of the thigh of the athlete's leading leg to horizontal or above at takeoff.

✓ Extension and backward rotation of the athlete's leading leg.

✓ Wide stride position in the air.

✓ Rotation of the athlete's arms to balance the cycling action of the legs.

✓ Flexion and extension of both legs for the landing.

✓ Forward rotation of the athlete's arms for the landing.

✓ Flexion at the athlete's hips and knees to allow the body to move beyond the point of contact with the sand.

3. **Hold graded competitions to help develop motivation and technique.**

   a. Athletes compete for distance using a standing long jump. Each uses a 2-footed takeoff, and then a single-footed takeoff with the take-off foot placed forward.

   b. Athletes compete for the total distance of 3 two-footed jumps in sequence, 3 bounding strides in sequence, and 3 hops in sequence.

   c. Athletes compete from an elevated takeoff and from a run-up of 5 strides. Require a selected technique (hang technique).

   d. Athletes compete for distance from a take-off area, using a 5-stride run-up. Require a selected technique (hang technique).

   e. Athletes compete for distance from a take-off area, using an extended run-up (9 strides or more). Require a selected technique (hang or hitch-kick).

   f. Athletes compete for distance from a take-off board, using an extended run-up (9 strides or more). Require a selected technique (hang or hitch-kick).

SUGGESTED STANDARDS OF PERFORMANCE—LONG JUMP

MALE

Age		Distance
12-13	Satisfactory	3.70 m (12'2")
	Good	4.00 m (13'1")
	Excellent	4.50 m (14'9")
14-15	Satisfactory	4.00 m (13'1")
	Good	4.50 m (14'9")
	Excellent	5.00 m (16'5")
16-17	Satisfactory	4.50 m (14'9")
	Good	5.00 m (16'5")
	Excellent	5.50 m (18'0")
18-19	Satisfactory	4.80 m (15'9")
	Good	5.30 m (17'5")
	Excellent	5.80 m (19'0")

FEMALE

Age		Distance
12-13	Satisfactory	3.00 m (9'10")
	Good	3.40 m (11'2")
	Excellent	3.80 m (12'6")
14-15	Satisfactory	3.40 m (11'2")
	Good	3.80 m (12'6")
	Excellent	4.10 m (13'5")
16-17	Satisfactory	3.60 m (11'10")
	Good	4.00 m (13'1")
	Excellent	4.30 m (14'1")
18-19	Satisfactory	3.80 m (12'6")
	Good	4.20 m (13'9")
	Excellent	4.50 m (14'9")

9

TRIPLE JUMP

The triple jump was included in the Olympic Games of 1896 and until recently was a men's field event. Triple-jump competitions in the Olympic Games are now held for men and women.

Like the long jump, the triple jump demands great speed and spring. The two events differ in that the triple jump involves three jumps in sequence (a hop, step, and jump), all of which are interdependent. To achieve the greatest possible distance, an athlete must have great rebound ability (the ability to jump, land, and jump again) and be able to balance the distribution of effort between all three jumps. A triple jumper must be an excellent sprinter and have the muscular power and resilience to be able to jump and rebound three times in succession.

SAFETY SUGGESTIONS

Although the triple jump is an attractive and fun event, be aware of the intense physical demands that training for this event places upon your athletes. The triple jump places considerable stress on the athlete's heels, knees, hips, and joints of the feet. Consequently, you should increase the intensity of training slowly and carefully. No instructional period should be devoted solely to triple jump until your athletes have developed adequate muscular power. When introducing your athletes to this event, keep repetitive jumping and rebounding to a minimum and limit the total number of jumps in any sequence to 3 or 4. To ease the shock of repetitive jumping and bounding, have your athletes perform on surfaces that provide adequate cushioning, such as grass or mats. During indoor training, gymnastic floor-exercise mats are excellent for this purpose. Heel pads provide additional protection.

This chapter will offer you some examples of rebound exercises, which are an integral part of power training for the triple jumper. Called *plyometrics*, *depth jumping*, or simply *rebound jumping*, these are activities in which your athletes simulate the bounce of a ball by repetitively jumping down from a height and immediately rebounding up again. This type of activity requires a lengthening contraction from the athlete's muscles during the landing and an explosive shortening contraction of the same muscles during the takeoff. Such exercises are very demanding and are recommended only for the mature and experienced athlete. Don't require your athletes to perform these activities until their legs have been strengthened through less stressful activities.

Be aware of the dangers that can arise from asking an athlete to compete in both the long jump and the triple jump. The demands of both events greatly increase the stress placed on your athlete's legs and feet. Keep in mind that there is also the technical conflict between the differing takeoffs in the long jump and the triple jump: The long jump requires great upward thrust at takeoff; the triple jump requires a low, flat trajectory.

A large instructional pit is useful for teaching the triple jump and the long jump. The larger the pit and the more run-ups that are available, the greater the opportunity for a high level of activity. Take-off distances for run-ups both from the side and the ends of the pit can vary according to athletes' ages and the drill being practiced. The adult distance of the take-off board for triple jump is 13 m from the pit. For school-age athletes, this distance can vary from 5–8 m up to the adult competitive distance.

A take-off area (recommended earlier for the long jump in chapter 8) is also useful for the triple jump. This large area is much easier to hit at the end of a run-up than a competitive take-off board. A take-off area virtually eliminates foul jumps, and you can make triple jump (and long jump) more pleasurable by measuring from the mark made by the athlete's foot at takeoff to the nearest point of the landing in the sand.

TECHNIQUE

Triple-jump technique has changed very little over the past 20 years. Some variations have occurred in the use of arms in gaining lift during each of the three jumps, but the main elements of the technique have remained basically the same (see figure 9.1).

THE HOP

After a fast run-up, the athlete takes off with a strong forward thrust from the jumping leg. The athlete's body is upright during takeoff,

and a flat horizontal trajectory conserves take-off speed for use in each of the following two jumps. The athlete drives the thigh of the leading (nonjumping) leg up to horizontal and then swings it back to the rear. The thigh of the athlete's jumping leg is then lifted upward so that a wide stride position exists at the midpoint of the hop. As the athlete's jumping leg lands, it flexes in preparation to drive the athlete forward in the step. The arms work vigorously to balance the athlete's body and assist in driving the athlete forward. The hop is approximately equal in length to the jump.

THE STEP

The step is usually slightly shorter than either the hop or the jump. The athlete's body is upright in the takeoff for the step, and the leading leg is flexed and swung forward vigorously to become the leg that will cushion the athlete's landing at the end of the step and then immediately drive the athlete forward in the final jump. At the midpoint of the step, the athlete has a wide stride position.

THE JUMP

The athlete vigorously swings the leading leg forward from the step into the jump, aiming for distance and a good landing position (feet together well in front of the athlete's body). Elite athletes occasionally use a hang technique during the flight of the jump. Many athletes will also use a technique that resembles the elementary long jump that was described in chapter 8.

TEACHING STEPS

STEP 1. Lead-Ups
STEP 2. The Triple Jump

STEP 1: LEAD-UPS

The lead-up drills used for the triple jump involve repetitive bounding, jumping, and hopping. These drills are designed to develop the athlete's leg power, muscular endurance, and coordination. They are also excellent for sprinters, high jumpers, long jumpers, and athletes competing in the throwing events.

Figure 9.1 Triple-jump technique: the hop, the step, and the jump.

Repetitive Bounding

As shown in figure 9.2, athletes bound with long, reaching strides (3 or 4 strides in total) from a standing start and from a short relaxed run-up (3–5 strides). Methods for measuring a run-up and choosing the jumping or favored leg are taught during your instruction in long jumping (see chapter 8).

COACHING TIPS

- Drive forward vigorously with your jumping leg.
- Swing the thigh of the leading leg up to horizontal with each of your bounding strides.
- Try to hold a wide stride position at the midpoint of each of your bounding strides.
- Swing your arms forward as powerfully as possible at the takeoff for each bounding stride.

Hopping for Distance

The athlete performs 3 or 4 hops for distance on the right leg (see figure 9.3). The same drill is then performed using the athlete's left leg. Have the athlete use a standing start or a short 3–5-pace run-up.

COACHING TIPS

- Swing your leading leg and the arms forward and upward to assist with each of your hops.
- Drive as powerfully as possible with your hopping leg.
- Use your arms and the swing of your free leg to help you with each hop.

Rabbit Hops

As shown in figure 9.4, each athlete performs 3 or 4 repetitive 2-legged jumps (rabbit hops). Who can cover the most distance with 3 rabbit hops in sequence?

COACHING TIPS

- Extend both your legs as powerfully as possible with each jump.
- Lean forward and swing your arms forward and upward to assist in driving you forward.

Figure 9.2 Repetitive bounding.

Figure 9.3 Hopping for distance.

Figure 9.4 Rabbit hops.

Standing and Running Long Jump

Athletes practice a standing long jump and a running long jump from a 3-stride run-up using a takeoff from the nonfavored leg (see figure 9.5). Because the triple jump requires 3 jumps in succession, the first of these jumps usually occurs from the nonfavored leg. This drill will familiarize your athlete with this action. If an athlete's favored leg is the right, then the athlete will start a 3-stride run-up from the left foot so that the takeoff occurs on the left (nonfavored) leg.

COACHING TIPS

- Make sure you start your run-up from the correct leg. If you normally jump from your right leg, you will start your run-up by taking your first stride with your left leg.
- Drive powerfully with your jumping leg at takeoff.
- Lift the thigh of your leading leg to horizontal.
- Swing your arms forward and upward as strongly as possible at takeoff.

Combinations of Hops, Jumps, and Bounding Strides

The step (the second of the three jumps in the triple jump) is really a long bounding stride. Athletes practice combinations of hops, jumps, and bounding strides initiated from a standing start and then from a short, controlled approach of 3 strides (see figure 9.6). The step can be combined with other jumping activities in the following manner:

Figure 9.5 Standing long jump.

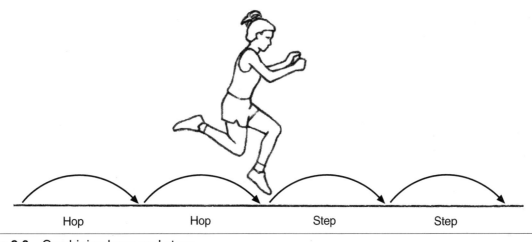

| Hop | Hop | Step | Step |

Figure 9.6 Combining hops and steps.

Hop, hop, step

Step, step, jump

Step, step, hop, jump

Hop, hop, step, step, jump

Distance and Time Competition

Have your athletes compete against each other using selections from the previous 4 sequences or from sequences that you design. Award points for the greatest distance achieved. For a time contest, each athlete has to cover a certain distance with a particular combination of hops and steps in a certain time. By restricting the amount of time available for performing the sequence of jumps, you force each athlete to jump as vigorously and as quickly as possible. A time and distance competition will make your athletes thrust low and forward as powerfully they can.

Repetitive Bounding and Jumping Over Low Obstacles

Place mats short distances apart and set up several low obstacles, such as bamboo canes balanced on traffic cones. Athletes perform combinations of hops, steps, and jumps over the obstacles and land from the hops, steps, and jumps on the mats (see figure 9.7). Increase the distances between the mats to make each athlete stretch and reach out with each jump.

STEP 2: THE TRIPLE JUMP

Learning the Sequence and Rhythm of the Triple Jump From a Standing Start

On grass, or on mats, have your athletes practice the sequence of jumps in the triple jump by hopping (left to left), stepping (left to right),

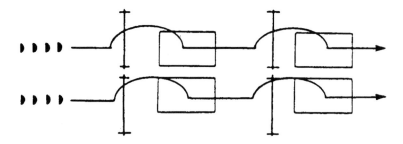

Figure 9.7 Repetitive bounding and jumping over low obstacles.

and jumping (from right to land with both feet together). All sequences begin with the athletes placing the left foot behind a line and attempting a triple jump from a standing start (see figure 9.8). You provide a verbal count similar to "left, right, together." Athletes can experiment by changing their starting foot to see if they feel more comfortable beginning with the opposing foot.

COACHING TIPS

- Try to make each of your 3 jumps in the hop, step, and jump equal in size.
- Take off into each of your 3 jumps with a long low powerful leg drive.
- Swing the thigh of your leading leg to horizontal at each takeoff and simultaneously swing your arms forward and upward.

Standing Triple Jump Into the Jumping Pit

Athletes practice the hop and the step on grass and land in the pit with the jump (see figure 9.9). Each athlete attempts to shift their starting position progressively further away from the pit. Make sure that each athlete tries to make the hop, step, and jump equal in length. Figure 9.10 shows the recommended ratios.

COACHING TIPS

- Lift the thigh of your leading leg as close to horizontal as possible on each of your three jumps.
- Swing your arms forward and upward as vigorously as you can on each of your three jumps.
- Claw back at the ground with the foot of your supporting leg at the end of each jump.
- Think of jumping long and low rather than upward.

- Try to make each jump equal in length. Don't jump a huge distance in the hop; otherwise, you'll have nothing left for the step and jump!

Triple Jump Using a Run-Up

Each athlete attempts a triple jump using a run-up and taking off from a take-off area. Place the take-off area 5–8 m from the sand pit (see figure 9.11). Be ready to modify this distance according to the ability of your athletes. A run-up of 9 to 11 strides together with check marks is worked out in the same manner as in the long jump (see chapter 8).

COACHING TIPS

- Drive long and low in your takeoff. Concentrate on horizontal rather than vertical movement (don't hop high in the air).
- Aim for equal distances in each of your jumps.
- Listen to the rhythm of your footfalls during the triple jump; the cadence should be regular (da—da—da).
- Lift the thigh of your leading leg to horizontal at the midpoint of your hop and your step and for the takeoff in the jump. Aim for a wide stride position each time you're in the air.
- Land flat-footed at the end of your hop and step.
- Pull your body forward with the foot of your supporting leg by using a clawing or pawing action. Do this at the end of your hop and your step.

Double-Arm Action

Your athletes can attempt a double-arm action during the three jumps as an alternative to the more natural alternating-arm action (left

Figure 9.8   A triple jump from a standing start.

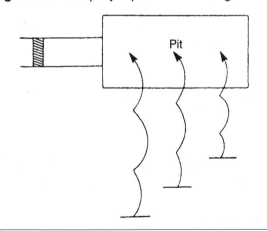

Figure 9.9   Standing triple jump into the pit.

leg forward, right arm forward). Many elite athletes use the double-arm action (see figure 9.12). It is not a difficult skill for young athletes to perform.

COACHING TIPS

- At the takeoff from your hop and your step, swing both arms simultaneously forward and upward to a point where they are horizontal and parallel to the ground; this arm swing will help to lift your body forward and upward.

- Keep your arms flexed at the elbows (approximately 120 degrees).

Repetitive Bounding Over Obstacles Varying in Height and Distance

The following drills are extremely demanding and are recommended for mature and experienced athletes. They are usually practiced in the off-season and only after the athlete's leg strength has been developed in other less-demanding activities. Progressively increase the height and distance between the obstacles. Make sure that your athletes become accustomed to landing from low heights before having them land and rebound from greater heights.

In these drills, the athlete bounds from one foot to the other over various obstacles (see figure 9.13). Be sure you carefully select

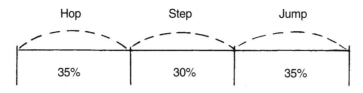

Figure 9.10 Recommended ratios for each segment of the triple jump.

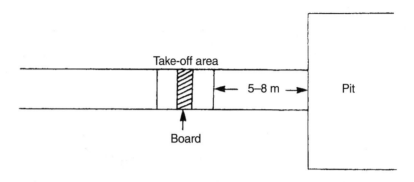

Figure 9.11 Triple-jump take-off area 5–8 m from the pit.

Figure 9.12 Double-arm action.

obstacles according to the maturity and ability of your athletes. You can choose one or two sections of a vaulting box, mats placed lengthwise or crosswise, bamboo canes placed on traffic cones, or low hurdles. Your athletes must be challenged but also capable of leaping the obstacles. Place the most challenging obstacles first and the easier obstacles afterwards so that fatigued athletes can clear them even though they are tired. Example: 3 or 4 bounding jumps in sequence, and then repeat the drill 3 or 4 times with rest periods in between each attempt.

These tips are applicable to all types of rebound and depth jumping:

- Cushion your landing by making sure you land on your full foot, not on the ball of your foot or on your heel.
- To absorb the shock of landing, partially flex at your knees and hips.
- Be sure to roll forward and push off the ball of your foot for your rebound.

Combination Hopping and Bounding Over Obstacles

To increase the workload placed on your athletes, make up a sequence of hopping and bounding. Have the athlete clear low obstacles as part of the sequence (see figure 9.14).

Rebound Jumping

The athlete jumps down from one vaulting box onto a mat, immediately rebounding up onto the next box (see figure 9.15). Boxes are varied in height.

Repetitive 2-Legged Jumps Over a Series of Low Hurdles

This activity allows no momentary pauses. Initially, have your athletes perform 2-legged

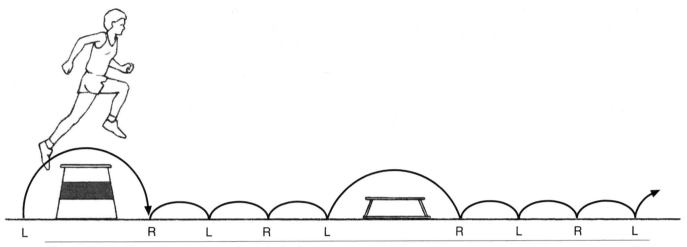

Figure 9.13 Bounding over varying obstacles.

L   R   L   R   L   R   L   R   L

Figure 9.14 Hopping and bounding over obstacles.

L   L   R   L   L   R

Figure 9.15 Rebound jumping.

jumps over bamboo canes set on traffic cones. When you are assured of your athletes' abilities, have them perform the same action over low hurdles (see figure 9.16). As an easier variation, have your athletes clear a hurdle first, and then have them jump over bamboo canes set on top of traffic cones. Carefully select the height of the obstacles according to the ability of your athletes. Example: 3 or 4 2-legged jumps in sequence, and then repeat the drill 3 or 4 times with rest periods in between each attempt.

Two-Legged Jump Up Onto a Vaulting Box, Followed by a Single-Legged Landing and an Immediate Rebound

This drill is very demanding. Your athletes must have sufficient power to control a single-leg landing and then immediately drive up onto the next vaulting box (see figure 9.17). Elite athletes frequently increase the demand on their legs by wearing weight belts and weighted jackets! The power to perform these drills takes a long time to develop and is achieved only after years of hard training. Example: 3 or 4 two-legged and single-legged jumps in total. Repeat the drill 3 or 4 times with rest periods in between each attempt.

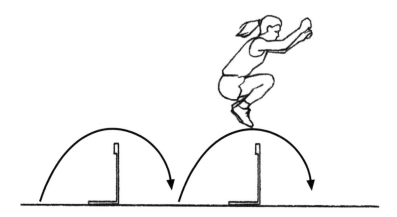

Figure 9.16 Two-legged jumps over a series of hurdles.

Figure 9.17 Jumping and rebounding.

COMMON ERRORS AND CORRECTIONS

Error	Reasons	Corrections
The athlete uses uses stutter steps in the run-up. The run-up is irregular.	The athlete is unsure of the run-up. Check marks on the run-up may be incorrect, and the athlete may be tense and anxious prior to jumping.	Have the athletes practice the run-up using the drills and lead-ups recommended for the long jump in chapter 8.
The athlete uses too much backward lean at takeoff.	The athlete's penultimate and final strides are too long, and the athlete overemphasizes height in the hop. The athlete's head is dropping back on the shoulders as the athlete incorrectly concentrates on height in the takeoff.	Have the athlete practice the run-up and the takeoff, aiming for a fast, flat takeoff. The athlete's upper body should be erect, and the athlete's vision should be directly ahead. Have the athlete concentrate on a low, flat trajectory in the hop. Shorten the length of the athlete's penultimate stride.
The hop has too much height and distance. The athlete "collapses" at the end of the hop and has no momentum for the step and the jump.	The athlete leans backward at the takeoff. The strides taken by the athlete in the run-up immediately prior to the takeoff are too long. The athlete overemphasizes the hop and forgets that two more jumps must follow.	The athlete must practice repetitive jumps, hops, and bounding strides with an upright torso or a slight forward lean at takeoff. The athlete should also practice hops and steps with the distances well defined by cones or markers. Have the athlete practice the run-up with a shorter penultimate stride.
The jumping leg is allowed to hang or drag during the hop.	The athlete relaxes the jumping leg instead of bringing it forward and upward so that it is ready for the step.	The athlete must practice sequential hopping, jumping, and bounding on grass or mats, emphasizing forward and upward drive with the thigh of the athlete's jumping leg.
The athlete performs the triple jump with stiff legs throughout.	The athlete fails to partially flex the legs at the midpoint of the hop, the step, and on the two landings at the end of the hop and step.	The athlete must practice sequential hopping, jumping, and bounding on grass or mats, emphasizing forward and upward drive with the thigh of the athlete's jumping leg.

→

Error	Reasons	Corrections
The athlete lands on the toes at the end of the hop or step and complains of painful landings at the end of the hop and step.	The athlete is reaching out with the toes for distance instead of reaching out with the heel and making each landing a flat-footed one.	Correct as for the previous 2 errors, emphasizing a flat-footed landing. The athlete should aim for a backward pawing or clawing action with the supporting foot and "drag" the ground backward when landing at the end of the hop and step.
The athlete's arm action is poor and haphazard during each of the 3 jumps.	The athlete is unsure of the correct technique.	Have the athlete repeat standing triple jumps, emphasizing a strong upward arm swing at the takeoff for each of the 3 jumps. Decide on whether the athlete should use an alternate- or double-arm action. The alternate-arm action is more natural and easier for beginners to perform.
The step is extremely short, and there is no drive for distance.	The athlete has too much height and distance in the hop, and the jumping leg "collapses" at at the end of the hop. The athlete is unable to drive forward with the leading leg in the step. The athlete's arm action is weak and ineffective.	Have the athlete practice repetitive jumps, emphasizing a vigorous arm action and a powerful leading-leg action (with the thigh driven forward and upward to horizontal on each occasion). Assign hop and step drills over low obstacles.
After the hop and the step, the jump is weak and achieves poor distance.	The athlete loses momentum in the hop and the step. Errors in the hop and the step produce a poor jump.	The athlete must practice sequential hops and steps on grass and mats, using a short run-up. Emphasize that the athlete must maintain good horizontal speed throughout. Have the athlete practice long jumps from short run-ups, taking off from the nonfavored leg.

ASSESSMENT

1. **Assess the following theoretical elements as taught during instructional sessions:**
   a. Fundamental rules governing the triple jump.
   b. Good safety habits for use in the triple jump.
   c. Basic elements of triple-jump technique.
   d. Basic elements of triple-jump training.

2. **Assess the performance of technique during the following stages of skill development:**
   a. Repetitive bounding, hopping, and jumping.
   b. Various combinations of bounding, hopping, and jumping.
   c. Triple jump using a short run-up (3–5 strides).
   d. Triple jump using a full-length run-up.

   CRITICAL FEATURES OF TECHNIQUE TO OBSERVE DURING ASSESSMENT

   ✓ Ability to use a run-up and 2 check marks.
   ✓ Achieving a strong forward drive with a flat trajectory in the take-off for the hop.
   ✓ Driving the leading leg back and stretching out with the take-off leg in the flight of the hop.
   ✓ Pawing or clawing backward with the foot of the supporting leg in the landing at the end of the hop.
   ✓ Driving forward and stretching out in a wide stride position in the step.
   ✓ Driving upward with the arms to horizontal at each takeoff for the hop, the step, and the jump.
   ✓ Clawing backward with the foot of the supporting leg in the landing at the end of the step.
   ✓ Swinging the thigh of the leading leg up and forward in the takeoff for the jump.
   ✓ Reaching out with the legs well in front of the body for a good landing position at the end of the jump.
   ✓ Achieving a distance ratio of 35 percent, 30 percent, 35 percent between the hop, step, and jump.

3. **Hold graded competitions to help develop motivation and technique.**
   a. Athletes compete for distance from a standing start using a jump from a single-legged takeoff and then a jump from a double-legged takeoff.
   b. Athletes compete for distance using selections from the following sequences: 3 bounding strides from a standing start, 3 hops from a standing start, 2 bounding strides and a jump taken from a standing start, and 2 hops and a jump taken from a standing start.
   c. Athletes compete for distance from 3- and 5-stride run-ups using a selection from the preceding sequences.

d. Athletes compete against each other and the stopwatch by doing a series of hops, bounds, and jumps that you designate. Who can complete the series covering a specified distance or further in the shortest time?

e. Athletes compete for distance in a triple jump from 3- and 5-stride run-ups.

f. Athletes compete for distance in a triple jump from an extended run-up of 9–13 strides. Takeoffs can occur from a take-off area rather than a take-off board.

g. Athletes compete under full competitive conditions.

SUGGESTED STANDARDS OF PERFORMANCE—TRIPLE JUMP

MALE

Age		Distance
12-13	Satisfactory	7.50 m (24'7")
	Good	8.50 m (27'10")
	Excellent	9.50 m (31'2")
14-15	Satisfactory	8.50 m (27'10")
	Good	9.50 m (31'2")
	Excellent	10.50 m (34'5")
16-17	Satisfactory	9.00 m (29'6")
	Good	10.00 m (32'7")
	Excellent	11.00 m (36'1")
18-19	Satisfactory	10.50 m (34'5")
	Good	11.00 m (36'1")
	Excellent	11.50 m (37'9")

FEMALE

Age		Distance
12-13	Satisfactory	7.00 m (23'0")
	Good	7.80 m (25'7")
	Excellent	8.40 m (27'7")
14-15	Satisfactory	7.50 m (24'7")
	Good	8.20 m (26'11")
	Excellent	9.20 m (30'2")
16-17	Satisfactory	7.90 m (25'1")
	Good	8.70 m (28'6")
	Excellent	9.60 m (31'6")
18-19	Satisfactory	8.50 m (27'10")
	Good	9.10 m (29'10")
	Excellent	10.00 m (32'7")

10

POLE VAULT

In the first modern Olympic Games in 1896, pole vaulting was included in the Olympic Games as a competition for males only. Now it is an event for males and females. Pole vault is included in the men's decathlon, but at present it is not in the women's heptathlon. Since its inclusion in the Olympic Games, the event has undergone dramatic changes. In the early years, athletes used wooden and aluminum poles and landed on grass, sand, or wood chips. Today's pole-vaulter combines superior training with the modern technology of fiberglass and graphite poles, high-speed runways, and immense foam-rubber pits that cushion landings from heights as great as 6 m (20′).

The modern composite vaulting pole has played a large part in the dramatic increase in heights that elite athletes have achieved. Made of graphite and/or fiberglass, it has many advantages over the stiff aluminum pole used during the early 1960s. The flexion of the much lighter composite pole eliminates the shock that athletes experienced with an aluminum pole when they were wrenched upward at takeoff. By flexing, the modern pole also allows an athlete to hold much higher on the pole. The energy stored in the flexed pole then helps to thrust the athlete higher when the pole straightens out.

The finer aspects of pole vaulting take time to learn well. Young athletes cannot be expected to hold high on the pole and sprint down the run-up in one or two instructional periods. Although they can master the basics of pole vaulting in a short period of time, it takes dedication and hard work to join the elite in this attractive and dynamic event.

SAFETY SUGGESTIONS

Athletes are now reaching tremendous heights in the pole vault. More height requires more attention to safety. The following sections list some recommendations that you can use when you teach this event to your athletes.

LANDING AREAS

An athlete using a modern composite pole flexes the pole considerably in the early part of the vault. Much of this flexion occurs while the athlete is suspended above or near the vaulting box. For the protection of the athlete, large landing pads have been designed with special sections that fit around the pole-vault box. Don't use landing pads that fail to satisfy these requirements. For example, don't use high-jump landing pads for pole vault. These pads are too small and lack the additional sections needed to surround the pole-vault box. Nor should you make up pole-vault landing pads out of a series of stacked gymnastic mats. Athletes can fall into the joins between the mats even when they're tied together.

Be aware that the rubber filling in landing pads deteriorates with time and can become waterlogged if allowed to stand uncovered in the rain. Keep the pads dry, and check their firmness regularly. Pay particular attention to the corner areas of the landing pads to make sure they give adequate support.

The minimum size of a pole-vault pit is 5 m by 5 m, excluding the front protection pads that rest around the pole-vault box. Although sand pits and wood chips are adequate for teaching the fundamentals, they should not be used for intermediate and advanced vaulting.

CROSSBARS

One of the problems you'll face when you coach pole vault is the time taken to replace a crossbar after it has been knocked off. You can overcome this problem by using thin 8 mm ($\frac{5}{16}$") rubber tubing that is stretched between the crossbar supports on the pole-vault uprights. You can obtain this rubber tubing from your local hardware store.

Two or three handkerchief-size pieces of brightly colored cloth can then be attached to the center of the tubing to aid in sighting the crossbar when your athlete runs up to vault. An alternative method for making your substitute crossbar visible is to slide your tubing through a series of brightly painted lightweight rubber plugs that replicate the diameter of the competitive crossbar. Position about six of these plugs in the center of your rubber crossbar.

Your rubber tubing must hold its horizontal position prior to a vault, but the tubing must also stretch easily all the way down to the landing pads when an athlete fails in an attempt. Rubber tubing comes in several different thicknesses and strengths. Be sure that you obtain

tubing that stretches easily. Don't use tubing that is thick and powerful. Competitive pole-vault standards have heavy base supports that easily resist the inward pull of the 8 mm rubber tubing recommended here. If you are using nonconforming pole vault standards, be sure to place additional weight on their bases to stabilize them.

You will be faced with one further problem when you have several athletes of different abilities vaulting together. You'll find that competitive pole-vault standards don't adjust low enough for some of your younger and less-experienced athletes. To solve this problem, attach 1 ½ m (4') wooden broom-handle size poles to the crossbar supports. Firmly attach these poles so that they extend vertically downward from the crossbar supports. Attach one line of your rubber tubing to the lower end of these poles. This line will be at a lower height for your less-experienced athletes. Attach a second line of tubing to the actual crossbar supports for your more accomplished athletes. Two lines of highly stretchable tubing separated by a fairly large gap will keep athletes of varying ability vaulting in quick succession. More time on task means more attempts and a greater rate of improvement!

For your young inexperienced athletes, you can use high-jump standards in place of competitive pole-vault standards. But the base of the high-jump standards must either be attached firmly to the ground or weighted down to stop them falling inward when your rubber tubing crossbar is stretched by one of your athletes.

RUN-UPS

All run-ups should be well-maintained, particularly at the take-off area. Grass and artificial surfaces can be slippery when wet for athletes not wearing spikes.

POLES

Using composite poles specifically designed for young vaulters will help you to teach the fundamentals of pole vault. These poles are shorter and lighter than the competitive models, and their small cross-sectional diameters make them easy for a young athlete to grip. Manufacturers specify the bodyweight for which a pole is designed. The greater the variety of these poles that you have available, the easier it is to accommodate differences in bodyweight and ability.

Tape each pole where the handholds occur. Tape, combined with resin and spray adhesives, assists in maintaining grip. Carefully check all poles for damage prior to each practice session, and do not allow athletes to leave composite poles lying flat on grass areas and stadium infields, where they can be punctured and cracked by spikes.

POLE-VAULT BOX

You can fabricate a pole-vault box without much difficulty, but be sure that it is built strongly and angled correctly at the sides to allow for the movement the pole. The box must be rigidly seated in the ground according to official specifications.

CHARACTERISTICS OF A POLE-VAULTER

A good pole-vaulter is a combination of a sprinter and a gymnast. These athletes tend to be fearless, and they enjoy the height and flight that the pole vault provides. Besides having an excellent strength-weight ratio, an excellent pole-vaulter is extremely flexible and able to withstand the hyperextension (back arch) that occurs at the moment of takeoff. Include in your program activities that emphasize stretching and flexibility plus drills that develop strength and power. In this way, your young athletes will be adequately prepared for the demands of the event.

In any instructional class, you are going to find those who want to vault and those who are afraid of this event. Many with a desire to vault may not have the strength to hang and swing on the pole, much less lift their legs above their handhold. It is important that you recognize these individual differences and make allowances for them. Don't force all of your athletes to attempt this event if there is any doubt concerning their desire or physical abilities.

TECHNIQUE

There are five basic stages in pole-vault technique: the run-up, the plant, the takeoff, the

ride and rock-back, and the bar clearance (see figure 10.1).

GRIP, CARRY, AND RUN-UP

It is a matter of individual preference on which side of the body an athlete will carry the pole. An athlete who carries the pole on the right side of the body will grip the pole from above with the fingers of the left hand. This hand is positioned just above waist height and approximately 30 cm (1′) in front of the athlete's hips. The right hand is positioned to the rear of the athlete's hips and is rotated so that the palm is facing forward. This hand grips the pole in the V formed between the fingers and the thumb. The right hand will press downward in order to balance the weight of the pole and hold the plant end of the pole off the ground. The right and left hand are approximately shoulder-width apart. (See figures 10.22a and 10.22b on page 186.)

The angle that the pole is held relative to the horizontal is a matter of individual preference. Some athletes begin their run-up with the pole pointing almost vertically skyward. Others begin their run-up with the pole at an angle of 45 degrees to the horizontal, and some athletes hold it in a horizontal position. The closer to vertical that the athlete holds the pole during the run-up, the greater the air resistance on the pole, and the greater the demand for accuracy as the pole is brought down to plant in the box. Irrespective of the angle of the pole, all athletes begin with a fast, relaxed run-up and aim to hit top speed just prior to planting the pole in the pole-vault box.

THE PLANT

The plant usually begins on the third-to-last stride. An athlete carrying the pole on the right side of the body pushes the pole forward and upward so that the right arm is extended above the head. The left arm pushes forward against the pole. The downward pull from the right arm combined with the forward push of the left arm causes the pole to flex.

THE TAKEOFF

The athlete thrusts forward directly behind the pole. The athlete's bodyweight is suspended

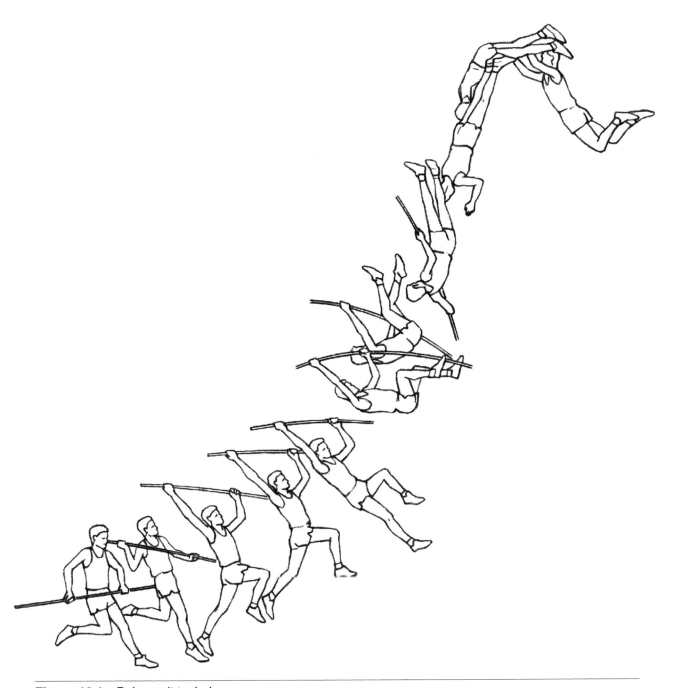

Figure 10.1 Pole-vault technique.

from the right arm, which is fully extended above the head, and the left arm, which is slightly flexed and holds lower on the pole. The leading leg is driven upward. The take-off leg trails to the rear in an extended position.

RIDE ON THE POLE AND THE ROCK-BACK PHASE

Following the takeoff, the athlete momentarily extends and hangs on the pole. The athlete then flexes at the waist and pulls upward toward the upper handhold. As the pole starts to straighten, the arms pull, and the athlete's body extends with the feet driven up close to the pole and toward the crossbar.

ACTION OVER THE BAR AND BAR CLEARANCE

A ½-rotation coupled with flexion at the hips rotates the athlete to a face-down position above the bar. The pole straightens out, helping to elevate the athlete. The athlete hyperextends (arches) the back and simultaneously pushes away from the pole. A relaxed fall onto the landing pads completes the vault.

TEACHING STEPS

STEP 1. Lead-Ups
STEP 2. Swing and ½-Rotation on the Pole
STEP 3. Intermediate Pole-Vault Skills

STEP 1: LEAD-UPS

Pole vaulting requires a combination of sprinting, jumping, and gymnastic ability. To improve sprinting and jumping ability, use the drills offered in chapters 1, 7, 8, and 9. Gymnastic floor exercises and apparatus skills on the low horizontal bar, parallel bars, rings, and ropes develop power and coordination. The teaching progressions and safety techniques for the following gymnastic skills can be obtained from most elementary and intermediate gymnastic manuals. Activities that emphasize pulling, pushing, and the development of abdominal strength are essential for success in pole vaulting.

Rope Climb

This drill develops the athlete's upper body strength and simulates the pull on the pole. Figure 10.2 shows the rope climb without the use of the legs and feet. This activity can be initially practiced on a knotted rope. The athlete uses the knots to help climb upward. Rope climb can be made more difficult by having the athlete hold the legs in a sitting V position during the climb and starting from a straddle-sit position on the floor. Remember that your athletes are most tired at the top of their climb. Make them climb small distances repeatedly rather than climb high off the ground. Be sure to teach the proper technique for holding the rope away from the body during the descent.

COACHING TIPS

- Don't climb more than 2–2½ m (6'–8') to begin with.
- Hold the rope away from your body with your feet on the way down.

- Rest and repeat the drill.
- If you want an extra challenge, try starting from a straddle-sit position on the floor.

Swinging on a Rope and Lifting the Knees

This drill develops abdominal and upper-body strength and simulates the swing and ride on the pole (see figure 10.3). Place gymnastic crash pads beneath the swing area.

COACHING TIPS

- Bend (flex) at the waist and lift your knees as you swing upward.
- Try to touch the rope as high as possible with your knees and feet.

Swinging on a Rope With Partner Assistance

The athlete runs, grabs the rope, and lifts the knees as high as possible. A partner provides assistance and more closely simulates the feel of elevation on the pole for the athlete by pulling and straightening the rope (see figure 10.4). This drill develops the athlete's upper-body and abdominal strength. Place gymnastic crash pads beneath the swing area and make sure that the partner correctly times the pull on the end of the rope.

Swinging on a Rope and Rotating Onto a Box Top

The athlete runs, grabs the rope, and swings upward to turn onto a vaulting box top or a stack of gymnastic crash pads (see figure 10.5). This drill simulates the elevation and rotation of the body on the pole and develops upper-body and abdominal strength. You may need to use spotters to stabilize the box and/or to stabilize the athlete.

COACHING TIPS

- Scissor your legs to help you rotate onto the box.
- If you fail to balance on the box top, you can hold onto the rope and swing back to the floor.

Pulling Up and Rotating on a Rope

The athlete lies on the floor and simultaneously pulls upward and rotates on the rope (see figure 10.6). This simulates the ½-rotation and upward drive on the pole. This drill also develops the athlete's shoulder and arm strength.

Figure 10.2   Rope climb.

• Pull hard and look back down at the floor to help initiate your rotation.

Pullovers on the Horizontal Bar

The athlete grips a horizontal bar and pulls up and over the bar (see figure 10.7). This drill simulates the athlete's upward pull on the pole and also helps to develop the athlete's general upper-body and abdominal strength. Initiating the action from a hang is considerably more difficult than from a jump off the floor. For beginners, use a chest-height horizontal bar and pad the bar where the athlete's body will contact it. Use undergrip, overgrip, and mixed grip (left hand over and right hand under or vice versa). Use two spotters to provide assistance and safety.

• Flex your legs and pull them up as close to the bar as possible.

• Drop your head back and pull vigorously with your arms.

Back Extension to Handstand

From a sitting position, the athlete rolls back and extends into a handstand (see figure 10.8).

Figure 10.3   Swinging on a rope and lifting the knees.

Figure 10.4 Partner-assisted rope swinging.

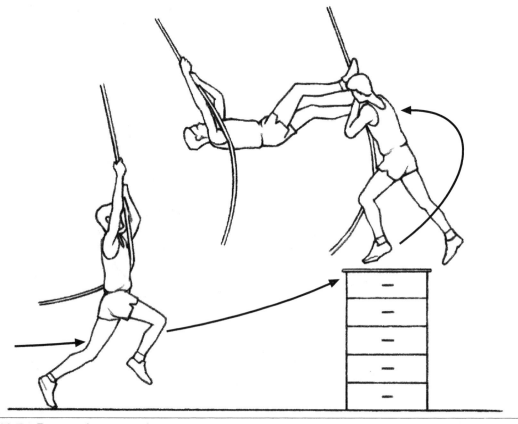

Figure 10.5 Rope swing onto a box top.

176

Figure 10.6 Pulling up and rotating on a rope.

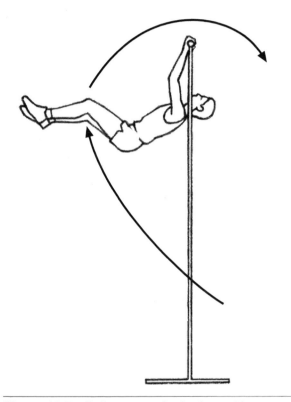

Figure 10.7 Pullovers on the horizontal bar.

This gymnastic drill should initially be practiced with spotters who grip the athlete's legs around the knees and lift upward. This drill simulates the athlete's upward drive on the pole for the bar clearance. It develops good explosive power in the athlete's arms and shoulders.

COACHING TIPS

Athlete

- Make sure your seat has rolled over past your head before you extend upward.
- Position your hands shoulder-width apart on each side of your head.

Spotters

- You stand on each side of the athlete and use a squeeze grip around the athlete's knees. As the athlete drives up into the handstand, lift the athlete's legs directly upward in a straight line above the athlete's hands.

Back Extension to Clear a Bar

The athlete does the same action as in the preceding drill, but this time the athlete does the handstand over a bar (see figure 10.9). The use of elastic tubing as a crossbar makes the back extension more closely resemble a pole-vault bar clearance. The crossbar provides the athlete with a target to clear. Begin by placing the bar at 30 cm (12") and progressively raise it with each successful clearance. See the previous drill for teaching points to emphasize.

Round-Off Along Single Sections of a Vaulting Box

The round-off is a gymnastic skill that should be learned with the help of spotters. Using single sections of vaulting boxes that you progressively increase in height will simulate the ½-rotation and the athlete's upward thrust, which occurs during the bar clearance (see figure 10.10).

COACHING TIPS

Athlete

- Practice this drill at floor level before trying it on sections of the vaulting box. Have spotters assist you in your handstand position and help you to complete your ½-turn.

Figure 10.8 Back extension to a handstand.

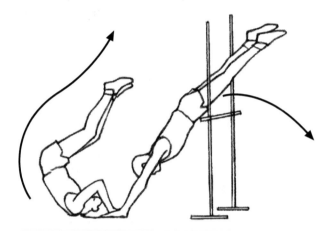

Figure 10.9 Back extension to clear a bar.

- Rotate your last hand placement and turn the fingers of this hand back toward your approach. Bring your legs together to assist in rotating your body.
- Your hips and legs must pass directly over your hands.
- Pull your stomach in, and don't arch your back.

Spotters
- Stand at the midpoint of the skill where the athlete passes through the handstand position. Face the athlete's back. Grip the athlete with one hand on either hip and help turn the athlete through the ½-rotation.

Underswing on a Low Horizontal Bar

An underswing on the low horizontal bar requires the athlete to swing under the bar

and thrust the legs vertically upward. The athlete simultaneously presses the arms backward and upward so that they are extended above the head. This motion pushes the athlete upward and outward from the bar (see figure 10.11). The athlete must remember to let go of the bar once the arms are fully extended. Spotters should be ready to cradle the athlete through the flight path to the landing.

Be sure this gymnastic skill is practiced with the help of spotters. It develops upper-body and abdominal strength and simulates the upward drive on the pole. Use gymnastic floor exercise mats under the bar.

COACHING TIPS

Athlete
- Flex (pike) at the hips and bring your feet close to the bar for the underswing.
- Extend your body and push away from the bar for the dismount.
- Try to get a high, arching flight path as you push away from the bar.

Spotters
- Stand on either side of the athlete at the midpoint of the flight path. Make sure that the athlete doesn't fall backward.

Underswing and ½-Turn Dismount on the Horizontal Bar

This skill is similar to the underswing dismount with the exception that a ½ rotation is initiated

Figure 10.10 Round-off along vaulting boxes.

Figure 10.11 Underswing on a low horizontal bar.

during the underswing and is completed after the bar has been released. The ½ rotation is initiated with a scissoring action of the legs. Once the ½ rotation has been set in motion, the athlete must release the bar (see figure 10.12).

Athletes should initially practice this drill on a low horizontal bar (set at chest height) with assistance from spotters. This drill simulates the athlete's elevation on the pole together with rotation of the athlete's body over the bar. This drill develops the athlete's upper-body and abdominal strength.

Athlete

- Perform the underswing and scissor your legs in the air to initiate your rotation.
- Release your right hand when rotating to the left or vice versa.
- Push away and release the bar for your dismount.

Spotters

- Stand on either side at the midpoint of the athlete's flight path and make sure

Figure 10.12 Underswing and $\frac{1}{2}$-turn dismount on the horizontal bar.

that the athlete doesn't stumble back toward the bar.

Dynamic Push-Ups to Clear a Low Obstacle

These explosive push-ups (press-ups) simulate the upward drive for bar clearance in pole vault (see figure 10.13). A small block of sponge rubber is a safe obstacle to use in this drill.

COACHING TIPS

- Flex your arms only slightly, not all the way. Then extend them explosively.
- Push hard from your fingertips.

STEP 2: SWING AND $\frac{1}{2}$-ROTATION ON THE POLE

A swing and $\frac{1}{2}$ rotation on the pole will require the athlete to run up, plant, and swing on the pole. During the swing on the pole the athlete will perform a $\frac{1}{2}$ rotation in order to land facing back toward the pole vault box. There are several fundamental skills that must be learned in order to perform the swing and $\frac{1}{2}$ rotation on the pole. These are discussed on the following pages.

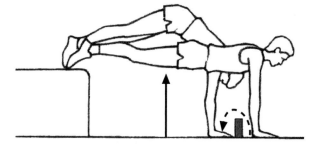

Figure 10.13 Dynamic push-ups to clear a low obstacle.

Finding the Direction of Bend in a Composite Pole

When a composite vaulting pole is flexed, the side of the pole on the outside of the curve is specifically manufactured to bend, stretch, and rebound back to its original shape. The side of the pole on the inside of the curve is designed to rebound back to its original shape after being compressed. By calling this side the soft side, manufacturers indicate what side of the pole should be on the inside of the curve when it is flexed.

Opposing this soft side is the strong side of the pole that must line up with the outside of the curve when the athlete flexes the pole. For an athlete who carries the pole on the right side of the body during the run-up, the side of the pole that will eventually be on the outside of the curve must face downward and be angled slightly toward the right. When the athlete plants the pole in the box for the takeoff, the pole is then lifted upward and rotated into a position directly ahead of the athlete's body. In this position, the strong side of the pole will end up facing forward and slightly to the left. The pole flexes toward the left, and the athlete swings up on the right side of the pole and on the inside of the curve. The soft side of the pole will be on the inside of the curve facing toward the athlete.

Athletes who carry the pole on the left side of the body will have the pole flex toward the right. The strong side will face forward and to the right, and the athlete will swing up on the left side of the pole with the soft side of the pole on the inside of the curve.

If you have an unmarked pole, you can find its direction of flex by having your athlete lift the pole to chest height at the grip end and letting the pole rotate freely in one hand with the tip of the pole on the ground. The strong side will face down, and the soft side will face up. Another method is to allow the pole to roll while it is supported on a hurdle (see figure 10.14). Again the strong side will face down, and the soft side will face up.

Swinging on the Pole From a Low Height

The athlete stands on 2 sections of vaulting box and plants the pole in the sand at the take-off end of a long-jump pit (see figure 10.15). This drill will also be effective if the pole is planted in the pole-vault box and the athlete swings forward onto the landing pads. An athlete who carries the pole on the right side of the body will grip the pole at shoulder height with the left hand. The right arm is fully extended, with the right hand gripping the pole above the head. In this drill, the pole will not flex.

- Look forward on the left side of the pole and swing on the right side of the pole.
- Push away with your feet from the vaulting box and swing as far out as possible onto the sand pit (or onto the landing pad).

VARIATION

Lay ropes across the sand pit to form distance zones. Athletes compete to reach the furthest zone that they can with their feet. This drill will encourage your athletes to flex at the waist and to pull with their arms. Make sure the sand pit is well dug.

Experiencing the Flexion of the Pole and Swinging From Greater Height Into a Sand Pit

Use all the sections of your vaulting box to create a height that requires a higher handhold on the pole. This higher handhold will give novices a feel for the flexion of a composite pole. As in the preceding drill, the athlete plants the pole in the sand at the take-off end of the long-jump pit or in the pole-vault box (see figure 10.16). If the pole-vault box is used, the athlete will land on the pole-vault landing pads.

COACHING TIPS

- Hang and swing on the pole. Don't try to raise your legs.
- Push away strongly from the box.
- Your higher handhold on the pole will cause the pole to flex a little.
- As you drop toward the sand (or the landing pads), you'll feel the pole straighten out.

Finding Vertical Reach on the Pole

Before swinging on the pole from a short run-up, the athletes need to find their vertical reach position on the pole. This is the spot reached

Figure 10.14 Finding the direction of bend in a fiberglass pole.

Figure 10.15 Swinging on the pole from a low height.

by the athlete's outstretched arm on a pole held vertically, with the tip of the pole in the pole-vault box (see figure 10.17). Holding 5–10 cm (2"–4") above this position on the pole will allow a novice to hang on the pole but be lifted a minimal distance from the ground.

Swinging on the Pole From a Short Run-Up

To have your athletes swing on a pole from a short run-up, you should hold the pole in the box ready for an athlete who will run up and then grip the pole. You can plant the butt end of the pole in the sand at the take-off end of the long-jump pit (or you can use the pole-vault box). Hold the pole at an angle so that approaching athletes will grip it approximately 5–10 cm (2"–4") above their vertical reach positions. A short unmeasured run-up can be used for this drill. The athletes run to grip the pole (see figure 10.18). You assist them in swinging through to land in the sand or onto the pole-vault landing pad. The athletes must

tell you which side of the pole they will swing on by calling out "left" or "right" before running up. You shift to the opposing side of the pole according to the athlete's call.

COACHING TIPS

These tips are for an athlete swinging on the right side of the pole:

- Run at a jogging speed with your right arm extended above your head and your left arm forward ahead of your chest in a flexed position. Your left hand will grip the pole in front of your chest. Your right hand will grip the pole above your head.

- Don't try to lift your legs upward when you're gripping the pole. Just hang on and swing on the pole.

Measuring a 5-Stride Run-Up

In order to pole-vault, an athlete must have a measured approach. A 5-stride run-up is adequate for young athletes. An athlete carrying

Figure 10.16 Swinging into a sand pit.

5–10 cm

Figure 10.17 Finding vertical reach on the pole.

the pole on the right side of the body measures a run-up in the following manner:

1. The athlete stands with the right arm extended upward beside a pole held vertically in the pole-vault box. A position 5–10 cm (2"–4") above where the athlete's hand touches the pole becomes the athlete's upper handhold on the pole. An athlete carrying the pole on the right side of the body will grip the pole at this spot with the right hand.

2. With the base of the pole still in the pole-vault box, the pole is angled downward so that the athlete can grip the spot designated for the upper hand hold. The athlete's right arm is fully extended above the head and the left hand grips the pole ahead of the body at shoulder height. The athlete stands directly below the upper handhold and to simulate the takeoff, raises the right thigh. A partner marks the position of the left foot on the ground. Holding the pole in the carry position and beginning

Figure 10.18 Swinging on the pole from a short run-up.

with the left foot, the athlete runs back 5 strides. A partner marks the fifth stride.

3. After the run-up is measured, the athlete runs up without carrying the pole. You hold the pole in the pole vault box ready at the correct angle. An athlete who would carry the pole on the right side of the body begins a 5-stride run-up with the first step taken with the left leg. On the fifth stride, the left foot should be beneath the upper handhold (the right hand). The athlete's right thigh is driven upward in preparation for the swing on the pole (see figure 10.19).

COACHING TIPS

- After you have found the position of your takeoff foot under the pole, turn around and place your feet together ready to start your run back.

- Starting with your feet together, run back 5 even strides at moderate speed.

- If you carry the pole on the right side of your body, start your run back by taking the first stride with your left foot.

- When you run up, start with your left foot and count your strides out loud as you run. I'll hold the pole ready for you.

- If your left foot is ahead of its correct position beneath the upper handhold after 5 strides, note the difference and shift back the start of your run-up an equal amount.

- Shift your starting position forward if your left foot is to the rear of its correct position.

Run-Up With the Pole Held in Plant Position

After running up without carrying the pole, the athletes now carry the pole themselves. You will still stand close to where the pole is planted in order to assist. To simplify the plant action for novices, the athlete can run up using a short practice pole held above the head in the plant position (see figure 10.20). The pole remains in this position throughout the 5-stride run-up. The pole can be planted in the sand of the long-jump pit, or you can use the pole-vault box.

COACHING TIPS

- Run directly behind the pole.

- Keep the pole in position with the tip just off the surface of the run-up.

- Keep your eye on the pole-vault box and be ready to plant the pole in the box.

Swing and ½-Rotation on the Pole

In this drill, the athlete uses a 5-stride run-up, holding the pole above the head in the plant position. The athlete plants the pole in the sand at the take-off end of the long-jump pit and

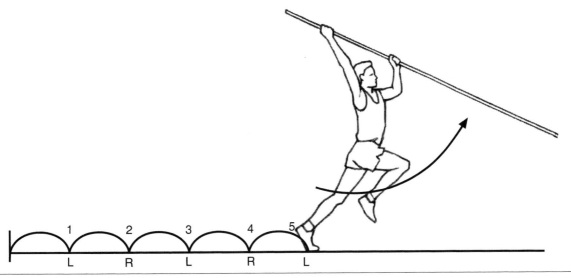

Figure 10.19 5-stride run-up (right-handed).

Figure 10.20 Run-up with pole in plant position.

swings both legs together on the same side of the pole (right side for a right-handed vaulter). A ½-rotation completes the swing, and the athlete lands standing in the sand (see figure 10.21).

COACHING TIPS

- Swing first, lift your legs, and then pull with your arms.
- Look back toward the takeoff and scissor your legs; your body will rotate.
- Hold on to the pole. There's no need to let go.

Elementary Pole Vault: No Pole Carry

Using a 5-stride run-up, a swing, and a ½-rotation, the novice now attempts to clear a cross-

bar set at chest height. You hold the pole in the pole-vault box at the correct angle for each athlete. In this way, the athlete experiences an elementary vault without having to carry the pole. Vaulters swinging on the right side of the pole will start their 5-stride run-up with the left leg.

STEP 3: INTERMEDIATE POLE-VAULT SKILLS

Figure 10.22a illustrates the pole carry as seen from the side. Figure 10.22b illustrates the pole carry as seen from behind. The athlete carries the pole at the side of the body with the tip of the pole elevated to approximately shoulder height. A wide

Figure 10.21 Swing and $\frac{1}{2}$ rotation.

grip makes the pole easy to carry. For an athlete carrying the pole on the right side of the body, the pole rests on the thumb of the left hand, which is at waist height and ahead of the hips. The fingers of the left hand grip the pole from above. The right hand is rotated palm forward and presses downward, balancing the weight of the pole.

Sprinting With the Pole

On grass, have your athletes run short sprints of 15–20 m with the pole (see figure 10.23). They start with the tip of the pole elevated to head height, and as they sprint they lower the pole to horizontal and then down to ground level to slide it along the grass.

COACHING TIPS

- Relax as you run.
- Avoid too much shoulder shrugging or pushing back and forth with the pole.
- Keep the tip of the pole directly ahead of you; don't let it wander from left to right.

Simulating the Pole Plant From a 5-Stride Run-Up

Athletes first practice this drill on grass. Athletes simulate the plant of the pole into the

Figure 10.22 Two views of the pole carry.

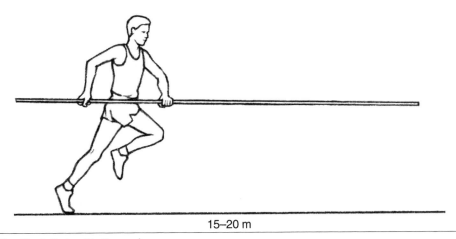

15–20 m

Figure 10.23 Sprinting with the pole.

pole-vault box by pushing the tip of the pole along the ground (see figure 10.24). The athlete initially walks through the sequence and then progressively increases the speed of action.

The sequence of a 5-stride run-up and pole plant for an athlete carrying the pole on the right side of the body is as follows.

1. The athlete starts with the feet together, holding the pole in carry position with the upper handhold at 5–10 cm (2"–4") above vertical reach position.

2. On stride 1 (left foot forward), the pole remains in carry position.

3. On stride 2 (right foot forward), the arms start to push the pole forward. The left arm is extended, and the right hand on the pole moves forward past the body.

4. On stride 3 (left foot forward), the athlete extends the left arm forward and uses the right hand to push the pole upward past the right shoulder.

5. On stride 4 (right foot forward), the athlete extends the arms with the right hand positioned directly above the head. The base of the pole is almost touching the ground.

6. On stride 5, the athlete steps forward with the left foot, drives the right thigh upward, and hops on the left foot. (The hop simulates the jump that the athlete takes at takeoff.) The right arm remains extended above the head, and the tip of the pole slides along the ground.

Instructor's

Count:	left	right	left	right	left	hop
Stride:	1	2	3	4	5	

Practicing the Pole Plant

Athletes can also practice the pole plant slowly and mechanically from a 3-stride approach. In this drill, you can put benches end to end to form an elevated platform along which the athletes can perform their 3-stride approach (see figure 10.25). The extra height of the benches allows the plant of the pole to be performed slowly and methodically. The pole is planted into the sand of a long-jump pit or slid along the grass. There is no takeoff in this drill.

Instructor's Count:	left	right	left
Stride:	1	2	3

Combining a 5-Stride Run-Up and Plant

The sequence for this drill is as follows:

1. Each athlete first measures a 5-stride run-up from the end of the long-jump pit.

2. The athlete plants the pole in the sand (take-off end of the long-jump pit) and holds the pole in the take-off position with the right thigh raised and upper arm extended. The left foot is directly below the upper handhold. The right hand holds the pole 5–10 cm (2"–4") above vertical reach with the lower hand at shoulder height. A partner marks the position of the left foot.

3. The athlete turns around on the mark and places both feet together, holding the pole in the carry position. Beginning with the left foot, the athlete runs 5 strides, and a partner marks the fifth stride.

4. The athlete starts the 5-stride approach with the feet together, taking the first stride with

Figure 10.24 Simulating the pole plant from a 5-stride run-up.

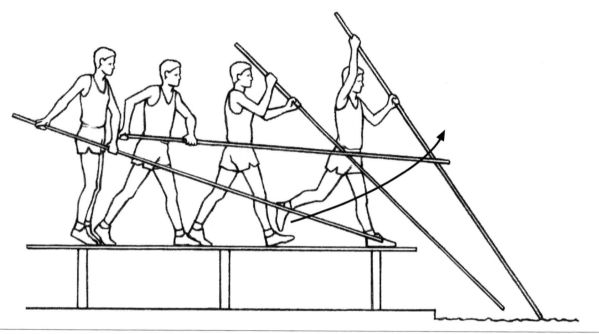

Figure 10.25 Practicing the pole plant using benches.

the left foot. The hopping action previously practiced on the grass now becomes a takeoff followed by an easy swing on the pole. The athlete makes no effort at this stage to elevate the legs and swings through to land standing in the sand. You stand by to assist at takeoff.

Transferring a 5-Stride Run-Up and Pole Plant to the Pole-Vault Run-Up

Athletes repeat the preceding drill, using the pole-vault run-up and planting the pole in the pole-vault box. At takeoff, athletes raise their legs and

swing to land on the pole-vault landing pads in a sitting position. No crossbar is used.

COACHING TIPS

- Drive the pole forward and upward during the last 2 strides of the pole plant.
- Stay directly behind the pole at takeoff.
- Extend your right arm.
- With your left arm, push forward into the pole.
- Raise your legs and swing on the pole and land in a sitting position.
- Hold onto the pole.

Increasing the Length of the Pole Vault Run-Up and Using Check Marks

With practice, the athlete progressively increases the run-up from 5 to 7 strides and from 7 to 9 strides. Later the run-up can be increased to 11 and 13 strides. Measure the longer run-ups in the same manner as for the 5-stride run-up. Use check marks on the longer run-up to ensure accuracy during the approach. In the 9-stride run-up illustrated in figure 10.26, the fifth stride has a check mark. Elite athletes will frequently use a second check mark, which is often placed at the first stride of the run-up.

Learning to Flex the Pole

This practice teaches the athlete to coordinate the plant with actions that emphasize flexion of the pole. No takeoff occurs, and all actions are performed at high speed. The complete action is initially performed from 2 or 3 strides. The athlete thrusts the pole forward in the pole plant action into the pole-vault box. The athlete's bodyweight moving forward flexes the pole (see figure 10.27). The pull of the athlete's upper arm and the push of the lower arm assists in this action. In this drill, make sure that

the athlete is ready for the rebound of the pole after it is flexed. The pole will drive the athlete back toward the run-up. This drill demands excellent timing and is extremely tiring.

COACHING TIPS

• Get the pole above your head as fast as possible in the pole plant.
• Straighten your right arm.
• Be sure your left elbow and wrist are directly below the bend of the pole.
• Drive your right knee upward toward your left hand.
• Be prepared for the rebound of the pole.

Emphasizing the Rock-Back Action After Takeoff

This practice requires the athlete to rock backward after takeoff so that the athlete's back is parallel to the ground. Backward rotation of the body occurs at the shoulder axis. The hips and knees are flexed as the rock-back occurs, so they are ready for the thrust of the athlete's body upward above the handhold (see figure 10.28).

To perform this drill, an athlete carrying the pole on the right side of the body must have

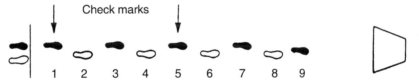

Figure 10.26 Using check marks on a 9-pace run-up.

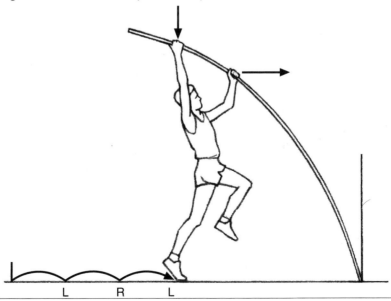

Figure 10.27 Flexing the pole.

enough speed in the run-up to force the pole into a bend that angles forward and across to the left side of the pit. Elite athletes will often perform this rock-back practice and then lower the legs after they have been driven upward so that they can land standing on the landing pads.

Use rubber tubing for a crossbar and set it at about 60 cm (24") above the height of the athlete's upper handhold. The pole-vault standards are placed 60 cm (24") to the rear of the pole-vault box. This positions the rubber tubing so that the athlete can use it as a target for the feet.

COACHING TIPS

- Hang from your upper hand-hold and drop your shoulders back.

- Flex your legs and swing them upward, driving your feet up toward the target (the crossbar).

- Try to touch the crossbar with your feet.

Elevating the Body Above the Handhold

After the rock-back, the pole will be flexed, and the athlete's hips will rise above the lower handhold. As the pole begins to straighten out, the athlete's hips and feet must be driven upward (see figure 10.29). The athlete pulls vigorously on the pole when the hips are as high as possible. The athlete's pull, coupled with a scissoring action of the legs, initiates the ½-rotation to put the athlete facing down-

ward for the bar clearance. The final push and release with the upper hand completes the vault. Rubber tubing set 60 cm (24") above the height of the upper handhold provides an adequate target. The standards are placed approximately 60 cm (24") to the rear of the box.

COACHING TIPS

- Keep your feet close to the pole during your upward pull.

- Remember to pull at the same time that your pole straightens out.

- Pull and turn to face down toward the crossbar.

Practicing the Pull, Rotation, and Push on the Pole

An athlete can practice the pull, rotation, and push with the pole in the box (see figure 10.30). The action is performed as dynamically and vigorously as possible.

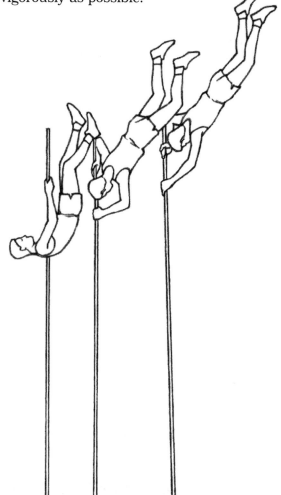

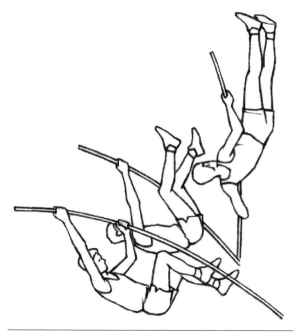

Figure 10.28 The rock-back action.

Figure 10.29 Elevating the body above the handhold.

COACHING TIPS

- Drop back against the pole to give it some flexion.
- As it rebounds, pull, rotate, and push as quickly as possible.

Bar Clearance

The bar clearance is a relatively easy movement to perform, although the timing has to be precise. The athlete drives as forcefully as possible against the pole in order to complete the upward push. An arch (hyperextension) of the athlete's back muscles helps to elevate the athlete's upper body and clear the bar (see figure 10.31).

COACHING TIPS

- Think of pushing your shoulders backward. This will help you arch away from the bar.

- Time your arch so that it occurs as the legs and trunk drop downward. This will help you rotate away from the bar.

Raising the Handhold and Lengthening the Run-Up

As confidence and ability increases, the athlete's run-up is progressively increased in length. Greater speed in the run-up allows for a higher handhold and more flexion in the pole. It also increases the time that the athlete has available to maneuver on the pole. Run-ups of 13 and 15 strides can produce 3½–4 m vaults.

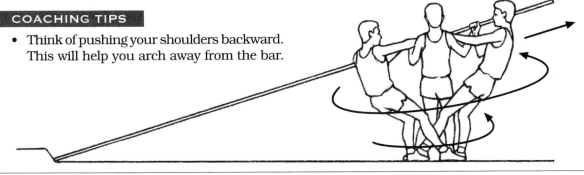

Figure 10.30 Practicing pull, rotation, and push on the pole.

Figure 10.31 Bar clearance.

COMMON ERRORS AND CORRECTIONS

Error	Reasons	Corrections
The upper arm is flexed during takeoff.	The athlete's grip is incorrectly positioned on the pole. The speed of the run-up and the body position below the pole at takeoff vary from one attempt to the next.	Have the athlete take off from a vaulting box and practice swinging on the pole with the upper arm extended. The athlete should remeasure the the run-up and swing on the pole from a 5-stride run-up. The athlete must hold the pole ready in the take-off position. The athlete should emphasize a fully extended upper arm.
The athlete's chest hits the pole during takeoff.	The athlete's left arm collapses and does not keep the athlete's body away from the pole. The athlete's chest rests against the pole during the vault.	Use a pole appropriate for the athlete's bodyweight and that the young athlete can flex easily. The athlete should hang from the pole with the right arm and use the effect of the run-up to push forward against the pole with the left arm.
The athlete takes off with the body too far to the side of the pole.	The athlete is afraid of swinging on the pole and raising the legs. The athlete is not directly to the rear of the pole at takeoff.	The athlete should work on having the chest directly behind the pole at takeoff. The takeoff and swing should be practiced slowly and mechanically from an elevated position (from a row of benches or a vaulting box top).
The athlete's legs are not elevated during the swing.	The athlete is trying to raise the legs by pulling upward with the arms by themselves. The athlete may be trying to raise the legs without any flexion at the knees. The athlete may have poor abdominal strength.	The athlete should keep the upper arm extended and raise the legs by dropping the the shoulders back and flexing the legs at the knees. The athlete should work on developing abdominal strength.
The athlete's swing and ½-rotation are incomplete. The athlete performs a ¼-rotation or no rotation at all.	The athlete's legs are not elevated. There's no pull-and-turn action from the athlete's arms, and the athlete's head is not turned back toward the run-up. The athlete probably has poor abdominal and shoulder strength.	Instruct the athlete to practice the swing and ½-rotation on a rope. The athlete should also practice the underswing dismount with ½-rotation on the low horizontal bar. The athlete should practice general upper-body and abdominal exercises.

→

INTERMEDIATE AND ADVANCED POLE-VAULT SKILLS
(performed without instructor assistance)

Error	Reasons	Corrections
The athlete's run-up is inaccurate and varies each time. The athlete slows down during the run-up.	The athlete's ability to run with the pole is poor. The athlete is afraid of the takeoff and the ride on the pole. The athlete's measurement of the run-up is incorrect. The athlete's run-up may be too long, and the position of check marks is incorrect.	Have the athlete remeasure the run-up. The athlete should practice sprinting with the pole and work to improve sprint endurance. To improve accuracy in the approach, have the athlete practice from a shorter run-up.
The athlete's take-off foot is not directly below the upper hand-hold at takeoff. The pole jerks in the athlete's hand at takeoff.	The athlete's run-up is poorly measured, or the speed of the athlete's run varies with each approach. The athlete's upper arm may not be extended at takeoff.	Have the athlete remeasure the run-up, making sure that the speed used running back from the take-off spot is the same speed as used in the approach run. The athlete should aim for smooth, regular acceleration in the run-up.
The athlete's take-off foot is too far to one side at takeoff. The athlete's take-off foot is not directly below the pole at takeoff.	The athlete overemphasizes the swing of the body to the side of the pole. The athlete is not directly behind the pole at takeoff.	Instruct the athlete to practice the pole plant from a short run-up. Place check marks on the ground to assist in foot positioning. The athlete must concentrate on having the body directly to the rear of the pole at takeoff.
The athlete's legs and hips are not elevated after takeoff.	The athlete is afraid of dropping the shoulders back and lifting the legs. The athlete may have insufficient abdominal power. There's no upward drive with the thigh of the athlete's leading leg at takeoff.	Assign the athlete strength and power exercises for the upper body, arms, and abdomen. Use gymnastic, rope, and pole activities in which the athlete lifts the lower body upward.
The athlete extends the body too early instead of maintaining the flexion at the waist and lifting the legs upward toward the crossbar.	The timing of the extension of the athlete's body is incorrect. The athlete is hurrying the extension of the body instead of waiting for the completion of the swing. The athlete's shoulders do not rock backward, and the athlete's feet are not raised upward.	Assign rock-back and extension activities using ropes and poles. Instruct the athlete to drive the feet upward parallel to the rope or the pole. Give the athlete verbal assistance on timing of the extension of the body.

→

Error	Reasons	Corrections
The pole does not flex sufficiently, and no energy is stored in the pole.	The pole may be too stiff for the athlete's bodyweight and strength. The athlete's grip is too close (right hand too close to the left hand), and the athlete's grip may be too low on the pole. The athlete's lower arm is not pushing forward into the pole. The athlete's run-up speed prior to the pole plant may be too slow.	Check the pole specifications relative to the athlete's body-weight. Check the athlete's grip height and grip width. Have the athlete practice the plant and pole flexion from a short run-up.
The athlete and pole slow down as they rise upward and they fail to reach a vertical position.	The athlete is running too slowly during the run-up, and the grip is too high on the pole. The athlete's legs and hips may be elevated too early.	Have the athlete work on improving sprinting ability with the pole. Check the athlete's grip height and lower it if it is too high. Instruct the athlete to wait until the pole begins to straighten before pulling the body upward. Provide verbal assistance on timing.
The athlete has too little time to complete the vault and knocks the bar off on the way up.	The athlete's grip on the pole may be too low. The athlete may have elevated the legs and hips when the pole was close to vertical. Extension of the body above the handhold occurs too late. The athlete's center of gravity may not be directly below the upper hand-hold at takeoff. The position of the standards and the crossbar may be incorrect.	The athlete must raise the grip on the pole and remeasure the run-up and takeoff so that the athlete's body is directly below the upper handhold at takeoff. Have the athlete practice the complete vault, working to correct the timing for the elevation and extension of the body above the handhold. Check that the position of the standards puts the crossbar directly below the high point of the athlete's bar clearance.
The athlete knocks the bar off on the way down.	The athlete swings up too early. The athlete's center of gravity is not directly below the upper handhold at takeoff. The position of the standards and the crossbar may be incorrect.	Have the athlete remeasure the run-up so that the athlete's center of gravity is directly below the upper handhold at takeoff. Provide verbal assistance during the takeoff and the pull and extension up toward the crossbar. Check that the position of the standards puts the crossbar directly below the high point of the athlete's bar clearance.

→

Error

The athlete fails to perform the ½-rotation and never achieves the face-down position over the bar.

Reasons

The athlete's feet are too far away from the pole during the upward pull. The legs and hips drop away from the pole.

Corrections

Have the athlete practice with the rope and pole, pulling and rotating with the feet as close to the rope and pole as possible. Work to improve athlete's abdominal and upper-body strength.

ASSESSMENT

1. **Assess the following theoretical elements as taught during instructional sessions:**

   a. Fundamental rules governing the pole vault.

   b. Good safety habits for the pole vault.

   c. Basic elements of pole-vault technique.

   d. Basic elements of training for the pole vault.

2. **Assess the performance of technique during the following stages of skill development:**

   a. Athletes run to swing on the pole, which you hold ready for them.

   b. Athletes run to swing and perform a ½-turn on the pole while you hold it.

   c. Athletes run up carrying the pole in plant position. They swing and perform a ½-turn on the pole.

   d. Athletes perform the plant action with the pole, using a 5-stride approach on grass.

   e. Athletes perform the run-up, pole carry (pole at the side of the body), plant, and swing. They don't elevate the hips and legs, and no ½-rotation is required.

   f. Athletes perform a run-up, pole carry (pole at the side of the body), plant, swing, and elevation of the hips and legs. No ½-rotation is included.

   g. Athletes use a short run-up and plant and flex the pole without taking off.

   h. Athletes perform the complete vault from an extended run-up.

   CRITICAL FEATURES OF TECHNIQUE TO OBSERVE DURING ASSESSMENT

   ✓ Gripping and carrying the pole.

   ✓ Accelerating through the run-up.

   ✓ Pushing the pole forward and upward and taking off with the athlete's body directly below an extended right arm.

   ✓ Flexing the pole from the forward push of the lower arm, combined with the downward pull of the upper arm.

   ✓ Flexing the legs and hips during the ride on the pole.

   ✓ Pulling with the arms and extending the body upward close to the pole as the pole straightens.

✓ Rotating 180 degrees and flexing at the hips to achieve a piked position above the bar.

✓ Hyperextending and pushing away from the pole for the release and landing.

3. **Hold graded competitions to develop motivation and technique. (Use the rubber tubing as a crossbar throughout.)**

   a. Athletes compete for distance in the long-jump pit using just the swing on the pole. (You assist with the pole at takeoff.)

   b. Athletes compete for height using an elementary swing and ½-rotation on the pole. (You assist with the pole at takeoff.)

   c. Athletes compete for height using a run-up, swing, and ½-rotation on the pole. The athletes carry the pole in plant position above the head during the run-up, and you assist with the pole at takeoff if necessary.

   d. Athletes compete using full competitive conditions.

SUGGESTED STANDARDS OF PERFORMANCE—POLE VAULT

MALE

Age		Height
14-15	Satisfactory	2.10 m (6'11")
	Good	2.40 m (7'10")
	Excellent	2.60 m (8'6")
16-17	Satisfactory	2.40 m (7'10")
	Good	2.70 m (8'10")
	Excellent	2.90 m (9'6")
18-19	Satisfactory	2.60 m (8'6")
	Good	2.90 m (9'6")
	Excellent	3.10 m (10'2")

FEMALE

Age		Height
14-15	Satisfactory	1.80 m (5'10")
	Good	2.00 m (6'7")
	Excellent	2.20 m (7'2")
16-17	Satisfactory	1.90 m (6'3")
	Good	2.20 m (7'2")
	Excellent	2.40 m (7'10")
18-19	Satisfactory	2.10 m (6'11")
	Good	2.40 m (7'10")
	Excellent	2.60 m (8'6")

Part III

THROWING EVENTS

11

SHOT PUT

The shot put is an individual event in the Olympic Games for males and females and is dominated by big, powerful athletes. It is also included as an event in the men's decathlon and the women's heptathlon.

A major advance in the technique of shot put occurred in the 1950s when Olympic champion Parry O'Brien changed his technique and began his glide (shift) across the ring facing the rear of the ring rather than facing to the side. This method, known as the *O'Brien* or *glide* technique, is used by the majority of modern shot-putters.

A technique gaining popularity is the *rotary* technique. This method of throwing employs a discus-style rotation across the shot-put ring rather than a glide. Both the glide and rotational techniques have been equally successful in achieving long throws.

There are two major reasons why the rotary method of throwing is more difficult to master than the backward shift required in the glide technique. First, the rotary technique has to be performed by a very big athlete in the tight confines of a shot-put ring—a ring that is only 2.135 m (7') in diameter. The shot-put ring is considerably smaller than a discus ring, which is 2.5 m

(8' 2½") in diameter. Second, the spinning rotary action of the shot put makes control of the shot more difficult than if the athlete uses the glide technique. Because of these technical difficulties it's best that you teach the glide technique first. After your athlete has been taught how to spin across the ring and throw a discus, then the athlete can experiment with the rotary shot-put technique.

One important feature with both the glide and rotary techniques is that the shot must stay in contact with the athlete's neck until the final putting (pushing) action occurs. In this chapter, we will talk about athletes throwing the shot. Keep in mind that the athlete can use any throwing action as long as the shot stays in contact with the athlete's neck up to the instant that the shot is pushed by one hand out into the throwing sector. The rules do not allow an athlete to spin around with the shot held at arm's length!

SAFETY SUGGESTIONS

When teaching the shot put, be sure that you choose shot that are appropriate to the strength and hand sizes of your athletes. A large selection of shot that vary both in weight and size will help you achieve this objective. Shot should range from .5 kg (1.1 lbs.) up to competitive weights, 7.25 kg (16 lbs.) for men and 4 kg (8 lbs., 13 oz.) for women. From experience, you will be able to assess whether a shot is too light or too heavy for the athlete using it. As a general rule, the shot should be heavy enough to require a putting (pushing) action, but not light enough to allow the athlete to throw it easily, like a ball.

A good warm-up of jogging, stretching, and light exercises is necessary. In particular, the ligaments and muscles of the wrists and hands should be warmed up for the explosive actions that characterize this event. Even when the athlete uses correct technique, a poor warm-up can cause ligament and muscle injuries.

All shot must be safely stored and then carried to the throwing circles for each instructional session. Don't allow athletes to throw or play with the shot (or any throwing implements) during the time that they are being transported from one area to another.

Although the shot travels a far shorter distance than the discus, javelin, or hammer, shot put still demands rigorous safety regulations to which all must adhere. Most problems occur from lack of communication between the athlete and whoever is (often unknowingly) in the line of flight. Shot-putters begin both the glide and rotational technique facing away from the direction of throw, so these athletes are momentarily blind to what is happening in the throwing sector. When athletes are practicing, those waiting to throw should act as observers. The observers make sure that no one has moved into the throwing sector, and they also make sure that athletes acting as officials have finished measuring and are well out of the line of flight before the next athlete throws.

During competition as well as during training, all spectators (and those waiting to throw) should stand at least 3–4 m (10'–14') to the immediate rear of the ring. Experienced officials will stand close to the ring in order to check for foot violations, but their proximity to the ring is based on a firm understanding of the particular characteristics of the event. Right- and left-handed throwers require different officiating positions.

The rotary technique of shot put has increased the need for vigilance by those conducting the event. This is particularly the case when athletes try the rotary technique for the first time. Because of the outward pull of the shot when the athlete rotates across the ring, it is not unusual for beginners to lose the shot at the midpoint of the rotation or when the shot is being pushed away from the athlete's body. This is one reason why it is better that mature athletes practice this technique under your supervision. Remember that the glide technique is far easier to perform than the rotating technique and has virtually the same rate of success in producing long throws. Nonathletes and spectators should stand at least 4 m (14') to the rear of the ring when the rotary technique is being practiced.

GLIDE TECHNIQUE

The fundamental movement pattern of the glide technique has not changed since its invention in the 1950s, even though bigger and more powerful athletes have dramatically increased the distances thrown. The following description of this technique refers to a right-handed thrower.

PREPARATION

The athlete stands at the rear of the ring with the back toward the direction of the throw. The athlete's weight is on the right leg, and the athlete's line of vision is directly to the rear. The athlete cradles the shot under the chin. The left arm is extended and pointed toward the rear.

GLIDE

The athlete flexes the right leg and lowers the upper body close to horizontal in preparation for the backward shift (glide) across the ring. The left leg is kicked backward, and simultaneously the right leg drives the athlete toward the center of the ring. The upper body stays in its lowered position. At the end of the glide, the athlete pulls the right leg in under the body and places the left foot in position at the front of the circle. At the end of the glide, the upper body is still inclined toward the rear of the ring.

THE PUT

The athlete begins the final putting action by applying force from the ground up in the following sequence: legs, hips, chest, and finally the throwing arm. The athlete's legs extend in a rotary fashion toward the direction of throw. Then the athlete's hips rotate in the same direction followed by a forward and upward thrust of the athlete's chest. The right side of the athlete's body rotates forward and upward around an extended left leg. A powerful extension of the athlete's throwing arm and fingers pushes the shot away from the athlete's neck. This characteristic putting (pushing) action completes the throw (see figure 11.1). After the shot has left the athlete's hand, the athlete's legs reverse positions. The athlete's left leg moves backward from the front of the ring, and the right leg moves forward against the stop board to prevent the athlete from falling out of the front of the ring and fouling the throw. This leg switch is called a *reverse*.

ROTARY TECHNIQUE

The rotary technique uses a discus thrower's footwork in the first ⅔ of the throw. The final putting action resembles that used in the glide technique. The following description of this technique refers to a right-handed thrower. The athlete stands in a shoulder-width stance at the rear of the ring with the back toward the direction of throw. The athlete cradles the shot in the neck. The legs are slightly flexed, and the vision and free arm are directed toward the rear.

ROTATION

A right-handed thrower first winds up by rotating the shoulders and shot toward the right. The athlete then rotates toward the left in discus style by pivoting on the balls of both feet. Continuing to pivot, the athlete pushes toward the center of the ring. The athlete places the right foot in the center of the ring and with additional rotation positions the left foot at the front of the ring. The body position that the athlete assumes at this phase of the throw is similar to that used in the glide technique. The right leg is flexed and the left leg extended to-

ward the front of the shot-put ring. The upper body is inclined toward the rear of the ring.

THE PUT

The athlete begins the final putting action in the rotary technique just like an athlete using the glide. Force is applied from the ground up in the sequence of legs, hips, chest, and throwing arm. The athlete's legs extend in a rotary fashion toward the direction of throw. The extension of the athlete's legs push the hips in the same direction. The action of the hips is followed by a rotary upward thrust of the athlete's chest. The right side of the athlete's body rotates forward and upward around an extended left leg. A powerful extension of the athlete's throwing arm and fingers pushes the shot away from the athlete's neck (see figure 11.2). After the shot has left the athlete's hand, the athlete's legs reverse positions to prevent the athlete from falling out of the front of the ring and fouling the throw.

The big difference between the glide and the rotary technique is the additional rotation that is included in the rotary technique. An athlete using the rotary technique must control the tendency of the shot to pull away from the athlete's neck. At the same time, the athlete must be precise in timing the application of force on the shot. If this thrust is mistimed, the shot can easily fly out of the sector and not be counted as a fair throw.

TEACHING STEPS

STEP 1. Lead-Ups
STEP 2. Shot Put From a Standing Position
STEP 3. Shot Put Using the Glide Technique
STEP 4. Shot Put Using the Rotary Technique

STEP 1: LEAD-UPS

Preparatory activities for shot put can begin with all forms of throwing by using soccer balls, basketballs, or light medicine balls. Initially, throwing is two-handed (from behind the head, between the legs, or around the side of the athlete's body). You can then have your athletes progress to one-handed or two-handed

Figure 11.1 Glide technique.

Figure 11.2 Rotary technique.

throwing, using a pushing or putting motion. This throwing will simulate the action required in the shot put.

A Push-Throw With a Medicine Ball

Athletes throw medicine balls against the wall using a pushing action (see figure 11.3). Whoever throws the ball catches it on the rebound.

COACHING TIPS

- Use your legs to push forward into the throw. Make sure your legs extend fully.
- Push your chest high and keep your head up.
- Extend your arms as vigorously as possible, and be sure to push with your fingers.

Push-Throws in Pairs

Pairs of athletes face each other and use one- and two-handed push passes to pass a medicine ball to each other (see figure 11.4).

COACHING TIPS

- If you are throwing with your right arm, before you throw be sure to step forward one long stride with your left leg. This step will give you a good throwing stance.
- Keep the elbow of your throwing arm at shoulder level; don't let it drop to the side of the body.

- Keep your chest up and extend your legs as you throw.

Putting the Medicine Ball for Distance

Athletes put the medicine ball for distance (see figure 11.5). Distance lines are marked on the ground.

COACHING TIPS

- Try to make your throwing action as long as possible. Push from as far back to as far forward as possible.
- Drive up onto your toes and push forward with your body. Use your whole body in the throw, not just your arms.
- To obtain the longest distance, a trajectory of about 40 to 43 degrees above horizontal is necessary. Release the medicine ball so that your arms are fully extended in front of you and just above head height.

Putting a Medicine Ball for Height and Distance

This drill emphasizes both height and distance. Surgical tubing is suspended to act as a crossbar between 2 high-jump or pole-vault standards 2–3 m (7'–10') above the ground. If your athlete can throw the medicine ball over the crossbar, then that athlete takes 2 paces back-

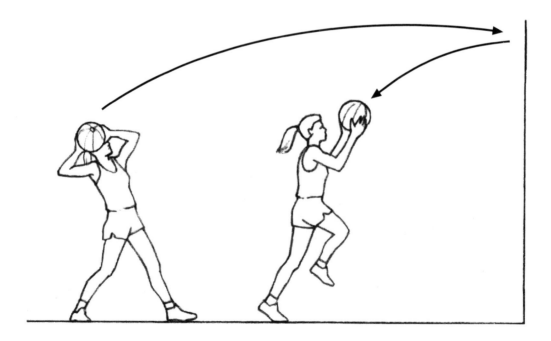

Figure 11.3 Push-throw with a medicine ball.

Figure 11.4 Push-throw in pairs.

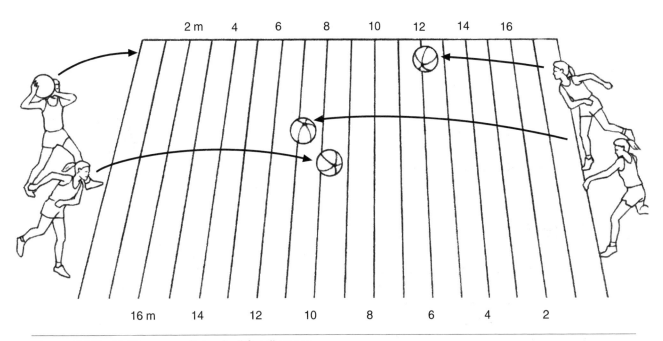

Figure 11.5 Putting a medicine ball for distance.

ward (see figure 11.6). Who can end up furthest from the standards? (Be sure that the
elastic will stretch sufficiently when hit. It is
also a good idea to add extra weight to stabilize the bases of the high-jump or pole-vault
standards.)

COACHING TIPS

- This lead-up will test whether you are using a good trajectory.
- Remember to extend your legs and push
your chest upward as you throw.

- Use the big muscles of your legs, back,
and chest before using your throwing
arm, not afterward.

Passing Relay

Athletes push-pass a medicine ball in zigzag
fashion from one end of a team to the other
(see figure 11.7). Which team is going to be the
quickest in passing the medicine ball? Make
sure that the medicine ball is light enough to
catch easily.

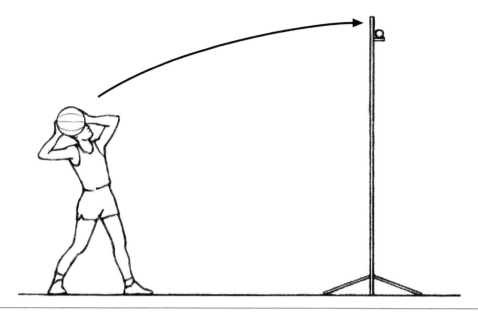

Figure 11.6   Putting a medicine ball for height and distance.

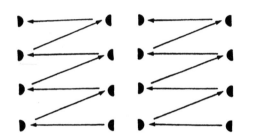

Figure 11.7   Passing relay.

- Be alert and ready to catch the ball.
- Reach out to catch the ball and absorb its energy by drawing your arms and body back the moment your hands contact the ball.
- Throw the ball accurately with the correct amount of force so that your partner can catch the ball easily.
- Whoever drops the medicine ball has to pick it up, so be accurate when you throw.

STEP 2: SHOT PUT FROM A STANDING POSITION

Each athlete begins a standing put facing away from the direction of throw, keeping the vision to the rear and cradling the shot under the chin. The athlete flexes the right leg and reaches back with the left leg into the putting stance, lowering the upper body approximately 30 degrees from the vertical by flexing at the hips. The shoulders at this point remain square

Figure 11.8   Shot put from a standing position.

to the rear. The athlete pushes upward and rotates toward the direction of the throw by extending the legs and thrusting the hips and chest forward. A powerful thrust of the throwing arm and the vigorous snap of the fingers complete the putting action (see figure 11.8).

The Correct Handhold for Cradling the Shot

Each athlete raises and lowers the shot from the shoulder to full arm's length several times. This drill develops a feel for the manner in which the shot rests between the athlete's fingers and thumb (see figure 11.9).

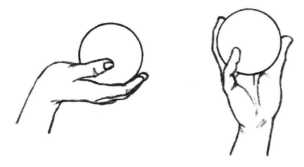

Figure 11.9 Cradling the shot.

- Hold the shot between your fingers and thumb; don't let it drop down into the palm of your hand. If you feel you cannot hold the shot between your fingers and the thumb, then the shot is too heavy, and you need to use a lighter one.

- Raise and lower your arm slowly. This action will give you a feel for the support given to the shot by the combined action of the thumb and the fingers.

Standing Put: Initial Stance Facing the Direction of Throw

Athletes stand facing the direction of throw and holding the shot in the correct hand position. A right-handed thrower steps forward with the left foot and then puts the shot (see figure 11.10).

- Keep the elbow of the throwing arm high (just below shoulder height) during the put.

- Begin the putting action by moving your body forward. Move your hips forward and keep your chest high and square (at right angles) to the direction of throw.

- Keep the elbow of your throwing arm up (in its original position). Don't let it drop down to the side of your body.

- Extend your legs and be sure to put the shot from your fingers (not from your palm).

- Finish the putting action with your throwing arm extended in front of your body and with the shot leaving your hand just above head level.

Figure 11.10 Standing put facing throwing direction.

Standing Put: Shoulders Rotate 90 Degrees From the Direction of Throw

A right-handed thrower steps toward the direction of the throw with the left leg. The athlete then rotates the shoulders 90 degrees to the right (away from the direction of throw). The put begins with the athlete's right leg extending and thrusting the hips and the chest toward the direction of the throw (see figure 11.11). The extension of the athlete's throwing arm and the thrust of the fingers holding the shot complete the putting action.

- Be sure to begin your throw by extending your legs first.

Figure 11.11 Standing put with 90-degree shoulder rotation.

- After your legs are extended, turn your hips and lift your chest upward and toward the direction of the throw before using your throwing arm.

- Be sure to keep the elbow of your throwing arm at shoulder level. Don't let it drop downward; otherwise, the shot will bend your fingers backward. Think of the putting action as an incline press in the weight room.

- Finish the put with a thrusting action from your fingers toward the direction of the throw.

Standing Put: Initial Stance Facing the Direction of Throw

A right-handed thrower begins facing the direction of the throw with the feet together, and then takes one pace forward (slightly wider than shoulder-width) with the left leg. This provides the correct foot positioning for the final throwing stance. The athlete then rotates 180 degrees on the balls of the feet to face directly away from the direction of the throw. The athlete's bodyweight is shifted back over the right foot. From this position, the athlete rotates on the balls of the feet while lifting upward. The athlete turns the legs, hips, and chest toward the direction of throw. The put is completed with a strong extension of the athlete's throwing arm and a thrust with the fingers (see figure 11.12).

COACHING TIPS

- Lift upward with your legs and back and simultaneously rotate toward the direction of the throw.

- Don't be in a hurry to use the throwing arm; wait until your body has lifted up and rotated toward the direction of throw.

- Try to apply force in the correct sequence: Your legs simultaneously extend and rotate, followed by your hips and chest, and finally the extension of your throwing arm.

- Keep the elbow of the throwing arm at shoulder level throughout.

- Your final contact with the shot is a strong push with your fingers.

Standing Put: Initial Stance 180 Degrees From the Direction of Throw

This is the complete action of a standing throw. A right-handed thrower begins facing 180 degrees from the direction of throw (facing the rear of the shot-put ring). There are two acceptable methods for performing the standing put: The athlete begins with both feet already in the putting stance (as in figure 11.13); or the athlete begins with both feet together, and then initiates the standing put by first reaching back with the left foot into the putting stance.

For a right-handed thrower, the standing put occurs in the following sequence. The athlete begins by lowering the upper body and flexing the right leg to approximately a $\frac{1}{4}$-squat position. The right leg then rotates and extends upward, forcing the hips around and toward the direction of throw. The athlete's hips pull the chest around and toward the direction of throw. The athlete's chest is thrust upward, and both legs extend fully. The extension of the throwing arm and the fingers holding the shot complete the standing put.

Figure 11.12 180-degree rotation followed by standing put.

Figure 11.13 Standing put with feet positioned in the putting stance.

When the left foot is positioned in the putting stance, the foot must be offset correctly in the manner illustrated in figure 11.14. This is explained in the next drill.

The Putting Stance

The foot positions used in the putting stance allow the athlete's body to rotate and move forward toward the direction of the throw. For a right-handed thrower facing the rear of the ring, the left foot is placed approximately one foot-width to the athlete's right of a line indicating the direction of throw. If the left foot is incorrectly positioned to the left, it will block and resist the athlete's efforts to rotate and drive forward into the throw. The distance between right foot and left foot in the putting stance is slightly more than shoulder-width.

STEP 3: SHOT PUT USING THE GLIDE TECHNIQUE

Now that your athletes have a good grasp of the standing throw, it is time to introduce them to the glide across the ring. The following drills will initially concentrate on the glide.

Learning the Glide With Partner Assistance

A partner holds the performer's hands, making sure that the athlete's upper body remains low and that the athlete's shoulders are horizontal and facing directly to the rear. As the athlete glides backward, the partner moves in the same

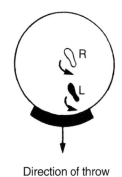

Direction of throw

Figure 11.14 Putting stance.

direction, making sure that the athlete's upper body stays low and does not rise upward (see figure 11.15). The athlete learning the glide concentrates on the following actions, *all of which must be performed simultaneously*:

(a) The left leg makes a low backward thrust with the left foot skimming across the ground.

(b) The left foot lands in the correct throwing position each time (offset to the athlete's right as indicated in figure 11.14).

(c) The right leg extends and makes a strong backward thrust. The right leg is then immediately flexed and pulled in directly below the upper body.

(d) The right foot and knee rotate approximately 45 degrees toward the direction of throw. The athlete must be sure that the right and left legs perform their separate actions almost simultaneously. Both feet should land in the putting stance at the same time.

Repetitive Glide Practice Without Partner Assistance and Without a Shot

A right-handed thrower assumes an initial stance similar to the standing put position. After lowering the upper body and flexing the right leg, the athlete drives backward to perform the glide (see figure 11.16). After a momentary pause, the next glide is performed. The athlete must concentrate on each glide separately, making sure that the movements are performed correctly. This drill must not become a series of aimless backward hops.

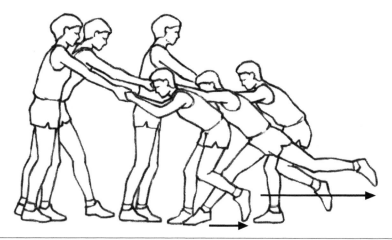

Figure 11.15   The glide with partner assistance.

Figure 11.16   The glide without partner assistance.

COACHING TIPS

- Your backward gliding action is not an upward jump. Don't raise your back or jump up in the air.

- Keep your feet close to the ground throughout. They should skim across the ground.

- After extending your right leg, pull it in under you so that it's in a flexed position directly below your upper body. (If you don't do this, your right leg will be unable to provide power for the throw.)

Glide and Shot Put Using a Short Glide and a Light Shot

The athlete's initial stance in this drill is the same as for the standing put. A short glide allows the athlete to concentrate on the rhythm of both the glide and putting action (see figure 11.17). In this way, the athlete is not concerned about the distance that must be covered in a normal glide.

COACHING TIPS

- Keep your upper body low until your glide is complete; then lift upward into the putting action, not before.

- Extend and flex your right leg so that it is pulled in directly below your upper body at the end of the glide. Don't leave your right leg behind you; otherwise, you'll land with both legs extended and you won't be able to push with them.

Glide and Shot Put Using a Full-Size Glide

This drill requires the complete putting action using the glide technique (see figure 11.1). The rhythm of the glide and putting action must be a fluid movement, not a stop-and-start jerky motion. A properly performed glide takes the athlete from the back of the ring into the putting stance in the center, so the athlete must shift backward approximately 60 cm (2'). The glide is immediately followed by an explosive

Figure 11.17 Using a short glide.

putting action. The momentum of the athlete's body pushing against the shot should force the athlete to step forward with the right leg and perform the reverse.

COACHING TIPS

- A longer glide will demand more effort from your right leg. Think of the action as a push followed by a pull-in with your right leg.

- Thrust your left leg backward to its position in the putting stance the same time that you push with your right leg.

- Remember to stay low until your feet are in position at the center and front of the ring.

- As soon as you've completed the glide, think of striking from the ground up by using your legs, hips, chest, and throwing arm in that sequence. Remember that your throwing arm is the last to act.

- Thrust forward into your throw as powerfully as possible. Perform your reverse only after the shot has left your hand.

The Reverse

Athletes use a reverse to keep from falling out of the front of the ring. Figure 11.18 shows the athlete bringing the rear leg forward against the stopboard for the reverse.

COACHING TIPS

- Make sure your hips and chest move forward beyond your left foot before initiating the reverse. Think of a post extending

Figure 11.18 The reverse.

vertically upward from your left foot. Your body must move past that post before you perform the reverse.

- Don't perform the reverse before extending your legs fully and driving your body forward into the throw.

STEP 4: SHOT PUT USING THE ROTARY TECHNIQUE

The rotational technique uses a discus-style rotation across the shot-put ring in place of a glide (figure 11.2). Once the athlete has completed the rotation, all else in the throw is basically the same as with the glide technique. The addition of the rotary action causes control problems that do not exist in the glide technique, problems due to the outward pull of the shot during the rotation across the ring. The athlete will feel that the shot "wants" to fly out sideways. Consequently, the athlete must generate additional force to hold the shot in tight against the neck. The timing required in the rotary technique is critical, because the athlete must be able to change, at the correct instant, a rotary action into one that is linear.

Athletes who have not mastered the rotary technique will find that they will do the following:

(a) Throw the shot out of the sector (right-handed athletes tend to throw the shot outside of the sector on the right side).

(b) Lose control of the shot during the rotation across the ring.

(c) Land in a poor (narrow) throwing stance at the end of the rotation.

Because of these problems, be sure that you teach the rotational technique to mature athletes as an alternative method only after they have mastered the glide technique.

Athletes Learn the Discus Rotation

Athletes who are going to use the rotary shot-put technique must first learn the discus rotation (see chapter 12).

Simulating the Position of the Shot During the Rotary Technique

Without using a shot, and with the throwing hand held at the neck, each athlete practices the rotary technique in the shot-put ring.

COACHING TIPS

• Be sure to make the rotation at the back of the ring tight enough so that it allows sufficient room in the front of the ring for a wide throwing stance.

• Concentrate on performing most of your rotation in the rear half of the ring. A straight-line (nonrotary) thrust in the direction of the throw must predominate after both your feet have landed in their final positions at the front of the ring.

• Put your left arm out horizontally during your rotation to maintain your balance.

A Rotary Shot Put Using a Light Shot

Choose a shot that is 1–2 kg (approximately 2–4 lbs.) lighter than the shot used by the ath-

lete in the glide technique. A right-handed thrower should rotate slowly into the putting stance (figure 11.2) by using the outward swing of the athlete's left arm to help initiate rotation from the rear of the ring. The athlete must hold the shot firmly in the neck. Once the rotation has been completed, the final part of the put is performed in essentially the same way as in the glide technique.

COACHING TIPS

• Squat down at the rear of the ring as though sitting on a stool. Don't tilt forward.

• Look forward and pivot on the balls of both feet to initiate the rotation.

• Keep pivoting on the balls of your feet until facing the direction of throw.

• Continue the pivot on your left foot, meanwhile bringing your right leg around to be positioned in the center of the ring.

• Land on the ball of your right foot at the center of the ring.

• Shift your left leg as quickly as possible into its position in the final putting stance.

• Try to keep your body weight to the rear of the ring so that when you land in the putting stance, your upper body will be over a flexed right leg.

• Throughout the rotation, hold the shot tightly against your neck and keep the elbow of your throwing arm at shoulder level throughout.

• Complete the putting action with a linear thrust at the shot. This action is similar to that used in the glide technique.

Rotary Shot Put Using a Competitive-Weight Shot

Have your athletes select shot that are the correct weight for their competitive age levels. Each athlete slowly performs the rotary technique. Don't allow the athlete to forfeit control over the shot (or a good throwing position at the end of the rotation) for increased rotary speed at the back of the ring.

COMMON ERRORS AND CORRECTIONS

STANDING PUT

Error	Reasons	Corrections
The athlete has no thrust from the fingers during the put.	The athlete's handhold on the shot is incorrect; the shot is thrown from the palm of the hand rather than being put (pushed) from the fingers of the throwing hand.	The athlete must support the shot with the pads of the fingers and thumb. Have the athlete practice standing puts, emphasizing extension of the athlete's arm and thrust of the athlete's fingers (be sure to use lightweight shots for this drill). The athlete can also practice the action of the hand and fingers without using a shot.
The shot is thrown or hurled rather than pushed (put). The novice complains of the shot bending the fingers backward during the put.	The shot is not cradled under the athlete's chin. The elbow of the athlete's throwing arm has dropped below the athlete's shoulder in the putting stance.	Correct the athlete's handhold and the position of the shot against the athlete's neck. The athlete must hold the elbow high, keeping the thumb of the throwing hand down and under and the little finger uppermost. Have the athlete practice the standing put after these factors are corrected.
The athlete's seat goes backward as the shot is thrust forward.	There's no extension and thrust from the athlete's legs, and the athlete's hips are not driven forward. The athlete's left foot is in the wrong position in the putting stance, and the left leg blocks the athlete's rotation toward the direction of throw.	Have the athlete practice the standing put, emphasizing the leg thrust and hip movement toward the direction of throw. The athlete's left foot in the putting stance must be offset in the manner shown in figure 11.14.
The left side of the athlete's body collapses during the final phase of the put.	There is no extension or resistance provided by the athlete's left leg and the left side of the athlete's body during the put. The athlete's shoulders are not square to the direction of throw.	Have the athlete practice the standing put, emphasizing upward thrust of the left leg and left side of the body. The chest should rotate toward the direction of throw around an an axis of the left side of the body. The shoulders should be square to the direction of throw.

→

Error	Reasons	Corrections
The shot is put with the athlete's body sideways to the direction of the throw. The shot is released over the top of the head.	There's no thrust from the athlete's right leg, and the athlete's hips and chest are not turning toward the direction of the throw. The athlete's rear leg is not extending toward the direction of throw, and the left foot is incorrectly positioned.	The athlete's left foot must be in the correct position in the throwing stance. The athlete should practice (without a shot) the correct positioning of the left foot, followed immediately by the correct rotary elevation of the legs and chest.
The shot is released with a low trajectory.	The athlete is not thrusting the body upward during the throw. Both the throwing arm and line of vision are too low. The athlete's seat goes backward as the shot is pushed forward.	The athlete should practice a standing put over a bar set high enough to emphasize extended legs, lifted chest, correct line of vision, and and correct trajectory.
The sequence and timing of the athlete's actions are incorrect (for example, the throwing arm performs its push on the shot prior to the thrust of the legs and chest).	The athlete is too eager to throw and has a poor understanding of the sequence and timing of actions.	Have the athlete practice a standing put without the shot and then a standing put without extending the arm from the neck. The athlete can practice using the thrust of the legs and the chest by themselves to push the shot forward. Emphasize the correct sequence of legs, followed by hips, chest, and throwing arm.

GLIDE TECHNIQUE

Error	Reasons	Corrections
The athlete swings the left leg back and forth in a pendular fashion before initiating the glide. The glide is performed with a large upward hop.	The athlete relies on the swing of the left leg to help shift the body across the ring and uses insufficient drive from the right leg. The athlete's left leg should be thrust backward long and low. Both of the athlete's feet should skim across the surface of the ring.	Have the athlete practice repetitive glides using the correct leg action.
The athlete jumps upward instead of gliding low and close to the ground. The athlete's left leg is kicked high in the air at the start of the glide.	The drive from the athlete's right leg is upward instead of backward and across the ring. The athlete's left leg is swung upward instead of thrust backward at the start of the glide.	Have the athlete practice glides without shot, emphasizing the powerful backward thrust of the athlete's left leg combined with a similar drive from the athlete's right leg.

→

Error	Reasons	Corrections
The athlete is upright at the end of the glide; the athlete's center of gravity is not over the rear (right) leg at the end of the glide. The athlete's center of gravity is positioned midway between the athlete's legs at the end of the glide.	The athlete's upper body is raised either at the start or during the glide. The athlete then falls backward during the glide. The right leg is not pulled in under the body at the end of the glide.	The athlete should practice repetitive glides while maintaining a low upper-body position, making sure both feet hit the ground at the same time with the athlete's upper body positioned above the right leg throughout.
The athlete turns prematurely toward the direction of the throw.	The athlete's left foot is incorrectly placed at the end of the glide. The athlete rotates toward the direction of throw either at the start of the glide or during the glide. The athlete turns the head and shoulders prematurely toward the direction of the throw.	Have the athlete practice the glide, keeping the athlete's vision to the rear throughout. Mark on the ground the final foot positioning at the end of the glide and have the athlete practice hitting these positions each time. The athlete's left arm should be extended and pointed to the rear throughout the glide.
The athlete's hips and seat move backward as the shot is driven forward by the throwing arm.	The athlete remains over the rear (right) foot during the final phase of the put. The athlete fails to extend the right leg or move the hips and chest toward the direction of the throw.	The athlete should practice the standing put, emphasizing upward lift and forward motion of the body over the left foot while moving forward toward the direction of the throw.
The athlete extends the throwing arm in the putting action before the legs, hips, and chest drive forward into the put.	The athlete is overeager to complete the throw. The timing and sequence of the athlete's actions are incorrect.	Have the athlete practice the standing put, emphasizing the sequential action of the legs, hips, chest, and finally the throwing arm. The athlete should practice these actions with and without a shot.
The athlete performs the reverse before the shot leaves the the athlete's hand.	The athlete is afraid of making a foul throw and is not moving the bodyweight toward the direction of the put. The athlete extends the left side of the body too soon.	Instruct the athlete to practice the standing put without a reverse. The athlete should push forward beyond the left foot position during the put and try to delay the extension of the left leg and the left side of the body.

$\rightarrow$

ROTARY TECHNIQUE

Error	Reasons	Corrections
The athlete uses too much rotation and has no linear thrust on the shot. The athlete loses control of the shot, and the shot lands outside of the sector. The hips open up (rotate too far) by the time the throwing stance is achieved.	The athlete's rotation continues for too long a time period. The athlete fails to achieve a strong throwing stance.	Have the athlete practice the the rotation and putting action slowly without a shot. The athlete should then practice the rotary motion slowly using a lightweight shot. Emphasis should be on making sure that the athlete lands in a good throwing position at the end of the rotation. Make the athlete slow down the rotation and concentrate on an excellent body position first.
The athlete is upright before assuming the throwing stance and achieves no power in the throw.	The athlete's upper body is elevated, and the athlete's legs are fully extended at the back of the ring and also in the middle of the ring. The athlete lifts upward when performing the rotation.	The athlete must practice keeping low during the rotation, and then lifting upward only after achieving the throwing stance where both feet are in contact with the ground at the front of the ring.
The athlete's rotation across the ring is not toward the direction of the throw.	The time spent by the athlete rotating at the back of the ring is either too long or too short.	Use lines on the ground and a rhythm count to assist the athlete with directional control.
The athlete loses control of the shot, which flies away from the neck before the final putting action is complete.	The athlete's throwing hand is not holding the shot firmly enough in the neck. The athlete's timing of the final thrust against the shot is incorrect. Rotation across the ring is too fast.	Instruct the athlete to practice slow rotational throws, waiting until the correct throwing position is achieved before initiating a final thrust on the shot.

ASSESSMENT

1. **Assess the following theoretical elements as taught during instructional sessions:**
   a. Fundamental rules governing the shot put.
   b. Good safety habits for use in the shot put.
   c. Basic elements of shot-put technique.
   d. Basic elements of training for the shot put.
2. **Assess the performance of technique during the following stages of skill development:**
   a. Standing put initiated with the athlete's side to the direction of throw.
   b. Standing put initiated with the athlete's back to the direction of throw.

c. The glide action across the shot-put ring without release of the shot.

d. The complete glide technique and putting action.

e. The rotary technique performed without a shot.

f. The complete rotary technique and putting action.

CRITICAL FEATURES OF TECHNIQUE TO OBSERVE DURING ASSESSMENT

Glide Technique

- ✓ Gripping the shot with the thumb and fingers of the hand and cradling it under the chin.
- ✓ Flexing the right leg and driving the body backward across the ring.
- ✓ Holding the upper body in a position where it is parallel to the ground and kicking the left leg back to its position in the throwing stance.
- ✓ Pulling the right leg directly under the upper body at the end of the glide.
- ✓ Rotating the foot of the right leg in its position under the upper body so that it is at right angles to the direction of throw.
- ✓ Offsetting the left foot correctly in the throwing stance.
- ✓ Holding the shoulders square to the rear of the ring and maintaining the backward lean of the upper body through the completion of the glide.
- ✓ Initiating the drive toward the direction of the throw with the right leg, followed by the hips.
- ✓ Thrusting the chest upward and extending the legs toward the direction of the throw.
- ✓ Extending the throwing arm and fingers at approximately 40 degrees from horizontal to complete the throw (put).
- ✓ Bringing the right leg forward in front of the left for the reverse.

Rotary Technique

- ✓ Gripping the shot with the thumb and finger of the hand and cradling it under the chin.
- ✓ Turning the shoulders and shot fully to the right rear prior to rotating across the shot-put ring.
- ✓ Squatting and rotating on the balls of both feet toward the direction of the throw.
- ✓ Performing a running rotation across the ring so that the athlete's legs rotate ahead of the shoulders.
- ✓ Landing in a wide throwing stance with the athlete's bodyweight well back over a flexed right leg.
- ✓ Offsetting the left foot correctly in the throwing stance.
- ✓ Initiating the final throwing (putting) action with a rotary extension of the legs.
- ✓ Driving the hips upward and forward toward the direction of the throw, followed by the chest, and lastly the extension of the throwing arm.
- ✓ Bringing the right foot forward in front of the left foot for the reverse.

3. Hold graded competitions to help develop motivation and technique.

a. Athletes compete for distance using a standing throw, which they initiate with their backs to the direction of the throw. Select shot according to age, size, and gender.

b. Athletes compete for distance using the glide technique. Select shot according to age, size, and gender.

c. Athletes compete for distance using the rotary technique. Select shot according to age, size, and gender.

SUGGESTED STANDARDS OF PERFORMANCE—SHOT PUT

MALE

Age	Weight of Shot		Distance
12-13	3 kg (6.61 lbs.)	Satisfactory	7.00 m (23'0")
		Good	8.50 m (27'10")
		Excellent	9.50 m (31'2")
14-15	3 kg (6.61 lbs.)	Satisfactory	8.00 m (26'3")
		Good	9.50 m (31'2")
		Excellent	10.50 m (34'5")
16-17	5.45 kg (12 lbs.)	Satisfactory	9.00 m (29'6")
		Good	10.50 m (34'5")
		Excellent	11.50 m (37'9")
18-19	7.260 kg (16 lbs.)	Satisfactory	8.50 m (27'10")
		Good	10.00 m (32'10")
		Excellent	11.00 m (36'1")

FEMALE

Age	Weight of Shot		Distance
12-13	3 kg (6.61 lbs.)	Satisfactory	5.00 m (16'5")
		Good	6.00 m (19'8")
		Excellent	7.00 m (23'0")
14-15	3 kg (6.61 lbs.)	Satisfactory	6.00 m (19'8")
		Good	7.00 m (23'0")
		Excellent	8.00 m (26'3")
16-17	4 kg (8.81 lbs.)	Satisfactory	6.50 m (21'4")
		Good	7.50 m (24'7")
		Excellent	8.50 m (27'10")
18-19	4 kg (8.81 lbs.)	Satisfactory	7.00 m (23'0")
		Good	8.00 m (26'3")
		Excellent	9.00 m (29'6")

12

DISCUS

The discus throw is included in the Olympic Games as an individual event for males and females. It is an event in the men's decathlon, but it is not included in the women's heptathlon.

The tremendous increase in distances thrown in the discus event have resulted from big, powerful, long-armed athletes who have spent years in weight training specifically related to the event. The technique of discus throwing has changed little over the past 30 years. You will see little variation in technique from one athlete to the next.

The athlete begins the throw facing to the rear of the 2.5 m (8' 2½") ring. Using approximately 1¾ rotations, the athlete is able (counting windup) to accelerate the discus through 2 full rotations during the throw. Some athletes have attempted to add an additional hammer-style spin at the start of the rotation across the ring. This spin has proved to be ineffective because it gives no additional acceleration to the discus.

Of all throwing implements, the discus most resembles an airfoil. Spin is essential for stability during flight, and a headwind gives lift to the discus and assists in producing the longest throws. A wind of about 16–25 kph (10–15 mph)

approaching the athlete from the front produces the most favorable conditions for the longest throws. Under these conditions, the wind combines with the aerodynamic shape of the discus to give it lift and hold it up in the air. At present, the rules of the event allow records to be set in any wind conditions.

SAFETY SUGGESTIONS

The discus event can be hazardous because of its rotary method of throwing. Young athletes will experience difficulty in gripping and releasing the discus, and their directional accuracy is often very poor. This chapter will recommend teaching progressions that will eliminate much of the risk, but you must still develop and reinforce good safety habits.

As with other throwing equipment, you should regularly check all discuses to see that they are in good order. The metal rim must be smooth and without burrs that could tear the skin. Substitute equipment that you use for training purposes must also be safe and designed to withstand repeated use.

All discuses should be stored safely and carried in an orderly fashion to the throwing area. Do not allow your athletes to throw, bowl, or fool around with the discuses in any way while they are being transported. In wet conditions, provide towels for wiping off the rim and the surface of the discus. A concrete throwing ring is the best type of throwing surface. Make sure that the ring drains properly and that the metal rim around the ring is the official height. Keep a broom handy for sweeping out the ring. Avoid teaching the discus throw on wet grass. Wet grass can be slippery and cause an athlete to release the discus in the wrong direction.

The organizational format used when the discus is rolled or thrown with an underarm swinging motion is different from that used when teaching standing and rotary throws. For rolling or tossing the discus up in the air, station athletes along a line, 3–4 m (10'–13') apart. On your command, the athletes all release the discuses together. Then on your command the athletes all retrieve together. Do not allow athletes to roll, bowl, or throw discuses back to the throwing area or to other athletes. Those who are late in following your commands must not throw, nor run out to collect the discus the instant they have thrown it. These athletes must wait until you give the command to do so. It's best if you station yourself centrally to the rear of your athletes. In this way, you can see everyone, and all are within earshot of your commands. Those waiting their turn must also stand to the rear of those performing.

Athletes use a slinging action in the discus for both standing and rotary throws. The centrifugal nature of this action causes problems with the handhold on the discus and also with the timing of the release. The safest arrangement for practicing standing and rotary throws is to position those waiting their turn well back to the rear (5–6 m or 16'–20'). Athletes then step forward individually to throw.

SPECIFIC CHARACTERISTICS OF THE DISCUS THROW

Experienced officials know that a discus can be difficult to see edge-on and that it will skip and bounce, particularly on wet grass. Allowances must also made for the wind shifting the flight path of a discus and causing throws to land outside of the throwing sector. Knowledgeable officials usually know the capabilities of the athletes competing in a discus event, and they are prepared for exceptional throws. Officials will keep other athletes well clear of the throwing sector, particularly those who have just finished another event and who are less likely to be aware of what is happening around them. Brightly colored netting set beyond the outer limits of the throwing sector is an excellent safety device for trapping bouncing discuses. It also stops athletes and spectators from wandering into the throwing area.

TECHNIQUE

The object of modern discus technique is to simulate a rotary cracking of a whip, with the whip (the discus arm) swung around the side of the body. A discus thrower "runs" in a rotary fashion across the ring, twisting the legs and hips ahead of the upper body as though coiling up a spring. When the athlete is in the throwing stance, the athlete unwinds the spring and cracks the whip. The tip of the whip moving at high speed is the discus.

GRIP AND WINDUP

The athlete holds the discus by the pads of the fingertips, the thumb resting against the side of the discus. The outward pull of the discus holds the discus in the athlete's hand. The athlete begins in a shoulder-width stance facing away from the direction of throw; vision is directly ahead. A right-handed athlete rotates the shoulders and discus arm as far as possible to the right. The athlete's bodyweight shifts momentarily over the right foot. The legs are slightly flexed.

ROTATION

A right-handed thrower shifts the bodyweight to the left and rotates on the balls of the feet toward the direction of throw. The discus trails behind the body. The athlete runs in a rotary fashion across the ring with the legs rotating ahead of the shoulders and discus arm. The athlete tries to get both feet into the throwing stance as quickly as possible.

THROW AND REVERSE

When the athlete's feet have landed in the throwing stance, the athlete powerfully extends the legs and drives the hips forward toward the direction of throw. The hips pull the chest and finally the throwing arm, which simulates the tip of a whip. Once the discus is released, the athlete arrests the forward movement of the body by reversing the feet, bringing the rear (right) leg forward against the inner edge of the rim of the circle.

TEACHING STEPS

STEP 1. Lead-Ups

STEP 2. Standing Throw Using a Discus Substitute

STEP 3. Rotary Throw Using a Discus Substitute

STEP 4. Standing Throw With the Discus

STEP 5. Rotary Throw With the Discus

STEP 1: LEAD-UPS

Small rubber rings (quoits) or hula hoops are excellent training substitutes for the competitive discus. They eliminate the problem of gripping the discus that a novice commonly experiences. An athlete grips the ring or hula hoop in a normal fashion and then is able to con-

centrate on other parts of the discus throw, in particular the footwork. Once the athlete has learned the footwork, then practice can begin with the discus itself. Rubber rings and hula hoops are excellent substitutes for the discus for the following reasons:

- They are safe to use and can be thrown both indoors and outdoors.
- They are easy to grip and light enough to be held at arm's length.
- They generate a certain amount of drag, which forces the athlete's throwing arm into a good trailing position.
- They cannot be thrown far, which means that young athletes can repeat throws more often.

Slinging a Small Rubber Ring

Each athlete steps forward toward the direction of throw and slings a small rubber ring (see figure 12.1). The throwing arm is kept extended throughout, and the athlete swings it around the body just below shoulder level. A right-handed athlete steps forward into the throw with the left foot, extending the legs powerfully and driving the hips and chest forward into the throw.

Figure 12.1 Slinging a rubber ring.

- As you swing your arm back, step forward with your left foot into the throwing stance.
- Thrust your hips and chest well ahead of your throwing arm.
- Keep your throwing arm just below shoulder level, and release the ring ahead of your body and just above eye level.

Accuracy Competition With Small Hoops

Set up a high-jump standard to use as a target. Individual athletes or teams compete against each other for points. Points are awarded for hitting the standard or dropping a hula hoop on the standard. The slinging action used earlier is repeated in this lead-up drill (see figure 12.2). Requiring height and distance in a throw teaches athletes to lift their bodies upward at the moment of release.

Slinging a Volleyball, Basketball, or Light Medicine Ball for Distance

You can use any slinging activity with volleyballs, basketballs, or light medicine balls as an introduction drill for the discus throw. Par-

ticularly beneficial are two-handed slinging drills. These drills teach the windup of the athlete's shoulders relative to the athlete's hips. Athletes can use various throwing positions, such as standing, sitting, or kneeling (see figure 12.3).

- Concentrate on thrusting your chest forward into the throw ahead of your arms and the ball.
- Extend your legs vigorously toward the direction of throw when you use a standing throw.

STEP 2: STANDING THROW USING A HULA HOOP AS A DISCUS SUBSTITUTE

Use a hula hoop with a diameter of 1 m (approximately 3') for the following drills. They can be gripped without any problem and easily held at arm's length by your young athletes. As the athlete practices the following drills, the hoop will simulate the drag of a discus held at arm's length yet eliminate the problems normally encountered by novices when they try to grip the rim of a discus for the first time.

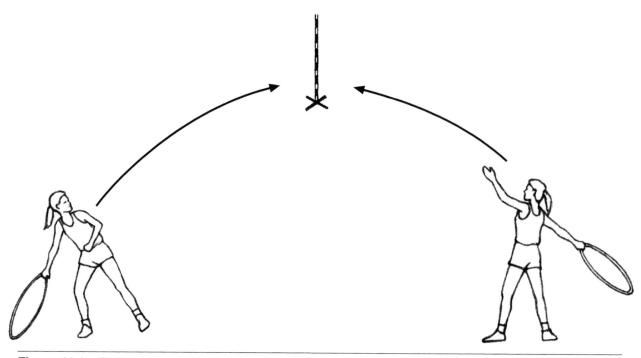

Figure 12.2 Accuracy competition with hoops.

Figure 12.3 Slinging a ball from a sitting position.

Standing Throw Initiated With the Athlete's Side Toward the Direction of Throw

A right-handed athlete stands side-on to the direction of throw (with the left shoulder toward the direction of throw). The athlete's feet are shoulder-width apart, with the left foot offset correctly in the throwing stance. (The offset position allows the athlete to drive the body fully into the throw. Any other stance will block this action. See figure 12.4.)

The athlete swings the hoop and the shoulders back and around to the right side of the body. This action will cause the athlete to rotate on the balls of the feet toward the right, simultaneously shifting the bodyweight over the right leg. The standing throw begins with the athlete's right leg extending and the hips rotating vigorously toward the direction of throw. The athlete's hips lead the chest and throwing arm, and the athlete's body drives upward and forward.

a   *b*

Figure 12.4 Standing throw initiated with the side of the athlete toward the direction of throw: whole view (*a*) and foot position only (*b*).

Figure 12.5 The step-back standing throw.

COACHING TIPS

- Swing your throwing arm back slowly as far as possible to the right and rotate your shoulders as far as you can in the same direction. This action will generate a muscular stretch across your waist that you can use to pull on the hoop.
- Start your standing throw by vigorously extending your right leg and turning your knees toward the direction of throw.
- Thrust your hips and chest forward before your throwing arm swings around. Extend your left leg.
- Keep your throwing arm just below shoulder level, and release the hoop in front of your body, just below eye level.

The Step-Back Standing Throw

The athlete begins with the back toward the direction of throw. As the athlete rotates the hoop and shoulders to the right for the windup, the left foot is placed backward into the throwing stance. The athlete's bodyweight remains to the rear over a flexed right leg during this action. The rotation of the athlete's knees drives the athlete's hips and chest toward the direction of throw. The athlete's throwing arm is pulled around by the action of the athlete's chest. The athlete's arm completes the throw with a whiplike action, releasing the hoop as far ahead of the body as possible (see figure 12.5).

COACHING TIPS

- Keep your weight back over your flexed right leg as you shift your left foot back into position.

- Be sure to step back into the correct offset position with your left foot (see figure 12.4b).
- Initiate the throwing (slinging) action from the ground up (rotate your knees toward the direction of throw, followed by your hips, chest, and finally your throwing arm).
- Stretch up into your throw. Extend your legs.

STEP 3: ROTARY THROW USING A RUBBER RING OR HULA HOOP AS A DISCUS SUBSTITUTE

A rotary throw using a rubber ring or small hoop requires the same footwork and body actions as a throw with the competitive implement (figure 12.6).

Rotary Throw Initiated Facing the Direction of Throw

Mark foot positions on the ground to guide your athlete through the rotary steps of this drill. The athlete begins facing the direction of throw with an initial stance in which the left foot is placed one step forward. The athlete gently swings the throwing arm (and the hoop or ring) back as far to the right as possible for the windup and then holds the arm in this position.

The athlete begins by pivoting on the left foot and stepping forward and rotating around onto the right foot. The athlete's right foot is positioned one pace forward with the heel now pointing toward the direction of throw (see figure 12.7). The athlete's weight remains to the

Figure 12.6 Rotary throw using a discus substitute.

Figure 12.7 Rotational throw initiated with the athlete facing the direction of throw.

rear. The remaining part of the throw is a repetition of the step-back standing throw, taught previously (see figure 12.5).

COACHING TIPS

- Put the hoop back for the windup and keep it back.
- Start with your left foot forward. Step forward with the right foot and turn your right heel toward the direction of throw.
- Step directly back into the correct throwing position with your left foot. Don't swing your foot out and around into position, because this takes too long. (For the correct foot positions in the throwing stance, see Figure 12.4b.)
- Initiate your throwing action by rotating your knees toward the direction of throw.
- Follow the rotation of your knees by turning your hips and chest toward the direction of throw.

- Bring your throwing arm around just below shoulder height to complete the throw.
- Stretch up into the throw.

Rotary Throw Initiated With the Athlete's Side Toward the Direction of Throw

Mark foot positions on the ground to guide your athlete through the rotation. A right-handed thrower now begins with the left side of the body toward the direction of throw. This position adds a further 90 degrees of rotation to the previous drill. The hoop is gently swung back as far as possible to the right for the windup. It remains in this position. The athlete then pivots on the left foot and steps forward and around on to the right foot. The athlete continues to pivot until the heel of the right foot points toward the direction of throw (see figure 12.8). The athlete now steps back with the left foot into the throwing stance. The remaining part of the throw is exactly the same as in the preceding drills.

Figure 12.8 Rotational throw initiated with the side of the athlete toward the direction of throw.

- Always keep your weight back toward the rear of the circle (don't shift it forward) as you pivot and step forward with the right foot.

- Continue to keep your weight to the rear as you thrust your left leg back into its throwing stance position. This will put you into a powerful throwing stance.

- In the throwing stance, your right leg should be partially flexed and your upper body inclined toward the back of the circle. From this position, you can rotate around, up, and forward into the throw.

Rotary Throw Initiated With the Athlete's Back Toward the Direction of Throw

Mark foot positions on the ground to guide the athlete through the rotation. A right-handed thrower begins with the back toward the direction of throw, adding yet another 90 degrees of rotation to the preceding drill. The hoop is gently swung back as far as possible to the right for the windup and is held in this position. The athlete begins to rotate, shifting the bodyweight over the left foot, and pivots on the balls of both feet until the left foot points toward the direction of throw. The athlete continues the pivoting motion while bringing the right foot around and placing it down close to the center of the ring, with the heel pointing toward the direction of throw. The remaining part of the throw is a repetition of the step-back standing throw (see figure 12.5).

- This drill simulates the complete discus throw.

- Flex your knees slightly and sit as though squatting on a stool during the rotation at the back of the ring.

- Keep your eyes on the horizon; don't look at the ground.

- Pivot on the balls of both feet until you face the direction of throw.

- Continue to pivot, placing your right foot in the center of the ring with the heel facing the direction of throw.

- Keep your bodyweight to the rear.

- Step back with your left leg into the throwing stance, but keep your bodyweight to the rear of the circle.

- Make sure your left foot is offset correctly in the throwing stance.

- Drive around into the throw, working from the ground up (extend and rotate your legs, followed by your hips, chest, and finally your throwing arm).

Rotary Throw in the Discus Circle Initiated With the Athlete's Back Toward the Direction of Throw

Mark foot positions in the discus ring, and have your athletes repeat the action of the preceding drill (see figure 12.9). Using this drill, the athletes now become accustomed to rotating within the confines of the 2.5 m (8' 2½") discus ring. The athlete begins in a shoulder-width stance, straddling the line of throw.

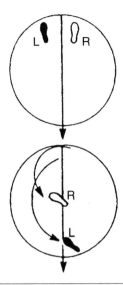

Figure 12.9 Foot positions in the discus circle.

COACHING TIPS

- Swing the hoop slowly as far to your right as possible and maintain this position throughout the rotation across the ring.
- Shift your weight over your right foot as you swing the hoop to the right.
- Enter your rotation by shifting your weight back over the left foot.
- Pivot on the balls of your feet until the left foot points toward the direction of throw.
- Step around your left foot with the right, placing the right foot in the center of the ring (heel toward the direction of throw).
- Place your left foot approximately 15 cm (6") from the front rim of the discus ring, offset to your right.
- Complete the forward rotary drive of your body into the throw, as before.

STEP 4: STANDING THROW WITH THE DISCUS

The athlete stands with the back toward the direction of throw. The athlete swings the discus back to the right and simultaneously steps back with the left foot, keeping the bodyweight over a flexed right leg. After placing the left foot in position, the athlete vigorously extends the legs and rotates the hips toward the direction of throw. The athlete's hips are followed by the chest and the throwing arm, which is swung around the body just below shoulder level (see figure 12.10). For a right-handed thrower, the squeeze of the athlete's throwing hand on the discus will give it a clockwise rotation. The index finger of the athlete's throwing hand is last to contact the discus.

Gripping the Discus

The athlete holds the discus on the pads of the fingers, resting the thumb against the side of the discus and flexing the hand slightly inward at the wrist (see figure 12.11). Some variations in grip can occur; for example, the index and second finger can be placed close together rather than spread apart.

COACHING TIPS

- As your throwing arm hangs beside your body, the discus will rest on the last fleshy pads of your fingers (the pads nearest the fingertips). Curl these pads around the rim of the discus.
- Your thumb does not hook around the edge of the discus but rests lightly against the side of the discus.

Swinging the Discus Backward and Forward Without Release

Athletes swing the discus lightly forward and back at the side of the body (20 degrees either side of vertical) with the arm acting as a pendulum (see figure 12.12). This motion provides a feel for the pressure of the discus against the pads of the athlete's fingers. The discus is not released in this drill.

COACHING TIPS

- Curl the last pads of the fingers around the rim of the discus. Spread your fingers, and be sure that you don't allow the pull of the discus to straighten out your fingers.
- Use your left hand to help control the discus at the apex of the forward swing. You can squeeze the discus between your left and right hand at the top of your swing.
- Gently swing the discus backward and forward like a pendulum.
- Keep your swings low. There is no need for you to swing the discus high in the front or to the back.

Figure 12.10 Technique for the standing throw.

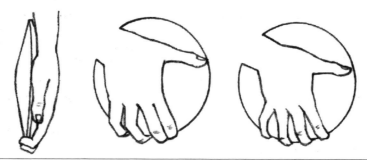

Figure 12.11 Three views of gripping the discus.

Figure 12.12 Swinging the discus backward and forward without release.

Bowling the Discus

Athletes bowl the discus along the ground for a distance of 5 m (16'–17'). In figure 12.13 the discus rolls off the index finger in a clockwise direction. On a flat surface, the discus should roll directly ahead.

COACHING TIPS

- Right-handed athletes step forward with your left foot. Left-handed athletes step forward with your right foot.

Figure 12.13 Bowling the discus.

- Swing the discus back gently and then bend forward and release it with your hand almost touching the ground.

- Squeeze the discus out of your hand, closing your hand into a fist by pulling your fingertips toward your palm in sequence from your little finger to your index finger. Perform this action quickly and vigorously.

Tossing the Discus in the Air With the Correct Spin

This drill teaches the athlete the correct spin that must be given to the discus when it is released. Place your athletes 3–4 m (10'–13') apart along a line. Each athlete steps forward with one foot. (Right-handed athletes will step forward with the left foot.) Each athlete swings the discus forward and then backward beside the body and then gently tosses it forward and up in the air so that it hits the ground 4–5 m (13'–16') ahead of the athlete. A squeezing action initiated from the athlete's little finger through to the index finger will cause the discus to roll out of the hand and rotate with a clockwise movement during flight. Athletes must throw one after the other according to your command. Make sure athletes throw the discus forward and not up above their heads.

COACHING TIPS

- Squeeze the discus out of your hand like a bar of soap, starting with the back of your hand and completing the action with your index finger.
- Your index finger is the last finger to be in contact with the rim of the discus, not your little finger.

Standing Throw With the Discus Initiated With the Athlete's Side Toward the Direction of Throw

An initial attempt at a standing throw using a discus must be performed with minimum effort and with little to no windup (backswing). A right-handed athlete begins in a shoulder-width stance with the left side toward the direction of throw. The left foot is offset to the left in the throwing stance. The athlete swings the discus loosely back and forth around the body with the discus at hip level (no higher) and no more than 30 cm (12") away from the side of the body during the swing. In this way the discus is still pressing down on the pads of the fingers.

When the discus has swung back and around the body as far as possible, the athlete rotates on the balls of the feet toward the direction of throw, pushing the hips and chest ahead of the discus arm (see figure 12.14a). The athlete throws the discus a distance of only 3–5 m (approximately 10'–16'). In subsequent attempts with this type of standing throw, the athlete will work toward swinging the discus around the body so that it follows an arc just below shoulder level. Figure 12.14b gives you a view from above of a right-handed athlete imparting spin to the discus.

COACHING TIPS

- Don't begin by trying to swing the discus a long way out from your body. You'll try this action later.
- As your throwing arm swings toward the direction of throw, your throwing hand will be above the discus with the thumb leading.
- Start the throw when the discus has been swung all the back in your wind-up. Turn on the balls of your feet and push your chest and hips toward the direction of throw. Try to make your hips and chest move around ahead of the discus.
- Don't turn your hand sideways to the direction of throw or turn your hand palm up so that it is underneath the discus.
- Squeeze the discus out of your hand, and start the squeezing action with your little finger first.
- Your index finger is in contact with the rim of the discus last of all.

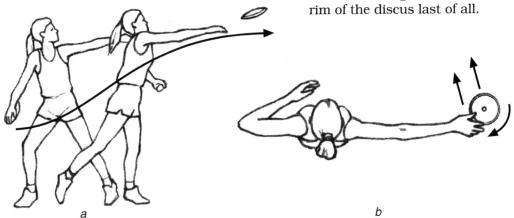

a   b

Figure 12.14 Standing throw with the discus initiated with the athlete's side toward the direction of the throw.

Step-Back Standing Throw With the Discus

The athlete begins in a shoulder-width stance with the back toward the direction of throw, loosely swinging the discus back and forth. As the discus is swung back in the windup, the athlete immediately places the left foot backward into the throwing stance, making sure that the bodyweight remains over the right leg as the left leg is thrust back into its position. Legs, hips, and chest then rotate in that sequence around and forward into the throw (see figure 12.15). The athlete's throwing hand is on top of the discus with the thumb leading. With the exception of gripping the discus, all actions replicate those performed earlier with a rubber ring and the hula hoop.

COACHING TIPS

- To begin with, don't try to swing the discus far out from your body. Keep the discus at hip level and about 30 cm (12") out from your body.
- As you get more confidence, try swinging the discus further away from your body.
- Try to make your body move ahead of your throwing arm.
- Thrust with your legs, hips, and chest toward the direction of throw.
- The pull on your discus arm is the last action that you perform.

STEP 5: ROTARY THROW WITH THE DISCUS

The drills leading an athlete to a full rotary throw with the discus progress in the same manner as when the athlete was using a hula hoop or rubber ring as a substitute for the discus. Gripping the discus will initially feel awkward and uncomfortable. The following drills are designed to minimize this discomfort.

Rotary Discus Throw Initiated Facing the Direction of Throw

Although this drill was performed earlier with a rubber ring or hoop, the use of the discus will present some control problems. Athletes can overcome these problems by using one of the two options:

(a) The athlete can swing the discus back gently for the windup with the discus kept low (at hip level) and 30 cm (12") from the body. When the discus can be swung back no further, the athlete immediately rotates into the throw (see figure 12.16). Carrying the discus low coupled with immediately starting the rotation when the discus is swung back as far as it will go will stop the discus from falling out of the athlete's throwing hand.

(b) The athlete can swing the discus back in the windup at hip level and then press it against the seat, holding it there throughout

Figure 12.15 Step-back standing throw with the discus.

Figure 12.16 Rotary discus throw initiated with the athlete facing the direction of throw.

the rotation. Holding the discus pressed against the seat allows a beginner to rotate more slowly and concentrate on the correct footwork without worrying about dropping the discus.

COACHING TIPS

- Trail the discus behind your body throughout the rotation. When the rotation is complete, drive your body forward into the throw ahead of your throwing arm.
- Keep your throwing hand on top of the discus, and remember that the index finger touches the discus last of all.
- If you are rotating with the discus pressed against your seat, remember to hold the discus in that position until you are pushing your hips and chest toward the direction of throw. At that point, you can let the discus move out and away from your body.

Rotary Discus Throw Initiated With the Athlete's Side Toward the Direction of Throw

The athlete begins with the left side of the body toward the direction of throw, controlling the discus in the same manner as discussed previously (see figure 12.17). The footwork used in this drill replicates the rotary throw initiated with the side toward the direction of throw when using a rubber ring or a hula hoop.

COACHING TIPS

- Try to keep your throw flowing and continuous from start to finish. This action will help you keep the discus under control. The more fluid your motion, the easier it is for you to hold the discus in the correct position.

- Remember the points that we worked on in the previous drills.

Rotary Discus Throw Initiated With the Athlete's Back Toward the Direction of Throw

This drill is the complete rotary discus throw. The athlete begins with the back toward the direction of throw, and then either swings the discus back low and close to the hip, using rotary speed to hold it in position, or swings the discus back and holds it on the seat during the rotation across the ring. The athlete's footwork in this drill replicates the same action practiced earlier using a discus substitute (see figure 12.18).

COACHING TIPS

- Keep the discus arm trailing to the rear of your body during your rotation across the ring.
- As you rotate, try to increase your speed of rotation and run into your throwing stance with the discus trailing behind.
- Work on getting both of your feet into your throwing stance simultaneously.
- The instant your feet land in the throwing stance, thrust forward into the throw with your hips by turning your knees as vigorously as possible toward the direction of throw. Think "knees, hips, chest, arm, discus" to help you remember the sequence.
- Make the right side of your body and the discus arm rotate around the left side of your body and your left leg. Imagine the left side of your body as the axle of a wheel around which everything is rotating.

Figure 12.17 Rotary discus throw initiated with the side of the athlete toward the direction of throw.

Figure 12.18 Rotary discus throw initiated with the back of the athlete toward the direction of throw.

- Once your throwing arm swings forward and releases the discus, bring your right leg forward for the reverse.

Variations in Starting Position at the Back of the Discus Ring

Many athletes begin their throws with a stance in which their feet straddle a line indicating the direction of throw. Some right-handed throwers will shift their starting position further to the right. By doing this they attempt to add more rotary pull to the discus at the back of the ring. You can have members of your class experiment with different starting positions (see figure 12.19).

COACHING TIPS

- The further you shift your starting position to the right, the longer you must pivot on the balls of both feet at the beginning of the rotation across the ring. Pivot across the ring; don't fall backward.
- Keep pivoting until your left foot points toward the direction of throw.

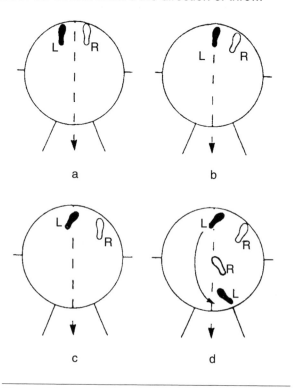

Figure 12.19 Four variations in discus starting positions.

COMMON ERRORS AND CORRECTIONS

STEP-BACK STANDING THROW

Error	Reasons	Corrections
The athlete steps back into the throwing stance with the wrong leg.	The athlete is unsure of the correct action.	Right-handed athletes must step back with the left leg. The athlete should practice the correct actions without the implement.
As the athlete steps back into the throwing stance, the athlete's bodyweight is shifted the same remain	The athlete is too eager to throw with the arm. The athlete is too erect or falls backward into the	The athlete's bodyweight must stay over the right leg when the athlete steps backward with the left leg into the throwing stance. The athlete's right leg must partially flexed until the left leg is in position. The throwing sequence is hips, chest, and finally the throwing arm.
The athlete turns prematurely toward the direction of throw as the athlete's left foot is placed into the throwing stance.	The athlete is too eager to throw and anticipates the throwing action. The athlete's hips rotate prematurely toward the direction of throw.	Instruct the athlete to practice the step-back action of the left leg with the seat toward the direction of throw. The athlete should begin rotating the hips toward the direction of throw only after the left foot is in position on the ground.
The athlete's left leg blocks the athlete from turning fully toward the direction of throw.	The athlete's left foot is not offset correctly during the step back into the throwing stance.	The athlete should practice shifting the left foot back into the correct throwing position without using the discus.
As the athlete's throwing arm and chest move forward into the throw, the athlete's hips and seat move backward.	There's no leg or hip action during the throw, and the athlete's chest drops forward toward the direction of throw.	Instruct the athlete to practice thrusting the hips forward and elevating the chest during the throw. The athlete's left foot must be offset correctly in the throwing stance.
During the release, the athlete's body falls to the left or right.	The athlete's foot positioning is incorrect, and the athlete's bodyweight is not shifting toward the direction of throw. The athlete's throwing arm is above shoulder level during the release, and the head and shoulders are dropped to the opposite side.	Mark correct foot positions on the ground. Have the athlete practice stepping back into the correct foot positions and driving the body ahead of the discus toward the direction of throw.

→

Error	Reasons	Corrections
The athlete releases the implement with the throwing hand close to the hip.	The athlete's throwing arm is too low following its arc around the athlete's body.	The athlete's throwing arm must be swung around the body just below horizontal (or just below shoulder level). The athlete should practice this action without the implement.
The discus has no spin; it flutters in flight.	The discus is not squeezed out of the hand; the athlete's fingers open up simultaneously to release the discus. The palm of the athlete's throwing hand is facing toward the direction of throw.	Have the athlete practice bowling the discus. The athlete should also practice standing throws, with the back of the throwing hand uppermost and the thumb leading. The discus must be squeezed out of the hand beginning from the little finger, with the index finger pulling last of all on the rim of the discus.
The athlete releases the discus out of the back of the hand.	The athlete is insure of the hand action to be used when releasing the discus. The athlete's throwing arm is flexed at the elbow immediately prior to release.	Have the athlete practice bowling and tossing the discus up and forward in the air, keeping the throwing arm extended throughout. The thumb of the throwing hand should lead the motion, and the index finger pull on the rim of the discus should be last of all. The athlete should practice easy standing throws with the discus.

ROTARY DISCUS THROW

Error	Reasons	Corrections
The discus does not trail behind the athlete's body during the rotation across the ring.	The discus is not held back at the end of the athlete's backswing. The athlete can also be spinning across the ring so slowly that the discus catches up and overtakes the athlete.	Instruct the athlete to practice rotary throws with the discus held on the athlete's seat. The athlete should also practice the rotation without the discus or using a light substitute for the discus and concentrate on having the discus trail behind.

→

Error	Reasons	Corrections
The athlete dives across the ring or falls backward across the ring.	The athlete's vision is not horizontal, and the athlete's shoulders are not parallel to the ground. The athlete's left foot is not pivoting toward the direction of throw at the start of the rotation at the back of the ring. There's no flexion in the athlete's knees.	The athlete's vision must be on the horizon, and the shoulders kept parallel to the ground. The athlete's head and left knee must lead into the rotation across the ring. The athlete should practice the correct footwork using a rubber ring or hula hoop. The athlete must sit and pivot as though squatting on a stool.
The athlete's rotation across the ring is not toward the direction of throw.	The athlete uses too much or too little rotation at the back of ring. The athlete's weight is not moving across the ring, and the athlete's line of vision is not correct.	The athlete must practice rotary throws without the discus or with a rubber ring or hula hoop. The athlete should concentrate on learning the correct legwork and the correct direction of rotation across the ring.
When the athlete is in the throwing stance, the athlete's bodyweight shifts prematurely over the front (left) leg.	The athlete's weight has not stayed over the flexed right leg as the left leg is thrust backward into the throwing position.	Instruct the athlete to repractice the step-back standing throw, emphasizing the correct positioning of the bodyweight over the athlete's right leg as the left steps back into position. Repeat this action using slow rotary throws.
In the throwing stance, the athlete has no windup and is unable to use the power of the hips and chest on the discus.	The athlete is not holding the discus back during rotation, and the athlete's legs and hips do not rotate ahead of the shoulders and throwing arm. The athlete's left leg is swung around to its position at the front of the ring instead of being thrust straight back into the throwing stance.	The athlete should work on the step-back standing throw, emphasizing the direct backward thrust of the left leg. Using a rubber ring or hula hoop, the athlete should practice running the legs ahead of the shoulders so that the feet are placed in throwing position with the discus trailing behind.

ASSESSMENT

1. **Assess the following theoretical elements as taught during instructional sessions:**

   a. Fundamental rules governing the discus throw.

   b. Good safety habits for the discus throw.

   c. Basic elements of discus-throw technique.

   d. Basic elements of training for the discus throw.

2. **Assess the performance of technique during the following stages of skill development.**

   The athlete uses a rubber ring, a hula hoop, or the competitive implement.

   a. A standing throw initiated with the side to the direction of throw.

   b. A step-back standing throw initiated with the back to the direction of throw.

   c. A rotary throw initiated facing the direction of throw.

   d. A rotary throw initiated with the side to the direction of throw.

   e. A rotary throw initiated with the back to the direction of throw.

   ### CRITICAL FEATURES OF TECHNIQUE TO OBSERVE DURING ASSESSMENT

   Rotary Throw (Right-Handed Thrower)

   ✓ Gripping the discus correctly.

   ✓ Turning the shoulders and discus arm to the rear of the body for the windup prior to the rotation across the ring.

   ✓ Squatting down and shifting the bodyweight over the left foot while initiating the pivot and rotation across the ring.

   ✓ Allowing the shoulders and discus arm to trail to the rear as the legs run across the ring to the throwing stance.

   ✓ Landing in a throwing stance with the bodyweight over a partially flexed right leg.

   ✓ Extending the right leg and rotating the hips forward toward the direction of throw.

   ✓ Extending both legs and thrusting the chest out toward the direction of throw.

   ✓ Pulling the discus arm around the body just below the line of the shoulder.

   ✓ Releasing the discus off the index finger and establishing a clockwise spin on the discus.

   ✓ Bringing the right leg forward in front of the left for the reverse to complete the throw.

3. **Hold graded competitions to help develop motivation and technique.**

   a. Athletes compete for distance using a discus substitute or using the competitive implement. Require a specific type of standing throw.

   b. Athletes compete for distance using a discus substitute or using the competitive implement. Require a specific type of rotary throw (i.e., beginning facing the direction of throw or with the side or back to the direction of throw).

SUGGESTED STANDARDS OF PERFORMANCE—DISCUS

MALE

Age	Weight of Discus		Distance
12-13	1 kg (2.2 lbs.)	*Satisfactory* *Good* *Excellent*	12.00 m (39'4") 16.00 m (52'6") 20.00 m (65'7")
14-15	1 kg (2.2 lbs.)	*Satisfactory* *Good* *Excellent*	18.00 m (59'0") 22.00 m (72'2") 26.00 m (85'3")
16-17	1.6 kg (3.52 lbs.)	*Satisfactory* *Good* *Excellent*	20.00 m (65'7") 25.00 m (82'0") 28.00 m (91'10")
18-19	2 kg (4.4 lbs.)	*Satisfactory* *Good* *Excellent*	21.00 m (68'11") 26.00 m (85'3") 30.00 m (98'5")

FEMALE

Age	Weight of Discus		Distance
12-13	750 g (1.61 lbs.)	*Satisfactory* *Good* *Excellent*	11.00 m (36'1") 14.00 m (45'11") 17.00 m (55'9")
14-15	1 kg (2.2 lbs.)	*Satisfactory* *Good* *Excellent*	13.00 m (43'4") 17.00 m (55'9") 20.00 m (65'7")
16-17	1 kg (2.2 lbs.)	*Satisfactory* *Good* *Excellent*	15.00 m (49'2") 19.00 m (62'4") 22.00 m (72'2")
18-19	1 kg (2.2 lbs.)	*Satisfactory* *Good* *Excellent*	17.00 m (55'9") 21.00 m (68'11") 24.00 m (78'9")

13

JAVELIN

Javelin throwing has been in the Olympic Games since 1908 as an individual event for men and women; it is also included as an event in the men's decathlon and the women's heptathlon.

Two historical developments have affected the conduct of competitive javelin throwing. The first was an attempt to use a discus-style rotation to throw. Although this method produced great distances, it was subsequently banned, and the rules now prohibit athletes from turning their backs toward the direction of throw. In effect, this law entrenched the traditional style of javelin throwing.

The second development resulted from the tremendous increase in distances (over 100 m) thrown by male athletes using super-aerodynamic javelins which at the time satisfied rule specifications. Worried rules makers subsequently changed the rules controlling the design of the javelin so that they would arc down toward the ground much sooner in their flight path. The change in javelin design temporarily reduced the distances that the men were able to throw. Modern research and training is now pushing these distances back up again. A simi-

lar design change has now been made to the women's javelin.

SAFETY SUGGESTIONS

Weighted balls and small lead shot are frequently used in javelin training. The weight of these items must be sufficient to produce some drag on the throwing arm, but not so much that it causes injury to the athlete's shoulder and elbow. Weighted leather beanbags filled with lead shot are also useful. Their great advantage is that they do not bounce or roll after being thrown.

If you are apprehensive about using competitive javelins with a class of young athletes, substitute ball throwing using javelin-style run-up and javelin-throwing technique. You can also have javelin-style competitions where the first impact of the ball indicates the distance thrown.

When you do decide to use the competitive implement, remember that both ends of the javelin can cause injury. Consequently, javelins must always be carried in an upright position and locked away after use. Young athletes must not be allowed to play with javelins or to treat them casually while they are being transported. When not in use, javelins must be stuck in the ground in an upright position, never stuck in the ground so that someone might walk or run into the tail end. When javelins are thrown, rigorously supervise the practice until safety habits become second nature and your athletes are deemed responsible enough to throw on their own.

Prior to javelin-style practices, make sure that your athletes go through a thorough and careful warm-up that includes stretching and flexibility activities specific to the event. Repetitive javelin throwing (or ball throwing) can place considerable stress on the athlete's back, shoulders, and elbow. This is particularly the case if a weighted ball or javelin is thrown incorrectly around the side of the body rather than over the shoulder. Use small lightweight javelin substitutes that are easy to grasp until the correct technique is well established.

During class instruction, position javelin throwers at least 3 m apart along a line. All athletes must be within earshot of your commands. Stand in a central position to the rear of the athletes. Those waiting to throw stand well back to the rear so that no one is struck by the tail of the javelin when a thrower extends the arm back to throw.

All athletes should throw at the same time or throw in sequence, according to your command. On command, make sure that all your athletes retrieve the javelins at the same time and carry them back in an upright position to the throwing area. If an athlete hasn't thrown at the same time as others in your group, then immediately command this athlete not to throw.

Care must be exercised when several javelins are stuck in the ground near each other. A javelin that is vigorously pulled out of the ground by one athlete can injure another who is standing to the rear. The javelin should be levered upward rather than pulled backward. However, if the javelin is stuck deep in soft ground, levering can break the tip. Athletes should first place a hand over the tail end and then carefully pull the javelin out backward.

Your athletes must never throw back toward their partners. This rule can be relaxed if you are teaching javelin technique using tennis balls.

Make sure that groups involved in other events are well beyond the javelin throwing

area. Allow for wind blowing a javelin off course, for throws landing outside of the designated area, and even for exceptional throws!

Wet conditions demand particular care. Run-ups on grass can be slippery unless your athletes use spikes. Always allow sufficient distance for the skidding of javelins on wet grass.

In competitive situations, you should provide a throwing area that conforms to the official specifications for the event. Officials should be fully qualified and well aware of the idiosyncrasies of the event. The javelin area, like other throwing areas, should be clearly marked and roped off well outside of the required 29-degree throwing sector. Officials must keep other athletes well clear of the throwing sector, particularly those who are exhausted from having just competed and who are less likely to be aware of what is happening around them.

Only experienced officials should be allowed to stand close to or facing the flight path of a javelin. Javelins viewed head-on are very difficult to see, and their speed of flight is highly deceptive. Landing flat, they may also bounce in a fashion similar to a discus. Officials with less experience should stand well to the side of the line of flight and then run out to mark the point of landing.

The technique of javelin throwing is the most natural action of the 4 throwing events, and youngsters who throw a ball well will have little difficulty grasping javelin fundamentals. Throwing tennis balls, softballs, and baseballs is a good introductory activity for javelin throwing, although you must remember that ball throwing must eventually be adapted to the specifics of javelin technique.

TECHNIQUE

Javelin throwing has shown little change in technique over the years, and today you will see little difference in technique from one athlete to the next. Some athletes will rotate the javelin arm forward, downward, and then extend it back prior to throwing. Others extend the throwing arm directly back without any forward motion. Some variations occur in the number of crossover (or impulse) steps that are used to tilt the athlete's body backward so that it is in a good throwing position. Some athletes use one; others use two crossover steps. Beyond these differences, the main elements of javelin technique are similar for all athletes.

RUN-UP

The athlete faces the direction of throw with the shoulders and hips square to the front. As the athlete accelerates through the run-up the javelin points toward the direction of throw with the tip slightly down. The athlete takes the javelin back to a full arm's length with the tip of the javelin now raised to the trajectory angle. The shoulders rotate 90 degrees to the right (right-handed athletes), and the hips remain facing the direction of throw.

CROSS-STEP, CROSSOVER, OR IMPULSE STEP

For a right-handed thrower, the cross-step is initiated by having the right leg stepping out and across in front of the left leg. This step helps to move the athlete's lower body ahead of the torso, tilting the athlete's body backward and away from the direction of throw. The athlete's shoulders and javelin arm are taken as far back as possible.

THROWING POSITION

The athlete's left leg steps out into a wide throwing stance, with the heel contacting the ground prior to the rest of the foot. The athlete's hips have rotated to the right so that the left hip is now toward the direction of throw. The athlete's rear leg (right) is partially flexed at

the knee and turned out to the side. The athlete's body is tilted backward, and the javelin arm is fully extended.

THE THROW

The athlete's right knee rotates vigorously toward the direction of throw and forces the hips in the same direction. The athlete's hips are followed by the chest, which the athlete thrusts toward the direction of throw so that the athlete's body resembles a bow. The javelin arm now acts like the end of a whip and is pulled forward at tremendous speed above the athlete's shoulder. The athlete's body is pushed forward, up, and over a straight left leg, and the javelin is released in front of the athlete's head (see figure 13.1).

REVERSE

After the javelin is released, the athlete continues to move forward, bringing the right leg forward and placing it in front of the left. This action, which is called a *reverse*, arrests any further motion and stops the athlete from stepping over the foul line (figure 13.22 on page 250).

TEACHING STEPS
STEP 1. Lead-Ups
STEP 2. A 3-Stride Throw With a Ball Using Javelin Technique
STEP 3. A Standing Throw With a Javelin
STEP 4. A Javelin Throw Using a Run-Up

Figure 13.1 Javelin technique.

STEP 1: LEAD-UPS

The following lead-up activities all involve throwing. They culminate with modified ball-throwing activities that are based on javelin-throwing technique.

Team Competition

Two teams of athletes stand on lines 20 meters apart, with a basketball placed on the ground equidistant from both teams (see figure 13.2). Each team throws volleyballs at the basketball, attempting to drive the basketball over their opponents' line. Allow one-handed and two-handed throws from above the head only.

Accuracy Competition

Basketballs are placed on a box top and must be knocked off by athletes throwing tennis balls or softballs (see figure 13.3). Throwing distances are appropriate for the age of the athletes. All athletes throw the same direction.

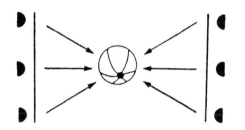

Figure 13.2 Team ball-throwing competition.

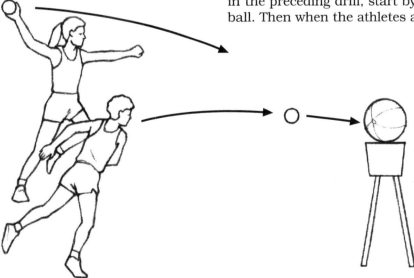

Figure 13.3 Accuracy competition.

Two-Handed Throw With a Basketball

While sitting, the athlete uses both hands to throw a basketball from behind the head (see figure 13.4). This activity forces the athlete to lean back and pull the basketball vigorously over the head. It helps the athlete to experience the stretch and pull action of the muscles of the chest and shoulders. Start by using a volleyball for this practice. Then when the athletes are experienced, they can use basketballs and then progress to lightweight medicine balls.

COACHING TIPS

- Reach back as far as possible behind your head with the basketball.
- Without overbalancing backward, let your elbows drop back as far as possible.
- Pull the ball forward and throw it as far as possible.
- Flex your arms at the elbows and lead the pulling action on the ball with your elbows.
- Extend the throwing action as far in front of your head as possible.

Two-Handed Basketball Throw From a Kneeling Position

This activity is similar to the preceding drill except that the athlete is in a kneeling position (see figure 13.5). This drill simulates the pull of the javelin over the athlete's head. As in the preceding drill, start by using a volleyball. Then when the athletes are experienced,

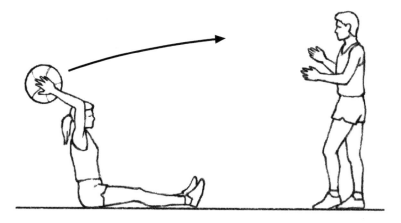

Figure 13.4 Two-handed throw with a basketball.

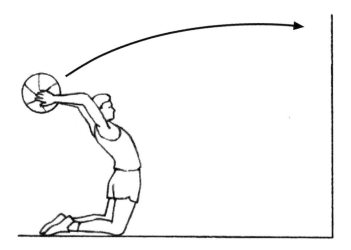

Figure 13.5 Two-handed basketball throw from a kneeling position.

they can use basketballs and progress to using lightweight medicine balls.

> **COACHING TIPS**
> - Tilt back to a position that you can comfortably control.
> - Pull the ball forward as vigorously as possible.
> - Contract your stomach muscles to help pull the chest forward.

Two-Handed Throw From a Standing Position

Each athlete begins in a standing position with the feet together. The athlete takes one stride (left foot forward for a right-handed athlete) and immediately performs a two-handed throw over the head (see figure 13.6). This practice simulates the athlete's forward body movement and

Figure 13.6 Two-handed throw from a standing position.

the pull of the javelin over the head. As in the preceding drill, start by using a volleyball. Then when the athletes are experienced, they can use basketballs.

COACHING TIPS

- Step out into a wide throwing stance.
- When you throw, make sure that you move your body forward and past your front foot. This foot will be your left foot if you are a right-handed thrower.
- Make your throwing action last for as long as possible. Pull from as far back as you can and drive the ball forward as far beyond the front foot as possible.

Running 2-Handed Throw

Add to the previous drill a short 2- or 3-stride run-up to simulate a run-up in a javelin throw (see figure 13.7). This practice is similar to a soccer throw-in. Volleyballs, soccer balls, and basketballs are all adequate for this drill. Start with the balls that are lighter. For a real challenge, use a lightweight medicine ball.

COACHING TIPS

- The addition of the 2- or 3-stride run-up will let you lean further back as you shift into the throwing stance.
- Step forward in the run-up quickly, and then lean back a little more as you shift into the throwing stance.

Two-Legged Jump and Throw

This practice is quite difficult and demands good coordination and quick explosive muscle actions. It simulates the athlete's pull on the javelin and in doing so strengthens the athlete's abdominal muscles. Novices should begin with a small jump and a push-throw from above the head. The action then progressively builds in intensity so that each athlete jumps higher and throws the ball from behind the head rather than pushing it from in front (see figure 13.8). As in previous drills, start by using the lightweight volleyball. Then when the athletes are experienced, they can use basketballs.

COACHING TIPS

- First practice this action without the ball.
- Think of jumping and then contracting the abdominals to pull the shoulders forward.
- Use the lightweight volleyball first. Then try it with the basketball.

Lift, Turn, and Throw

A lift, turn, and throw simulates the hip rotation that the athlete will use in the javelin throw (see figure 13.9). This drill should be performed slowly until the required actions are well-learned. Thereafter, it can be made more vigorous and explosive.

Figure 13.7 Running 2-handed throw.

Figure 13.8 Two-legged jump and throw.

Figure 13.9 Lift, turn, and throw.

COACHING TIPS

- A right-handed athlete will turn the hips to the front by rotating the knees first in the same direction.

- Imagine a corkscrew action, with your knees turning to the front followed by your hips, chest, and arms. Spinning on the balls of your feet will help to rotate your knees.

- Practice the action slowly to begin with, and don't concern yourself with distance.

- As you get used to the motion, speed up and throw for distance.

STEP 2: THREE-STRIDE THROW WITH A BALL USING JAVELIN TECHNIQUE

The athlete begins by facing the direction of throw with the feet together. The athlete's shoulders are turned 90 degrees, with the left shoulder toward the direction of throw and the right shoulder back. The athlete extends the left arm in the direction of throw and the throwing arm to the rear. The ball (tennis ball or baseball) is gripped in the athlete's right hand with the palm uppermost.

The athlete's left foot steps one stride forward, and the shoulders remain rotated with the throwing arm fully extended to the rear. The athlete's right foot steps across and ahead of the left foot, and the athlete's body leans backward (this is the cross-step). The athlete's throwing arm remains fully extended to the rear, palm uppermost. Next, the athlete's left foot steps forward into the throwing stance, with the heel placed down first. The athlete's bodyweight begins to shift forward.

To begin the throw, the athlete's hips and chest rotate toward the direction of throw. Thrusting the chest forward, the athlete pulls the throwing arm in the same direction, with the hand passing above the shoulder. The athlete's throwing arm flexes, and the elbow leads the throwing hand in the throw. The left leg and left side of the athlete's body straighten, and the right side of the body moves forward and rotates around the left. The athlete releases the ball above and in front of the head. After the ball is released, the athlete's right leg steps in front of the left leg to arrest further forward motion (see figure 13.10).

Reaching Back to Throw

Place several tennis balls or baseballs (4 or 5) on a box top to the rear of the athlete. The athlete stands in a wide stance (slightly wider than shoulder-width). The athlete reaches back, grasps a ball, turns to the front, and completes the throw (see figure 13.11). The balls must be placed far enough to the rear to ensure that the athlete reaches well back with a straight arm. The athlete's bodyweight must shift back over the right foot, and the right leg must be partially flexed. As a variation, a partner can offer balls individually on an open palm to the athlete. The athlete must be forced to reach well back to get each ball.

COACHING TIPS

- Once you grasp the ball, start your throw by turning your right knee (right-handed athlete) vigorously in the direction of throw. Push your hips toward the direction of throw.
- Your hips will pull your chest around towards the direction of throw.
- Your chest then pulls your throwing arm; be sure that you flex your throwing arm at the elbow. Remember that your elbow leads your hand in the throwing action.
- Release the ball well ahead of you and above shoulder level.
- Concentrate on the action of each throw individually; don't rush.

Throwing at Targets

Suspend hoops from soccer goalposts or draw circular targets on a wall. Athletes throw tennis balls at the targets from various distances (see figure 13.12). All athletes throw the same direction and begin the throw with their weight over their rear leg and with the throwing arm extended. The targets should be positioned to make the athletes to throw both forward and upward. You can award scores for accuracy.

COACHING TIPS

- Reach well back with an extended throwing arm, and make sure your weight is well over your rear leg.
- Move your weight forward toward the target and rotate your right knee (right-handed athlete) toward the direction of throw.
- Finish your throw with your body extended upward, and step with your right foot one more pace ahead of your left foot. This action will make sure that your body moves forward into the throw.

Practicing a 3-Stride Throw

Athletes practice a 3-stride throw using the technique explained previously (figure 13.10). A right-handed athlete begins a 3-stride throw with the throwing arm fully extended to the rear. The athlete takes the first stride with the left foot. All actions are initially performed slowly and mechanically so that they are fully understood.

COACHING TIPS

- Keep your throwing arm extended as you walk forward into the 3-stride throw.

Figure 13.10 Three-stride throw with a ball.

Figure 13.11 Reaching back to throw.

- Tilt your body backward as your right leg steps forward in the cross-step (right-handed athlete).
- Step out into a wide throwing stance with the heel of your left foot.
- Initiate the throwing action from the ground up in the following sequence: right knee rotated toward the direction of throw, followed by your hips, chest, and finally your throwing arm.
- Keep your body moving forward all the time.
- Release the ball well ahead of your body at an angle of 30 to 40 degrees above the horizontal position.

Increasing the 3-Stride Throw to a 5-Stride Throw

The athlete now adds 2 additional strides at the start of the 3-stride throwing sequence, making it a 5-stride throw. The athlete walks through the sequence with the throwing arm extended to the rear. A right-handed athlete begins the 5-stride throw in the same manner as the 3-stride throw (for example, taking the first stride with the left foot). The athlete turns the shoulders 90 degrees away from the direction of throw and keeps the throwing arm extended throughout the approach (see figure 13.13). The position of the athlete's shoulders is maintained until the actual throwing action occurs.

A 5-stride throw is as follows:

Sequence: left right left cross-step left throw
Stride: 1   2   3   4   5

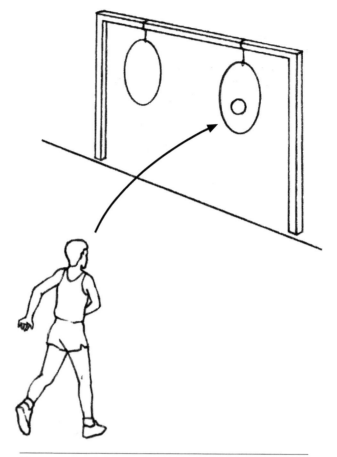

Figure 13.12 Throwing at targets.

The cross-step (in which the right leg steps across in front of the left) occurs on the fourth stride, and the throw occurs after the fifth and last stride has been completed.

COACHING TIPS

- Remember that this drill is similar to the 3-stride throw. The only difference is the addition of 2 strides at the start.
- Be sure to keep the palm of your throwing hand uppermost and your throwing arm extended so that it is parallel to the line of throw.
- Turn your shoulders 90 degrees so that your right shoulder is directly to the rear. Walk through the approach with your hips facing the direction of throw.

Extending the Throwing Arm During the Approach

This drill teaches your athlete to extend the throwing arm during the approach rather than

Figure 13.13 The 5-stride throw.

have it extended throughout. Holding a ball in the throwing arm, athletes repeatedly rotate their shoulders 90 degrees and extend their throwing arms as they jog (see figure 13.14). They do not throw the ball.

COACHING TIPS

- Rotate your shoulders a full 90 degrees so that your left shoulder is forward and your right shoulder is back. When you rotate your shoulders, they should be turned so that they are parallel to the direction of throw.

- Keep your hips square to the direction you are jogging. Don't turn your hips. Bring your shoulders back to the starting position (square to the front), and then repeat the drill again.

- Extend your throwing arm each time you rotate your shoulders so that your throwing arm is extended parallel to the direction of throw.

A 3-Stride Walk and Throw With the Throwing Arm Extended on the First and Second Strides

The athlete begins this drill with the throwing arm flexed and the ball held at chest height in front of the body. On the first and second strides, the athlete rotates the shoulders 90 degrees from the direction of throw and extends the throwing arm to the rear (see figure 13.15). The remaining portion of the 3-stride throw is performed as before.

COACHING TIPS

- Be sure to turn your shoulders a full 90 degrees, no less! Keep your hips facing the front until you complete the cross-step.

Figure 13.14 Extending the throwing arm.

- Extend your left arm and point it toward the direction of throw. This will keep your left shoulder in front and your right shoulder and throwing arm to the rear.

A 5-Stride Walk and Throw With the Throwing Arm Extended on the First and Second Strides

The athlete adds 2 strides to the start of the 3-stride walk and throw. The athlete extends the throwing arm during the first and second strides. The athlete's throwing arm stays extended until the throwing action itself is performed (see figure 13.16). Stress the same coaching points as in the preceding drill. Once the athletes have learned the 5-stride walk and throw, they can increase the speed of approach from a walk to a slow jog.

STEP 3: STANDING THROW WITH THE JAVELIN

The athlete places the left foot forward in a wide throwing stance, keeping the throwing arm fully extended, palm uppermost, tip of

Figure 13.15 Extending the throwing arm on the first and second strides of a 3-stride walk and throw.

Figure 13.16 Extending the throwing arm on a 5-stride walk and throw.

javelin at eye level, and vision forward. The athlete's left shoulder and left arm are forward, and the left arm points in the direction of throw. The athlete's right knee rotates in the direction of throw, forcing the hips and chest in the same direction. The left arm swings to the left to help pull the athlete's chest forward. The athlete pulls the javelin forward above the shoulder. The athlete's throwing arm flexes at the elbow. The left leg and left side of the athlete's body extend upward.

After the javelin has left the athlete's hand, the forward movement of the athlete's body will cause the athlete to step forward with the right leg so that it is ahead of the left. Called a reverse, this action is used to arrest any further forward motion (figure 13.17). Teach the sequence of actions so that they become fast and explosive. Beginners initially practice slowly, thereafter increasing their speed of movement.

Learning to Grip the Javelin

Athletes try 3 javelin grips, each of which is shown in figure 13.18 and described in the following sections. The index-finger grip is most commonly used and is the one you should teach. The second-finger grip is often called the Finnish grip and is moderately popular. The V grip is used least.

Index-Finger Grip The athlete's index finger grips the javelin shaft to the rear of the binding. The athlete's thumb lies along the side of the binding. The javelin lies in the center of the palm of the hand and is gripped by the athlete's fingers.

Second-Finger Grip The athlete's second finger grips the shaft of the javelin to the rear of the binding. The index finger is extended along the shaft of the javelin, and the thumb lies along the side of the binding. The javelin lies in the palm of the athlete's hand and is gripped by the fingers.

V Grip The shaft of the javelin is gripped in the V formed by the index and the second finger. This grip is immediately to the rear of the binding. The athlete's thumb lies along the side of the binding. The javelin lies in the

Figure 13.17 Standing javelin throw.

palm of the hand and is gripped by the fingers.

Securing the Grip on the Javelin

The athlete sticks the javelin in the ground and slides the throwing hand down the javelin from the tail to the binding to establish the grip that is being practiced (see figure 13.19).

COACHING TIPS

- The javelin must lie in the valley formed from the center of the base of the athlete's hand to the division between the thumb and index finger.
- The index finger (for the index-finger grip) wraps to the rear of the binding, and the thumb lies along the side of the binding.
- The remaining fingers of the hand wrap around the binding.

Throwing the Javelin Forward Into the Ground

Beginning with a flexed throwing arm, the athlete slowly takes the javelin back to arm's length. The palm of the throwing hand is uppermost. Stepping forward with the left leg (right-handed athletes), each athlete throws the javelin down into the ground 3–4 m (10'–13') ahead (see figure 13.20).

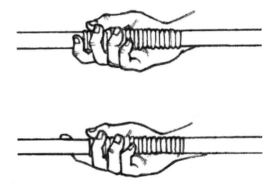

Figure 13.18 Three methods of gripping the javelin.

COACHING TIPS

- Keep the point of the javelin just below eye level and directed down at the ground.
- Pull on the javelin as though pulling a rope past your ear.
- Flex your throwing arm at the elbow as you pull your javelin forward.
- Pull your throwing arm forward, keeping the elbow of your throwing arm close to the javelin and well ahead of your throwing hand.
- Don't let the point of the javelin stray from its target directly ahead on the ground.

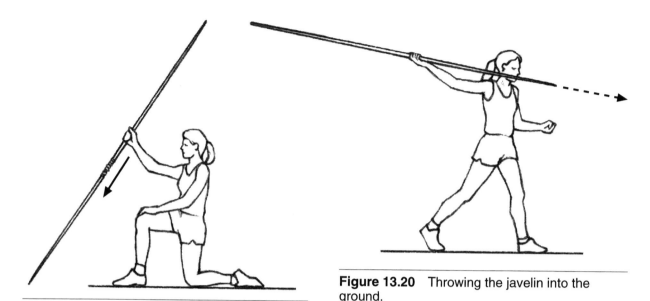

Figure 13.19 Securing the grip on the javelin.

Figure 13.20 Throwing the javelin into the ground.

Preparation for Standing Throws

Athletes work in pairs without releasing the javelin. A partner stands to the rear of the athlete, holding the tail of the javelin (see figure 13.21). The partner provides gentle but mobile resistance. Beginning in a throwing stance with the javelin arm fully extended, the athlete practices rotating the right knee, hips, and chest under the javelin and toward the direction of throw. This action should produce the bow position that the athlete's body passes through during the throw. Led by the elbow of the throwing arm, the athlete pulls the javelin forward over the head. The partner holding the tail of the javelin moves forward, still providing gentle resistance. Both athletes maintain their grip on the javelin; the javelin is not released.

COACHING TIPS

- Aim for smooth, nonjerky actions, beginning with the rotation toward the direction of throw with your right knee, hips, and chest.
- You must pull your throwing arm forward last of all. Remember that your throw starts from your legs.
- Keep the elbow of your throwing arm close to the javelin throughout.
- Perform the action slowly and precisely at first and then increase your speed.

A Standing Throw With the Javelin

Each athlete throws the javelin from a wide stance with the throwing arm fully extended

to the rear (figure 13.17). Athletes no longer throw the javelins down at the ground, but perform 8–10 m (25'–30') throws.

COACHING TIPS

- Begin the throw by rotating your hips and chest toward the direction of throw.
- Remember to initiate the hip rotation by the forward movement of the right knee.
- Keep the palm of your throwing hand uppermost.
- Pull the javelin forward, with your elbow leading the hand, and release the javelin above and in front of your head.

STEP 4: JAVELIN THROW USING A RUN-UP

The athlete faces the direction of throw, holding the javelin in the carry position. The athlete's body is square to the direction of throw, the throwing arm is flexed at the elbow, and the palm of the throwing hand is uppermost. In a 5-step sequence, a right-handed thrower steps forward with the left foot for the first step of the approach and begins to take the javelin back to arm's length. By the second step, the athlete has extended the javelin arm and rotated the shoulders 90 degrees from the direction of throw. The athlete's hips are still square to the direction of throw. On the third step, taken with the left foot, some backward lean is apparent (5 to 10 degrees).

Figure 13.21 Partner practice.

The cross-step and the fifth step occur one after the other in quick succession. The cross-step will put the athlete into a backward lean with the right knee slightly flexed and turned outward. The shoulders remain rotated 90 degrees away from the direction of throw, with the left shoulder toward the direction of throw. On the fifth stride, the athlete's left leg steps out into a wide throwing stance with the heel of the left foot contacting the ground first. Once in the throwing stance, the athlete rotates the right knee vigorously towards the direction of throw, pushing the hips and chest in the same direction. The athlete's body resembles a bow with the javelin being pulled whiplike over the shoulder. The athlete's body rises up, forward, and over an extended left leg. A sixth stride occurs when the athlete performs the reverse, bringing the right leg in front of the left. This action arrests any further movement forward (figure 13.22).

Extension of the Javelin Arm

The athlete practices the backward extension of the javelin arm (see figure 13.23). Initially this action is practiced at a walk, and then at a jog.

COACHING TIPS

- Hold the javelin with the grip just in front of your head. The javelin will be parallel to the direction you are moving.
- Keep your body square to the front and your shoulders relaxed.
- Rotate your shoulders and take the javelin back to arm's length. Keep your hips square to the direction you are running. Turn your shoulders, not your hips.
- Keep the palm of the throwing hand uppermost.
- Look to the front and keep your hips square to the line of the run-up.
- Keep the tip of the javelin at eye level when you extend the throwing arm.

A 3-Stride Javelin Throw at Walking Speed, Throwing Arm Extended on the First Stride

In this drill, the athlete extends the javelin arm directly backward on the first stride of the approach while keeping the javelin parallel with the direction of throw (see figure 13.24). As the athlete's right foot steps forward into the cross-step, the athlete's upper body tilts backward slightly. The left foot steps well out into the throwing stance. Once the athlete is in the throwing stance, the athlete's right knee pushes the hips and chest toward the direction of throw. This action must occur before the athlete pulls the javelin arm forward over the shoulder.

A 3-Stride Javelin Throw With the Throwing Arm Extended Throughout the Approach

When the approach speed approximates a fast run, the athlete must try to shift both feet into the throwing stance as quickly as possible. This fast shift of the athlete's feet can be practiced using a 3-stride approach. With this approach, the athlete should try to

Figure 13.22 Javelin throw using a 5-stride approach.

Figure 13.23 Extension of the javelin arm.

Figure 13.24 Extending the arm on the first stride of a 3-stride javelin throw.

use a rhythm pattern in which both feet land in the throwing stance almost simultaneously. Immediately after the feet have landed, the athlete concentrates on driving the hips and chest toward the direction of throw before pulling forward on the javelin with the arm.

- Listen to the sound of your feet landing, and try to make them land almost simultaneously in your throwing stance. You should hear a fast "da-da" as your feet land in the throwing position.
- Drive your hips and chest into the throw as soon as your feet land.
- Keep your body moving forward.
- Pull on the throwing arm last of all.

A 5-Stride Javelin Throw With the Throwing Arm Extended Throughout the Approach

This 5-stride throw at walking speed adds 2 more strides to the start of the 3-stride throw. The athlete begins this drill with the javelin arm extended. The sequence of actions is schematically laid out as follows, with the sixth stride occurring as the reverse.

Sequence	Stride
Left	1
Right	2
Left	3
Right (cross-step)	4
Left (throwing stance)	5
Throw	
Right (reverse)	6

A 5-Stride Javelin Throw With the Throwing Arm Extended During the First 2 Strides

In this drill, the athlete starts the approach with the javelin held in the carry position (figure 13.22). The athlete then takes the javelin directly back to an extended arm position during the first and second strides of the approach. This drill is practiced at walking speed.

- Keep the javelin parallel to the direction of throw as you extend your throwing arm.
- Keep the tip of the javelin just below eye level.
- Aim for a fast shift with both legs into the throwing stance.
- As soon as you place your left leg down in the throwing stance, strike forward toward the direction of throw with your right knee, followed by your hips, chest, and, lastly, your throwing arm.
- Brace your left leg and the left side of your body.
- Make the right side of your body move forward, upward, and around the post formed by the left leg and the left side of the body.

Increasing the Approach to 9 to 11 Strides

Now the athlete adds additional strides to the approach. For beginners, a 9–11-stride approach is recommended. Elite athletes frequently use a 25–30 m (80'–100') approach, in which 10–15 strides are devoted to a smooth acceleration into the throwing stance. Elite athletes will also use one or two check marks, the most important of which is commonly placed at the fifth stride prior to throwing (the most important phase of throwing). The recommended teaching sequence for increasing the size of the run-up is as follows:

1. The athlete repeats the 5-stride throw, extending the javelin arm during the first and second strides. The athlete begins with a walking approach, counting out the strides, and then attempts the same actions using a slow jog.

2. Add 4 strides for a 9-stride throw. The athlete begins with a walking approach, using a verbal count. Check marks indicate where the athlete should extend the javelin arm and where to enter the throwing stance.

3. Add 2 more strides for an 11-stride throw (see figure 13.25). The athlete increases the speed of the approach and adjusts check marks accordingly. Using spikes specially designed

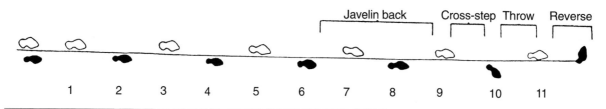

Figure 13.25 An 11-stride approach.

for javelin throwing will help the athlete obtain a good backward body lean without fear of slipping.

- Drive your foot forward into the cross-step and tilt your body backward.

- With the heel of your left foot, step out long and low into the throwing stance.
- Drive your hips and chest ahead of your throwing arm.
- Think of your body as the handle of a whip and the javelin as the tip of the whip; strike forward with the handle and crack the whip.

COMMON ERRORS AND CORRECTIONS

3- AND 5-STRIDE THROW WITH A BALL

Error	Reasons	Corrections
The ball is not taken back to arm's length prior to the throw.	The athlete is overeager to throw, and the timing of the throw is incorrect.	Have the athlete practice standing throws and 3- and 5-stride throws at walking speed, emphasizing the full extension of the throwing arm.
There is no backward body lean prior to entering throwing stance. The athlete is upright throughout the throwing sequence.	The athlete is using only the arm during the throwing action and is too eager to throw.	The athlete should practice the 3-stride throw, emphasizing backward lean as the right leg steps across for the cross-step.
During the cross-step, the athlete's right foot steps to the rear of the left foot instead of across the front of it.	The athlete is unfamiliar with the correct action of the right leg in the cross-step.	The athlete should slow down the required action and practice a single stride throw beginning with the right leg forward and already positioned across the left. Foot positions marked on the ground will help the athlete during a 3- or 5-stride throw.
The athlete has the wrong leg forward in the throwing stance.	The sequence of actions is too hurried. The athlete uses stutter steps in the approach.	The athlete must practice standing throws with the correct foot placed forward, and then progressively add additional strides to the approach.
The athlete falls toward the left during the throwing action.	The athlete is not extending the left side of the body upward during the throw. The athlete's hips may be moving backward during the throw and the head and left shoulder may be dropping to the left during the throw.	Have the athlete practice standing throws, keeping the left foot forward and lifting the body forward, up, and over a braced left leg during the throw.
The ball is put in shot-put style rather than thrown like a javelin.	The athlete has poor timing and has difficulty coordinating the the actions of the throwing arm.	Instruct your athlete to practice standing throws, moving the arm slowly through the throwing action. A partner can guide the athlete's motion from the rear by controlling the movement of the athlete's hand and elbow must lead (move ahead of) the throwing hand in the throwing sequence.

→

Error	Reasons	Corrections
The athlete throws the ball around the side of the body. The athlete's throwing hand passes below shoulder level.	Although this is a comfortable and adequate method for throwing a ball, it is not the correct way to throw the javelin because the throwing arm is not pulled forward above the shoulder.	Correct as you did for the preceding error. The athlete must apply javelin technique to ball-throwing action. The athlete's throwing hand must pass above the shoulder. The athlete should practice the required action slowly with a partner guiding the motion of the throwing arm.
The athlete fails to extend the throwing arm in a direct line to the rear, but rather swings the arm back around the body from right to left.	The athlete's right leg is not stepping directly forward in the cross-step but to the right of the direction of throw. The athlete's shoulders are rotating more than 90 degrees relative to the direction of throw.	The athlete must practice reaching back and throwing a ball placed or held directly to the rear. The athlete should walk slowly through a 3-stride throw, extending the throwing arm directly to the rear and parallel to the direction of throw.
The athlete is side-on throughout the whole approach. The athlete is moving sideways like a crab and using multiple crossover steps.	The athlete is overemphasizing the crossover action of the cross-step in the approach and is unsure of the required motions at each phase of the approach.	The athlete must rotate the shoulders so the right shoulder and throwing arm are directly to the rear. The athlete's hips should be kept square to the direction of throw until the athlete begins the cross-step.
The athlete throws the ball from ahead of the body like a dart.	The athlete is unfamiliar with the action of taking the throwing arm back to full extension. The athlete doesn't know correct sequence of activating the legs, hips, chest, and throwing arm.	The athlete must practice the sequence of hip, chest, and arm action in a standing position with a partner guiding the throwing arm through the correct path. The athlete then practices alone slowly, speeding up actions only when they are occurring in the correct sequence.

→

STANDING THROW WITH THE JAVELIN

Error	Reasons	Corrections
The athlete holds the javelin in the center of the binding and uses the a fist grip on the javelin, rotating the palm of the hand over the javelin.	The athlete does not know the correct grip or hand position.	Have the athlete stick the javelin point in the ground and slide the hand down to gain the correct grip. The index or second finger should be to the rear of the binding, and the javelin should lie along the valley formed from the center of the base of the athlete's hand to the division between the thumb and index finger.
The point of the javelin is not in line with the direction of throw.	The athlete's hand is not gripping the javelin forcibly enough. The javelin is also being allowed to swing away from the direction of throw. The athlete's shoulders are not rotated a full 90 degrees when the javelin arm is extended.	The athlete should practice keeping the tip of the javelin at eye level and under the chin. The javelin should rest on the palm of the hand, with the fingers pointing to the rear. The athlete's shoulders must be rotated so that the left shoulder is to the front and pointing toward the direction of throw. The athlete's left arm is extended, and the hand points toward the direction of throw.
The athlete throws the javelin around the side of the body. The tail of the javelin hits the athlete's back.	The athlete is not bringing the throwing hand forward over the shoulder and past the ear. The athlete has poor hip and chest rotation toward the direction of throw.	The athlete should practice a slow-motion throwing action (without release) with a partner gripping tho tail of the javelin and guiding the athlete through the correct motion. The athlete should emphasize the correct arm action, with the hip and chest rotation leading the action of the throwing arm.
The athlete uses an extreme angle of release. The javelin stalls in flight and hits the ground tail first.	The tip of the javelin is too high. The athlete's throwing hand has rotated upward at the wrist, allowing the tip of the javelin to lift. The athlete's throwing arm is angled down far too low. The tail of the javelin is dragging on the ground.	The athlete should practice a slow-motion throwing action with partner assistance. Have the athlete work on standing throws, keeping the tip of the javelin at eye level.

→

Error	Reasons	Corrections
The athlete throws the javelin with the wrong leg forward.	The athlete is unsure of the correct throwing stance.	Instruct the athlete to practice standing throws using a numbered sequence of actions: for example, 1) extend throwing arm, 2) step forward with the left foot, and 3) throw.
The athlete's body has no arch or bow position during the throwing action. The athlete's seat moves backward as the upper body and throwing arm move forward.	The athlete's hips and chest are not rotating and thrusting forward ahead of the throwing arm. The athlete is throwing with the arm by itself, instead of using the body first.	The athlete must emphasize driving the hips and chest forward into the throw prior to the strike of the throwing arm. The athlete must keep the body moving forward.
The javelin is thrown with the athlete's bodyweight continuously over the rear foot. The javelin lands tail first.	The athlete's bodyweight is not shifting forward during the throw. The athlete is using insufficient hip and chest rotation toward the direction of throw.	The athlete should temporarily overemphasize the reverse (stepping forward with the right leg after throwing, with the bodyweight moving forward over the left leg).
The athlete throws the javelin with a straight arm throughout the throwing action.	The athlete's throwing arm is not flexing at the elbow, and the athlete's elbow is not leading the throwing hand as it pulls on the javelin.	Instruct a partner to guide the athlete's hand and arm through correct actions (no javelin is used). Then the athlete repeats this practice with the partner guiding the javelin.

JAVELIN THROW USING A 9- TO 11-STRIDE RUN-UP

Error	Reasons	Corrections
The athlete's run-up is not in line with the direction of throw. A right-handed athlete drifts to the right side of the run-up or begins to shuffle sideways.	The athlete anticipates entry into the throwing stance. The hips turn to the side too early so that the athlete approaches the throw sideways.	The athlete must practice rotating the shoulders and taking the throwing arm back while the athlete's hips remains square to the direction of throw. An athlete's flexibility should be sufficient to allow the shoulders to rotate 90 degrees in relation to the hips. Draw lines along the length of the run-up to help keep the approach straight.
The athlete hits the ground with the tail of the javelin during the cross-step.	The athlete's angle of carry of the javelin is incorrect, and the extension of the athlete's throwing arm is not flat enough. The palm of the athlete's throwing hand may not be directly below the javelin.	Correct the athlete's angle of carry. The athlete must maintain this angle when the throwing arm is extended backward. The athlete should practice driving the right leg low and forward rather than upward in the cross-step.

Error	Reasons	Corrections
The athlete falls to the left during the throw (right-handed athlete).	The athlete's head drops toward the left during the throw, and the left side of the body collapses toward the left during the throw.	Have the athlete practice 3- and 5-stride throws, keeping the left shoulder high and vision toward the direction of throw. The athlete must brace the left side of the body and drive the right side of the body up and around the left.
The athlete places the right foot at right angles to the direction of throw in the cross-step (points directly to the right in the cross-step).	The athlete may be running up to throw with the body sideways to the direction of throw. The athlete rotates the hips too far (and too early) prior to assuming the throwing stance.	Instruct the athlete to practice 3- and 5-stride throws with the right foot crossed over and positioned with toes pointing 30 to 40 degrees to the right of the direction of throw.
The athlete performs a series of shuffle steps in the run-up. The right leg is placed to the rear of the left leg instead of in front.	The athlete is unsure of the correct leg actions prior to the entry into the throwing stance.	The athlete should practice 3- and 5-stride throws at walking speed with the javelin extended throughout, concentrating on the correct leg action and footwork.
During the throwing action, the athlete has no forward thrust toward the direction of throw.	The athlete's head is dropped forward, and the stride with the left leg into the throwing stance may be too big. As the athlete's shoulders move forward, the seat moves backward.	The athlete must keep the vision toward the direction of throw and correct the stride length of the left leg in the throwing stance. The athlete can also practice 3- and 5-stride throws with an emphasis on stepping forward onto the right foot for the reverse after the throw.
The athlete runs up much too fast and is unable to assume a good throwing position.	The athlete feels that run-up speed is a dominant factor in the throw and has poor knowledge of the importance of body position in the throwing stance.	Have the athlete practice walking and jogging throws from 3 to 5 strides, emphasizing correct throwing position. A partner gives a verbal count to provide a cadence for the approach. The athlete must slow down the approach and aim for body lean in the cross-step.
The athlete slows down too much during the run-up.	The athlete is unsure of the run-up and feels that it serves no real purpose. The athlete anticipates the throw and is unable to transfer the speed of the run-up into the throw.	Have the athlete practice acceleration into optimal throwing position after taking the throwing arm back. The speed of the athlete's run-up must complement the ability to enter the throwing position.

ASSESSMENT

1. **Assess the following theoretical elements as taught during instructional sessions:**

   a. Fundamental rules governing the javelin throw.

   b. Good safety habits for use in the javelin throw.

   c. Basic elements of javelin-throw technique.

   d. Basic elements of training for the javelin throw.

2. **Assess the performance of technique during the following stages of skill development:**

   a. A standing throw with a ball using javelin-throw technique.

   b. A throw with a ball initiated from a 3- and 5-stride approach and using javelin-throw technique.

   c. A standing throw with a javelin.

   d. A javelin throw initiated from a 3- and 5-stride approach.

   e. A javelin throw initiated from an extended 9- to 11-stride run-up.

   ### CRITICAL FEATURES OF TECHNIQUE TO OBSERVE DURING ASSESSMENT

   ✓ Running up with the javelin (or ball), taking the throwing arm back, and rotating the shoulders 90 degrees to the direction of throw.

   ✓ Stepping across the body with the rear leg in the cross-step and tilting the upper body backward.

   ✓ Stepping out into a wide throwing stance.

   ✓ Rotating the right knee and hips toward the direction of throw ahead of the chest and the throwing arm.

   ✓ Thrusting the hips and chest forward so the body resembles a bow.

   ✓ Driving the body forward and up over a straight supporting leg.

   ✓ Pulling the javelin directly toward the line of throw, leading with the elbow, and releasing the javelin above the shoulder.

   ✓ Bringing the rear foot forward for the reverse.

3. **Hold graded competitions to help develop motivation and technique.**

   a. The athlete throws a ball from a standing position using javelin-throw technique.

   b. The athlete throws a ball from 3- and 5-stride approaches using javelin-throw technique.

   c. The athlete throws a ball from a 9- to 11-stride run-up, using javelin-throw technique.

   d. Athletes compete for distance throwing a javelin from a standing position.

   e. Athletes compete for distance throwing a javelin from 3- and 5-stride run-ups.

   f. Athletes compete for distance throwing a javelin from an extended run-up. Use full competitive conditions.

SUGGESTED STANDARDS OF PERFORMANCE—JAVELIN

MALE

Age	Weight of Javelin		Distance
12-13	600 g (1.32 lbs.)	*Satisfactory* *Good* *Excellent*	16.00 m (52'6") 20.00 m (65'7") 24.00 m (78'9")
14-15	600 g (1.32 lbs.)	*Satisfactory* *Good* *Excellent*	22.00 m (72'2") 28.00 m (91'10") 32.00 m (105'0")
16-17	800 g (1.76 lbs.)	*Satisfactory* *Good* *Excellent*	27.00 m (88'7") 31.00 m (101'8") 35.00 m (114'10")
18-19	800 g (1.76 lbs.)	*Satisfactory* *Good* *Excellent*	30.00 m (98'5") 35.00 m (114'10") 39.00 m (127'11")

FEMALE

Age	Weight of Javelin	Distance	
12-13	400 g (.88 lbs.)	*Satisfactory* *Good* *Excellent*	15.00 m (49'2") 18.00 m (59'0") 22.00 m (72'2")
14-15	600 g (1.32 lbs.)	*Satisfactory* *Good* *Excellent*	15.00 m (49'2") 18.00 m (59'0") 22.00 m (72'2")
16-17	600 g (1.32 lbs.)	*Satisfactory* *Good* *Excellent*	18.00 m (59'0") 21.00 m (68'11") 25.00 m (82'0")
18-19	600 g (1.32 lbs.)	*Satisfactory* *Good* *Excellent*	21.00 m (68'11") 25.00 m (82'0") 30.00 m (98'5")

14

HAMMER

The hammer throw was first contested in the Olympic Games in 1900. For many years, it was solely a male event. Today it is an event for males and females. Males throw a hammer that weighs 7.25 kg (16 lbs.), and the females throw a hammer that is 4 kg (8 lbs., 13 oz.).

The hammer throw is considered one of the most technical and complex of the throwing events. It is unique in that the athlete repeats 3 or 4 rotations at high speed across the 2.13 m (7') ring. Each rotation successively increases the velocity of the hammer. If the athlete makes mistakes, they are progressively magnified from one turn to the next.

Although hammer throwing is claimed to be one of the most satisfying of all throwing events, it suffers from being confined to relative obscurity because athletes must practice on waste tracts of land. To a large degree, this rejection stems from the fact that the event can be dangerous to all but the thrower. Even with elite throwers, this event always requires the most rigorous of safety precautions.

During the 1980s, athletes from the Soviet Union revolutionized the technique of hammer throwing. They changed the athlete's footwork and altered the arc of movement that the hammer followed. These changes increased the acceleration applied to the hammer, and distances exceeded 86 m (284'). For the beginner, the traditional technique of throwing is more than adequate, and this is the technique taught in this chapter.

You can begin teaching the fundamentals of hammer throwing with a variety of training implements. Athletes can use 1–1.2 m (3'–4') broom handles or wooden poles to simulate the hammer. These substitutes allow the athlete to concentrate on learning the footwork. A basketball in a net with a handle attachment is also excellent for teaching hammer basics. Using this equipment, the athlete can safely practice preliminary swings, turns, and the delivery (release) of the hammer both indoors and outdoors.

SAFETY SUGGESTIONS

The hammer throw is a rotary event that exerts a tremendous outward pull on the thrower. This force increases from one rotation to the next as the athlete accelerates the hammer.

The athlete must counteract this pull at all times. Because the athlete is accelerating the implement far longer than in other throwing events, minor errors committed early in the swings and turns become major errors later in the throw. Frequently beginners (and sometimes even elite throwers) lose control and release the hammer in the wrong direction. Consequently, a safety cage surrounding the thrower is absolutely essential. This cage protects those watching, coaching, and officiating. The cage must be built to the required standards and regularly inspected and repaired.

All hammers should be safely stored and carried in an orderly manner to the throwing areas. Don't allow young athletes to play with throwing implements or treat them casually while they are being transported. Prior to each throwing session, closely examine each hammer, checking the hammer pivot (in the head of the hammer), the wire, and the handle. Replace worn parts immediately. Also inspect any training equipment that you use in place of the hammer.

A multipurpose concrete pad can be laid on an area of waste land. You can paint the smaller 2.13 m (7') hammer and shot circles inside the larger 2.50 m (8' 2½") discus circle. This arrangement allows athletes in different throwing events to practice in sequence from within the same protective cage. The only difficulty you will have with this setup is that competitive shot-put circles are equipped with a large curved stop board at the front of the circle. This board will have to be removed if discus throwers, hammer throwers, and shot-putters are throwing from the same concrete pad.

The following safety suggestions are recommended for training sessions in which your athletes throw the competitive hammer or use substitutes for the hammer:

- You (or other qualified personnel) supervise all throwing sessions.
- Don't allow group throwing—even if you have a concrete pad large enough to allow this to occur. Have your athletes throw one at a time.
- Require those waiting their turn to stand well behind the hammer cage.
- Be sure your athletes carry the hammers back to the throwing circles. Under no

circumstances are hammers (or any other implements) thrown back.
- The athlete who is throwing, with the help of observers, first checks the area where the hammer will land to make sure it is clear before any throw is attempted.
- Take particular care in wet conditions. Sweep out the throwing circles and make sure that your athletes wear athletic shoes that provide adequate traction.
- Be sure that the substitute equipment that you use for training purposes is safe and designed to withstand repeated impact with the ground.
- Require the thrower to use a glove protecting the inner hand. Make several gloves of different sizes (right-handed and left-handed) available for practice sessions.

TECHNIQUE

Modern hammer throwers use 2 or 3 preliminary swings and 3 or 4 turns to rotate across the hammer ring. If the athlete is able to apply continuous acceleration to the hammer and can fit 4 heel-toe rotations in the 2.13 m (7') ring, then 4 turns should be used. The following descriptions and illustrations show the main elements of a hammer throw using 1 swing and 3 turns (see figure 14.1).

INITIAL STANCE

A right-handed thrower grips the hammer handle with the left hand and wraps the right hand over the top of the left hand. The athlete stands at the rear of the ring, with the back toward the direction of throw and the feet approximately shoulder-width apart.

PRELIMINARY SWINGS

A right-handed thrower places the hammer on the ground to the right rear and turns the shoulders to the right so that a straight line exists between the hammer head and the athlete's left shoulder. To begin the preliminary swings, the athlete pulls the hammer upward toward the left. When the hammer has rotated as far to the left as possible, the ath-

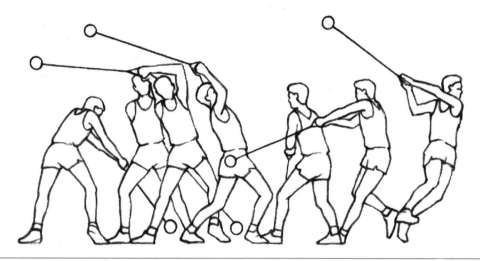

Figure 14.1   Hammer-throw technique.

lete ducks under the hammer and accelerates it in its arc from left to right. The pathway that the hammer follows has a high point to the left rear of the athlete and a low point to the right front. The high point is progressively raised through each of the athlete's 3 or 4 rotations across the ring, until it becomes the final trajectory angle when the athlete releases the hammer.

As the hammer follows its rotary pathway in the preliminary swings, the athlete counteracts the pull of the hammer by shifting the hips in the opposing direction. Each full rotation of the hammer around the athlete's body prior to the athlete's entering the turns is called a preliminary swing or simply a swing.

THE TURNS

When the head of the hammer reaches its lowest point in the last preliminary swing, the thrower fixes the arms and hammer in front of the body and rotates into the first of 3 or 4 turns. The left foot is rotated 180 degrees on the heel toward the direction of throw, and the right foot rotates 180 degrees on the toe. The athlete rolls (or rocks) along the outer edge on the left foot at the midpoint of the turn and performs another 180 degrees of rotation on the ball of the left foot. The athlete then picks up the right foot, brings it fully around, and places it on the ground parallel to the left foot. This series of actions completes one turn. Elite athletes perform 3 or 4 turns. Beginners can compete in hammer competitions using only 1 or 2 swings followed by 1 or 2 turns. It is also quite legal for

an athlete to compete in a hammer throwing competition using swings only, with no turns. Standing with their feet at the front of the ring and with their backs initially to the direction of throw, athletes use 2, 3, or even 4 swings before delivering (releasing) the hammer. This technique is used in Highland Games competitions when athletes throw the Scottish hammer.

For each turn that is performed across the ring, the athlete attempts to rotate the lower body (legs and hips) as quickly as possible around and ahead of the torso (and hammer). The faster the athlete gets the feet around and down on the ground ahead of the torso and hammer, the more the athlete can accelerate the hammer up toward its high point and down toward its low point. In essence, the athlete is towing the hammer through 3 or 4 turns and trying to make it move faster and faster. With each turn, the high point of the hammer is raised toward its final angle of release.

As the hammer ball moves around its circular pathway faster and faster, its outward pull on the athlete progressively increases. The athlete flexes the legs and sits back to counteract this pull. The athlete's arms stay fully extended. In this way, the athlete maintains balance while at the same times maintaining the maximum distance from the axis of rotation out to the hammer ball. The further out from the athlete that the hammer ball travels and the faster the athlete spins, the greater the speed of the hammer. Coupled with an optimal angle of release, these factors produce a great distance when the hammer is thrown.

Figure 14.1 (*continued*)

THE DELIVERY (RELEASE)

After placing the right foot down at the end of the third (or fourth) turn, the athlete explosively extends the body and pulls the hammer in an upward spiral by lifting the chest and extending the legs and the back. The athlete's pull on the hammer occurs when the hammer is in front of the body and passing through the low point of its arc. When the hammer is released, the athlete is fully extended with the left shoulder toward the direction of throw.

THE REVERSE

After releasing the hammer, the athlete concentrates on staying in the ring and not fouling the throw by stepping on the rim of the circle or outside of it. The athlete rotates on the right foot and brings the left foot around and back to the rear. The athlete may also flex both legs and lower the body back and away from the forward edge of the ring.

TEACHING STEPS

STEP 1. Lead-Ups

STEP 2. Hammer Swings

STEP 3. Hammer Turns

STEP 4. Combining Hammer Swings, Turns, and Delivery

STEP 1: LEAD-UPS

All 2-handed swinging and slinging drills are good lead-ups for the hammer throw. These drills simulate the delivery (final throwing action and release) in the hammer throw.

2-Handed Throws With the Medicine Ball

The athlete throws a medicine ball in 2-handed fashion for height (see figure 14.2). This activity resembles the upward thrust of a hammer thrower's body during the delivery (release) of the hammer.

Figure 14.2 Two-handed medicine ball throw.

Figure 14.3 Two-handed overhead throw.

- Extend your legs and lift up onto your toes.
- Throw your head back and lift your torso upward.
- Use both arms to throw the ball as high as possible.

Two-Handed Overhead Throw With a Medicine Ball

An overhead throw for distance emphasizes not only the upward thrust of the athlete's body, but also the backward lean required in the delivery of the hammer (see figure 14.3). Athletes can compete for distance and/or height in this activity. Set up pole-vault standards and a crossbar and have your athletes compete to see who can hurl the medicine ball the highest and farthest.

- Use your legs and back as powerfully as possible to drive the ball backward and upward as far as possible.
- Lift up high onto your toes.

Two-Handed Overhead Throw With the Medicine Ball Against a Wall

Athletes throw the medicine ball overhead against the wall and then quickly rotate to catch it on the rebound (see figure 14.4). This activity combines an extension of the body with quick reactions and rotation of the athlete's body.

- As soon as you throw the ball backward against the wall, pivot on the balls of your feet for a $^1/_2$-rotation to catch the ball again. This pivoting action is used both in the hammer turns and in the delivery of the hammer.

Two-Handed Slinging of a Medicine Ball Over the Shoulder

This lead-up drill emphasizes the upward rotary lift of the athlete's body during the delivery and release of the hammer. The athlete's legs and body extend upward, and the extended arms sling the medicine ball over the shoulder (see figure 14.5). The two-handed slinging action simulates the two-handed motion used in the hammer deliv-

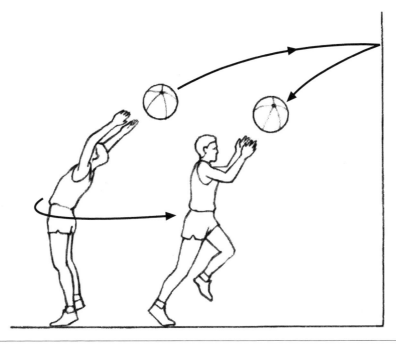

Figure 14.4 Two-handed overhead throw, turn, and catch.

Figure 14.5 Slinging a medicine ball over the shoulder.

ery. Athletes can compete in this activity for distance.

COACHING TIPS

- Extend your legs and back simultaneously and pivot on the balls of your feet toward the direction of throw.

- Release the ball high over your left shoulder (right-handed thrower).

STEP 2: HAMMER SWINGS

A right-handed athlete grips the hammer handle with the left hand inside the right. The athlete begins the swings with the hammer laid back on the ground to the right rear. The athlete rotates the shoulders to the right and fully extends the left arm, forming a straight line from the shoulders, down the arms, wire, and out to the hammer ball. The legs are flexed.

The athlete begins by pulling (towing) the hammer upward to the left so that the plane of the hammer has a high point to the athlete's left rear. When the hammer has rotated as far to the left as possible, the athlete rotates his shoulders quickly toward the right, shifts the bodyweight in the same direction, and pulls the hammer down to its low point on the right side. This sequence of actions completes the first swing. The athlete may repeat this sequence for 2 more swings, increasing the hammer's speed each time. When the hammer passes in front of the right foot in the final swing, the athlete shifts the bodyweight above the left foot in preparation for the entry into the turns (figure 14.6).

Hammer Swings Using a Pole

Introduce your athletes to the hammer swings with the use of 1–1.2 m (3'–4') broom handles or poles (see figure 14.7). The athlete's left hand grips the end of the pole, and the right hand grips the pole just beyond the left. Both arms are extended.

Figure 14.6 Hammer-swings.

Figure 14.7 Hammer swings with a pole.

COACHING TIPS

- Make sure your arms are extended in front of your body.
- Flex your legs slightly and look forward.
- Swing the pole as far to the left as possible, and at the same time move your hips to the right.
- Swing the pole upward on your left side so that the arc of its movement has a high point to your left rear and a low point to the right front of your body.
- When the pole is swung as far to the left as possible, drop your head underneath your arms and rotate your chest and shoulders to meet the pole on the right. Repeat this action for several swings.

- Remember that as the pole swings to the left, your hips shift to the right. The same action occurs in the opposing direction.

Hammer Swings Using a Basketball in a Net

A basketball or light medicine ball in a net with a string extension is an excellent substitute for the competitive hammer. Make it the same length (1.2 m or 4') as the competitive hammer. Swings practiced with this equipment will be much faster than those performed with a pole (see figure 14.8). It is very important to establish the correct body positions first by using the slower actions of the pole. Athletes can then work on the swings using the following sequence with both hands gripping the net handle

Figure 14.8 Hammer swings with a ball in a net.

and then with only the left hand gripping the net handle (for an athlete rotating toward the left).

COACHING TIPS

- Stand in a shoulder-width stance.
- Place the ball (in the net) on the ground to your right rear.
- A straight line should extend from your left shoulder down the string extension to the ball itself.
- Drag the ball upward to your left by extending your legs and body and pulling with your shoulders. This action initiates the first of your swings.
- As soon as you have swung the ball as far to your left as possible, duck your head under your hands and turn to meet the ball again on your right side.
- Balance the pull of the ball by moving your hips in the opposing direction.
- Throughout the swings, think of the ball and net as an extension of your arms and shoulders.
- Avoid bending (flexing) your arms when the ball is in front of your body.

Hammer Swings and Delivery (Release) Using a Basketball in a Net

The athlete adds a delivery (release) to 2 or 3 hammer swings using a basketball in a net (see figure 14.9).

COACHING TIPS

- Perform 2 or 3 swings, setting the high point of the ball's arc over your left shoulder.

- Shift your hips to your right when the ball rotates to your left.
- Begin the final pull on the ball for the delivery after 2 or 3 swings when the ball is at its low point in front of your body.
- Extend your legs and back vigorously and throw your head back. This action will help you pull the ball in the direction that you want to release it.
- Pivot on the balls of your feet toward the direction of throw, and release the ball over your left shoulder.

The Grip on the Hammer Handle

A right-handed thrower (who will release the hammer over the left shoulder) wears a protective glove on the left hand. The left hand grips the hammer handle, and the right hand is wrapped over the left (see figure 14.10). The reverse arrangement occurs for left-handed throwers.

COACHING TIPS

- When you grip the hammer, avoid making a tight fist with your hands.
- Form a long hook with the fingers of both hands and use this hook to grip the handle of the hammer.

Hammer Swings and Delivery (Release) Using a Light Hammer

In this drill, athletes practice hammer swings and delivery (release) using a hammer that is

Figure 14.9 Hammer swings and delivery using a ball in a net.

Figure 14.10 Gripping the hammer.

approximately ½ of the competitive weight for their age range; in most cases, a 4 kg (8.8 lb.) hammer is adequate. The hammer is placed on the ground to the right rear of the athlete, who tows it into the first swing in the same manner as when using the ball in the net. The high point of the hammer's arc is to the athlete's left rear, whose hips are simultaneously shifted to the right to counterbalance the pull of the hammer. With each swing, the high point of the hammer is raised in preparation for the delivery.

The delivery is performed with an upward extension of the athlete's legs and back. The athlete pivots on the balls of the feet toward the direction of throw and releases the hammer over the left shoulder (see figure 14.11). Athletes practicing this drill can compete against each other for distance.

COACHING TIPS

- Keep the high point of the arc to the left rear of your body.
- Fully extend your arms when the hammer is in front of you.
- Drive up with your legs and chest in the delivery.

- Keep your arms extended during the delivery.

STEP 3: HAMMER TURNS

After completing 2 or 3 swings, the athlete enters the turns with the hammer fixed in front of the body. The athlete's arms are extended, and the athlete's vision is toward the hammer ball. A right-handed thrower begins the first turn with 180-degree rotation on the heel of the left foot and 180-degree rotation on the ball of the right foot The right knee is turned inward to the rear of the left knee during the rotation to the left.

The athlete rolls along the side of the left foot and then rotates 180 degrees on the toe of the left foot, simultaneously lifting the right foot off the ground and bringing it around so that the body rotates a full 360 degrees. As the athlete enters each of the turns, the hammer ball is raised on the left side and lowered on the right. This establishes a high point and low point in the arc that the hammer follows. It also sets the angle of trajectory for the hammer when it is released.

With each turn, the athlete attempts to rotate the lower body ahead of the upper body. By carrying out this action, the athlete winds up like a spring being coiled. Because the athlete's feet are on the ground ahead of the torso in each turn, the successive winding and unwinding of the spring progressively accelerates the hammer.

Figure 14.11   Hammer swings and delivery using a light hammer.

Rotation With the Arms Extended

Athletes rotate on the spot with the arms outstretched in front (see figure 14.12). No implement is used, and no specific footwork is demanded. A shuffling rotation with the feet is adequate.

VARIATION

The athlete performs the same action, gripping the end of a 1–1.2 m (3'–4') pole.

COACHING TIPS

- Squat down, look forward, and extend your arms, holding them out horizontally in front of your body.
- Don't worry about footwork; shuffle around in a circle, turning on the same spot.

Footwork for Hammer Turns

Athletes practice the heel-toe footwork used in hammer turns. The athlete's arms are outstretched in front of the body. No implement is used. Figure 14.13 shows the footwork for one complete turn.

Practicing a Sequence of Hammer Turns

Draw 2 parallel lines shoulder-width apart on the ground to assist the athlete in the alignment of the feet during the turns (see figure 14.14). The athlete performs 1, 2, and then 3 turns in sequence.

COACHING TIPS

- Squat down and look forward.
- Pivot a full 180 degrees on the heel of your

Figure 14.12   Rotation on the spot with the arm extended.

left foot and the toe of your right foot.

- Press the knee of the right leg in behind the left leg.
- Pivot 180 degrees on the toe of the left foot, simultaneously picking up your right foot to rotate around and complete the turn. Keep your legs close together during each turn.
- Don't swing your right leg out wide. Keep your legs close together.
- Make sure that your feet line up parallel at the end of each turn.
- Look forward throughout the whole action.

Hammer Turns Using a 1–1.2 m (3'–4') Pole

In this drill, athletes perform the same action as previously, but they now use a 1–1.2 m (3'–

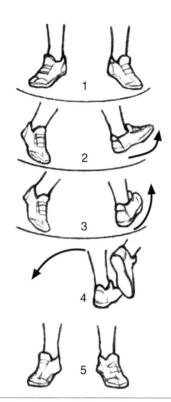

Figure 14.13 Footwork for each hammer turn.

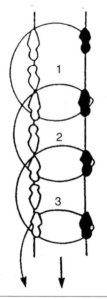

Figure 14.14 A sequence of hammer turns.

4') pole. Each athlete squats down and holds the pole at arm's length and directly ahead of the body throughout each turn.

COACHING TIPS

* Look forward and keep your arms fully extended.
* Don't raise or lower the pole during the turns.
* Concentrate on completing each 180-de-

gree turn and ending up with both feet on the parallel lines.

Hammer Turns Without a High or Low Point Using a Basketball in a Net

Each athlete uses a basketball in a net instead of the pole. The athlete can pass the ball around the body to give it some initial movement, and then enter the first turn holding the basketball in the net in an extended position directly in front of the body. The athlete makes no effort to achieve a high point on the left side of the body, nor a low point on the right side of the body. Providing that the first turn is completed correctly, the athlete then moves immediately into the second turn. Turns using a basketball in a net tend to be faster than with a pole. If the athlete gets confused and performs the footwork incorrectly, the slower movements with the pole should be practiced again.

COACHING TIPS

* Complete each turn so that your feet land on the parallel lines.
* Maintain a balanced squatting position throughout.
* Look forward.
* Concentrate on completing a full 180-degree rotation on your left heel, and then repeat it on the ball of your left foot.
* Keep your arms extended and the implement directly in front of your body.
* Make the first 180 degrees of the turn as slow and precise as you can, and then finish the last 180 degrees of the turn quickly.
* Keep your knees close together during the turn.

Adding a High and Low Point to the Turns

In order to release a hammer at the optimal trajectory angle, the athlete must tilt the arc of the hammer during the turns. In this way, the hammer will have a high point and a low point as it circles around. An elite athlete will progressively raise the high point through each turn. A right-handed thrower will have the high point to the left rear and the low point to the right front of the body. A novice can practice this action with the arms extended, holding a basketball or volleyball between the hands (see figure 14.15). An alternative is to use a 1–1.2 m (3'–4') pole. The athlete raises the ball or pole upward to a high point to

Figure 14.15   Practicing high and low points using a basketball.

the left rear during the first half of the turn, and then lowers it to a low point to the right front during the second half of the turn.

- Keep your arms fully extended during the turns.

- Raise your arms for the high point as you complete the first 180-degree rotation on the heel of your left foot. Lower your arms for the low point when the final 180 degrees is completed.

- Keep your legs flexed and knees together during the turns, and squat down (as though sitting on a stool) and look forward to maintain balance.

Combinations of Swings and Turns

Athletes now put swings and turns together in various combinations to familiarize themselves with the transition from swings to turns. Use a light hammer for this drill. This drill stresses the importance of the shift of the athlete's hips back and forth to counteract the pull of the hammer during the swings. This drill also emphasizes the shift of the athlete's bodyweight to the left for the entry into each turn.

Try these combinations of swings and turns:

(a) 2 swings followed by 1 turn

(b) 2 swings followed by 2 turns

(c) 2 swings, 1 turn, 2 swings

(d) 1 swing, 1 turn, 1 swing, 1 turn

(e) 2 swings, 2 turns, 2 swings, 2 turns

- Establish a high point and a low point during the swings, and maintain these high and low points through your turns.

- Shift your weight over your left foot in the transition from swings to turns.

- Keep your knees close together in each of your turns.

- Keep your left foot in contact with the ground, and shift your right foot through the last half of each turn as fast as possible.

- Keep the implement fixed at arm's length in front of your body during your turns.

- Shift your hips away from the hammer in the swings and squat down and lean away from the hammer in the turns. Don't try to flex your arms.

STEP 4: COMBINING HAMMER SWINGS, TURNS, AND DELIVERY

The swings, turns, and delivery (release) performed in sequence make up the complete throw. Remember that your athletes can progressively add more swings (up to a maximum of 3) to the turns (up to a maximum of 4) and each combination will make up a complete throw. The addition of more swings and turns is only worthwhile if they successfully accelerate the hammer.

The Complete Throw

The complete throw combines 1, 2, or even 3 preliminary swings, followed by 1, 2, 3, or 4 turns. The throw is completed with the delivery or release (see figure 14.1). Athletes slowly practice this action (without release) using the 1–1.2 m (3'–4') pole, and then with a release they practice turning faster using a basketball in a net or a lightweight hammer. Thereafter, the athlete practices with progressively heavier hammers until the athlete is throwing with the competitive-weight hammer.

A typical practice sequence is as follows:

(a) 2 or 3 swings, followed by 1 turn and the delivery.

(b) 2 or 3 swings, followed by 2 turns and the delivery.

(c) 2 or 3 swings, followed by 3 turns and the delivery.

(d) 2 or 3 swings, followed by 4 turns and the delivery.

COACHING TIPS

- Don't rush; perform the swings fairly slowly and increase speed in the turns and delivery action.

- Be sure to keep your arms extended and the hammer in front of your body.

- Try to bring your right leg around your body as fast as possible to complete each turn.

- Flex your right knee and make your right leg brush against your left as you rotate in each turn.

- Make sure your feet line up parallel to the direction of throw at the end of each turn.

Delivery and Reverse

The delivery (the actual release of the hammer) at the end of 3 or 4 turns demands extremely fast actions and precise timing. The rotation of the athlete's legs and hips in the third turn must occur at great speed so that both feet are on the ground well ahead of the athlete's upper body (and the hammer). In this way, the athlete can exert tremendous pull on the hammer.

The athlete's pull on the hammer in the delivery begins when the hammer ball is moving down in front of the body. The athlete rotates on the balls of the feet toward the direction of throw, lifting the chest upward and extending the legs and back. The action simulates an upward spiral. The athlete's body is fully extended when the hammer is released over the left shoulder. The athlete avoids stepping on the rim of the circle, or outside of the circle, by performing a reverse. This move can be done by withdrawing the left leg from the rim of the hammer circle and flexing or rotating on the right foot (see figure 14.16).

COACHING TIPS

- Begin the throw slowly and accelerate from swings to turns to the final release

- Make the acceleration smooth throughout.

- Start with the plane of the hammer fairly flat, and then successively raise the high point in each turn.

- Straighten your back and extend your legs as powerfully as possible in the delivery. Spiral upward toward the direction of throw.

- Throw your head back and deliver the hammer over your left shoulder.

Practicing the Reverse

The athlete practices the reverse (or recovery after releasing the hammer) at any time that the hammer is released.

COACHING TIPS

- Complete the delivery, release the hammer, and then consciously pull your left foot back from the inside edge of the rim of the circle.

- Flex your right leg and lower your weight backward.

- Don't perform this action until you have released the hammer.

Alternative Technique for Performing the Reverse

In an alternative technique used to prevent fouling, the athlete continues to rotate on the balls of the feet after releasing the hammer and rotates back toward the center of the circle.

COACHING TIPS

- After you release the hammer, rotate another ½-turn on the balls of the feet so that you face the direction of throw.

- Flex your legs simultaneously to lower your weight backward toward the center of the ring.

Figure 14.16 The delivery and reverse.

COMMON ERRORS AND CORRECTIONS

HAMMER SWINGS

Error	Reasons	Corrections
The athlete flexes the arms during the swings.	The athlete is fighting the hammer. The thrower fears loss of balance and uses no leg flexion. The athlete lowers the head and bends forward.	The athlete should allow the hammer to hang as an extension from the shoulders and flex the legs and squat down as though sitting on a stool. Instruct the athlete to practice one-handed and two-handed swings, extending the arms out in front of the body during the swings.
The athlete loses balance during swings.	The athlete is using no leg flexion and is looking downward. There is no shift of the hips in opposition to the pull of the hammer. The arms may be flexed when the hammer is in front of the body.	The athlete must practice the swings slowly using a pole. The athlete should also practice sitting and shifting the hips in opposition to the movement of the hammer. The faster the swings, the more pronounced the athlete's hip shift.
No high or low point occurs during the swings. The low and high points are in the wrong position.	The athlete is not taking the hammer to the left as far as possible during the swings. The The arc of the hammer is not elevated to the left side of the body.	Have the athlete practice establishing the correct plane of the hammer using a pole and and then a basketball in a net. The athlete should sweep the the implement upward to the left with each swing.
The athlete swings the arms and hammer like a windmill or propeller in front of the body. The hammer fails to travel to the rear of the thrower during the swings.	The thrower stands too erect and is afraid of swinging the hammer to the rear of the body and losing balance. The athlete's arms are flexed, and the hammer is not swept far enough to the athlete's left rear during each swing.	The athlete must squat down, look forward, and sweep or tow the hammer upward to the left. The athlete must also shift the hips to the right and rotate the shoulders to the right as the hammer moves from left rear to right rear. The athlete must practice flattening the plane followed by the hammer (but still keeping the high point on the left side of the body).

→

273

HAMMER SWINGS AND TURNS

Error	Reasons	Corrections
The athlete lands heavily on the right foot at the end of each turn.	The athlete's body is tilting toward the right. The bodyweight is not shifted over the left foot during the transition from swing to turn. The athlete may also be swinging the right leg around the body in a wide arc during each turn.	The athlete must consciously shift the bodyweight to the left and over the left foot when entering the turns. The athlete should practice turns with the arms extended (but without holding anything), and then practice with a pole. The right leg must be taken around the body quickly during the turns with both knees brought close together. The athlete must avoid falling to the right as the right foot is placed on the ground at the end of each turn.
The athlete loses balance, particularly during the second and third turns.	The athlete is not counteracting the increasing pull of the hammer by leaning away from the hammer. The athlete's legs are not flexed, and the athlete's arms may be flexed, or the vision may be directed downward.	Instruct the athlete to hang on the hammer with "long arms," flex the legs, squat, and shift the hips away from the hammer to maintain balance as the athlete's rotational speed increases.
The hammer and athlete appear to rotate as a block. The athlete's legs are not shifting ahead under the athlete's torso during each turn.	The movement of the athlete's hips is slow. The athlete's knees are not pressed together during the turns, and the athlete's non-supporting leg is allowed to swing outward during the turns.	The athlete must rotate the right leg around in each turn as fast as possible. Have the athlete practice rotating the legs and hips ahead of the torso without the hammer. Then the athlete can use the hammer substitutes and finally the hammer.
The athlete is unable to make the transition from swings to turns. The athlete attempts to perform another preliminary swing while entering the first turn.	The athlete is failing to hold the hammer at arm's length in front of the body when entering the turns.	Instruct your athlete to practice swings plus one turn using a pole. At the end of the second swing, the athlete holds the pole at arm's length in front of body and performs a turn. The athlete can practice using a basketball in a net or with a lightweight hammer.

→

Error	Reasons	Corrections
The athlete rotates on the spot or travels sideways during the turns. There is no movement across the ring in the direction of throw.	The athlete's heel-toe pivot is poorly performed. The athlete may be pivoting continuously on the toe of the left foot.	Have the athlete practice the turns without the hammer, accentuating the heel-toe action with each turn. The athlete should pivot 180 degrees on the heel of the left foot and then rock over the side of the foot to the ball of the foot to repeat the next 180 degrees. Use parallel lines to help establish the correct footwork.
The plane of the hammer is incorrect—either too flat or too high. The hammer hits the ground.	The athlete's upper body is tight and not relaxed. The angle of the athlete's arms at the shoulders varies and is not held constant.	Have the athlete first practice turns slowly using a pole to establish the correct angle of the arms. When practicing with the hammer, the athlete should progressively raise the arc followed by the hammer in each turn so that it reaches the correct angle for the release.

HAMMER DELIVERY FOLLOWING 3 OR 4 TURNS

Error	Reasons	Corrections
The athlete flexes the arms during the delivery.	The athlete feels that by flexing the arms, there will be more pull placed on the hammer. The athlete's legs are extended too early.	The pull on the hammer comes from a powerful extension of the athlete's legs and back. The athlete must think of long arms and loose, relaxed shoulders. The athlete's legs must be flexed during the turns. The athlete should practice the correct action slowly using a pole.
The athlete loses balance and falls over during the delivery.	The athlete is not shifting the bodyweight over the left foot during delivery. The athlete's pull during the delivery is not directed down the length of the hammer wire to the head of the hammer. The timing of the pull is incorrect.	The athlete should shift the bodyweight over the left foot during the delivery. The pull on the hammer occurs when the hammer head passes in front of the body. The athlete then extends the legs and back and rotates toward the direction of throw. The athlete should practice the timing using hammer substitutes.

→

Error	Reasons	Corrections
The athlete fails to generate any power in the delivery.	The athlete's legs and back are already extended prior to the delivery. The plane of the hammer may be too flat immediately prior to the delivery. The timing of the athlete's pull on the hammer during the delivery is incorrect.	Have the athlete first practice the swings and delivery action without turns and without an implement. Then have the athlete shift back to practicing with the hammer and including the turns. The athlete must raise the high point progressively through through each successive turn and emphasize throwing the head back and extending the legs and back in the delivery. The upward thrust of the athlete's body should pull directly along the wire of the hammer and out to the hammer ball.
The hammer head hits the ground during the delivery.	The athlete's upper body has dropped forward during the final turn and during the delivery. The high point of the hammer is too high in the last turn, or the high and low points are in the wrong positions.	The athlete should work on the correct action of the hammer by using a pole. The athlete must lower the high point (and raise the low point) but still maintain the position of the high point over the left shoulder The athlete must flex the legs and keep the upper body perpendicular to the ground.
The athlete is thrown or pulled out of the ring during the delivery.	The timing of the extension of the legs and the position of the hammer head during the pull of the delivery are incorrect.	Have the athlete practice swings and delivery using a single turn. The athlete must pull on the hammer by extending the legs as the hammer passes in front of the right foot. The athlete then extends the body in an upward spiral and performs the reverse immediately after the hammer is released.
The hammer flies out of the sector boundary, and the throw is declared as a foul.	The athlete's turns are not moving progressively toward the direction of throw. The athlete may be off-balance during each of the turns.	Have the athlete speed up rotation of the right leg and placement of the right foot, keeping the knees close together in the turns. Check that the athlete's feet are parallel to the direction of throw at the start and at the end of each turn. See that the athlete is sitting back and counteracting the pull of the hammer. Using a pole, the athlete can practice sitting and rotating the hips and legs around and head of the shoulders and hammer.

ASSESSMENT

1. **Assess the following theoretical elements as taught during instructional sessions:**
   a. Fundamental rules governing the hammer throw.
   b. Good safety habits for the hammer throw.
   c. Basic elements of hammer-throw technique.
   d. Basic elements of training for the hammer throw.

2. **Assess the performance of technique during the following stages of skill development:**
   a. Hammer swings.
   b. Hammer swings and delivery.
   c. Hammer turns performed along two parallel lines.
   d. Combinations of swings and turns performed along 2 parallel lines. Examples are 1 swing, 1 turn, 1 swing, 1 turn; 1 swing, 2 turns; or 2 swings, 2 turns, 2 swings, 2 turns.
   e. Hammer swings (2 or 3) and delivery (release).
   f. Hammer swings (2 or 3), turns (1, 2, 3, or 4), and delivery (release).

   CRITICAL FEATURES OF TECHNIQUE TO OBSERVE DURING ASSESSMENT
   - ✓ Gripping the hammer handle correctly.
   - ✓ Extending the arms in front of the body and achieving a high point to the left rear (right-handed thrower) during preliminary swings.
   - ✓ Dropping the head and shoulders under the hammer and shifting the hips in the opposing direction to the hammer during the preliminary swings.
   - ✓ Holding the hammer with extended arms in front of the body for each of the hammer swings.
   - ✓ Performing the 180 degree rotations on the heel and toe during the hammer swings.
   - ✓ Lowering the center of gravity by sitting as though on a stool during the entry to each of the turns.
   - ✓ Raising the hammer to achieve a high point to the left in each of the turns.
   - ✓ Counteracting the pull of the hammer in each turn by shifting the bodyweight in the opposing direction.
   - ✓ Pulling the legs in close together for each of the turns.
   - ✓ Performing an upward spiraling extension of the body in the delivery of the hammer.
   - ✓ Rotating on the toes and shifting the bodyweight back into the ring for the reverse after releasing the hammer.

3. **Hold graded competitions to help develop motivation and technique.**
   a. Throwers compete for distance using 2 or 3 swings and delivery. (No turns are used.)
   b. Throwers compete for distance using 2 or 3 swings, 1 turn, and delivery.
   c. Throwers compete for distance using 2 or 3 swings, 2 turns, and delivery.
   d. Throwers compete for distance using 2 or 3 swings, 3 turns, and delivery.
   e. Throwers compete for distance using 2 or 3 swings, 4 turns, and delivery.

SUGGESTED STANDARDS OF PERFORMANCE—HAMMER

MALE

Age	Weight of Hammer		Distance
12-13	3 kg (6.61 lbs.)	Satisfactory	10.00 m (32'9")
		Good	15.00 m (49'2")
		Excellent	20.00 m (65'7")
14-15	4 kg (8.81 lbs.)	Satisfactory	15.00 m (49'2")
		Good	20.00 m (65'7")
		Excellent	25.00 m (82'0")
16-17	5.45 kg (12 lbs.)	Satisfactory	20.00 m (65'7")
		Good	25.00 m (82'0")
		Excellent	30.00 m (98'5")
18-19	7.26 kg (16 lbs.)	Satisfactory	25.00 m (82'0")
		Good	30.00 m (98'5")
		Excellent	35.00 m (114'10")

FEMALE

Age	Weight of Hammer		Distance
12-13	3 kg (6.61 lbs.)	Satisfactory	10.00 m (32'9")
		Good	15.00 m (49'2")
		Excellent	20.00 m (65'7")
14-15	3 kg (6.61 lbs.)	Satisfactory	15.00 m (49'2")
		Good	20.00 m (65'7")
		Excellent	25.00 m (82'0")
16-17	4 kg (8.81 lbs.)	Satisfactory	20.00 m (65'7")
		Good	25.00 m (82'0")
		Excellent	30.00 m (98'5")
18-19	4 kg (8.81 lbs.)	Satisfactory	25.00 m (82'0")
		Good	30.00 m (98'5")
		Excellent	35.00 m (114'10")

THE COMBINED EVENTS

The two combined-event competitions in the modern Olympic Games are the 10-event men's decathlon and the 7-event women's heptathlon. The men's decathlon has changed dramatically from its original format, and the women's heptathlon (a recent addition to the Olympics) has grown out of the 5-event women's pentathlon competition.

In the 1904 Olympics, the men's decathlon included an 800-yd. walk, a hammer throw, and the 56-lb. weight throw. In the same Olympics, there was a triathlon for males consisting of a long jump, shot put, and 100-yd. dash. From 1906 through 1924, a pentathlon was offered for males as well as a decathlon. At that time, the pentathlon replicated the event held by the ancient Greeks and consisted of a standing long jump, discus, javelin, 192-m sprint, and wrestling! Today males have the opportunity of competing in a non-Olympic calendar pentathlon that consists of a long jump, javelin, 200-m sprint, discus, and a 1,500-m race. These events are all held on a single day. The events chosen in 1912 for the men's decathlon have remained unchanged to this day and are listed later in this section.

Females had to wait until 1964 before a women's combined events competition was included in the Olympic program. At this time, it was a pentathlon consisting of 80-m hurdles, shot put, high jump, long jump, and a 200-m sprint. By the time of the Los Angeles Olympic Games in 1984, the women's pentathlon had grown to a seven-event heptathlon. In the near future, a women's decathlon is expected to take the place of the heptathlon.

Both the decathlon and the heptathlon are spread over two days. The following lists show the order of events for these two multi-event competitions.

Decathlon: First Day

100 m
Long jump
Shot put
High jump
400 m

Decathlon: Second Day

110-m hurdles
Discus
Pole vault
Javelin
1,500 m

Heptathlon: First Day

100-m hurdles
High jump
Shot put
200-m run

Heptathlon: Second Day

Long jump
Javelin
800 m

The rules for the events in the decathlon and the heptathlon differ from those applying to similar individual events. Here are some rules applying specifically to the decathlon and heptathlon:

(a) In the running events, an athlete is disqualified after the third false start.

(b) In the throwing events, only three throws are allowed.

(c) Athletes have to start in every event; otherwise, they are disqualified.

(d) An athlete's standing in the combined events is determined by adding the scores gained in each of the individual events. This is done in accordance with a point system set out by the International Amateur Athletic Federation. The point scoring system is continuously upgraded as standards in track and field improve.

Athletes who compete in the combined events tend to be either superb runners who are also good jumpers but less accomplished at throwing, or powerful throwers who are moderately good as jumpers and runners. This division tends to occur because the physical requirements for superiority in some events can be disadvantageous in others. Muscle mass, which is helpful in throwing, is detrimental in the longer running events. A lean, lightweight athlete who is excellent in the jumps and runs is likely to be too small to produce superior performances in the discus and shot.

Multi-event athletes train to be strong, fast, and well coordinated and to have good endurance. Training for aerobic endurance is normally one of the less enjoyable activities for multi-event athletes, but this type of training is necessary because it helps the athletes to get through the physical discomfort of the 800-m run in the heptathlon and the 1,500-m run in the decathlon. These two events occur at the end of the competition when the athletes are most fatigued from having competed in all of the other events. Aerobic endurance also helps the athlete to better withstand the rigors of training for so many different events.

INTRODUCING COMBINED EVENTS COMPETITIONS

After you have taught the fundamentals of a number of individual events, you then have the opportunity of making up a series of 2-event biathlons, 3-event triathlons, 4-event "quadathlons," and 5-event pentathlons. These multi-event competitions provide an extra stimulus to your athletes, particularly those who are not event specialists. Multi-event competitions also give your athletes the chance of experiencing the point scoring system used in the decathlon and heptathlon. Consider using a small multi-event competition periodically as a highlight at the end of a series of your training sessions. You can also include a multi-event competition as part of a grand finale to your regular instructional program.

Following are some examples of multi-event competitions:

- A run and a throw; for example, a 50-meter or 100-m sprint and shot put

- A run, jump, and a throw; for example, a 5-hurdle race, high jump, and javelin

- 2 runs, a jump, and a throw; for example, a 100-m sprint, pole vault, discus, and a 300-or 400-m run

- 2 runs, 2 jumps, and one throw; for example, a 100-m sprint, high jump, long jump, javelin, and an 800- or 1,500-m run

Single-day pentathlon competitions are commonly held for young athletes in the following manner:

- For females aged 9 to 15 and males aged 9 to 13, the events are 80-m hurdles, shot put, high jump, long jump, and an 800-m run.

- For male athletes aged 14 and 15, the 100-m hurdles is substituted for the 80-m hurdles. The four remaining events in the pentathlon are the same as for females aged 9 to 15 and males aged 9 to 13.

- For athletes 16 years and older, heptathlon and decathlon competitions are used. Hurdle heights and the weights of throwing implements are adjusted according to age.

Because of the stress of training and the huge time commitment, it is better that you encourage only your more talented and mature athletes to try out for the decathlon and heptathlon. These multi-event competitions can require training sessions of 2 hours or more and frequently require 2 training sessions per day. This is obviously a large time commitment for your athlete and for you, too!

If you examine the choice of events in the decathlon and the heptathlon, you will see that the majority of events emphasize power. Eight out of the 10 events in the decathlon are power events, and 6 of these place great emphasis on technical skill. The heptathalon has 6 power events, and all of these emphasize technical skill. Such an emphasis on power and technical skill greatly influences the training of the decathlete and heptathlete.

Throughout the year, multi-event athletes (who must have great self-discipline and a capacity for hard work) will train to improve their strength, power, flexibility, coordination, and anaerobic endurance while continuing to recognize the importance of aerobic endurance. When working on technical skills, the athletes should concentrate on characteristics shared by several events in order to use their time most efficiently. For example, sheer speed is essential in the 100 m, the 400 m, and the hurdles, and is also vital in the jumps and the throws. Explosive power is needed in the throws, but it also helps in the jumps and the shorter running events. Technical similarities also overlap from one event to the next. For example, they occur in the takeoffs for the jumps and in important body positions used in the throws.

BASIC COMPONENTS OF A YEAR'S TRAINING PROGRAM

The basic components of a year's training program for a multi-event competitor is laid out in this section. The year has been divided into 3 parts, with the summer as the competitive season. As a general rule, the winter season is the time for working on basic conditioning and for building up strength and general endurance. Spring is used for more specific event-related training while still working on building up power and general conditioning. Summer is the time for major competitions and for the continuation of event-related training. To reach the elite level as a multi-event competitor, the athlete is faced with at least 7 years of extremely hard training.

Off-Season

- Long runs, interval training, Fartlek, and other types of aerobic training are performed.
- Weight training and circuit training are used to develop basic strength and power.
- General flexibility and mobility exercises are coupled with activities that promote coordination.
- Technique work concentrates on the athlete's weaker events.

Precompetitive Season

- Training becomes more event-related although work still continues on basic conditioning.
- The athlete trains on groups of 2 and 3 events which are technically related.
- Power training and weight training continues with greater emphasis on speed and explosiveness.
- Short fast runs are used to develop anaerobic endurance.
- Occasional long runs maintain aerobic endurance.
- Technical training continues as before, but it is now applied to a greater number of events.

Competitive Season

- The athlete takes part weekly in individual event competitions and, on several occasions during the competitive season, takes part in 4 or 5 events in a day.

- Light, fast weight training continues.

- The athlete trains on pairs of events that follow each other in competition. For example, in the decathlon, long jump and shot put, hurdles and discus, discus and pole vault. In the heptathlon, hurdles and high jump, high jump and shot put, long jump and javelin.

- The athlete competes in 2 or 3 decathlon/heptathlon competitions.

- Several days rest occurs after a decathlon or a heptathlon competition to allow the athlete's body to rejuvenate.

If you intend to assist an athlete who shows talent for becoming a combined events competitor, remember that patience, discipline, and hard work are essential. It takes time to develop the kind of all-around ability required in the decathlon and the heptathlon. Even though the athlete can be very good at certain individual events, there is no reward in a multi-event competition for the single event specialist. Your athlete must learn to work at less interesting events (weaker events) as well as those that provide the athlete with more pleasure. The key to success is the development of ability across the full range of events.

SUGGESTED READINGS

AAF/CIF coaching program: Track and field. (1995.) California: Amateur Athletic Foundation of Los Angeles.

Anderson, R. (1980.) *Stretching.* Bolinas, California: Shelter. Baert, J.P. (1980.) *The throws.* Canadian Track and Field Association, Level II Theory and Training. Vanier, Ontario: C.T.F.A.

Ballesteros, J.M. and Alvarez, J. (1979.) *Track and field: A basic coaching manual.* London: I.A.A.F.

B.C. Athletics Junior Development. (1997.) *Personal best performances and top ten for 1997 and all-time top ten 1997.* B.C. Athletics #206-1367 West Broadway, Vancouver, British Columbia, Canada.

Beynon, Robin. (1997.) *1997 British Columbia Athletics outdoor track and field rankings for juveniles, juniors, and seniors.* B.C. Athletics #206 1367 West Broadway, Vancouver, British Columbia, Canada.

Bompa, T. O. (1983.) *Theory and methodology of training: The key to athletic training.* Dubuque, Iowa: W.C. Brown.

Bowerman, W. J. and Freeman, W.H. (1990.) *Training for track and field.* Illinois: Leisure Press.

British Amateur Athletic Board. (1989.) *How to teach the jumps, throws, track events.* Surrey, England: B.A.A.B./A.A.A.

Burrows, R. (1997.) *Race walking to fitness.* Athletics Canada, 1600 James Naismith Drive, Gloucester, Ontario, Canada.

Canadian Track and Field Association. (1975.) *Elementary coaching manual.* Canadian Track and Field Association, Level I Theory and Training. Vanier, Ontario: C.T.F.A.

Carr, G. (1997.) *Mechanics of sport: A practitioner's guide.* Champaign, Illinois: Human Kinetics.

Chu, D.A. and Signier, R. (1986.) *Plyometrics for fitness and peak performance.* New York: Doubleday.

Costello, F. (1984.) *Bounding to the top.* Mountain View, CA: TAFNews.

Dellinger, W. (1996.) *Track and field fundamentals* (video series). Eugene, OR: VideoSports Network.

Dick, F.W. (1980.) *Sports training principles.* London: Lepus.

Doherty, K. (1985.) *Track and field omnibook* (4th ed.). Los Altos, California: TAFNews.

Drowatzky, J. N. (1984.) *Legal issues in sport and physical education management.* Champaign, Illinois: Stipes.

Ecker, T. (1996.) *Basic track and field biomechanics* (2nd ed.). Mountain View, CA: TAFNews.

Fleck, S. J. and Kraemer, W.J. (1987.) *Designing resistance training programs.* Champaign, Illinois: Human Kinetics.

Freeman, W.H. (1996.) *Peak when it counts: Periodization for American track and field* (3rd ed). Mountain View, CA: TAFNews.

Gambetta, V. (1989.) *TAC track and field coaching manual* (2nd ed.). Champaign, Illinois: Leisure Press.

Gambetta, V. (1987.) Principles of Plyometric Training. *Track technique.* Fall, pages 3099 to 3102.

Harre, D., editor. (1982.) *Principles of sports training* (English language edition). Berlin (East): Sportverlag.

International Amateur Athletic Federation. (1989.) *I.A.A.F. official handbook.* London: I.A.A.F.

International Amateur Athletic Federation. (1989.) *I.A.A.F. scoring tables for men's track and field events.* London: I.A.A.F.

International Amateur Athletic Federation. (1989.) *I.A.A.F. scoring tables for women's track and field events.* London: I.A.A.F.

International Amateur Athletic Federation. (1989.) *Designs for 400 meter track and field terrain (4 designs).* London: I.A.A.F.

International Amateur Athletic Federation. (1989.) *Track and field athletics—A basic coaching manual (Development programme book no. 1).* London: I.A.A.F.

International Amateur Athletic Federation. (1989.) *Athletics officiating—A practical guide (Development programme book no. 2).* London: I.A.A.F.

Jacoby, E. (1983.) *Applied techniques in track and field.* Champaign, Illinois: Leisure Press.

Knudson, L., director. (1994.) *Track and field instructional videotapes.* Indianapolis, IN: USA Track and Field.

Mach, G. (1980.) *Sprints and hurdles.* Canadian Track and Field Association, Level II Theory and Training. Vanier, Ontario: C.T.F.A.

Markham P. (1989.) *Race walking.* British Amateur Athletics Board.

National Federation of State High School Associations (1997.) *Track and field rules update* (video). Kansas City, MO.

Nygaard, G. and Boone, T. (1985.) *Coaches' guide to sport law.* Champaign, Illinois: Human Kinetics.

Pearl, W. and Moran, G. T. (1986.) *Getting stronger.* Bolinas, California: Shelter.

Powell, J. (1987.) *Track and field—Fundamentals for teacher and coach* (4th ed.). Champaign, Illinois: Stipes.

Premier's Sport Awards Program Instructor's Resource Manual. (1995.) *Track and field.* Vancouver, B.C., Canada: British Columbia Ministry of Housing, Recreation, and Consumer Services.

Radcliffe, J.C. and Farentinos, R.C. (1985.) *Plyometrics: Explosive power training* (2nd ed.). Champaign, Illinois: Human Kinetics.

Reid, P. (1982.) *The jumps.* Canadian Track and Field Association, Level II Theory and Training. Vanier, Ontario: C.T.F.A.

Rosen, M. and Rosen, K. (1988.) *Track: Championship running.* New York: Sports Illustrated.

Rudow, M. (1992.) *Advanced race walking* (3rd ed.). Technique Publications.

TAFNews. (1995.) *Track and Field News' big red book* (conversion and scoring tables). Mountain View, CA. TAFNews.

Tulloh, B.(1994.) *Track athletics.* London: Blandford.

Walker, L.T. (1984.) *Track and field: A guide for the serious coach and athlete.* Chicago: Athletic Institute.

Walker, L.T. (1989.) *Track and field: For men and women.* Chicago: Athletic Institute.

Ward, T. (1997.) *Track and field.* Crystal Lake, IL: Rigby Interactive Library.

World-class track and field video series. (1991.) Ames, IA: Championship Books and Video Productions.

ABOUT THE AUTHOR

Gerry Carr, PhD, is a professor in the School of Physical Education at the University of Victoria, British Columbia, where he teaches biomechanics to physical educators and coaches. During a noteworthy track and field career, he threw the discus for Great Britain in the Olympic Games and competed for the UCLA Bruins in the discus, shot put, and hammer throw. He has coached and taught track and field to physical educators and elite athletes in Europe, the United States, and Canada.

An accomplished writer, Carr has published six books and more than 30 articles on sport and physical education, including *Mechanics of Sport: A Practitioner's Guide* (Human Kinetics, 1996), which explains the mechanical principles involved in the performance of sport techniques. Carr resides in Victoria, British Columbia.